Behavior, Society, and Nuclear War

BEHAVIOR, SOCIETY, AND NUCLEAR WAR
A Series of Review Volumes

edited by Philip E. Tetlock, Jo L. Husbands,
Robert Jervis, Paul C. Stern, and Charles Tilly

Committee on Contributions of Behavioral and Social Science
to the Prevention of Nuclear War
Commission on the Behavioral and Social Science and Education
National Research Council/National Academy of Sciences

BEHAVIOR, SOCIETY, AND NUCLEAR WAR

VOLUME TWO

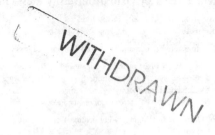

Philip E. Tetlock
Jo L. Husbands
Robert Jervis
Paul C. Stern
Charles Tilly
Editors

Committee on Contributions of Behavioral and Social Science
to the Prevention of Nuclear War
Commission on Behavioral and Social Sciences and Education
National Research Council

New York   Oxford
OXFORD UNIVERSITY PRESS
1991

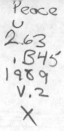

Peace

U
263
.B45
1989
V.2
X

Oxford University Press

Oxford   New York   Toronto
Delhi   Bombay   Calcutta   Madras   Karachi
Petaling Jaya   Singapore   Hong Kong   Tokyo
Nairobi   Dar es Salaam   Cape Town
Melbourne   Auckland

and associated companies in
Berlin   Ibadan

Copyright © 1991 by Oxford University Press, Inc.

Published by Oxford University Press, Inc.,
200 Madison Avenue, New York, New York 10016

Oxford is a registered trademark of Oxford University Press

Library of Congress Cataloging-in-Publication Data
(Revised for vol. 2)
Behavior, society, and nuclear war.
"Committee on Contributions of Behavioral
and Social Science to the Prevention of Nuclear War,
Commission on Behavioral and Social Sciences
and Education, National Research Council."
Includes bibliographies and indexes.
1. Nuclear warfare—Psychological aspects.
2. Nuclear warfare—Social aspects.   I. Tetlock, Philip.
II. National Research Council (U.S.). Committee on Contributions of Behavioral and
Social Science to the Prevention of Nuclear War.   III. National Research Council (U.S.).
Commission on Behavioral and Social Sciences and Education.
U263.B45   1989   355.02′17   88-33043
ISBN 0-19-505765-1 (v. 1)   ISBN 0-19-505766-X (v. 1 : pbk.)
ISBN 0-19-505767-8 (v. 2)   ISBN 0-19-505768-6 (v. 2 : pbk.)

987654321

Printed in the United States of America
on acid-free paper

Foreword

In recent years, scientists have been prominent among those expressing concern about the risk of nuclear war. New programs and research groups have sprung up at universities, and professional associations have paid increasing attention to the danger. In the National Academy of Sciences, many members believed it was time to move beyond the academy's traditional focus on technical questions to explore the potential contributions of behavioral and social science research to the issue. The creation of the Committee on Contributions of Behavioral and Social Science to the Prevention of Nuclear War in the spring of 1985 thus reflected the recognition that scientists can work to reduce the risks of nuclear war by improving understanding of the cultural, institutional, political, and cognitive processes involved in making war or preventing it.

The National Research Council assembled a committee that brings knowledge and concepts from across the behavioral and social sciences to bear on international security issues. Committee members thus include individuals with experience in relevant international policy issues and individuals with broad knowledge in the behavioral and social sciences. The committee has three major objectives: (1) to foster innovative, multidisciplinary applications of social and behavioral science knowledge and methods to preventing nuclear war and enhancing global security; (2) to foster relevant cooperative research between the Soviet and American behavioral and social science communities; and (3) to disseminate the results of its own work, as well as existing knowledge in the behavioral and social sciences, to potential users of these findings, including the academic community, policymakers, and the interested public.

As one of its first tasks, the committee set out to identify knowledge about behavior and society that might be valuable in developing policies to reduce the risk of nuclear war. To that end, it called on behavioral and social science scholars to review work in specified areas to determine its relevance to understanding current defense and foreign policy issues. This volume is the second in a series that presents those reviews.

The series takes a measured approach out of conviction that scholars need to be especially cautious and self-critical when they seek to advise on practical decisions of grave consequence. Much that has been offered as knowledge in the past cannot be defended as more than educated opinion, and one aim of this series is to keep that distinction clear. The primary audience for the series consists of scholars and students interested in international security issues and in the possible applications of knowledge in the behavioral and social sciences to those issues. The committee hopes that the critical distillations of knowledge presented here can offer a basis for developing more focused knowledge and better informed advice for preventing nuclear war.

The series is edited by committee members Philip E. Tetlock, Robert Jervis, and Charles Tilly, and staff members Jo L. Husbands and Paul C. Stern. The editors have been responsible for developing ideas for chapters, selecting the authors, and managing the review process. Each chapter has been reviewed by the editors, additional members of the committee, and scholars and practitioners who brought diverse perspectives to the topics. The views expressed in the chapters, however, are those of the authors.

We are indebted to the Carnegie Corporation of New York, the John D. and Catherine T. MacArthur Foundation, and the National Research Council Fund for their support of the committee. We wish also to acknowledge the important role of the Commission on Behavioral and Social Sciences and Education of the National Research Council, which was responsible for organizing this committee. Special thanks are due Kenneth Arrow, Timothy Colton, Clifford Geertz, Catherine Kelleher, Harold Kelley, Charles Townes, and Amos Tversky, former members of the committee, who helped select and review contributions to this volume, and especially to William K. Estes, founding chair of the committee, and David A. Goslin, former executive director of the commission, for their leadership and support of the committee's efforts from its inception through the planning stages of this volume.

Herbert A. Simon and Charles Tilly, *Cochairs*
Committee on Contributions of Behavioral and Social Science
to the Prevention of Nuclear War

NOTICE: The project that is the subject of this report was approved by the Governing Board of the National Research Council, whose members are drawn from the councils of the National Academy of Sciences, the National Academy of Engineering, and the Institute of Medicine. The members of the committee responsible for the report were chosen for their special competences and with regard for appropriate balance.

This report has been reviewed by a group other than the authors according to procedures approved by a Report Review Committee consisting of members of the National Academy of Sciences, the National Academy of Engineering, and the Institute of Medicine.

The National Academy of Sciences is a private, nonprofit, self-perpetuating society of distinguished scholars engaged in scientific and engineering research, dedicated to the furtherance of science and technology and to their use for the general welfare. Upon the authority of the charter granted to it by the Congress in 1863, the Academy has a mandate that requires it to advise the federal government on scientific and technical matters. Dr. Frank Press is president of the National Academy of Sciences.

The National Academy of Engineering was established in 1964, under the charter of the National Academy of Sciences, as a parallel organization of outstanding engineers. It is autonomous in its administration and in the selection of its members, sharing with the National Academy of Sciences the responsibility for advising the federal government. The National Academy of Engineering also sponsors engineering programs aimed at meeting national needs, encourages education and research, and recognizes the superior achievements of engineers. Dr. Robert M. White is president of the National Academy of Engineering.

The Institute of Medicine was established in 1970 by the National Academy of Sciences to secure the services of eminent members of appropriate professions in the examination of policy matters pertaining to the health of the public. The Institute acts under the responsibility given to the National Academy of Sciences by its congressional charter to be an adviser to the federal government and, upon its own initiative, to identify issues of medical care, research, and education. Dr. Samuel O. Thier is president of the Institute of Medicine.

The National Research Council was organized by the National Academy of Sciences in 1916 to associate the broad community of science and technology with the Academy's purposes of furthering knowledge and advising the federal government. Functioning in accordance with general policies determined by the Academy, the Council has become the principal operating agency of both the National Academy of Sciences and the National Academy of

Engineering in providing services to the government, the public, and the scientific and engineering communities. The Council is administered jointly by both Academies and the Institute of Medicine. Dr. Frank Press and Dr. Robert M. White are chairman and vice chairman, respectively, of the National Research Council.

Committee on Contributions of Behavioral and Social Science to the Prevention of Nuclear War 1989–1990

HERBERT A. SIMON
Cochair, Department of Psychology, Carnegie-Mellon University

CHARLES TILLY
Cochair, Center for Studies of Social Change, New school for Social Research

ROBERT M. AXELROD
Institute of Public Policy Studies, University of Michigan

BARRY M. BLECHMAN
Defense Forecasts, Inc., Washington, D.C.

GEORGE W. BRESLAUER
Department of Political Science, University of California, Berkeley

JOHN L. COMAROFF
Department of Anthropology, University of Chicago

PHILIP E. CONVERSE
Center for Advanced Study in the Behavioral Sciences, Stanford, California

LYNN R. EDEN
Department of History, Carnegie-Mellon University

BARRY EICHENGREEN
Department of Economics, University of California, Berkeley

RICHARD E. ERICSON
Department of Economics, Columbia University

WILLIAM K. ESTES
Department of Psychology, Harvard University

WILLIAM A. GAMSON
Department of Sociology, Boston College

ALEXANDER L. GEORGE
Department of Political Science, Stanford University

ROBERT JERVIS
Institute for War and Peace Studies, Columbia University

GAIL W. LADIPUS
Department of Political science, University of California, Berkeley

ROBERT PUTNAM
John F. Kennedy School of Government, Harvard University

ROY RADNER
Mathematical Sciences Research Center, AT&T Bell Laboratories

JACK P. RUINA
Center for International Studies, Massachusetts Institute of Technology

PHILIP E. TETLOCK
Department of Psychology, University of California, Berkeley

PAUL C. STERN
Study Director

JO L. HUSBANDS
Senior Research Associate

DANIEL DRUCKMAN
Senior Staff Officer

MARY E. THOMAS
Senior Program Assistant

Contents

Behavior, Society, and Nuclear War

Introduction

PHILIP E. TETLOCK, JO L. HUSBANDS, ROBERT JERVIS, PAUL C. STERN, AND CHARLES TILLY

N ow is a time of potentially fundamental change in East–West relations. The rapid internal and foreign policy changes underway in the Soviet Union, the prospects for major nuclear and conventional arms agreements, and the warming of U.S.–Soviet relations promise to transform the international system. American public opinion no longer regards the Soviet Union as the primary threat to U.S. security. Many expert observers see the U.S.–Soviet conflict as a fading security issue: writers have proclaimed the "end of history" (Fukuyama, 1989) as a result of the triumph of liberal capitalist democracy; redefined international security to put ecological threats, rather than military conflict, at the center (Matthews, 1989); and theorized on the declining significance of military force (Mueller, 1988) and the growing significance of economic power and technological innovation (Gilpin, 1987).

If such is the new thinking about international security, it is reasonable to ask why we continue to publish volumes whose guiding motivation is the prevention of nuclear war. Our answer is that we believe reducing the risk of nuclear war remains a vital concern. In some respects the world situation may be changing rapidly for the better; the motivation for direct U.S.–Soviet confrontation is certainly on the wane, and support for indirect confrontations between proxy states is also declining. These trends, if they continue, are cause for optimism. Nevertheless, many of the old scenarios for "World War III" remain as plausible as they were in the past, and new sources of instability may arise in changed world conditions.

The world is still one of nation-states where concern for sovereignty is paramount, where weapons of mass destruction still fill the arsenals of major powers, and where institutions and norms to regulate conflict remain weak. Nuclear weapons are still controlled by complex technologies capable of unpredicted failure and by large and far-flung military organizations that may not be fully understood by the political authorities who have, in theory, ultimate control. And the problems of nuclear proliferation remain. Nuclear weapons are already available to states whose conflicts are little affected by superpower détente, and they may become available to other states and non-state groups that may be more willing to use them than are the superpowers.

A new U.S.–Soviet détente may also create new uncertainties in the world. Already, the future of Eastern Europe has become much less certain. It is possible to imagine scenarios, unthinkable a few years ago, of the peaceful transformation and integration of Europe. It is equally possible, however, to imagine scenarios of armed conflict in Europe that could draw in Western powers. In other areas of the world, a respite from U.S.–Soviet competition might encourage the resolution of regional conflicts, or it might lead to the eruption of festering disputes that had been suppressed by the fear of super-power involvement. And the changing relations between East and West are bringing new economic opportunities—and conflicts—that introduce further uncertainties to the international scene.

The net effect of the current changes in the climate of international relations may well be a decreased probability of nuclear war. What is more certain is that the range of phenomena relevant to causing or preventing nuclear war has grown. The old list of possible proximate causes of nuclear war has not been rendered obsolete, even if some of the scenarios now seem less likely. Because the new world conditions suggest new scenarios of conflict, it is increasingly important to understand the basic, underlying processes that affect international conflict and cooperation, such as political and economic interdependence, nationalism, changing international economic balances of power, the emergence of international norms and regimes, and change in public and elite opinion.

If moderation in superpower conflict continues, the next historical period may provide a "policy window" (Evangelista, Chapter 5) for putting into place institutional arrangements to reduce the risk of nuclear war. Opportunities may arise to shift some attention from crisis management to crisis prevention, from reducing conflict to building international institutions, and from the use of deterrence and other forms of "threat power" in international relations to what Boulding (1989) calls economic and integrative power. If such opportunities arise, it will be important to have knowledge at hand about the possibilities and pitfalls attached to pursuing them in the international arena. Accordingly, in this second volume of *Behavior, Society, and Nuclear War*, we are presenting a broadened agenda: the content now includes analyses both of possible proximate causes of nuclear war and of underlying processes.

The series will thus include chapters that address the enduring issues of war and peace, as well as the changing conditions of international relations. The enduring issues are represented in this volume by chapters on judgment and decision making in foreign policy contexts (Fischhoff, Chapter 3) and on the role of arms races in international conflict (Downs, Chapter 2). The chapter on third-party intervention (Wallensteen, Chapter 4) addresses a basic issue of peacemaking, but also implicitly recognizes the growing relative importance of conflicts between small powers. Changing international conditions are most strongly reflected in Chapter 1, by Janice Stein, which focuses specifically on techniques of reassurance as alternatives to and complements of deterrence, and Chapter 5, by Matthew Evangelista, which considers the sources of moderation in Soviet security policy.

As set out in Volume One, a central purpose of the series is to help disentangle the factual and moral issues that underlie disagreements about how best to prevent nuclear war. Toward this goal, the behavioral and social sciences contribute in two categories: methodological and theoretical. On the methodological side, the behavioral and social sciences can identify the dangers of making vague causal claims that are difficult to falsify and that rest on superficial and subjective readings of the historical record. For instance, the quality of analysis that underlies public debates about the political and strategic functions of nuclear weapons is often strikingly inferior to the quality of analysis that was required to invent and construct these weapons in the first place. The discussion of international politics and East–West relations that accompanies broader policy debates is often equally weak. One rarely hears policy advocates specify the types of evidence that would induce them to change their minds, clearly articulate the causal assumptions that undergird their prescriptive recommendations, or dispassionately assess the strengths and weaknesses of alternative research methods for testing their causal assumptions. Although the contributors to this series are asked to explore the policy implications of the research literatures they review, they are also asked not to slip into roles of policy advocacy. We encourage contributors to be methodologically self-conscious—to make careful note of both the strengths and weaknesses of the data and methods that underlie their theoretical and policy conclusions.

On the theoretical side, the behavioral and social sciences can identify the dangers of making undifferentiated, sweeping claims concerning the causes of war and peace. Simple theoretical generalizations tend to have poor empirical track records in the arena of public policy. The causes of international conflict are extremely complex; variables operating at a number of levels of analysis appear to play key causal roles (Tetlock, 1989). Moreover, the effects of these variables appear to be both interactive (the effects of variable A on war depend on levels of variables B, C, D, . . .) and probabilistic (variables influence the likelihood of various types of war and peace but rarely make a particular outcome inevitable).

The behavioral and social sciences have established lines of research and theory that promise to clarify the factors affecting the likelihood of war in general and of nuclear war in particular. Although there is no well-accepted theory of the conditions that promote nuclear war, there is knowledge about important parts of the problem, including: the behavior of decision makers under uncertainty, the effects of different kinds of organizations on their members, the circumstances under which threats do or do not deter dangerous behavior, and the processes of negotiation when stakes are high. There is also knowledge about parts of the problems of the causes of war in general (in this series, Levy, 1989) and of change in specific policies or broader social systems that decrease the likelihood of war (e.g., Evangelista, Chapter 5; Stein, Chapter 1).

Our strategy in developing this series has been to identify existing work that bears on these issues and then to persuade a well-informed researcher to summarize the current state of the literature and reflect on its implications for reducing the risk of nuclear war and enhancing international security. Given the difficulties of conducting research on these issues—the limited number of observations, the large number of confounding variables, and the fallibility of the research methods at our disposal—it is impressive, as Tetlock argues (1989), that we have achieved as much as we have. Given the magnitude of the problem, it is discouraging, as Tetlock also argues, that so much remains to be accomplished.

The behavioral and social sciences do not offer decisive solutions to the international predicaments confronting the world today; they do, however, identify considerations that prudent policymakers should take into account in choosing among policies aimed at reducing the risk of nuclear war. They can help illuminate and specify for the policy community the dangers of cognitive conceit (of thinking we know more than we do); the limitations of deterrence theory, the most widely accepted theory of international influence, and the strengths and limitations of the alternatives; the impact of crisis-induced stress on human thought and the difficult trade-offs in crisis management; the pitfalls of international communication; and the egregious errors that can arise from relying on selective and superficial readings of the historical record.

In brief, we draw on the behavioral and social sciences to make a case for new intellectual approaches to the subject of international security. The approaches need to be conceptually rigorous, with key ideas well defined and their links to empirical reality explicitly noted; theoretically eclectic in drawing upon a broad range of interacting levels of analysis, from the psychological to the international; and methodologically self-conscious, with careful scrutiny of the distinctive strengths and weaknesses of the different research methods that underlie claims to knowledge about the sources of war and peace. Taking a new approach, to be sure, is not easy; it requires increased tolerance of ambiguity and complexity. There are no neatly packaged answers to the pressing policy dilemmas posed by the multifaceted and rapidly changing international environment. To contribute to policy deliberations, researchers must try to understand and take account of the complex interactions of human and societal processes. Appreciating the difficulties, we attempt here to mobilize new resources for the task.

References

Boulding, K.E. 1989. *Three Faces of Power*. Newbury Park, Calif.: Sage Publications.
Fukuyama, F. 1989. The end of history. *The National Interest* 16(Summer):3–18.
Gilpin, R. 1987. *Political Economy of International Relations*. Princeton, N.J.: Princeton University Press.
Levy, J. 1989. The causes of war: A review of theories and evidence. In P.E. Tetlock, J.L. Husbands, R. Jervis, P.C. Stern, and C. Tilly, eds., *Behavior, Society, and Nuclear War*, Vol. 1. New York: Oxford University Press.
Matthews, J.T. 1989. Ecological security. *Foreign Affairs* 68(2):162–177.
Mueller, J. 1988. *Retreat from Doomsday: The Obsolescence of Major War*. New York: Basic Books.
Tetlock, P.E. 1989. Methodological themes and variations. In P.E. Tetlock, J.L. Husbands, R. Jervis, P.C. Stern, and C. Tilly, eds., *Behavior, Society, and Nuclear War*, Vol. 1. New York: Oxford University Press.

1

Deterrence and Reassurance

JANICE GROSS STEIN

Introduction

Deterrence is not uniformly appropriate as a strategy of conflict management among adversaries. On the contrary, evidence drawn from different kinds of studies now suggests important limiting conditions that constrain the utility of deterrence. This chapter briefly reviews the cumulating evidence of the strengths and weaknesses of deterrence as a strategy and attempts to delimit its utility. It then looks at strategies of "reassurance" that might substitute for or supplement deterrence and compensate for some of its obvious risks in the management of a relationship among adversaries.

Strategies of reassurance are conceived broadly as a set of strategies that adversaries can use to reduce the likelihood of a threat or use of force. In assessing these strategies, this chapter looks at their underlying theoretical assumptions, at the quality of the evidence that sustains arguments of their strengths and weaknesses, and at the conditions that constrain their effectiveness. Finally, it assesses the likely interaction between strategies of deterrence and reassurance under different conditions.

Deterrence: A Critique

There is currently no single theory of deterrence. Rather, there are several theories of deterrence that have developed in successive waves over time (Jervis, 1979). Moreover, as recent reviews of the theoretical literature conclude, theories of deterrence remain seriously underspecified (Morgan, 1983:15; Zagare, 1987:1). A major controversy in the literature on international conflict management centers on the validity of theories of deterrence and, consequently, on deterrence as a strategy of conflict management. Although the two are related, they are not synonymous.

Theories of deterrence are a subset of theories of rational choice. They include far more, however, than the assumption of rational calculation. A theory of international behavior must go beyond models of instrumental rationality and import assumptions from other theories if it is to model the context of international choice (Nye, 1988:248; Snidal, 1985; Lebow and Stein, 1989a; Jervis, 1989). Although there is no single theory of deterrence in international conflict, existing theories tend to share a set of common postulates and assumptions.

Deterrence seeks to prevent undesired action by convincing the party who may be contemplating such action that its cost will exceed any possible gain. Generally, theories of deterrence treat hostility as a constant and assume

intent by a would-be challenger to engage in undesirable action (Mearsheimer, 1983). The fundamental concern then becomes how the calculations
of a would-be challenger can best be manipulated from the outside. Second,
and closely related, theories of deterrence look at the ways in which one actor
can manipulate threats to influence another's calculation of likely cost and
benefit (Jervis, 1979:292). In so doing, they emphasize the manipulation of
an adversary's calculation of relative costs.

Deterrence strategy focuses on the application of the theory to the management of international conflict. The analysis of deterrence as a strategy of
international conflict avoidance generated its own body of theory about the
conditions of its success and failure. Although analyses of the strategy of
deterrence differ widely, two variants can be identified.

The first variant was almost entirely deductive in nature (Brodie, 1959;
Kahn, 1960, 1962, 1965; Kaufman, 1954; Schelling, 1960, 1966; Snyder,
1961, 1972; Wohlstetter, 1959). Drawing heavily on models from game
theory, it defined the strategy of deterrence as the attempt ". . . to persuade
an adversary, through the threat of military retaliation, that the costs of using
military force to resolve political conflict will outweigh the benefits"
(Howard, 1982/1983:315). In postulating the requirements for successful
deterrence, it emphasized the importance of the credibility of threats and
commitments. Credibility, analysts argued, is based only in part on the requisite military capabilities. Through the manipulation of models drawn from
game theory and rational choice, it examined how policymakers could reinforce the credibility of their commitments.

If deterrence is to work, the defender must carefully define the unacceptable action, communicate the commitment to punish transgressors or to deny
them their objectives, possess the capability to carry out this threat, and
demonstrate the resolve to do so. Deterrence theories explored the tactics of
commitment that could enhance credibility (Schelling, 1960, 1966; Snyder,
1972). In deductive theories of deterrence, capability and commitment were
the crucial variables. A second, revisionist wave of scholarship broadened the
scope of the analysis and evaluated the effectiveness of deterrence as a strategy in light of evidence from historical cases (Russett, 1967; George and
Smoke, 1974; Morgan, 1983; Mearsheimer, 1983; Snyder and Diesing, 1977;
Huth and Russett, 1984, 1988). In particular, in their analysis of deterrence
failures, George and Smoke rooted the strategy of deterrence in a theory of
initiation, distinguished among types of deterrence failures, and analyzed the
obstacles to the effective implementation of deterrence. Drawing on empirical
evidence of deterrence failure under different kinds of conditions, they urged
modification and revision of some of the postulates of deterrence theories.
Generally, most of these empirical analyses of deterrence recommended more

relaxed assumptions of choice that were nevertheless compatible with models of subjective expected utility.

To explain the failures of deterrence and, simultaneously, the poor fit between the predictions of the theory and observed behavior in important cases, three strands of criticism have developed. Those persuaded by the deductive logic of deterrence theory emphasize the faulty execution of the strategy and dispute the allegation of an unsatisfactory fit between theory and evidence (Quester, 1989). Drawing on evidence of conventional deterrence failures, they document the ineptness of leaders who, they insist, failed to specify the behavior that was unacceptable, signal their commitment, develop adequate military capabilities to support deterrence, or communicate their resolve. In reasoning that is analogous to that of some economists, proponents of deterrence insist that the theory is "right" but that the people who use it are "wrong."

Others, however, point to improperly specified models. In particular, those who examined cases of deterrence failure urge the need for a reformulation of the theory of deterrence as a series of contingent propositions that vary with the context (George and Smoke, 1974). Some suggest that models of subjective expected utility that include a broader set of estimates of the likely costs and benefits of action and inaction will provide a more valid basis for the analysis of the effectiveness and limits of deterrence strategies (Bueno de Mesquita, 1981, 1985; Bueno de Mesquita and Lalman, 1986).

A third group of critics goes further. They insist that deterrence fails because the theoretical assumptions on which the strategy is based are inherently inadequate (Jervis, Lebow, and Stein, 1985; Lebow and Stein, 1987a, 1989a). Empirical analyses of deterrence failures, they contend, have identified anomalies that cannot be accommodated by revision of existing theories and obstacles that cannot be transcended by better execution of the strategy.

First, deterrence is oversimplified as a theory of motivation. Leaders can be motivated not only by "opportunity" but also by "vulnerability," by a sense of political and strategic weakness that drives them to consider a challenge. Deterrence theories do not model the critically important political and psychological needs that can constrain the strategy of deterrence. Nor do they examine how preferences are formulated and how "learning" occurs (Nye, 1988). Because they do not, they provide no theoretical guidance for revision of the models of instrumental rationality that are at their core and for the construction of appropriate models of subjective expected utility.

Even if these obstacles could be overcome, differentially weighted, subjected expected utility models cannot accommodate the evidence that leaders deviate from processes of rational choice in important and distorting ways in interpreting relevant information and in weighing relative costs and benefits.

Insofar as the evidence suggests, for example, that would-be challengers distort information about the chances of success of military action or ignore critically important value trade-offs in making their decisions, theories of deterrence premised on variants of rational choice will provide a poor guide to strategy.

Before examining the evidence relevant to this debate, it is important to introduce three caveats. First, very little of the evidence is drawn from cases of deterrence success (Huth and Russett, 1984, 1988; Stein, 1985a; Lebow and Stein, 1987a, 1989c, 1990). This is largely a function of the extraordinarily difficult problem of inferring success through counterfactual argument (George and Smoke, 1974; Lebow and Stein, 1987a). The success of deterrence generally results in no action and can remain largely invisible to outsiders.

To identify a universe of cases of successful deterrence, analysts must first establish what would-be challengers intended to do and, far more problematic, what they would have done had the defender not threatened retaliation. Both tasks are most easily accomplished in cases of "immediate" deterrence when defenders anticipate a challenge and threaten to punish or to deny a would-be challenger its objectives in an attempt to deter (Morgan, 1983:28). At times the historical evidence does establish that a challenger did consider the use of force, but was deterred. Egyptian leaders, for example, did consider a limited attack in the Sinai peninsula in December 1971, and again in November 1972, but were deterred by Israel's military superiority and unquestioned resolve (Stein, 1985a). The more complete and reliable the historical evidence of both the challenger's and defender's calculations, the easier it is to define the relevant universe of cases.

Even then, restricting the analysis to cases of immediate deterrence biases the results in important ways. Because leaders have already begun to consider a use of force, these cases constitute the most demanding and rigorous test of deterrence. Undoubtedly, the bias that is built into the selection of cases inflates the rate of deterrence failure.

The alternative is to identify cases of "general" deterrence. General deterrence refers to the existing power relationships between adversaries and works by preventing a would-be challenger from even considering a use of force because of the obviously adverse consequences of military action. When it works, it leaves no evidentiary trail whatsoever and provides no criterion for case selection. Consequently, the success of general deterrence can be inferred only through counterfactual argument rather than evidence and is often subject to intense controversy (Lebow and Stein, 1987a, 1989c, 1990). For these reasons, analysts of deterrence face little alternative but to restrict their selection to cases of immediate deterrence, and it is this evidence that is examined here. Although this test of deterrence is demanding, it is not inherently unfair; proponents of deterrence argue its merits as a strategy of war avoidance under precisely these conditions.

Second, the evidence that is reviewed here is drawn principally from cases of conventional rather than nuclear deterrence. This is largely because empirical evidence relating to the success or failure of nuclear deterrence is largely unavailable (but see Betts, 1987). There are, of course, significant differences between cases of conventional and nuclear deterrence that limit the capacity to extrapolate directly from the one to the other (Stern et al., 1989a). When one nuclear power attempts to deter another, the most important factors are mutual vulnerability and absolute costs of the consequences of a use of force (Jervis, 1984). Nevertheless, many of the most important empirically based generalizations from studies of conventional deterrence relate to the impact of distortions in leaders' processes of attribution, estimation, and judgment under different kinds of political and strategic conditions. Because some of these distortions are likely to occur even in a nuclear environment, it is appropriate to consider carefully their relevance to the use of deterrence as a strategy of conflict management in a context of "immediate" nuclear deterrence.

Third, the relevant evidence is of two kinds. Some of the evidence is drawn from the relationship between structural and behavioral variables across cases (Huth and Russett, 1984, 1988; Huth, 1988). However, these variables have an impact on deterrence only as they are mediated by leaders' perceptions and decisions. Especially when the universe of cases is neither fully identified nor large, an explanatory model cannot rely ultimately on the associations between situational factors and the outcome of deterrence, but must "trace the process" through which these factors affect the outcome of deterrence (Russett, 1967; George, 1982; Huth, 1988).

The critical processes that mediate the impact of situational variables are the psychological processes of inference, estimation, and judgment. Much of the evidence relevant to these processes is qualitative and drawn from detailed analyses of historical cases. As I will argue, however, the available evidence suggests that these processes intervene in critically important ways to affect the outcome of deterrence.

Strategic Factors

There is surprisingly little quantitative analysis of the causes of deterrence failure (Levy, 1989). Those studies that have been done, moreover, are correlational and do not provide a robust basis for causal explanations of the success and failure of deterrence.

These studies suggest, at best, a weak correlation between superior military capability and deterrence success. In an analysis of the determinants of success in 77 cases of military threat, for example, Karsten, Howell, and Allen find that weaker or smaller states are no more likely to yield than are stronger or larger states (1984:54, 70). Their sample does not distinguish carefully, however, between deterrence and compellence, or between the use of threats to convince an adversary to do something it does not want to do and to stop doing something it is already doing (Schelling, 1960, 1966). In their more focused examination of 54 cases of immediate extended deterrence in this century, Huth and Russett (1984) find that although the local balance of military capabilities is important, it is not most heavily correlated with the success of deterrence. In a subsequent study of 51 cases of immediate extended deterrence, they distinguish between immediate or mobilized forces, short-term mobilizable forces, and long-term military capabilities. They find that deterrence was more likely to succeed when the immediate or short-term balance favored the defender, but the long-term balance of forces was basically irrelevant as were nuclear capabilities (Huth and Russett, 1988; Huth, 1988). Their evidence is consistent with George and Smoke's distinction between gross military capabilities and usable military options as a component of deterrence success (1974; George, Hall, and Simons, 1971:5–9). It appears that the overall balance of military capabilities between adversaries has at most a secondary impact on the success or failure of deterrence.

The interpretation of the evidence is made more difficult, however, by problems of selection bias. Karsten, Howell, and Allen (1984) do not make their criterion of case selection explicit. Huth and Russett (1984, 1988) include those cases where a would-be attacker threatens the use of force, a defender attempts to deter, and the would-be challenger clearly perceives the threat. It is entirely possible that a would-be challenger threatens force only when its leaders consider the balance of military capabilities to be reasonably favorable; if this is so, then the selection of cases would significantly bias the analysis of the impact of military capabilities.

A second difficulty of interpretation arises from the classification of deterrence as a success or failure. Huth and Russett (1984, 1988) classify deterrence as successful when an attack is repelled with only small-scale combat. They treat the Berlin blockade, for example, as a success when it is more appropriately classified as a deterrence failure followed by successful compellence. A more appropriate criterion of deterrence failure in international conflict is a use of force by a challenger despite a defender's threat to retaliate (Morgan, 1983; Lebow and Stein, 1989c, 1990).

Even more troubling is the lack of systematic evidence of the intentions of the would-be challenger. In the classification of their cases, Huth and Russett

(1984, 1988) do not specify how they establish the intentions of the challenger. A recent reexamination of the data sets constructed by Huth and Russett eliminates a large majority of their cases (Lebow and Stein, 1990), partly because the indicators of intentions are inadequate. A threat to use force does not always equate to intention to use force. Huth and Russett do not make clear, for example, how they distinguish between a bluff and the intention to attack, or how they determine whether a would-be challenger was deterred by the threat of retaliation or chose not to use force for reasons wholly unrelated to the actions of the defender.

In May 1973, for example, President Sadat of Egypt decided not to go to war against Israel because he did not wish to disrupt the forthcoming summit meeting between the United States and the Soviet Union (Stein, 1985*a*). Can this be considered a successful case of deterrence by Israel? Much of the evidence of a challenger's intentions is open to more than one interpretation and is frequently the subject of considerable controversy among contemporary historians (Orme, 1987; Lebow, 1987; Lebow and Stein, 1987*b*).

Qualitative studies of conventional deterrence failure permit more careful investigation of these controversies and more detailed presentation of the evidence. Evidence drawn from some case studies does support the findings of the quantitative studies on the limited impact of relative military capabilities. They document how challengers have proceeded to use force even when they considered the balance of capabilities to be unfavorable and the defender's commitment to retaliate credible. Japan did so in 1941, as did Egypt in 1973 (Russett, 1967; Stein, 1985*a*). In an analysis of six attempts by the United States to extend deterrence in the Middle East, Stein (1987*a*) finds that challengers considered a use of force even when the local balance of capabilities was unfavorable. Lebow (1987) reviews other cases of deterrence failure where leaders considered a use of force despite their adverse estimates of the balance of military capabilities. As George and Smoke (1974:522, 543) note, moreover, a would-be attacker who considers the local balance of capabilities unfavorable may be deterred from choosing one military option but not another. Quantitative and qualitative evidence converge to suggest that estimates of military inferiority by a would-be attacker are neither necessary nor sufficient to prevent a challenge. The empirical support for this proposition is robust.

Some theories of deterrence have paid attention to the impact of strategic vulnerability on the outcome of deterrence. In his analysis of the "reciprocal fear of surprise attack," Schelling explored the consequences of the vulnerability of weapons systems for the stability of deterrence (1960:207–229). Most of the analysis, however, has concentrated on the consequences of the vulnerability of strategic systems for crisis stability.

Empirical studies of deterrence failure have examined a broader set of strategic factors that create a sense of weakness and endanger deterrence. Among the most important are changes in the balance of military capabilities that work against a challenger and an inhospitable strategic environment characterized by a "security dilemma." Both these strategic factors are important as they are perceived and evaluated by decision makers, and both can defeat deterrence even when military capabilities favor the defender and credibility and resolve are not in question.

Analyses of Egyptian decision making in 1973 and Japanese decision making in 1941 identify a common pattern (Stein, 1985a; Russett, 1967; Lebow and Stein, 1987a). In both cases, leaders acknowledged their military inferiority but also anticipated unfavorable changes in the balance of capabilities. In the autumn of 1973, President Sadat considered that Egyptian military capabilities had peaked and would deteriorate in the future; he estimated that the longer he postponed war, the stronger Israel would become. Japanese leaders also judged that time was working against them; they opted for war only after they were persuaded that the military balance between themselves and their adversaries would never again be as favorable as it was in 1941. Although it is qualitative and partial, the evidence suggests that, contrary to the expectations of those theories of deterrence that emphasize the importance of capability and credibility, leaders who anticipate an unfavorable decline in the relative balance of power may see no alternative to military action.

In principle, theories of deterrence premised on rational choice should be able to build these kinds of factors into their models. A revised model of subjective expected utility could accommodate leaders' estimates of adverse trends in the military balance in their weighting of relative costs to predict the outcome of deterrence. Theories of deterrence, however, which focus on the creation and manipulation of credible threats, reinforced by usable military options, would not provide a useful basis for the design of this kind of model. Three distinct kinds of problems are at issue (Lebow and Stein, 1989a).

First, theories of deterrence, as distinct from theories of rational choice, are silent about the relative costs of inaction; the weighting of this kind of cost cannot be deduced from the postulates of deterrence theories. Second, the tone of much of deductive deterrence theory, which emphasizes the manipulation of threats, is counterintuitive to the design of this kind of revised model; it creates "blind spots" for those who analyze and for those who use deterrence (Stern, 1986). Third, as I shall argue next, estimates of vulnerability may result in significant distortions in information processing, insensitivity to warning, and biased estimates of relative costs that may make deterrent threats irrelevant. Models of rational choice cannot accommodate these kinds of consequences.

Under certain kinds of strategic conditions, deterrence may not only fail, it may provoke the action it is designed to deter because it intensifies the pressure on the challenger to act. The distinguishing characteristic of an international "security dilemma" is that behavior perceived by adversaries as threatening and aggressive is a defensive response to an inhospitable strategic environment (Butterfield, 1951; Herz, 1950; Jervis, 1978). To enhance their security, leaders take measures that simultaneously diminish the security of others. They are likely to do so when geography is harsh and provides no buffer zone or margin for error, when offensive and defensive technology are difficult to distinguish, and when the relative power balance between adversaries is changing so that for one of the two, the advantages of striking first are substantial. Under these kinds of strategic conditions, a deterrent threat is likely to be misread, the hostility of an adversary is likely to be exaggerated, and defensive action designed to reinforce deterrence may be interpreted as preparation for offense. In the strategic environment of 1914, for example, the attempt by Russia to deter Germany through mobilization of its forces provoked the use of force it was designed to prevent (Snyder, 1985).

Evidence drawn from the analysis of cases of conventional deterrence failure provides one possible interpretation of the association between a challenger's military inferiority and deterrence failure identified in the quantitative studies. When would-be challengers anticipate adverse military trends, or cannot distinguish offensive from defensive action and anticipate great costs if they are attacked first, then their military inferiority will not prevent a use of force. On the contrary, in an unstable strategic environment, an attempt to reinforce deterrence through threat or a show of force may increase crisis instability and provoke the action it is designed to prevent.

Domestic Political Factors

Quantitative studies of deterrence have not systematically investigated the impact of domestic political factors. Comparative analyses of cases of conventional deterrence do not look directly at the relationship between domestic politics and the outcome of deterrence. They do suggest, however, that the impact of domestic politics may be powerful but mediated through the perceptions of political leaders in at least three ways.

First, would-be challengers who have felt politically vulnerable and pressed have chosen at times to use force, even though they considered the prospect of military success uncertain or even unfavorable. Indeed, it is the interaction between strategic and political factors, external and internal pressures that has at times driven leaders to choose force. German strategy in 1914, for example, can be explained not only by its strategic dilemmas, but also by the impact of domestic political, economic, and institutional processes. A school of German historians argues that the structural contradictions of German society were powerful inducements to the deliberate exaggeration of external threat (Fischer, 1975). Important industrial and economic groups benefited directly, they suggest, from the heightened perception of threat, the emphasis on offense by the military, and the military spending that followed. The political leadership alleviated the social tensions and sharp class conflict in Germany at the time, at least in part, by their emphasis on the hostility of their adversaries and the growing external threat (Gordon, 1974; Van Evera, 1984).

In Egypt as well, President Sadat confronted a badly deteriorating economy and growing political pressure in 1973. He was persuaded that foreign investment and economic growth were impossible unless Egypt broke the military and political stalemate with Israel. He also alluded repeatedly to the escalating political crisis that could be arrested only if Egyptian forces eradicated the humiliating defeat of 1967 through military action. Moreover, the use of military force to regain even part of the Sinai peninsula captured by Israel in 1967 was politically legitimated and broadly sanctioned by the Egyptian body politic; that a challenge was legitimate increased the political costs to the Egyptian president of continuing inaction. Partly because he felt so vulnerable at home, Egypt's president chose to use force in 1973, even though he acknowledged Israel's military superiority and estimated very high costs for even a limited military challenge (Stein, 1985a).

The Egyptian decision to go to war in 1973 is seriously damaging to deductive theories of deterrence, although not to theories of rational choice. On the face of it, the decision is countertheoretical: Israel had clear and acknowledged military superiority. Proponents of deterrence might argue that Israel's leaders failed to reinforce deterrence and, consequently, the Egyptian leadership miscalculated; if Egyptian leaders had miscalculated, then deterrence might have failed because of faulty implementation and human error. Reliable evidence does not sustain such a proposition. Despite the failure of Israel's leaders to reinforce deterrence, Egypt's leaders did not miscalculate. They considered their military capabilities inferior to those of Israel, and acknowledged the risks of military action—indeed, exaggerated the risks and anticipated considerable losses—but nevertheless chose to use force because they considered the foreign and domestic political and economic costs of inaction unbearably high. Their challenge to deterrence was a calculated act of desperation.

Theories of deterrence generally do not accommodate evidence of these kinds of calculations by a challenger (but see George and Smoke, 1974). Again, it can be argued that the high cost of the status quo and the consequent urgency of action can be built into a revised model of subjective expected utility to predict the outcome of deterrence. However, guidelines for the weighting of these factors cannot be derived from the postulates, axioms, or assumptions of deterrence theories that do not consider, much less model, the impact of domestic political variables and needs on net expected utility (Lebow and Stein, 1989*a*).

Existing theories of deterrence treat states as unitary actors, do not allow for important political divisions, and ignore the motivated errors in calculation that can flow from pressing political need. Nor do they consider the possible contradiction between individual and collective rationality in modeling the likelihood to deterrence success. If, for example, the leader of a would-be challenger were to lose a great deal personally if no action were taken, then it would be rational for the leader to attack at the least unfavorable time, even if the chances of success were small. This argument can be extended, of course, to the preferences of leaders of large, important bureaucracies. Thus, what is rational for the individual may not be rational for the state. Theories of deterrence, because they treat the state as a unitary actor, do not consider the contradiction between individual and collective rationality, which is so central to models of public choice. Insofar as they do not, they create important "blind spots" for the strategy of deterrence.

Domestic politics may have an impact on the defender as well as the challenger. Unfortunately, the impact of domestic politics on a defender's calculations has not been the subject of systematic investigation. The limited evidence that is available suggests that in a domestic political climate inhospitable to a use of force, defenders have felt constrained when they considered reinforcing deterrence. British and French leaders felt that their publics would not support a show of force against Hitler in 1938, and Henry Kissinger complained repeatedly of the constraints imposed on U.S. strategy in Vietnam by a public antagonistic to the commitment of U.S. forces (Lebow and Stein, 1987*a*; Kissinger, 1979:288–296). In a political climate that is suspicious of an adversary, leaders may also exaggerate the hostility of their opponent, resort to threat to reinforce deterrence, and, in an unstable strategic environment, risk provoking military action by an adversary. On the other hand, although the evidence here too is correlational rather than causal, limited, and indirect, analysts of U.S. public opinion have documented a significant and reliable increase in public support after a president threatens or uses limited force abroad (Mueller, 1973; Ostrom and Simon, 1985). Moreover, the United States has been especially likely to use force when economic growth is slow or negative and in preelection periods (Ostrom and Job, 1986; Huth and Russett, 1988).

Even though the importance of domestic political factors is widely acknowledged, evidence of their impact on deterrence is still limited, episodic, and uneven. We need to know a great deal more about the direction and scope of their impact. The data that we do have suggest that when leaders feel themselves politically constrained and vulnerable, their strategic choices can at times be understood, at least in part, as a deliberate response to their political needs and interests.

Psychological Factors

Strategic and political factors have an impact on deterrence only as they are mediated by leaders' perceptions and decisions. Deterrence theories assume that leaders are "rational" in their handling of information and in the choices they make. Evidence drawn from a broad range of cases of deterrence failure shows overwhelmingly, however, that political leaders depart in important ways from the norms of rational choice (George and Smoke, 1974; Jervis, 1976, 1979, 1982a; Jervis, Lebow, and Stein, 1985; Lebow, 1981, 1987; Lebow and Stein, 1987a; Stein, 1987a).

Psychologists trace flaws in information processing and decision to fundamental cognitive processes or to error motivated by human needs. Cognitive factors have received greater attention, but the evidence of motivated error and its impact on decisions is impressive. A great deal of the evidence, however, is experimental and derived from studies of ordinary people performing ordinary tasks.

Cognitive psychologists have examined the distorting impact of cognitive "schemata" and "scripts," as well as a series of heuristics and biases on the crucial decisional processes of attribution, estimation, and judgment. The most important of these is the overwhelming impact of people's prior concepts and theories on leaders' perceptions and inferences; people see what they expect to see. Leaders' perceptions are heavily theory-driven. Their organizing schemas constrain and condition how and what they perceive, what types of information are relevant, and, therefore, what types of information are noticed and stored. Schemata also guide the recall and interpretation of information in memory (Abelson, 1973, 1981; Schank and Abelson, 1977; Thorndyke and Hayes-Roth, 1979; Kelley, 1972; Anderson, 1982; Reder and Anderson, 1980; Lau and Sears, 1986; Axelrod, 1976; George, 1969; Jervis, 1976).

In October 1973, for example, Israel's intelligence analysts believed that Egypt would not attack until the Egyptian air force could strike at Israel in depth and at Israel's airfields in particular, and that Syria would attack only in conjunction with Egypt (Stein, 1985b:64). Using this as an organizing concept to interpret a great deal of evidence of Egyptian military activity, intelligence analysts discounted the possibility of preparation for an attack and interpreted the activity in the field as annual military maneuvers. Their low estimate of the likelihood of attack was reinforced by their confidence in Israel's military superiority; beliefs reinforced one another. The "theory" of analysts in military intelligence drove the interpretation of the evidence and led to a serious underestimation of threat and to a failure to reinforce deterrence.

Closely related to the overwhelming impact of schemata is the limited ability of leaders to empathize. Individuals are inherently limited by cognitive processes in their capacity to understand how others see the world, and these limits are further exacerbated when there are important differences in cognitive contexts (Fiske and Taylor, 1984). This may be an especially serious problem in deterrence, that assumes that leaders can reconstruct the cost-benefit calculus of would-be challengers, that they can communicate a credible threat effectively, that they can signal their resolve, and that their adversary will accurately perceive their intentions. When sender and recipient use quite different contexts to frame, communicate, and interpret signals, however, the opportunities for miscalculation and misjudgment multiply; it becomes even more difficult for one set of leaders to imagine how another sees them and interprets their actions (Jervis, 1985; Lebow, 1985a; Lebow and Stein, 1987a). In addition to these deeply rooted substantive impediments to the communication and perception of threat, cognitive psychologists have identified a number of specific heuristics that can impair processes of perception and attribution. Evidence in support of these heuristics is drawn both from laboratory studies and historical analysis. People are "cognitive misers:" because of well-defined cognitive limits, their processing of information is selective (Anderson, 1982; Fiske and Taylor, 1984). Heuristics refer to the rules people use to test the propositions embedded in their schemas; they describe how individuals process information. When challengers resort to heuristics of "availability" and "representativeness," for example, they interpret deterrent threats in terms of what is easily available in their cognitive repertoire and exaggerate the similarity between one threat and a prior class of threats (Tversky and Kahneman, 1973; Ajzen, 1977; Jervis, 1986a). This can lead to serious miscalculation.

Cognitive psychologists have also established the impact of a series of cognitive biases on the handling of new information as well as on processes of estimation and judgment. These cognitive biases are widespread; they derive from human limitations that are inherent (Kahneman, Slovic, and Tversky, 1982; von Winterfeldt and Edwards, 1986). Among the most important are the discounting and denial of information that is inconsistent with prevailing beliefs, a discounting that makes leaders insensitive to warning (Abelson et al., 1968; Jervis, 1976:143–201; Jervis, 1982a; Lebow, 1981:101–147); the "egocentric" bias, where leaders exaggerate the degree to which the behavior of others is the result of their prior action and overestimate the extent to which an adversary's behavior is targeted at them (Ross and Sicoly, 1979; Fiske, and Taylor, 1984); overconfidence in the accuracy of their estimates of the likely consequences of their actions (Fischoff, Slovic, and Lichtenstein, 1977); the "proportionality" bias, where leaders make inappropriate inferences about the intentions of others from the costs and consequences of the actions they initiate (Komorita, 1973; Jervis, 1985:15; Lebow and Stein, 1989b); the "fundamental attribution error," where leaders exaggerate the importance of dispositional over situational factors in explaining the undesirable behavior of others and, consequently, overestimate threat (Jones and Nisbett, 1971; Ross, 1977; Kelley and Michela, 1980; Nisbett and Ross, 1980); and, the attribution of greater coherence and centralization than the evidence warrants, which also contributes to the exaggeration of threat (Jervis, 1976:319–329; Levy, 1983).

These heuristics and biases contribute in important ways to errors by both a defender and a would-be challenger that can result in the defeat of deterrence. Because they are pervasive and distorting, they frequently lead to the misperception of intentions, commitment, resolve, or values, and to major errors in the cost-benefit calculations required by deterrence (Jervis, 1979; Lebow, 1981; Lebow and Stein, 1987a, 1989a). Moreover, in many cases of inaccurate threat perception, biases interacted with one another to aggravate misperception (Stein, 1987b). Although the case evidence suggests that cognitive errors occur in clusters, existing psychological theory tends to treat these biases singly. Exploring the covariation among biases is an important theoretical and research challenge (Lebow and Stein, 1989b).

The near ubiquity of cognitive biases and heuristics is a serious problem for deterrence theory and strategy. Because they are generally characteristic of processes of attribution, estimation, and judgment, they do not appear to vary systematically with either specific kinds of needs and interests or types of political and strategic situations. This does not appear to be the case for motivated errors.

Motivational psychologists identify many of the same errors as do cognitive psychologists, but explain these errors by the impact of deeply rooted fears and needs rather than expectations. "Push" models of behavior explain observable biases in information processing in terms of individual personality structures and the diverse ways in which they mediate deep-seated, universal human needs. "Pull" models emphasize the needs, fears, and anxieties that situations arouse in individuals (Hoyenga and Hoyenga, 1984). Both traditions emphasize, however, that when needs are pressing, people will make fundamental errors in attribution, estimation, and judgment. Motivational explanations are based in part on the premise that there is a strong association between certain types of external situations, internal needs, and decisional processes. Scholars have drawn on motivational psychology to explore the impact of political and strategic needs on leaders' calculations (Lebow, 1981; Snyder, 1984; Jervis, Lebow, and Stein, 1985; Lebow and Stein, 1987a; 1989b).

Motivated error, like cognitive biases, can lead to the discounting or denial of unpleasant or threatening information, and thereby to the underestimation of threat and insensitivity to warning (Stein, 1988b). Janis and Mann, in their analysis of decision making, identify a pattern of "defensive avoidance," characterized by efforts to avoid, dismiss, and deny warnings that increase anxiety and fear (1977:57–58, 107–133). This kind of information processing has serious implications for the perception by a would-be challenger of a deterrent threat. Once leaders have committed themselves to a challenge, efforts by defenders to make their commitments credible may only have a marginal impact. Lebow's analysis of 13 cases of brinkmanship suggests that even elaborate demonstrations of resolve may be insufficient to discourage a challenger who is convinced that a use of force is necessary to preserve vital strategic and political interests (1981:57–97).

Motivated discounting of alarming information may also have a serious impact on the estimate by a defender of the likelihood of a challenge to deterrence. A careful reading of the evidence of some studies of intelligence failures suggests a process of motivated misperception by a defender (Betts, 1982; Handel, 1976). In the autumn of 1973, for example, Israel's leaders were preparing for a general election and, in their campaign rhetoric, members of the governing coalition emphasized the calm along the borders and the improved strategic situation. In this kind of political climate, political leaders may have unconsciously discounted the growing evidence of Egyptian and Syrian military preparation. In part because they did not wish to alarm the public unnecessarily, Israeli leaders were reluctant to increase military preparedness unless they were certain the measures were necessary.

A recent analysis of President Carter's decision to attempt to deter Soviet military action in the Persian Gulf in the wake of its intervention in Afghanistan has explained this decision in part as a motivated response to changing political needs (Lebow and Stein, 1989b). Indeed, cognitive explanations cannot wholly account for the dramatic change in Carter's estimate of Soviet intentions, a change that was largely inconsistent with his prior beliefs and expectations. The sharp increase in his estimate of the Soviet threat is even more unexpected given the espousal of a "defensive" interpretation of Soviet motives by some of his senior advisers; the evidence did not speak for itself. In a changed political climate, it is likely that a vulnerable president adjusted his policy so that it became congruent with political needs and interests. The change in Carter's attitude is best explained by the complex interaction among cognitive and motivational processes: the inertia produced by cognitive consistency was overwhelmed by need.[1]

Not only domestic political needs but also strategic fears and needs can motivate error by political leaders. In 1973, for example, the strategic as well as the political needs of Israel's leaders may have been served by a discounting of the probability of attack. They represented a status quo power that had no interest in war, and this satisfaction created incentives for wishful thinking and motivated denial of threatening information. They tended, in consequence, to discount evidence indicating Egyptian preparation to attack and conjointly to inflate evidence suggesting that deterrence was secure. Predictably, the result of such a pattern of information processing was strategic and tactical surprise when Egyptian and Syrian forces attacked. Unlike their counterparts in intelligence, the evidence suggests that the errors of the political leadership were motivated at least in part by their political and strategic needs (Stein, 1985b).

German military decisions in 1914 also can be explained in part by the mediated impact of motivated error. Although German military leaders confronted elements of a security dilemma, they greatly exaggerated the dangers and reasoned inside out to create a "perceptual security dilemma" (Snyder, 1985:170). They overrated the hostility of their adversaries and consequently assumed the inevitability of a two-front war. Once they did, they saw preventive war as the only alternative to strategic vulnerability, emphasized its benefits, and discounted its risks. The German military did not overestimate their offensive capabilities and then choose force, as some deterrence theories would predict; rather, they exaggerated the hostility of their adversaries as psychological explanations of affect would expect and then insisted that an offensive strategy was the only option. In the late summer of 1914, deterrence was inappropriate as a strategy of conflict management. The Russian mobilization, designed to deter Germany and Austria, only enhanced their fears of strategic vulnerability and pushed the German military leadership, already committed to an offensive strategy, to urge their civilian counterparts to preempt. As the outbreak of war in 1914 illustrates, when unfavorable strategic assessments by a would-be challenger are reinforced by estimates of exaggerated hostility and a sense of acute vulnerability, an attempt at deterrence is especially likely to provoke motivated error and, consequently, the use of force it is designed to deter.

Unlike the distortions produced by cognitive heuristics and biases, the motivated errors of political leaders appear to be situation specific. We need to know more, however, about the conditions that arouse deeply felt political needs and strategic fears and their relative impact on leaders' calculations about a challenge to deterrence. In some of the cases that have been analyzed, for example, the two sets of needs were reinforcing; under these conditions, their interaction is especially likely to motivate error. Research has yet to be done, however, on whether vulnerabilities at home and abroad are equally likely to predispose leaders to make errors in judgment that can defeat deterrence. The limited evidence that is available suggests only that when leaders feel vulnerable, anticipate threat abroad or at home and can see no attractive military or diplomatic option, they are especially likely to engage in defensive avoidance, wishful thinking, and bolstering. When they do so, the obstacles to the success of deterrence multiply.

The evidence of the distorting impact of psychological processes on deterrence is drawn from detailed studies of processes of attribution, estimation, and judgment by political leaders. Consequently, the data are qualitative rather than quantitative, historical rather than experimental, and often indirect because psychological processes leave no direct behavioral traces. Nevertheless, although the data are often open to different interpretations, the evidence of different kinds and magnitudes of distortion and error across cases is substantial.

Paradoxically, the difficulties lie principally with the available theory rather than with the evidence. The theoretical challenge is twofold. First, cognitive psychologists have yet to develop a set of theoretically integrated propositions to explain distorted attribution, estimation, and judgment. The impact of heuristics and biases is well-documented, but we do not know when they occur or how they interact. Second, psychologists have not yet integrated the cognitive and affective dimensions in a theoretically coherent explanation. The following section reviews briefly each of these challenges and their implications for the analysis of deterrence.

Cognitive psychology analyzes the organizing schemas and belief systems that are fundamental to cognition but does not satisfactorily explain processes of change in the crucial elements of a cognitive repertoire (Jervis, 1986*b*:327–328; Lebow and Stein, 1989*b*). Processes of cognitive change are central, however, to theories of deterrence that attempt to model change in a would-be challenger's judgments. Cognitive psychology has yet to specify when one or another schemata is invoked to guide the processing of new information, when people assimilate inconsistent information into a schema, when they adjust the schema to the evidence, and when they reject one schema in favor of another. Moreover, cognitive theories do not specify the external conditions or mediating causes of any of these changes.

Cognitive psychologists also identify a set of discrete heuristics and biases whose relationship to one another and to substantive and situational factors remains as yet unexplicated. A recent examination of the misperception of strategic threat by political leaders suggests that at times these biases appear in patterned clusters rather than independently of one another (Stein, 1987*b*). Drawing on propositions from cognitive psychology, the underestimation of the likelihood of an Egyptian attack by Israel's leaders in 1973 and the consequent failure to reinforce deterrence can be explained in part as a "theory-driven" process of judgment, by the heuristic of availability, and by the reinforcing impact of the bias toward self-image (Stein, 1985*b*). Similarly, examination of President Carter's decision to attempt to deter Soviet military action in the Persian Gulf indicates that the bias toward proportionately interacted with a tendency toward overconfidence, egocentricity, and fundamental errors of attribution to inflate his perception of the Soviet threat (Lebow and Stein, 1989*b*).

In both these cases, heuristics and biases reinforced one another and were easily interpreted. When biases contradict each other, however, existing theory does not specify their relative importance, the likelihood that one will supercede the other, or the conditions when each is likely to occur. If cognitive theories are to be more useful in explaining the outcome of deterrence, analysts must first identify clusters of biases that are theoretically coherent and integrated. They must also examine the interactive effects of contradictory heuristics and biases. These biases must then be related to the kinds of errors that can defeat deterrence: Are leaders insensitive to their adversary's values and interests, for example, because of an inability to empathize, because of a bias towards egocentricity, or because of the tendency to discount inconsistent information?

Third, cognitive explanations generally have paid inadequate attention to the context in which people make their estimates and choices. Many of the relevant propositions in cognitive and motivational psychology have been tested in controlled laboratory studies, involving ordinary people facing ordinary decisions. Psychologists debate whether biases identified in the laboratory are replicated outside (Ebbeson and Koncini, 1980; Jungermann, 1983). Jervis (1986*b*:324) suggests, for example, that cognitive processing may vary with the importance of the issue to the decision maker, and that performance may improve on problems that are central rather than trivial (but see Nisbett and Ross, 1980:220–222). If this proposition is sustained in a political and strategic context, leaders may be far less prone to errors in their judgments when the intrinsic interests at stake are central to a would-be challenger. On the other hand, a great deal of evidence suggests that arousal tends to narrow the cognitive field; well-learned responses are performed more efficiently, but less familiar responses are performed more poorly (Easterbrook, 1959). Similarly, psychologists and political scientists have found that moderate stress tends to enhance effective information processing, while extreme stress degrades performance (Janis and Mann, 1977: 391–432; de Rivera, 1968:150–

151; Holsti and George, 1975; Lebow, 1981:115–147, 268–273; George, 1986). To the extent that deterrence requires judgments that are not routine in situations where important interests are at stake and leaders are under great stress, its success becomes more problematic.

Psychological theories must also attempt to integrate cognitive and affective dimensions in their explanations of attribution, estimation, and judgment. Cognitive and motivated error are often treated dichotomously, partly because they are derived from different theoretical assumptions and organizing principles. One tradition within psychology treats cognition and affect as separate systems that operate largely independently of one another (Zajonc, 1980; Zajonc, Pietromonaco, and Bargh, 1982). This separation is contested, however, and the failure to specify the relationship between cognition and affect is troubling both when the two sets of theoretical expectations diverge and when they converge (Lazarus, 1982).[2]

When cognitive and motivational explanations differ in their theoretical predictions, interpretation of the evidence permits some assessment of their relative importance even in the absence of good theory. The lack of an integrated explanation is far more serious when the evidence is incomplete. To return to an earlier proposition, insofar as the "importance" of an issue and affect are not entirely independent of one another, motivational explanations would qualify the proposition that performance outside the laboratory may improve on problems that are central rather than trivial. They would predict that if intense affect were associated with "important" interests, performance would be degraded and, consequently, deterrence failure would become more likely when vital interests were at stake. Motivational theories, consequently, would expect deterrence to work best when the issues at stake are not central to leaders who make the critical judgments.

A second kind of controversy stems not from divergent expectations but rather from an inability to separate the cognitive and affective components of a central theoretical concept. In Germany in 1914, in India in 1962, and in Israel in 1973, cognitive and motivational explanations converge; the political needs of leaders reinforced the impact of cognitive biases and heuristics (Lebow, 1981:119–147, 216—223; Stein, 1985b; Lebow and Stein, 1987a). Because the expectations converge, the evidence cannot discriminate between the two explanations nor establish the relative impact of cognition and affect.

Current analysis of the impact of leaders' perceptions of "legitimacy" on deterrence illustrates this problem. It has been suggested that when a would-be challenger sees its action as "legitimate," then deterrence is more likely to fail (Stern et al., 1989b). It is unclear from the argument whether "legitimacy" is a cognitive or an affective concept. In all likelihood, it is both. Leaders derive criteria of legitimacy from personally held norms that are embedded in their organizing schemas and from attribution of intentions to others, but frequently feel intensely about what is and what is not "legitimate." Insofar as judgments of legitimacy are a product of both cognition and affect, specification of its mediating impact on deterrence remains ambiguous and even contradictory.

If psychological explanations of deterrence are to become more precise and more powerful, analysts must address the relative importance of affect and cognition on the distortions in processes of attribution, estimation, and judgment that defeat deterrence. This is no easy task, both because the theory is only beginning to develop and because behavioral evidence often does not permit distinction between the two perspectives. Nevertheless, analysts of deterrence can attempt to improve the power and precision of their explanations and their prescriptions.

The situational and structural factors that give rise to the two kinds of errors must be identified through carefully controlled historical comparison. Evidence drawn from cases of conventional deterrence failure does suggest, for example, that domestic political crises and security dilemmas create a heightened sense of vulnerability among political leaders (Jervis, 1976:58–113; Lebow, 1981; Lebow and Stein, 1987a; Stein, 1987a). These feelings of weakness and need increase the likelihood of the kind of motivated error and distorted decision making that can defeat deterrence.

This kind of proposition must be the subject of further research across cases of deterrence success and failure. If a relationship between strategic and political vulnerability and deterrence failure can be substantiated, for example, it would have implications not only for theory but also for policy. In deciding whether or not to attempt to deter, and if so, how to do so, leaders could be advised to pay special attention to the political and strategic environment of their adversaries and to their sense of vulnerability. Insofar as the political and strategic preconditions of vulnerability can be identified, leaders can be given a rough rule of thumb to distinguish those conditions that are especially likely to defeat deterrence.

Summary

Since George and Smoke's pioneering empirical analysis of deterrence in 1974, the comparison of evidence drawn from cases of conventional deterrence failure has permitted the development of some contingent generalizations about the conditions of its failure. Before summarizing these generalizations, however, two caveats are in order. First, these generalizations derive largely from cases of conventional deterrence failure and must be tested systematically against evidence drawn from cases of "immediate" deterrence success. Should some of the same political, strategic, and psychological conditions hold when deterrence succeeds as a strategy of war avoidance, then they are far less important and powerful as components of an explanation of deterrence failure. Second, some of these propositions are themselves preliminary and require both further conceptual clarification and additional research.

The available evidence suggests indirectly that deterrence as a strategy of conflict management may be most appropriate when adversarial leaders are motivated largely by the prospect of gain rather than by the fear of loss, have the political and strategic freedom to exercise restraint, are not mislead by grossly distorted assessments of the political-military situation, and are vulnerable to the kinds of threats that a would-be deterrer is capable of making credible. If challengers do not share these cognitive, motivational, and political attributes, a strategy of deterrence is more likely to fail.

The timing of deterrence may be important to its success or failure. Deterrence is more likely to succeed if it is attempted early, before an adversary commits itself to a challenge. Some psychological and historical evidence suggests that once challengers have made such a commitment, they are more likely to engage in bolstering and less likely to be sensitive to warnings that their action is likely to meet with retaliation (Janis and Mann, 1977; Lebow, 1981). This kind of insensitivity to warning is especially likely when challengers are motivated by acute political need or strategic fear.

One of the most robust findings is that the military superiority of a defender may be neither a necessary nor a sufficient condition of deterrence success. This proposition is generally supported across cases and across different kinds of evidence. Consideration of the relative military balance is not the primary determinant of the outcome of deterrence.

Finally, some evidence suggests that when would-be challengers feel politically vulnerable or consider trends in the military balance unfavorable, deterrence as a strategy of conflict management may provoke the response it is attempting to prevent. Under these conditions, deterrence may not only be ineffective, it may also be dangerous. Domestic political instability or strategic vulnerability or both may provoke motivated distortion of basic processes of inference, estimation, and judgment that can defeat deterrence.

These conditional propositions, although promising, still leave important policy and theoretical questions unanswered. Examination of the needs and fears of would-be challengers, for example, has emphasized their distorting impact on leaders' subsequent calculations. In so doing, it stresses the importance of need as well as opportunity as a motive for a challenge to deterrence. Although opportunity and need are theoretically distinct concepts, in practice they are not mutually exclusive. *Opportunity* has generally been defined in the theoretical literature as a defender's vulnerable commitment, while *need* has been conceived of as strategic or political weakness or both. The dichotomy between the two as motives for a challenge to deterrence, however, is almost always blurred in specific historical cases; many, if not most, challenges contain elements of both. Analysts suggest, for example, that Iraq decided to attack Iran both because it saw the *opportunity* to exploit the political divisions within Iran and because it feared the export of Iran's revolution to the large Shi'ia population within Iraq (Heller, 1984; Tripp, 1986). The important question for strategy, however, is the relative weight of need and opportunity as motivating factors. It is significant because it speaks to the approximate mixture of deterrence with other strategies of conflict management.[3]

Development of a broader typology of motivation is also important to the theory of deterrence. Evidence from psychological research in the laboratory suggests that people tend to pay greater attention to value rather than to probability and are more sensitive to potential loss than they are to potential gain. Individuals tend to be risk-averse with respect to gains and risk-acceptant with respect to losses (Slovic and Lichtenstein, 1968; Kahneman and Tversky, 1979, 1984; Hershey and Shoemaker, 1980). If these propositions are valid outside the laboratory, they suggest by implication that would-be challengers would be more likely to challenge deterrence to avoid loss than to achieve gains.

Attention to leaders' estimates of the costs of inaction as well as the costs of action would capture a more complex set of motives. Analyses of deterrence have at times considered these factors. Daniel Ellsberg (1961), for example, modeled leaders' critical risks and Glenn Snyder analyzed the "critical risk tactics" that can reduce an opponent's incentives to defect (1972). Neither of these studies paid attention, however, to leaders' estimates of the domestic political consequences of inaction. Generally, deductive theories of deterrence have paid greater attention to opportunity than to need.[4] The failure to emphasize need as well as opportunity has created important blind spots for the strategy of deterrence.

The fact that theories of deterrence have not emphasized need in the past does not preclude a revised theory from doing so in the future. Indeed, as noted, some analysts suggest that a theory of deterrence built on a model of subjective expected utility could treat loss as negative gain and thereby accommodate challenges to deterrence even if the challenger expected to lose. When the costs of perpetuating the status quo are greater than the costs of a military action, a decision to challenge is rational. There are, however, serious obstacles to the specification of a model of subjective expected utility appropriate to a theory of deterrence.

Existing theories of deterrence provide no guidelines to specify the weight of domestic political needs in a reformulated, subjective expected utility model. Theorists of deterrence would have to look beyond existing theories to determine appropriate weighting of this kind of variable and its interaction with other relevant variables in the model. In short, they need a far broader, better formulated theory of motivation anchored in international politics (Lebow and Stein, 1989*a*).

Even more serious, as I have argued, subjective expected utility models cannot accommodate the impact of systematic distortion in processes of estimation, attribution, and judgment. These processes would be theoretically unimportant, although historically interesting and policy relevant, if they did not intervene to affect behavior in ways unanticipated by theories of deterrence. The cumulating evidence from comparative case studies suggests, however, that especially when leaders feel threatened and vulnerable at home or abroad, their processes of inference are likely to be biased in ways that systematically distort their choices and, consequently, their strategic behavior.[5] Under these conditions, existing theories of deterrence provide poor explanations and inadequate guidance to policymakers.[6]

Existing theories of deterrence are a poor guide to strategy for other reasons. They do not distinguish systematically between different levels of conflict nor between different kinds and degrees of deterrence failure (George and Smoke, 1974). Most important, as George and Smoke (1974) noted over a decade ago, the theory fails to define its scope as an instrument of foreign policy. Indeed, critics of deterrence strategy in the United states have argued that, at times, it has replaced foreign policy (MccGwire, 1987). Because deterrence is an instrument of foreign policy, the uses and limitations of deterrence strategy in any given situation depend inescapably on the broader context of foreign policy. Especially because deterrence as a strategy of conflict management may be ineffective, uncertain, and risky under certain conditions, it must be nested within the broader context of foreign policy and supplemented by other strategies of conflict management. These strategies, which are grouped together broadly under the rubric of "reassurance," may substitute for or complement deterrence and reduce some of its obvious risks.

Deterrence and Reassurance

Strategies of reassurance begin from a different set of assumptions than does deterrence. They too presume ongoing hostility but, unlike deterrence, root the source of that hostility not only in adversaries' search for opportunity, but in adversaries' needs and weaknesses as well. Reassurance strategies are conceived broadly as a set of strategies that adversaries can use to reduce the likelihood of resort to the threat or use of force.[7]

To examine the utility of reassurance strategies and the conditions that constrain their effectiveness, this chapter looks at five strategies that differ in the scope of their objectives and in their combinations of the elements of reassurance. They also vary in their relevance to different kinds of deterrence. First, leaders can attempt through restraint not to exacerbate the pressures and constraints that operate on their adversary. A strategy of restraint is relevant largely when leaders anticipate a use of force. Second, they can try informally to develop "norms of competition" to regulate their conflict and reduce the likelihood of miscalculated war. Third, leaders can also try to break out of habitual threat or use of force through less conventional methods of irrevocable commitments. These strategies can be used as substitutes for or complements to immediate deterrence and in the context of general deterrence as well. Fourth, leaders can attempt to establish informal or formal regimes designed specifically to build confidence, reduce uncertainty, and establish acceptable limits of competition. Fifth, they may attempt to initiate a process of tension reduction through reciprocal strategies like "tit-for-tat" and gradual reciprocation in tension-reduction (GRIT), which may make immediate deterrence less necessary. These last two strategies are most appropriate in the context of general deterrence.

Strategies of reassurance are, of course, particularly appropriate for a defender who is trying to deter. Some may also be useful, however, to a would-be challenger in a deterrence relationship who, while actively considering the option of a resort to force, nevertheless attempts to persuade a defender of the limits of its objectives, the benefits of negotiation, and the importance of acceptable limits of competition. Consequently, this chapter looks as broadly as possible at the utility of reassurance strategies from the perspective of both parties to an adversarial relationship.

Strategies of reassurance are useful in the first instance insofar as they reduce the risks of deterrence. As we have seen, deterrence can fail at times regardless of how well it is executed. It can provoke rather than prevent a challenge from a frightened or vulnerable adversary, because it intensifies the pressures on a would-be challenger to act. It can also fail because a defender or a challenger misinterprets the other's intentions and signals; under these conditions, it becomes ineffective. Finally, it can be irrelevant when initiators are insensitive to threats and their consequences. This is most likely to happen when their attention is focused on their own needs. In short, deterrence can at times be provocative, ineffective, or irrelevant.

Different strategies of reassurance attempt to compensate for these three kinds of difficulties. The exercise of restraint, both in the language leaders use and in the deployment of military forces, can reduce the risk of provocation. Leaders can also attempt to reduce the difficulties of interpreting their own and their adversary's intentions by providing more valid, consistent, and reliable information. They may seek to reassure each other, for example, by communicating through third parties who are credible to all sides. Syria and Israel have communicated through the United States repeatedly in the last decade in an attempt to reassure each other of the limits of their intentions. Strategies of reassurance can also attempt to reduce the uncertainty that is endemic to adversarial relationships by clarifying the acceptable limits of conflict and developing shared norms of competition; in so doing, they reduce the likelihood of miscalculation.

Strategies of reassurance can also attempt to prevent an anticipated challenge by persuading an adversary that it has more to gain through diplomacy than force. For a defender, reassurance of this kind can complement or substitute for deterrence; it attempts to alter the context in which leaders consider a use of force. A defender can convey to a would-be challenger its willingness to negotiate important issues in an attempt to make diplomacy more attractive than force. The important step is to persuade an adversary that negotiation is a serious alternative. In this context, a strategy of reassurance attempts to change the conditions under which leaders consider a use of force; it is distinct, however, from the process and substance of negotiation that may follow.[8] This kind of strategy is especially useful when leaders are heavily constrained by political weakness or allied pressure. To the extent that an alternative to the use of force can be made politically salient and visible, an adversary may decide to postpone a use of force in order to explore negotiation as an alternative. Similarly, leaders who are actively considering a use of force can clarify the limits of their objectives and, in so doing, encourage a defender to consider concessions in the expectation that negotiation is a credible option (Stein, 1989).

These short-term strategies of reassurance are likely to be more relevant to conflicts that are propelled by mutual hostility, misperception, and mistrust than to those that are largely issue driven. They are useful to the latter insofar as they attempt to create alternatives to force and make an option of negotiation credible and politically salient. They are, however, especially helpful to the former insofar as they attempt to clarify intentions, minimize uncertainty, reduce the likelihood of miscalculation, and develop a discourse that is less likely to inflame leaders and citizens. However, even when they are successful, short-term strategies of reassurance may accomplish no more than deterrence does when it succeeds; they achieve a temporary military stand down and buy time. More ambitious strategies of reassurance seek to minimize the need of both parties to manipulate the risk of war.

Leaders can, for example, attempt to create informal or formal "regimes" to build confidence, reduce uncertainty, and establish acceptable limits of competition. In so doing, they attempt to change the context of an adversarial relationship, alter stereotypes and misconceptions, reduce uncertainty about intentions, and establish rules of the road that limit the likelihood of miscalculation. Leaders can also try to initiate a process of tension reduction. Two variants of reciprocal strategies, "tit-for-tat" and GRIT, have received particular attention. These strategies attempt to change the context in which leaders assess one another's intentions. To the extent that any of these strategies of reassurance succeed, they make deterrence less necessary and create opportunities for alternative strategies of conflict management. In assessing the effectiveness and limits of these strategies, the analysis of reassurance moves beyond the framework of deterrence to the broader context of foreign policy. Indeed, it is precisely this broad perspective that is often missing in the analysis of deterrence.

Reassurance can be used as an alternative to or together with strategies of immediate deterrence. Before the Falklands/Malvinas War, for example, British leaders attempted through restraint to reassure Argentina's leaders rather than to deter. Leaders can also attempt to reassure even as they are trying actively to deter. In October 1973, Secretary of State Kissinger simultaneously attempted to deter the Soviet Union and to reassure its leaders of U.S. intentions. Under these conditions, the mix and sequencing of strategies are likely to be important to the outcome.

Strategies of reassurance, like deterrence, are difficult to implement. They too must overcome strategic, political, and psychological obstacles. Cognitive barriers to signaling, for example, can just as readily obstruct reassurance as they can deterrence. Other obstacles are specific to strategies of reassurance and derive from the political and psychological constraints leaders face when they seek to reduce tension and reassure an adversary. This chapter attempts to identify these obstacles and assess their interaction with strategies of deterrence.

Unlike deterrence, there is no "theory" of reassurance. There are, however, islands of theory in several of the behavioral sciences that address its fundamental purposes. Generally, strategies of reassurance have received less attention in the strategic literature than has deterrence, and there is less known about incentives for their use and the conditions of their success.[9]

The five strategies of reassurance examined here—the exercise of restraint, the creation of norms of competition, the making of irrevocable commitments, regime-building, and tension reduction—are only a few among many possible variants. They are neither mutually exclusive nor logically exhaustive. Moreover, the evidence in support of these strategies is an uneven mixture of quantitative and qualitative data, single-case study, comparative -case analysis, and laboratory experiment. These five strategies of reassurance have been chosen for analysis largely because there is some relevant evidence of their interaction with deterrence. The test of the effectiveness of strategies of reassurance is their contribution to the avoidance of war, the reduction of tension, and, ultimately, the creation of alternatives to the threat or use of force among adversarial leaders who are hostile and suspicious of one another.

Reassurance Through Restraint

Leaders may recognize that political conditions can compel an opponent to use force in the immediate future and attempt to prevent these pressures from becoming dangerously intense. This is no easy task. It may be very difficult to reduce the domestic political and economic pressures that are so often critical to a challenger's decision to use force. These kinds of factors are often not subject to manipulation, especially from the outside. However, even if leaders cannot directly affect the political environment of their opponent, at least they can try to refrain from actions that would be likely to exacerbate the pressures on their adversary to attack.

Restraint can also be important in reducing the likelihood of miscalculation when adversaries find themselves caught up in an escalating series of threats and military deployments. In 1987, India and Pakistan found themselves caught up in a cycle of escalating troop movements. In the autumn of 1986, India announced plans for unusually large war games scheduled for February and March 1987, at a newly completed training site in the Rajasthan desert near the border of the Pakistani province of Sind. Prime Minister Rajiv Gandhi described the operations as routine and assured Pakistan that India had no hostile intent. Given the unprecedented size of the Indian maneuvers, however, verbal reassurances were not enough to allay the fears of military leaders in Pakistan. Pakistani leaders also expressed concern that secessionists in Sind might ally with Indian forces. In response, Pakistan deployed military divisions just across the border from the Indian states of Punjab and Jammu and Kashmir; these areas have been the site of fighting between India and Pakistan in the past.

Officials in India and Pakistan admitted that neither wanted war. None of the disputes was sufficient, in and of itself, to provoke war, and both recognized India's military superiority. Despite the mutually acknowledged differences in military capability, however, leaders in Pakistan and India sent additional troops to the border area even as they expressed alarm that an accidental shot by either side could lead to full-scale fighting.

As India and Pakistan became increasingly alarmed, both pledged to exercise restraint and agreed to high-level discussions designed to ease tension and allay mutual fear. The two delegations to the talks, led by Adbus Sattar, the foreign secretary of Pakistan, and Alfred Gonsalves, the acting foreign secretary of India, approved a partial withdrawal of approximately 80,000 of the 340,000 heavily armed soldiers who faced each other along the north-central border and agreed to further negotiations to arrange withdrawal of the remainder. The agreement provided further that until the Indian army exercises had ended, Pakistan would continue to deploy its armor and troops in the Punjab. The two sides also exercised "the maximum restraint" and avoided all provocative actions along the border. Neither side was confident that deterrence alone could prevent war, and each recognized the need for restraint. The language each used to describe the agreement is revealing: Humayan Khan, the Pakistani ambassador to India, explained that "it was a question of mutual reassurances," given that each side felt provoked by the other, and Gonsalves, India's chief negotiator, added that Pakistan had been reassured of India's intentions (*New York Times*, 5 February 1987).

A strategy of restraint can reduce some of the obvious risks of deterrence. Because it uses the language of reassurance rather than threat, it can allay the fears of leaders caught in a process of escalation. In this case, mutual restraint by both India and Pakistan reduced the likelihood of miscalculation and of escalation. However, restraint can be demanding of and dangerous for those who use it.

It is demanding because it requires leaders to monitor their adversary's political pressures, its strategic dilemmas, its leaders' estimates of the political and strategic costs of inaction, and their assessment of the alternatives. A strategy of restraint encourages leaders to consider their adversary's calculus within the broadest possible political and strategic context. Like deterrence, it requires leaders to view the world through the eyes of their adversaries and, as we have seen, there are formidable cognitive and motivational impediments to reconstructing the calculus of another set of leaders. Perhaps because leaders pay attention to the vulnerabilities and opportunities of their adversary when they consider restraint, they may be able to overcome some of these impediments. At a minimum, they are more likely to do so than leaders who consider only deterrence.

A strategy of restraint is not only demanding but also dangerous if it culminates in miscalculated escalation. When deterrers are attentive to the weaknesses of an opponent, to the possibility that they may provoke an adversary who is as yet uncommitted to a use of force, then they are more likely to exercise restraint. Would-be challengers, however, may misinterpret restraint and caution as weakness and lack of resolve (Jervis, 1976:58–113). Great Britain's attempt to reassure Argentina in 1982 is a case in point.

Great Britain was extremely sensitive to what its leaders considered important domestic constraints on the Argentinian leadership. Attuned to the political weakness of their opponents, British leaders refrained from making overt threats or visible military preparations to defend the Falklands. Lord Carrington, British foreign minister at the time, later confessed "[We] feared that it would lead to war by strengthening the hand of extremists in the *Junta*" (*London Times*, 5 April 1982). The British government also responded with extraordinary timidity to a private Argentinian attempt to assert sovereignty over the South Georgia Islands, an obvious prelude to a challenge in the Falklands. HMS *Endurance*, an Antarctic survey ship sent to the Islands in the aftermath of the incident, was then hastily withdrawn when three Argentinian warships appeared on the scene. Nicanor Costa Méndes, then Argentina's foreign minister, subsequently explained that the retreat of *Endurance*, after Lord Carrington's earlier promise to Parliament that it would remain on station as long as necessary, succeeded in convincing the junta that they had nothing to fear from Great Britain (Lebow, 1985*b*). The impact of the strategy of restraint was the obverse of what British leaders had intended: it strengthened the resolve of those committed to military action and allayed the anxieties of more moderate men like Costa Méndes, who were now persuaded that a use of force would probably succeed.

Argentina's leaders went to war largely because of their expectation that Great Britain would tolerate a use of force. The British dilemma—whether to seek to prevent miscalculated escalation through restraint or to deter a premeditated challenge through threat and demonstration of resolve—is a recurrent problem in choosing a strategy of conflict management. The policy problem is compounded by the fact that strategies designed to prevent the occurrence of one often tend to exacerbate the likelihood of the other. More troublesome still, it may not be apparent before the fact which of the two routes to war is the more likely.

The Sino–Indian border conflict, which erupted into war in 1962, illustrates the kinds of difficulties leaders face when they try to design a mixed strategy of deterrence and reassurance to avoid both miscalculated escalation and a calculated challenge (Lebow, 1981:148–228). In 1961, Chinese soldiers surrounded Indian outposts that had been set up in contested areas of Ladakh. After they demonstrated their ability to cut off several of these outposts, the Chinese subsequently withdrew, leaving the Indian pickets unharmed. Hoping to deter further encroachments by India, China intended the limited action as a demonstration of resolve that would nevertheless allow Indian leaders to back down without loss of face because violence had been avoided. Government officials in New Delhi, however, misinterpreted the Chinese reluctance to fire on the pickets as a sign of timidity. They reasoned that Chinese forces had failed to press their tactical advantage because China feared the consequences of a wider conflict with India. As a result, Indian leaders became more optimistic about the prospects of a successful challenge and bolder in their efforts to occupy as much of the disputed territory, east and west, as they could.

China's mixed strategy of a limited demonstration of resolve followed by restraint failed to prevent war. It failed because of serious miscalculations by India's leaders of China's intentions and its capabilities (Lebow, 1981:153–168). Prime Minister Nehru and Defense Minister Menon were persuaded that China would want to avoid the condemnation by the nonaligned bloc that would follow if it were to use force. Indian leaders also incorrectly saw themselves as militarily superior and interpreted the apparent Chinese reluctance to fire on the Indian pickets as evidence of fear of military defeat. This faulty assessment of the military balance can be traced to a series of self-serving and unrealistic intelligence reports from a highly politicized military bureaucracy. The Chinese, who formulated their military assessment on the basis of a more thorough and careful analysis of the capabilities of the two sides, could not know how badly the Indian leadership was misinformed. Unaware of the nature and extent of India's miscalculations, they acted with restraint. In so doing, the Chinese reinforced precisely those expectations among Indian leaders most likely to promote rather than prevent a challenge.

Evidence of the interactive impact of restraint and deterrence is fragmentary and episodic. Analysts have not yet examined the documentary record to identify the relevant universe of cases. The limited evidence that is available of the interactive use of restraint and demonstration of resolve suggests that each carries with it the risk of serious error. An exercise of restraint may avoid provocation of a beleaguered or frightened adversary, but may also increase the likelihood of miscalculated escalation. The language of threat and demonstration of resolve, on the other hand, may reduce the probability that a challenger will underestimate a deterrer's response, but it may also provoke a vulnerable and fearful opponent.

Reassurance Through Norms of Competition

Adversaries can also attempt to reassure one another of the limits of their intentions through the development of informal, even tacit norms of competition in areas of disputed interest. Informal, shared norms among adversaries may delegitimate certain kinds of mutually unacceptable action and, consequently, reduce the need to manipulate the risk of war. They may also establish mutually acceptable boundaries of behavior and reduce some of the uncertainty that can at times lead a would-be challenger to miscalculate.

The experimental literature is relevant only indirectly because it examines the impact of shared norms on the propensity of players to cooperate. In one experiment, players were allowed pregame discussion; they subsequently invoked social sanctions against "cheats" and "greed" and continued to cooperate despite the experimenter's use of increasing payoffs for defection (Bonacich, 1972). Shared norms may also transform players' preference structures and consequently change the game matrix to permit cooperation (Axelrod, 1986). More directly related to deterrence, it has been suggested that a concession that is readily interpreted as adherence to a shared norm is less likely to be interpreted as evidence of weakness and provoke a miscalculated challenge (Stern et al., 1989*b*).

Analyses of historical cases also deal with the impact of shared norms on war avoidance. The United States and the Soviet Union attempted to develop explicit understandings of the limits of competition when they signed the Basic Principles Agreement in 1972 and, a year later, a more specific agreement on consultation to deal with crises that threatened to escalate to nuclear war. These agreements were not a success, in part because the formal documents masked significant disagreement and differences in interpretation. If anything, the unrealistic expectations they aroused, the dispute over interpretation of the agreements, the consequent allegations of cheating and defection, and the ensuing distrust and anger exacerbated the management of the conflict between the two nuclear adversaries (George, 1983; Stein, 1987*b*).

The United States and the Soviet Union were far more successful in establishing less formal and less explicit norms of competition in Cuba and then in the Middle East (George, 1983, 1985). In both cases, they did so because of a shared fear that their competition could escalate easily to a serious and dangerous confrontation. In 1962, President Kennedy declared that the United States would not invade Cuba in return for an assurance that the Soviet Union would not again deploy offensive weapons on the island. There was some ambiguity, however, in subsequent years about the scope of the agreement and its duration. In August 1970, the Soviet Union inquired through diplomatic channels whether the agreement still remained in force. The Nixon administration reiterated its commitment to the shared norm and, shortly thereafter, invoked this understanding to object to the construction of a base in Cuba to service Soviet submarines.

Again in 1978, diplomatic discussions between Soviet and U.S. officials focused on the replacement of older fighter-interceptor aircraft with newer ground-attack planes capable of carrying nuclear weapons. The Soviet Union reassured the United States of its intention to deploy only a limited number of aircraft and the matter was resolved. The United States and the Soviet Union were less adept at handling the deployment in Cuba of a brigade of Soviet combat forces later that year. Although the shared norms did not appear to include ground forces, the Carter administration, under pressure from vocal critics in the Senate, nevertheless objected publicly that their introduction violated the common understanding and was illegitimate. The Soviet Union refused to withdraw the forces or to change their configuration but reaffirmed the training mission of the forces that were present (Duffy, 1983). Although the shared norm of competition was ambiguous, capable of multiple interpretation, and sensitive to domestic political processes, it nevertheless focused the attention of Soviet and U.S. leaders on the boundaries of competition and generally led to the mutual clarification of intentions and to a clearer definition of acceptable limits.

The usefulness of norms of competition in the Middle East provides a more dramatic illustration of their capability to regulate conflict and reduce the risks of deterrence. The United States and the Soviet Union have acknowledged tacitly that each may come to the assistance of its ally if it is threatened with a catastrophic military defeat by the ally of the other. To avoid such an intervention, the superpower must compel the regional ally who threatens to inflict such an overwhelming defeat to cease its military action (George, 1983; 1985:11; Dismukes and McConnell, 1979:276–278; Jonsonn, 1984; Evron, 1979:17–45). The Soviet Union invoked this tacit norm in 1967 and again in 1973, and although the United States attempted to deter Soviet intervention, it moved to compel Israel to cease it military action and to reassure the Soviet Union immediately of its intention to do so. Deterrence and reassurance worked together and, indeed, it is difficult to disentangle the impact of one from the other on the effective management of that conflict (Stein, 1987a).

In 1970, when Egypt's air defense capability had been destroyed, the Soviet Union also warned of its intention to intervene. This time, the Nixon administration responded only with a deterrent warning and made no attempt either to compel its ally to cease its air raids or to reassure the Soviet Union; not unexpectedly, deterrence failed when the Soviet Union introduced ground and air forces into Egypt. When the Soviet Union did so, however, the United States tacitly accepted the legitimacy of their presence and sought only to prevent their use in offensive activity. Implicitly, it acknowledged the legitimate Soviet interest in preventing a catastrophic military defeat of Egypt (George, 1983, 1985:11; Stein, 1987a).

Evidence of the preconditions of effectiveness of shared norms of competition is again episodic and unsatisfactory. Very little analysis has been done; there is as yet no systematic comparative analysis across cases of the interactive impact of shared norms and deterrence. George (1983, 1985) notes that these tacit and informal norms of competition in and of themselves do not provide a sufficiently stable basis for the management of conflict between the two superpowers; they lack both institutionalized arrangements and procedures for clarification of their ambiguities and extension to new situations. He suggests that, in the conflict between the United States and the Soviet Union, shared norms of competition are likely to vary in utility according to the resources and strategies the superpowers can use, the domestic and international constraints they face, leaders' capacity to formulate and differentiate their own interests as well as to evaluate the interests at stake for their adversary, the magnitude of each superpower's interest, and the symmetry of the distribution of interest. Tacit norms and patterns of restraint are more likely to emerge, for example, in areas of high-interest asymmetry than in areas of disputed or uncertain symmetry.

The preconditions for the development of effective norms of competition are rigorous, demanding, and unlikely to be met in many adversarial relationships. Indeed, the obstacles to success of shared norms are no less than those confronted by the strategy of deterrence. The cognitive and motivational limits to leaders' capacities to differentiate their own interests, as well as to evaluate the interests at stake for their adversary, are as severe as those that limit defenders' capacities to assess the interests of would-be challengers. Political pressures may encourage leaders to probe the limits of shared norms even as they incite would-be challengers to test the limits of commitment. Given these obstacles, it is surprising that in an area of disputed symmetry like the Middle East, the United States and the Soviet Union were able to agree tacitly on a shared norm. When norms of competition were shared, the available evidence suggests that they did reduce some of the real risks of deterrence.

It is possible, however, that the association between the development of norms and the reduction in the risks of deterrence is spurious—that norms develop only when the conflict is easily managed or both sides are strongly committed to avoiding overt conflict. Under these conditions, shared norms would have little independent impact on reducing the risks of deterrence (Jervis, personal communication—letter, March 1988; Kegley and Raymond, 1986:224). The evidence of their impact of U.S. deterrence of the Soviet Union in the Middle East, however, suggests that they were important in clarifying intentions and establishing limits in a conflict that has been very difficult for the United States and the Soviet Union to manage. Paradoxically, they did so by motivating the United States not only to deter but to reassure the Soviet Union that its fundamental demands would be met. Additional research is needed, however, both to identify those cases where shared norms of competition have succeeded and where they have failed to reduce the risks of deterrence, and to assess the relationship of shared norms to other variables that contribute to the success and failure of deterrence.

Reassurance Through Irrevocable Commitment

When leaders recognize that misperception and stereotyping govern their adversary's judgments as well as their own, they can try, by making an irrevocable commitment, to reassure their adversary of their benign intentions and to create incentives for negotiation. Analysts of deterrence have explored the usefulness of irrevocable commitments in reinforcing the credibility of deterrent threats (Schelling, 1960:131–137; 1980). This kind of commitment can be useful, however, to a defender in a deterrence relationship to signal its intention to negotiate and thereby reduce the costs to a would-be challenger of the status quo.

It can also be useful to a challenger who anticipates great cost both from the perpetuation of the status quo and a resort to force. Indeed, under these conditions, a challenger may be more willing to run the serious risks of a strategy of irrevocable commitment. As we have seen, when leaders consider the status quo unacceptable and illegitimate, they are especially likely to consider a challenge to deterrence. Simultaneously, however, they may attempt through a strategy of irrevocable commitment to persuade their adversary to enter into serious negotiation to reduce the costs of the status quo. This is precisely the strategy adopted by President Anwar el-Sadat in 1977.[10]

Dissatisfied with the progress of negotiations in the autumn of 1977 yet unprepared to accept the status quo, Sadat began again to consider seriously a use of force and simultaneously searched for a dramatic move that would both reduce the tension and distrust between Egypt and Israel and induce Israel to make major concessions. It was the distrust built up over decades, he argued, that constrained the attempt to negotiate the issues at stake and fueled the cycle of wars. He first considered asking the five permanent members of the Security Council to meet in Jerusalem with the parties to the Arab–Israeli conflict, but was dissuaded by President Carter, who warned that such a strategy would fail (Sadat, 1977:306–307; Carter, 1982:307). Secret negotiations between Egypt's deputy prime minister and Israel's foreign minister followed in Morocco, where each agreed to make a critical concession: Israel indicated its willingness to return most of the Sinai peninsula to Egyptian sovereignty, and Egypt agreed to peace and the establishment of diplomatic relations with Israel (Dayan, 1981:44–52). Although neither side was fully satisfied, both sides began to consider negotiation as a credible option. Yet neither was convinced of the sincerity of the other's intentions.

Shortly thereafter, in a speech to the People's Assembly in Cairo, President Sadat offered to travel to Jerusalem to address Israel's parliament personally in an effort to persuade its members of the sincerity of Egyptian intentions. The reaction was outrage in the Arab world, incredulity among the Israeli public, and alarm among some of the senior military in Israel, who considered the proposed visit a ruse to provide cover for a renewed attack. Within days, however, Sadat came to Jerusalem and spoke to the *Knesset* of the Egyptian terms for peace. Egyptian demands were unchanged but Israel's leaders and public paid attention to the deed rather than to the words. In large part through this single, dramatic act of reassurance, Sadat changed the trajectory of the conflict by changing Israel's incentives to negotiate.

Why did reassurance succeed? Several factors were at play, some general and some specific to the historical context. First, the initiative was irreversible: once the president of Egypt traveled to Jerusalem, he could not undo the deed. Because it could not be reversed, the action was treated as a valid indicator of Egyptian intentions rather than as a signal that could be manipulated (Jervis, 1970). Israel's leadership and public recognized the irreversibility of the action and, consequently, gave it great weight.

Second, the substantial political cost to President Sadat of breaking the long-standing Arab taboo of not dealing directly with Israel was also apparent to Israel's leaders. Dissension within the Egyptian government was pronounced; the Egyptian foreign minister resigned in protest. A tidal wave of criticism from the Arab world engulfed the Egyptian leader, and Arab states moved in near-unison to sever diplomatic relations with Egypt. Experimental studies suggest that people determine the motives of a donor by how much the gift cost the giver in utility: the greater the relative cost to the donor, the less likely ulterior motives (Komorita, 1973; Pruitt, 1981:124–125). These studies in attribution are consistent with evidence of the impact of the cognitive heuristic of "proportionality" (Lebow and Stein, 1989b): Israel's leaders reasoned that Egypt's president would not incur such heavy costs were he not sincere.

Third, Sadat's arrival in Jerusalem challenged the most important set of beliefs about Arab goals among Israel's leadership and public. A broad cross section of Israelis had assumed that Arab leaders were unrelentingly hostile, so much so that they were unprepared to meet Israel's leaders face to face. Once these core beliefs were shaken, it became easier for Israelis, as cognitive psychologists predict, to revise associated assumptions and expectations.

Fourth, President Sadat spoke over the heads of Israel's leadership directly to Israel's public. With his flair for the dramatic, he created the psychological and political symbols that would mobilize Israeli citizens to press their more cautious and restrained leaders. In so doing, he removed a constraint on Israel's leaders and created a political inducement to action. The strategy of reassurance had multiple audiences and multiple constituencies.

Fifth, the president of Egypt adopted a strategy of reassurance only when he judged that the conflict between Egypt and Israel had "ripened for resolution" (Zartman, 1985; Stein, 1983). In 1977, both leaders shared a common aversion to war. Sadat's initiative took place after a war that both sides lost. The military outcome of the war in 1973 persuaded civilian and military leaders in Egypt of Israel's superior military capability under almost any set of conditions. Moreover, Sadat was reluctant to risk the gains he had made with such difficulty in 1973. Nevertheless, he was unwilling to perpetuate the status quo and began again to consider a use of force, even though it was an unattractive option. As we have seen, estimates of inferior military capability and a committed adversary are not sufficient to deter. Equally important, Israel's leaders had become pessimistic for the first time about the efficacy of deterrence as an exclusive strategy of conflict management. Because one side was pessimistic about the benefits of a further use of force and the other about the stability of deterrence, both were willing to consider seriously alternative strategies that required major political concessions, even though they knew these concessions would be politically costly among their respective constituencies.

Under this very special set of conditions, reassurance through irrevocable commitment succeeded brilliantly. One must be very careful, however in extrapolating from this single case. The two critical components that make an irrevocable commitment reassuring to an adversary are its obviously high cost to the leaders who issue the commitment and its irreversibility. The strategy has been used infrequently, partly because it is often very difficult and very risky to design a commitment that is both high in cost and irreversible (Maoz and Felsenthal, 1987:198). Leaders frequently have neither the resources nor the information necessary to make irrevocable commitments.

Reliance on verbal declaration of good intentions to reduce an adversary's fears may not persuade. The aphorism "Words are cheap" is especially apt; promises made can be withdrawn. A suspicious adversary is likely to discount a reassuring verbal message because it can be reversed, often with little cost. A recent simulation of tacit bargaining in arms control finds, moreover, that leaders are rarely certain enough about an opponent's response to make a large gesture, while the opponent is rarely trusting enough to respond enthusiastically to a small one (Downs and Rocke, 1987). In designing strategies of reassurance, therefore, leaders face a difficult trade-off: they are more likely to make offers that are reversible and less costly, but reversible low-cost offers are far less persuasive to an adversary as an indicator of intentions.

Like deterrence, outside the laboratory reassurance through irrevocable commitment also requires a degree of freedom from domestic political and bureaucratic constraints. In Egypt, after the October War 1973, Sadat had great autonomy in decision making and, indeed, could withstand the resignation of his foreign minister. This kind of autonomy is far more difficult to achieve in highly institutionalized and open societies where interests are vested in existing strategies. The making of an irrevocable commitment to leaders long identified as antagonists can also be difficult to justify to the public. Yet, it is the public nature of the commitment that contributes to its irreversibility and credibility (Maoz and Felsenthal, 1987:191–192). For all these reasons, the making of irrevocable commitments that reassure effectively is likely to be difficult for both a would-be challenger and a defender.

Reassurance Through Limited Security Regimes

In an effort to reduce the likelihood of an unintended and unwanted war, adversaries have agreed, at times informally, on principles and put in place procedures to reduce the likelihood of accidental or miscalculated war. Technically, these arrangements are referred to as *limited security regimes*.

The concept of regime was borrowed from international law and broadened to incorporate the range of shared norms, principles, rules, and procedures around which leaders' expectations converge (Krasner, 1982a). These principles and procedures may be formal or informal, tacit or explicit, but because some norms are shared, the behavior of leaders is constrained. A rich literature explores the creation and impact of regimes in the international political economy, but far less attention has been devoted to the analysis of the creation and impact of limited security regimes (Lipson, 1984; Keohane, 1984; Axelrod and Keohane, 1985; Stein, 1985c; Krachtowil and Ruggie, 1986; Nye, 1987; Young, 1986; Smith, 1987).

The creation of limited security regimes is most likely when leaders share a common aversion to war and to its consequences (Stein, 1982; Stein, 1985c). A shared fear of war is not restricted only to the nuclear powers; it occurs with surprising frequency in the contemporary international system as military technology, conventional as well as nuclear, threatens ever greater destruction. The evidence that is available suggests that limited security regimes among adversaries are more likely to be created in the context of general deterrence that enhances the shared aversion of war; under these conditions, there is synergism between deterrence and reassurance (Stein, 1985c; Nye, 1987; Lebow and Stein, 1987a).

Also important is the configuration of interests among prospective members of a regime. Limited security regimes can accommodate "egoists" more easily than "competitors" as their principal participants.[11] Leaders need not be interested in the common good but can pursue their self-interest, irrespective of those of other participants. This capacity to accommodate egoists fits nicely with the evidence that at times would-be challengers are inwardly focused, preoccupied with their own needs and vulnerabilities. Regimes cannot, however, accommodate "competitors" who seek to maximize the relative difference between their own gains and those of their adversary (Messick and McClintock, 1968; Shubik, 1971). In practice, however, as distinct from the theoretical modeling of preferences, it is very difficult to determine the orientation of an adversary.

The distribution of power also contributes in important ways to the creation of international regimes. Analysts have speculated on the impact of different configurations of power. Jervis (1982b) suggests that in the classical balance-of-power system, the weaker states had little option but to accept the security regime put in place by the great powers. Security regimes have also been created in the aftermath of an important change in the distribution of power, especially after a major war (Jervis, 1982b:369–371; Kegley and Raymond, 1986). Analysts have suggested as well that the existence of a "hegemon" facilitates the creation of limited regimes; their evidence is drawn primarily, however, from the international political economy rather than from issues of international security (Keohane and Nye, 1977:38–60; Keohane, 1984). As a recent analysis of the nonproliferation regime demonstrates, however, the presence of a hegemon is not a necessary prerequisite of the creation of a limited security regime. On the contrary, collective action occurred in a period of hegemonic decline (Smith, 1987:268–269; Keohane, 1984:46).

Limited security regimes can be attractive to adversaries because they fulfill important functions and provide valuable resources to their members. Insofar as even limited security regimes provide reliable, low-cost information about members' activities, they make intentions less opaque and estimation less difficult, and they reduce the likelihood of miscalculation. They reduce uncertainty both about the behavior of adversaries and about the boundaries of the conflict. In the limited security regime in place between Egypt and Israel from 1974 and 1979, for example, the United States routinely circulated intelligence information about the military dispositions of one to the other. Limited security regimes also link issues together, lengthening the "shadow of the future" and increasing the incentives to sacrifice immediate for future gain (Keohane, 1984:88; Oye, 1985).[12]

Finally, adversaries may consider participation in a limited security regime if it improves the accuracy of detection and reduces the likelihood of defection. A regime may permit adversaries to monitor each other's actions with increased confidence by providing more complete and reliable information, by increasing surveillance capabilities for all parties, or by invoking the assistance of outsiders as monitors. It can give leaders more leeway than they otherwise would have to meet a prospective defection by increasing available warning time (Stein, 1985c).

Evidence drawn from the Middle East illustrates the possibilities and benefits of limited, informal security regimes that, although they were created under the most adverse conditions, nevertheless endured for a considerable period of time. It is not difficult to illustrate their utility in the management of conflict between Egypt and Israel in the last decade. Building on a series of limited arrangements agreed upon in the context of a deterrent relationship, Egypt and Israel, with the help of the United States, were able ultimately to agree on a set of principles and to put in place a complex series of procedures designed to reduce the probability of miscalculated escalation. Limited arms control provisions, creation of buffer zones, sharing of intelligence information, deployment of an international force, and involvement of the United States as a third-party guarantor presently work together within the framework of a formally agreed-on limited security regime to reduce uncertainty, clarify intentions, and minimize the risk of unintended war.

While it is not difficult to establish the relevance of a limited security regime in the favorable military and political conditions created by the war in 1973, the prospects of creating and maintaining a limited regime in the far harsher climate after the Suez War in 1956 are not as obvious. In this sense, the experiment after 1956 can serve as a critical case. In the mid-1950s, Egypt and Israel were parties to a bitter conflict that had twice erupted into war, and each suspected the other of the intention to expand. Analysts argue that these conditions preclude the creation of even a limited security regime (Jervis, 1982*b*; Lipson, 1984). Yet, some important preconditions were present.

After the war in 1956, general deterrence was reestablished. Israel, the deterrer, was then a status quo power with obvious military superiority and little interest in a use of force. Egypt, the challenger, was unprepared militarily and economically at the time for further fighting. Politically, however, Egypt was unable and unwilling to consider any agreement whose function was more extensive than the avoidance of unwanted war; an adversarial relationship was still very much present. Nevertheless, both sides perceived war as costly and unattractive, at least for the moment, and both were interested in procedures that could reduce the probability of an accidental conflict and simultaneously minimize the risk of a surprise attack. They were prepared to consider informally, indeed indirectly and tacitly, a limited set of principles and procedures narrowly focused on the management of security in the Sinai peninsula.

The informal and limited regime had several components. Israel insisted publicly and Egypt acquiesced tacitly that there was to be no blockade of the Straits of Tiran at the southeastern tip of the peninsula. Egypt also agreed to the deployment of a United Nations Emergency Force (UNEF) just inside the eastern border of the Sinai peninsula, on Egyptian territory. This force was formally charged with patrolling, manning sensitive border positions, and preventing infiltration across the border.

The United Nations' force was not so much a fire brigade as a fire alarm. Its most important function was not explicit but tactic: it could not prevent an attack, but it could provide valuable warning time of an impending attack in at least two ways. Bot Egypt and Israel expected that the withdrawal of the force would require time-consuming multilateral discussions at United Nations' headquarters in New York. This would provide valuable advance warning to the deterrer of an impending defection by the challenger. Moreover, because a demand for the withdrawal of the UNEF would signal a clear change in purpose, the challenger's intentions became far less opaque and easier to read. Consequently, agreement by Egypt to the deployment of an international force reassured Israel.

Another important component of the informal regime was a tactic consensus on the deployment of Egyptian forces in the Sinai peninsula. Egypt deployed only two divisions, well back in the western half of the desert, reinforced by no more than 250 tanks; this configuration of force did not represent an immediate threat to Israel (Evron, 1975). Although the scope of the arms control arrangements was limited and tactic, they nevertheless functioned as a hedge against accidental war and again as an effective early warning system. By limiting contact between the crack units of Israel's and Egypt's armed forces, the likelihood of war arising out of a chance, accidental encounter was reduced; in this sense, the limited, informal, and tacit components of the regime worked effectively to avoid an outcome that neither side wanted.

Because a massive deployment of the Egyptian army in the Sinai desert would have to precede any ground action, violation of these tacit rules would alert Israel to an impending attack. Israel's confidence in its general deterrent capability was therefore considerable as long as these rules were observed. Consequently, its leaders felt less need to resort to the language of threat and to engage in the conscious manipulation of the risk of war.

The informal, limited regime also permitted expectations to stabilize and converge about the management of security in the Sinai peninsula. The management of conflict therefore became easier as the actions of both parties became more predictable. Contrary to much of regime theory, expectations stabilized after, rather than before, the limited regime was in place as both sides began to "learn."

Although the limited security regime was tacit and narrowly focused, it persisted for 11 years and reassured both Egypt and Israel through important changes in the distribution of political and military power. Indeed, at times it protected President Nasser from the pressures of his Arab constituency. The proposition that even limited reassurance in the context of general deterrence was of considerable value to both challenger and defender is sustained by the special conditions that attended the disruption of the regime.

The regime was not destroyed through premeditated repudiation, but rather as a result of serious miscalculation, first by President Nasser and then by the secretary-general of the United Nations, U Thant. The president of Egypt, under considerable pressure from his Arab constituency, asked for a partial withdrawal of the UNEF but the secretary-general insisted on a complete withdrawal of the force if changes in its status were made. In so doing, U Thant not only removed the smoke detector from an overheated environment, but also dismantled a system of crisis management that provided time for outsiders to search for political solutions. When the peacekeeping force was pulled out, both Egypt and Israel immediately recognized that a war that neither had sought directly was now unavoidable. The experiment in reassurance, however, was not in vain; some learning had taken place. Seven years and two wars later, Egypt, Israel and the United States began the painstaking process of creating a better institutionalized, more explicit, more broadly focused security regime. This successor regime permitted considerable learning and a change in both Egypt's and Israel's definition of their interests. Today, in the context of ongoing general deterrence, these revised definitions of interests set the parameters for the management of the conflict between Egypt and Israel.

Reassurance through the creation of limited security regimes has not been restricted only to Egypt and Israel. The United States and the Soviet Union have established a series of limited regimes designed to reduce accident and miscalculation and to delimit the scope of their conflict. They began with efforts to improve communications in crisis through the establishment and then the modernization of the hotline. Other limited regimes followed: in 1967, the demilitarization of outer space; in 1970, a nonproliferation regime; in 1971, a set of measures to reduce the risks of accidental war; and in 1972, a limited regime to reduce the likelihood of accident and miscalculated conflict at sea (Lynn-Jones, 1985). In 1986, the superpowers and their allies negotiated a limited security regime designed to build confidence in central Europe. Advance notification and inspection of large military maneuvers are expected to reduce uncertainty, reassure an alarmed adversary, clarify intentions, and diminish the likelihood of accidental war. Most recently, in 1987, the United States and the Soviet Union agreed to the establishment of nuclear-risk-reduction centers. They have also regulated their conflict in central Europe through the Austrian State Treaty, the Berlin Agreements, and the Final Act of the Conference on Security and Cooperation in Europe.

All of these limited security regimes were created in the context of an ongoing adversarial relationship in which both sides continued to rely on general deterrence to prevent war. Within this context, both sets of leaders attended not to the aggressive intentions of the other but rather to their shared fears and common aversion to war.

Reassurance through the creation of limited and focused security regimes can be of considerable help in reducing fear, uncertainty, and misunderstanding between adversaries. At a minimum, adversaries gain access to more reliable and less expensive information about each other's activities, which can reduce uncertainty, the incidence of miscalculation, and an inappropriate manipulation of the risk of war. In a complex international environment that is often information-poor and technologically driven, lower cost and more valid information can be a considerable advantage in more effective management of conflict.

There are, however, serious obstacles to the creation of limited security regimes, even when adversaries share a powerful common aversion to war. First, the cost of unreciprocated participation is inordinately high because security is prerequisite to all other values, and even minor miscalculations can have large consequences (Jervis, 1982b). The defection of an adversary from a regime is almost certain to have graver consequences when the issue is security than, for example, when it is economic. The magnitude of the consequences of error makes limited security regimes especially difficult and risky to build. Closely related to the absolute scope of potential loss in security disputes is the difficulty in estimating the probability of loss. As the earlier analysis of deterrence suggests, estimation of the motives and intentions of adversaries is very difficult, as is the interpretation of an opponent's behavior. Precisely because the consequences of error are so great, leaders have an understandably pronounced fear of deception (Lipson, 1984).

Fear of a surprise attack can encourage leaders to try to build limited security regimes, but it can also make their attainment immeasurably more difficult. Leaders who otherwise might prefer to participate in a limited security regime may nevertheless refrain if they fear a devastating surprise attack. If the advantage to the side that strikes first is large, then leaders are not likely to weigh future benefits heavily in an uncertain and dangerous present. On security issues it is often difficult and dangerous to forego present advantage for future benefit (Oye, 1985). In short, the critical obstacles to the creation of security regimes lie in the unique dangers and consequences of error, dangers that are manifest in the extraordinary difficulties of detection and the grave consequences of defection (Stein, 1985c).

Nevertheless, analysis of the creation and maintenance of limited security regimes is valuable insofar as it highlights the frameworks adversaries have created to improve the management of their conflict. The episodic evidence that is available suggests that creation of a limited security regime is more likely when adversaries share a mutual aversion to war, when general deterrence is in place, and when neither party seeks to maximize relative gain on the specific issue. A careful reading of the very small number of studies of limited security regimes suggests that the relationship between deterrence and reassurance is interactive: general deterrence can be a critical precondition of limited security regimes among adversaries, and reassurance can eliminate some of the discourse of threat that might otherwise inflame a frightened adversary. In this sense, general deterrence and reassurance can become reinforcing strategies of conflict management.

There is still a great deal more to be learned, however, about how limited security regimes are created and maintained. Current theories give inadequate weight to the cognitive and motivational factors that are crucial to the formation of regimes. Although the distribution of power and the configuration of interests are important variables, they do not adequately explain the creation of the nonproliferation regime or the limited security regimes in the Middle East (Smith, 1987; Stein, 1985c). What leaders know and what they learn is central; it is, after all, leaders' expectations and preferences that are treated as the critical intervening variables by analysts of international regimes. Nevertheless, there is no explicit theory of cognitive change, no explanation of how leaders' expectations stabilize, converge, and change.

There has been little systematic analysis, for example, of the impact of cognitive schemas, heuristics, and biases on leaders' expectations, nor is the analysis of the maintenance and demise of security regimes informed by an explicit theory of learning (but see Nye, 1987; Rosenau, 1986). How do leaders interpret and reinterpret shared norms? One of the significant benefits of international economic regimes is their autonomous impact, their "lag" effect, even after underlying political and economic conditions have changed. Even though interests change, the international institutions that were created remain in place and continue to regulate conflict in the international political economy (Krasner, 1982b). Can we expect the same beneficent impact from limited security agreements? Do leaders change their definition of their interests partly because of their participation in limited security agreements? Does sufficient "learning" occur to mitigate the intensity of some international conflicts (Nye, 1987)? If so, under what political and strategic conditions does this occur?

Existing theories also do not pay sufficient attention to motivational explanations of leaders' definitions of their interests. Although interests are an essential variable in the explanation of regime creation, they generally are specified through microeconomic reasoning (Keohane, 1984). Insofar as leaders are motivated by the fear of war, however, models of rational choice may obscure the impact of fundamental psychological processes on leaders' preferences. Political and strategic needs may also significantly affect the way leaders value the costs and benefits of a limited security regime. The impact of fears and needs on leaders' evaluations of the prospect of gain and loss through participation in limited security regimes remains unexplored and unspecified.

Analyses of the creation, maintenance, and impact of limited security regimes have only just begun. The empirical studies are few (Jervis, 1982b; Stein, 1985c; Nye, 1987; Smith, 1987) and the theory is still developing. Through controlled comparative analysis, historical cases can be identified for investigation and richer theoretical models developed. Explanations must assess the impact of domestic political processes as well as strategic conditions on leaders' needs and expectations and model processes of learning and change. In short, the research agenda must explore when and how, in the context of general deterrence, adversaries' fears and needs can best be exploited to establish limited security regimes to reduce the likelihood of unwanted war.

Reassurance Through Reciprocity

In a protracted conflict characterized by repeated crises and attempts at deterrence, leaders may attempt to initiate a process of tension reduction in an effort to change the context of the relationship and reduce the risks of miscalculation. Reciprocity has long been at the center of theoretical concerns among sociologists, psychologists, game theorists, and analysts of the international political economy. Its utility as a strategy of reassurance on security issues, however, has only recently begun to receive serious attention (Axelrod, 1984; Keohane, 1986; Larson, 1986, 1987, 1988).

When the issue is one of security, reciprocal behavior is most usefully conceived as a pattern of contingent, sequential, and diffuse exchange among interdependent adversaries (Larson, 1986). Different streams of evidence from experimental studies, computer simulation, analyses of international interaction, and historical case studies converge to suggest that, at times, a strategy of reciprocity can be effective in initiating a process of tension reduction.

The experimental literature generally has focused on the effectiveness of reciprocal strategies on eliciting cooperation rather than on the narrower objective of the reduction of tension. Some of the findings should be relevant, however, to the more limited purpose of tension reduction in the context of a deterrence relationship.

In laboratory studies, reciprocal strategies do better than either consistent cooperation or consistent competitiveness in eliciting cooperation. The player who cooperates consistently is frequently exploited by the other (Shure, Meeker, and Hansford, 1965; Deutsch et al., 1967; but see Oskamp, 1971). Indeed, in games of "chicken," where the payoffs for a fight are lower than those for being exploited, a strategy of consistent competition was more successful in eliciting cooperation from the other side than was consistent cooperation (Sermat, 1964, 1967). However, an unconditionally competitive strategy can result in a "lock-in" of competitive responses (Rapoport and Chammah, 1965; Sermat, 1964, 1967). This is especially true when both sides are about equal in strength and resolve. Contingent strategies are more effective than any of the variants of noncontingent strategies in eliciting cooperation from an adversary (Patchen, 1987; Oskamp, 1971; Wilson, 1971).

Evidence from analyses of international bargaining suggests that a graduated strategy that begins with competition and then moves to cooperation is more successful in avoiding escalation (Leng and Walker, 1982). An analysis of bargaining strategies during international crises suggests that an initial period of coercive bargaining is sometimes necessary to establish resolve; after this initial period, one or the other parties is able to make concessions without appearing weak (Snyder and Diesing, 1977). Huth and Russett (1988) similarly find that a "firm but fair" strategy is strongly associated with the success of deterrence. However, an opening strategy of coercion risks a spiral of escalation that can be difficult to break (George, Hall, and Simons, 1971).

Two variants of reciprocal strategies, "tit-for-tat" and GRIT, have received special attention from analysts of international conflict management. In a series of computer tournaments designed by Robert Axelrod (1984), the first variant, tit-for-tat, proved most effective in inducting cooperation among egoistic players in an anarchic environment. Tit-for-tat succeeds because of its special attributes; it cooperates on the first move and thereafter replicates what the previous player has just done. It is therefore "nice," "forgiving," but "firm:" nice, because it begins cooperatively in an effort to promote reciprocal concession; forgiving, because although it retaliates for one defection, it subsequently forgives an isolated defection after a single response; firm, because it reciprocates defection with defection and thereby reduces the risk of exploitation for those who use the strategy (Axelrod, 1984:54). It is even more effective if retaliation is marginally less than provocation. Largely because of this admixture of controlled firmness and conciliation, Axelrod suggests, tit-for-tat holds broad promise as a strategy of conflict management.

Several of the characteristics of tit-for-tat may limit its applicability as a strategy of tension reduction on security issues. Proponents of tit-for-tat extol its simplicity: unlike deterrence, it does not assume rationality, or altruism,

trust, and communication, and it can be self-policing. As long as the participants value their future relationship, as long as the "shadow of the future" is
long, players will learn to cooperate through trial and error (Axelrod,
1984:125–126, 173–174; Oye, 1985). Paradoxically, the attractions of tit-for-
tat can become liabilities when the strategy is used outside the laboratory to
reduce tension in an adversarial relationship.

The preferences of the participants are likely to be critical to the outcome of
the strategy. It is questionable whether participants in a controlled experiment
are comparable to leaders in an adversarial relationship. Axelrod experiments
only with self-interested egoists, not with participants who concentrate on
relative gain. Experimental studies suggest that players do not optimize when
they seek to obtain higher relative gains (McClintock and McNeel, 1966a,
1966b; Kuhlman and Marshello, 1975; Messick and Thorngate, 1967;
Messick and McClintock, 1968; Kuhlman and Wimberley, 1976). When ex-
perimenters separate players who emphasize relative gain, they find that
competitors are likely to defect regardless of the strategy they encounter, even
tit-for-tat.[13] Moreover, cooperators are frequently assimilated to competitors;
when matched against competitors, they defect out of self-defense. Even
more alarming, competitors do not recognize that their opponent responded in
self-defense; on the contrary, they believe that their adversary was motivated
very much by the factors that governed their behavior (Kuhlman and Marshello, 1975; Kelley and Stahelski, 1970).

Tit-for-tat also pays no attention to the cognitive schematas of the players,
nor to the impact of standard heuristics and errors on attribution, estimation,
and judgment, a deficiency that, as we have seen, gravely weakens theories of
deterrence. Experimental studies show that people learn to reciprocate by
reasoning and making inferences about the other side's motives and future
action (Oskamp, 1971:243, 256). A cooperative move is unlikely to be reciprocated if an adversary has long-standing and deeply held negative images
that have been reinforced over time. Secretary of State John Foster Dulles held
such a "bad-faith" image of the Soviet Union. Consequently, he dismissed
almost every conciliatory Soviet action as designed to deceive the United
States and create an illusory and dangerous sense of complacency (Holsti,
1967; Stuart and Starr, 1982; Larson, 1985:29–34).

Drawing on theories of social exchange, Larson (1986:21) suggests that the
way a target interprets the initiator's motives is crucial to the success of
reciprocity. Particularly important is the attribution that an adversary made the
concession freely and voluntarily, rather than accidentally or through compul-
sion (Gouldner, 1960; Blau, 1964; Kelley and Thibaut, 1978; Enzle and
Schopflocher, 1978; Greenberg and Frisch, 1972). People are also more inclined to be receptive if they consider their opponent's motives to be be-

nign. If they estimate that their opponent is engaged in deceit or has ulterior motives, they do not feel obliged to reciprocate (Nemeth, 1970; Schopler and Thompson, 1968). Whether leaders interpret an action as conciliatory or aggressive is often a function of their perception of the goals and strategy that motivate the action (Jervis, 1976:58–113).

Not only do cognitive schemata, heuristics, and biases affect the interpretation of the meaning of action, but motivational biases do as well. Frequently, leaders give opposite labels to the same behavior when they initiate the action and when it is carried out by an adversary (Larson, 1985:37–38; Larson, 1988). The United States, for example, labeled Soviet arms supplies to Egypt and Syria in October 1973 as obstructionist and dangerous, but described its own substantial supply to Israel as an essential prerequisite to the termination of the war. Affect and cognition interacted to shape the inferences U.S. leaders made about their own as well as Soviet behavior. The action does not speak for itself.

Experimental and simulated studies of tit-for-tat also ignore the political and strategic context in which the strategy is used. Much like formal theories of deterrence, analysis of tit-for-tat remains largely acontextual. Experimental studies, for example, have identified asymmetries of power as a crucial explanatory variable of the type of strategies players use (Marwell, Ratcliff, and Schmitt, 1969). An opponent is also more likely to respond to a conciliatory action when the initiator of the action is equal or stronger in capabilities than the target (Lindskold and Aronoff, 1980; Chertkoff and Esser, 1976). Differences in capability have not yet been systematically built into analyses of tit-for-tat. Nor have the strategic fears and needs that can compound strategic dilemmas and culminate in motivated error been given systematic attention; the success of tit-for-tat has not been explored in different kinds of strategic environments.

Finally, the social context in which tit-for-tat is used is largely ignored in most of the experimental, simulated, and interaction studies. Leaders may differ, for example, in their perceptions of reciprocity and in the functional measures of equivalence that they use. These differences between the United States and the Soviet Union, for example, were starkly evident as the process of détente unraveled. Measures of equivalence in international security are defined by leaders' perceptions and expectations rather than by objective criteria and subject to cognitive and motivated bias.

The difficulty in establishing common criteria of reciprocity can be mitigated to some extent if leaders share social norms. As Axelrod (1986) observes, shared norms may increase the salience of collective interests and influence people's preference structures. In so doing, they decrease competitive play and make reciprocal bargaining more likely. However, systematic evidence of the impact of shared norms and of common criteria of legitimacy on reciprocation is still scarce (Gouldner, 1960). Moreover, as is evident from the analysis of shared norms of competition, obstacles to their development among adversaries are considerable.

A more sophisticated version of a reciprocal strategy designed specifically to reduce international tension between long-term adversaries is GRIT (Osgood, 1962). The initiator announces in advance that it is beginning a series of conciliatory actions designed to reduce tension and then implements these actions whether or not the other side reciprocates. The actions, moreover, should be easily verifiable. As each step is implemented, the initiator invites its adversary to reciprocate but does not specify the appropriate response. Further, a reciprocal response by an adversary should be rewarded by a somewhat more conciliatory action. These actions, however, should not impair the defensive capacity of the initiator and, if the other side attempts to exploit, the initiator should respond with an appropriate action but only to the degree necessary to restore the status quo. Larson (1987) finds that GRIT provides the best explanation for the capacity of the United States and the Soviet Union to reduce tension sufficiently so that they could agree on the neutralization of Austria and then on a summit meeting in 1955.

Experimental studies concur that strategies like GRIT, which build in a series of conciliatory initiatives taken independently of the other's actions, are more effective than tit-for-tat in eliciting a reciprocal response (Lindskold, 1978; Lindskold and Collins, 1978; Lindskold, Walters, and Koutsourais, 1983; Osgood, 1980; Pilisuk and Skolnick, 1968). Moreover, they were as effective among players who were judged generally competitive by their previous play as they were among those who were generally cooperative. A second variant that is also effective is a reciprocal strategy that is slow to retaliate and slow to return to conciliation; this variant of reciprocity allows for initial misperception (Bixenstine and Gaebelein, 1971; Pruitt and Kimmel, 1977). Similarly, the strategy of the "reformed sinner" elicits reciprocity; it begins with defection for a few moves to establish resolve before moving to contingent cooperation (Harford and Solomon, 1967; Benton, Kelley, and Liebling, 1972).

Evidence of the success of reciprocal strategies of tension reduction in the international environment is limited. There are few historical case studies, and the evidence that does exist is often ambiguous. The experimental evidence in support of reciprocal strategies is much stronger, but it is largely acontextual. At most, we can suggest that insofar as leaders can modify their strategies to accommodate the political, strategic, cultural, and psychological context of their adversary, reciprocal strategies of tension reduction may be useful in changing the context of an adversarial relationship so that deterrence becomes less risky in the short-term and ultimately less necessary.

Conclusion

This analysis of deterrence and reassurance has reviewed their theoretical assumptions, the fit of the theories with the available evidence, and the quality of the evidence that sustains arguments of their strengths and weaknesses. It has also explored their respective advantages and disadvantages under different conditions. It pointed to significant weaknesses within existing theories of deterrence that create important blind spots for those who use it as strategy. Analyses of reassurance strategies draw widely from the behavioral sciences, but little attempt has been made either to integrate discrete sets of theoretical propositions or to test their validity in different kinds of international environments. Finally, scholars have yet to agree on the relevant universe of cases that can be used to test both sets of theories. Consequently, the evidence that is available is fragmentary, often episodic, frequently open to multiple interpretation, and difficult to evaluate. It is, however, drawn increasingly from a wide rage of experimental, simulated, and historical studies. It is within this context of partial and, at times, flawed theory and uneven evidence that the following tentative propositions are put.

Evidence is beginning to cumulate from a range of historical studies about the factors that contribute to the failure of deterrence, but not enough is known about the conditions associated with its success. The evidence suggests indirectly that deterrence is most likely to succeed when adversarial leaders are motivated largely by the prospect of gain. In practice, then, leaders must determine whether an adversary is driven largely by opportunity before determining whether the theory is likely to be relevant. That determination, unfortunately, lies outside the scope of the theory; consequently, policymakers encounter serious difficulties in assessing the appropriateness of an attempt at deterrence. The evidence also suggests that deterrence is more likely to succeed when an adversary has the political and strategic freedom to exercise restraint, is not misled by grossly distorted assessments of the political-military situation, and is vulnerable to the kinds of threats a deterrer is capable of making credible. The timing of deterrence may also be important. The effectiveness of deterrence is likely to be enhanced if it is used early, before an adversary becomes committed to a use of force and becomes correspondingly insensitive to warnings and threats. Insofar as these strategic, political, and psychological conditions are not met, deterrence is increasingly likely to become ineffective, irrelevant, or even provocative.

When would-be challengers are motivated largely by need and are seriously constrained at home and abroad, strategies of reassurance can supplement or substitute for deterrence. Strategies of reassurance attempt directly to reduce the incentives to the threat or use of force and indirectly to make the use of force less likely through reduction of uncertainty and the establishment of norms that can regulate the management of conflict. As in deterrence, however, the theoretical literature is frequently insufficiently sensitive to the cognitive, motivational, political, and strategic factors that can limit the effectiveness of these kinds of strategies.

Preliminary historical and comparative research suggest that strategies of reassurance may at times be effective in reducing some of the obvious risks of deterrence. Restraint, the development of informal norms of competition, and irrevocable commitments can help to reassure a vulnerable adversary, reduce the likelihood of miscalculation, and create alternatives to the use of force. Longer-term strategies of reassurance designed to gradually reduce international tension and create limited security regimes can, in addition, help the parties to move away from the use of threat of force as their dominant mode of discourse. To succeed, however, all these strategies must overcome some of the same psychological, political, and strategic obstacles that confound deterrence.

Strategies of reassurance are most likely to succeed with an adversary who is concerned largely about its own security and does not seek primarily to exploit. Determining whether a would-be challenger is motivated primarily by opportunity or vulnerability is extraordinarily difficult, however, for the policymaker as well as for the scholar who subsequently has access to historical evidence. Leaders' explanations of their decisions, moreover, traced through the historical evidence, may not always provide the basis for an accurate attribution of their motives. They may see an opportunity, but in justifying their decision to use force, bolster through an emphasis on weakness and need.

Although opportunity and need are theoretically distinct concepts, in practice they are not mutually exclusive. The dichotomy between the two is almost always blurred in specific historical cases. What one leader sees as an avoidance of loss, another may interpret as the pursuit of gain. Indeed, the way goals are framed may have important consequences for the behavior of national leaders. After the Soviet Union intervened in Afghanistan, for example, debate raged among responsible U.S. officials as to whether the Soviet Union was motivated primarily by the attempt to avoid loss, or to seek gain and exploit an opportunity (Lebow and Stein, 1989b). This difference in attribution had important implications for policy. Those who considered that the Soviet Union was motivated by gain were more punitive in their policy recommendations than were those who considered that Soviet motivation was primarily defensive.

The way goals are framed and interpreted is, of course, conditioned by preconceptions as well as by evidence. Determining the relative weight of need and opportunity as motivating factors of an adversary's strategic choices is extraordinarily difficult. In most cases, both are likely to be present in different degrees. This determination is critical, however, because it speaks to the appropriate mixture and sequencing of deterrence with strategies of reassurance (George, Hall, and Simons, 1971). Pruitt and Rubin (1986) suggest, for example, that a combination of firmness and concern is most effective in managing social conflict. Not enough is known, however, about the interactive effects of deterrence and reassurance in different sequences under different conditions. Only through systematic comparison of cases of deterrence and reassurance, both when they succeed and when they fail, can contingent generalizations about their limiting conditions be established.

It is also important to analyze the outcome of reassurance strategies both in and outside the context of deterrence. An adversary's mixture of need and opportunity, for example, may be important in determining the effectiveness of reassurance strategies. If an adversary is driven largely by domestic political needs or strategic weaknesses, then reassurance may be more appropriate as a substitute for deterrence. If adversarial motives are mixed, reassurance may be more effective as a complement to deterrence. When an adversary is motivated primarily by opportunity, reassurance is likely to misfire and encourage the challenge it is designed to prevent.

Designing strategies of conflict management that combine components of deterrence and reassurance in appropriate mixtures and sequences is no easy task. There are formidable obstacles to the success of these strategies, individually and collectively, and the risks of one are often the benefits of the other. No single strategy is likely to work across cases under different strategic, political, and psychological conditions. Nevertheless, sensitivity to the limiting conditions of each strategy, to its relative strengths and weaknesses, and to its interactive effects is essential to the management of international conflict short of war.

Notes

This chapter draws in part from "Beyond Deterrence," coauthored with Richard Ned Lebow, *Journal of Social Issues* 43:5–71. Research and writing of the chapter was supported by a grant from the John D. and Catherine T. MacArthur Foundation to Richard Ned Lebow and Janice Gross Stein and from the Canadian Institute for International Peace and Security to Janice Gross Stein. I would like to acknowledge the helpful comments of Alexander George, Robert Jervis, Paul Stern, and the anonymous reviewers for the Commission on Behavioral and Social Sciences and Education at the National Research Council.

1. Cognitive and motivational models generally offer competing explanations for the same observable phenomena. This is in part a function of the elasticity of cognitive models. As Tetlock and Levi note, because the cognitive paradigm has so many theoretical degrees of freedom, it can explain almost anything (1982:83). They suggest that "between-theory" confirmation is premature until the conceptual ambiguities in cognitive and motivational models are clarified.

2. Two traditions within psychology do examine the relationship between cognition and affect. The first asks how thought processes shape what people feel and treats cognition as the antecedent variable. Experimental studies have examined how arousal, cognitive complexity, cognitive organization, and the fitting of new information to affect-laden schema shape affective reactions to new stimuli (Mandler, 1975; Strongman, 1978; Linville, 1982a, 1982b; Tesser, 1978, Fiske, 1981, 1982). Research has also demonstrated that both attributions about the results of past outcomes and thoughts about one's alternative outcomes contribute to emotion (Weiner, 1980, 1982; Kahnman and Tversky, 1982).

Somewhat less attention has been devoted to how feelings shape the way people think. Some studies suggest that intense emotion affects information processing and interrupts attention and memory (Nielson and Sarason, 1981; Brown and Kulik, 1977). Fear and anxiety in particular interrupt cognitive processes and can culminate in distorted processes of defensive avoidance and hypervigilance (Janis and Mann, 1977; Fiske and Taylor, 1984:332–333). Generally, the relationships between affect and cognition are complex, difficult, and just beginning to be understood (Fiske and Taylor, 1984:338–339; Lau and Sears, 1986:359).

3. For a more extensive discussion of the interactive effects of need and opportunity as motives to a challenge to deterrence, see Lebow (1989).

4. There are, of course, important exceptions in the larger strategic literature: the analysis of crisis stability, prevention, and preemption. This literature, however, is not directly relevant to the analysis of deterrence. The analysis of prevention focuses on leaders' perceptions of the extent to which military power and potential are shifting in favor of a particular adversary and, consequently, on the likelihood of a future attack (Levy, 1987:97). Similarly, analyses of crisis stability and preemption examine the impact of leaders' assessments of vulnerability on their estimate of the likelihood of attack by an adversary (Schelling, 1966).

5. Achen and Snidal (1989), in their analysis of the assumptions and requirements of rational deterrence theory, misunderstand this critical point.

6. Some analysts contend further that because subjective expected utility models suppress important structural information about the relationship of players' preferences, they ignore the impact that the interdependence of utilities can have on the choices that players make (Bueno de Mesquita, 1985, 1986; Zagare, 1987:20). It is therefore an inappropriate model of the strategic interdependence that is characteristic of deterrent relationships (Schoemaker, 1982).

7. The term *reassurance* is misleading in that it suggests principally the attempt to reduce miscalculation through verbal assurances. The focus here is on a broad set of strategies that adversaries can use to reduce the incentives to resort to the threat or use

of force. For want of a better term, I group these strategies broadly under the rubric of reassurance.

8. Strategies of reassurance are analytically distinct from those of negotiation. Negotiation generally refers to the exchange of proposals to reach mutually satisfactory joint agreements in a situation of interdependence (Stein, 1988a). A reassurance strategy is closer to one of "prenegotiation," which attempts to make negotiation a salient and attractive option; it is used in the process of getting to the table rather than at the table itself (Stein, 1989).

9. Strategies of reassurance are conceptually distinct from those of cooperation. Cooperation between adversaries on security issues can take place across a broad spectrum of issues, even when the parties do not consider a use of force likely (George, Farley, and Dallin, 1988). In his analysis of the incentives that facilitate security cooperation, George and his colleagues suggest that leaders' perceptions of the centrality of the issue and the tightness of mutual dependence are particularly important.

10. Maoz and Felsenthal (1987) similarly analyze President Sadat's strategy as "self-binding" commitment. Self-binding commitments are useful to resolve paradoxes in games in which equilibrium outcomes are Pareto, or socially inferior, but in which actors who have dominant strategies are harmed more than those who do not. Their analysis suggests that President Sadat's strategy can usefully be seen as a self-binding commitment to resove this kind of paradox.

11. In game theory, egoists seek to maximize their own gains, irrespective of the gains of others, while competitors seek to maximize the relative difference between their gains and the gains of others. Competitors, therefore, treat conflict as zero–sum, while egoists can choose a strategy that leads to a win–win outcome.

12. This "functional" theory explains regime maintenance rather than creation of regimes. In so far as the functions a limited security regime can perform are known to would-be members, however, they can become incentives to participate when adversaries share a common aversion to war.

13. Play in prisoner's dilemma does not distinguish players with a relative gain orientation. The matrix does not permit the analyst to distinguish the motives behind a competitive move: the same choice, "D," maximizes both individual and relative gain (McClintock, 1972; Larson, 1988).

References

Abelson, R. 1973. The structure of belief systems. In Roger Schank and Kenneth Colby, eds., *Computer Models of Thought and Language*, pp. 287–339. San Francisco: Freeman.

———. 1981. The psychological status of the script concept. *American Psychologist* 36:1715–1729.

Abelson, R., E. Aronson, W.J. McGuire, T.M. Newcomb, M.J. Rosenberg, and P.H.

Tannenbaum, eds., 1968. *Theories of Cognitive Consistency*. Chicago: Rand McNally.

Achen, C.H., and D. Snidal. 1989. Rational deterrence theory and comparative case studies. *World Politics* 41:143–169.

Ajzen, I. 1977. Intuitive theories of events and the effects of base rate data on prediction. *Journal of Personality and Social Psychology* 35:303–314.

Anderson, J.R. 1982. *The Architecture of Cognition*. Cambridge, Mass.: Harvard University Press.

Axelrod, R. 1976. The cognitive mapping approach to decision making. In Robert Axelrod, ed., *Structure of Decision: The Cognitive Maps of Political Elites*, pp. 3–17. Princeton: Princeton University Press.

———. 1984. *The Evolution of Cooperation*. New York: Basic Books.

———. 1986. An evolutionary approach to norms. *American Political Science Review* 80:1095–1111.

Axelrod, R., and R. Keohane. 1985. Achieving cooperation under anarchy. *World Politics* 38:226–254.

Benton, A.A., H.H. Kelley, and B. Liebling. 1972. Effects of extremity of offers and concession rate on the outcomes of bargaining. *Journal of Personality and Social Psychology* 24:73–83.

Betts, R. 1982. *Surprise Attack*. Washington, D.C.: The Brookings Institution.

———. 1987. *Nuclear Threats and Nuclear Blackmail*. Washington, D.C.: The Brookings Institution.

Bixenstine, E., and J. Gaebelein. 1971. Strategies of 'real' opponents in eliciting cooperative choice in a prisoner's dilemma game. *Journal of Conflict Resolution* 15:157–166.

Blau, P. 1964. *Exchange and Power in Social Life*. New York: Wiley.

Bonacich, P. 1972. Norms and cohesion as adaptive responses to potential conflict: an experimental study. *Sociometry* 35:357–375.

Brodie, B. 1959. The anatomy of deterrence. *World Politics* 11:173–192.

Brown, R., and J. Kulik. 1977. Flashbulb memories. *Cognition* 5:73–99.

Bueno de Mesquita, B. 1981. *The War Trap*. New Haven, Conn.: Yale University Press.

———. 1985. The War Trap Revisited. *American Political Science Review* 79:156–177.

Bueno de Mesquita, B., and D. Lalman. 1986. Reason and war. *American Political Science Review* 80:1113–1130.

Butterfield, H. 1951. *History and Human Relations*. London: Collins.

Carter, J. 1982. *Keeping Faith: Memoirs of a President*. New York: Bantam.

Chertkoff, J.M., and J.K. Esser. 1976. A review of experiments in explicit bargaining. *Journal of Experimental Social Psychology* 12:464–456.

Dayan, M. 1981. *Breakthrough: A Personal Account of the Egypt–Israel Peace Negotiations*. New York: Knopf.

de Rivera, J. 1968. *The Psychological Dimension of Foreign Policy*. Columbus, Ohio: Bobbs-Merrill.

Deutsch, M., Y. Epstein, Y.D. Canavan, and P. Gumpert. 1967. Strategies of inducing cooperation: An experimental study. *Journal of Conflict Resolution* 11:345–360.

Dismukes, B., and J.M. McConnell, eds. 1979. *Soviet Naval Diplomacy.* New York: Pergamon.

Downs, G.W., and D.M. Rocke. 1987. Tacit bargaining and arms control. *World Politics* 39:297–325.

Duffy, G. 1983. Crisis prevention in cuba. In George, Alexander. *Managing U.S.– Soviet Rivalry: Problems in Crisis Prevention,* pp. 285–316. Boulder, Colo.: Westview Press.

Easterbrook, J.A. 1959. The effect of motion on cue utilization and the organization of behavior. *Psychological Review* 66(3):183–201.

Ebbeson, E.B., and V.J. Koncini. 1980. On the external validity of decision making research: What do we know about decisions in the real world? In Wallsten, T.S., ed., *Cognitive Processes in Choice and Decision Behavior,* pp. 21–45. Hillsdale, N.J.: Erlbaum.

Ellsberg, D. 1961. The crude analysis of strategic choices. *American Economic Review* 61:472–478.

Enzle, M., and D. Schopflocher. 1978. Instigation of attribution processes by attributional questions. *Personality and Social Psychology Bulletin* 4:595–599.

Evron, Y. 1975. The demilitarization of the Sinai. Jerusalem Papers on Peace Problems. Leonard Davis Institute for International Relations: Jerusalem.

———. 1979. Great powers' military intervention in the Middle East. In M. Leitenberg and G. Sheffer, eds., *Great Power Intervention in the Middle East.* New York: Pergamon.

Fischer, F. 1975. *War of Illusions: German Policies from 1911 to 1914.* Trans. by M. Jackson. New York: Norton.

Fischoff, B., P. Slovic, and S. Lichtenstein. 1977. Knowing with certainty: The appropriateness of extreme confidence. *Journal of Experimental Psychology: Human Perception and Performance* 3:522–564.

Fiske, S. T. 1981. Social cognition and affect. In J. Harvey, ed., *Cognition, Social Behavior, and the Environment,* pp. 227–264. Hillsdale, N.J.: Erlbaum.

———. 1982. Schema-triggered affect: Applications to social perception. In M.S. Clark and S.T. Fiske, eds., *Affect and Cognition: The 17th Annual Carnegie Symposium on Cognition,* pp. 55–78. Hillsdale, N.J.: Erlbaum.

Fiske, S.T., and S.E. Taylor. 1984. *Social Cognition.* New York: Random House.

George, A.L. 1969. The "operational code": a neglected approach to the study of political leaders and decision making. *International Studies Quarterly* 13:190–222.

———. 1982. Case studies and theory development. Paper presented to the Second Annual Symposium on Information-Processing in Organizations. Carnegie-Mellon University, Pittsburgh, Pa.

———. 1983. *Managing U.S.–Soviet Rivalry: Problems of Crisis Prevention.* Boulder, Colo.: Westview.

————. 1985. U.S.–Soviet global rivalry. Norms of competition. Paper presented to the XIIIth World Congress of the International Political Science Association, Paris.

————. 1986. The impact of crisis-induced stress on decision making. In Institute of Medicine, *The Medical Implications of Nuclear War*, pp. 529–552. Washington, D.C.: National Academy of Sciences.

George, A.L., J.P. Farley, and A. Dallin, eds. 1988. *U.S.–Soviet Security Cooperation: Achievements, Failures, Lessons*. New York: Oxford University Press.

George, A.L., D.K. Hall, and W.E. Simons. 1971. *The Limits of Coercive Diplomacy: Laos, Cuba, and Vietnam*. Boston: Little, Brown.

George, A.L., and R. Smoke. 1974. *Deterrence in American Foreign Policy: Theory and Practice*. New York: Columbia University Press.

Gordon, M.R. 1974. Domestic conflict and the origins of the First World War: the British and the German cases. *Journal of Modern History* 46:191–226.

Gouldner, A. W. 1960. The norm of reciprocity: A preliminary statement. *American Sociological Review* 25:161–178.

Greenberg, M.S., and D.M. Frisch. 1972. Effect of intentionality on willingness to reciprocate a favor. *Journal of Experimental Social Psychology* 8:99–111.

Handel, M. 1976. Perception, deception, and surprise: The case of the Yom Kippur War. Jerusalem Peace Papers 19. Leonard Davis Institute of International Relations: Jerusalem.

Harford, T., and L. Solomon. 1967. "Reformed sinner" and "lapsed saint" strategies in the prisoner's dilemma game. *Journal of Conflict Resolution* 11:104–109.

Heller, M. 1984. *The Iran–Iraq War: Implications for Third Parties*. Cambridge, Mass.: Center for International Affairs, Harvard University.

Hershey, J.C., and P. Schoemaker. 1980. Risk taking and problem context in the domain of losses: An expected utility analysis. *Journal of Risk and Insurance* 47:111–132.

Herz, J. 1950. Idealist internationalism and the security dilemma. *World Politics* 2:158–180.

Holsti, O.R. 1967. Cognitive dynamics and images of the enemy: Dulles and Russia. In D.J. Finlay, O.R. Holsti, and R.R. Fagen, eds., *Enemies in Politics*, pp. 25–96. Chicago: Rand McNally.

Holsti, O.R., and A.L. George. 1975. The effects of stress on the performance of policy-makers. In C.P. Cotter, ed., *Political Science Annual: An International Review*, pp. 255–319. Indianapolis: Bobbs-Merrill.

Howard, M. 1982/1983. Reassurance and deterrence: Western defense in the 1980's. *Foreign Affairs* 61 (Winter):309–324.

Hoyenga, K., and K. Hoyenga. 1984. *Motivational Explanations of Behavior*. Monterey, Calif.: Brooks/Cole.

Huth, P. 1988. *Extended Deterrence and the Prevention of War*. New Haven, Conn.: Yale University Press.

Huth, P., and B. Russett. 1984. What makes deterrence work? Cases from 1900 to 1980. *World Politics* 36:496–526.

————. 1988. Deterrence Failure and Crisis Escalation. *International Studies Quarterly* 32(March):29–46.

Janis, I.L., and L. Mann. 1977. *Decision Making: A Psychological Analysis of Conflict, Choice, and Commitment.* New York: Free Press.

Jervis, R. 1970. *The Logic of Images in International Relations.* Princeton, N.J.: Princeton University Press.

————. 1976. *Perception and Misperception in International Politics.* Princeton, N.J.: Princeton University Press.

————. 1978. Cooperation under the security dilemma. *World Politics* 30:167–214.

————. 1979. Deterrence theory revisited. *World Politics* 31:289–324.

————. 1982a. Deterrence and perception. *International Security* 7:3–30.

————. 1982b. Security regimes. *International Organization* 36:357–378.

————. 1984. *The Illogic of American Nuclear Strategy.* Ithaca, N.Y.: Cornell University Press.

————. 1985. Perceiving and Coping with Threat. In R. Jervis, R.N. Lebow, and J.G. Stein. *Psychology and Deterrence,* pp. 13–33. Baltimore: Johns Hopkins University Press.

————. 1986a. Representativeness in foreign policy judgments. *Political Psychology* 7:483–506.

————. 1986b. Cognition and political behavior. In R.R. Lau, and D.O. Sears, eds., *Political Cognition,* pp. 319–336. Hillsdale, N.J.: Erlbaum.

————. 1989. Rational deterrence theory. *World Politics* 41:183–207.

Jervis, R., R.N. Lebow, and J.G. Stein. 1985. *Psychology and Deterrence.* Baltimore, Md.: Johns Hopkins University Press.

Jones, E.E., and R.E. Nisbett. 1971. The actor and observer: Divergent perceptions of the causes of behavior. In E.E. Jones, D.E. Kanouse, H.H. Kelley, R.E. Nisbett, S. Valins, and B. Wiener, eds., *Attribution: Perceiving the Causes of Behavior,* pp. 79–94. Morristown, N.J.: General Learning Press.

Jonsonn, C. 1984. *Superpowers: Comparing American and Soviet Foreign Policy.* London: Frances Pinter.

Jungermann, H. 1983. The two camps on rationality. In R.W. Scholz, ed., *Decision Making Under Uncertainty,* pp. 63–86. Amsterdam: Elsevier.

Kahn, H. 1960. *On Thermonuclear War.* Princeton: Princeton University Press.

————. 1962. *Thinking About the Unthinkable.* New York: Horizon Press.

————. 1965. *On Escalation.* New York: Praeger.

Kahneman, D., and A. Tversky. 1979. Prospect theory: An analysis of decision under risk. *Econometrica* 47:263–291.

————. 1982. The simulation heuristic. In D. Kahneman, P. Slovic, and A. Tversky, eds., *Judgment Under Uncertainty: Heuristics and Biases,* pp. 201–208. New York: Cambridge University Press.

————. 1984. Choices, Values, and Frames. *American Psychologist* 39:341–350.

Kahneman, D., P. Slovic, and A. Tversky. 1982. *Judgement Under Uncertainty: Heuristics and Biases.* New York: Cambridge University Press.

Karsten, P., P.D. Howell, and A.F. Allen. 1984. *Military Threats: A Systematic*

Historical Analysis of the Determinants of Success. Westport, Conn.: Greenwood Press.

Kaufman, W.W. 1954. *The Requirements of Deterrence*. Princeton, N.J.: Center of International Studies.

Kegley, C.W., and G.A. Raymond. 1986. Normative constraints on the use of force short of war. *Journal of Peace Research* 23(3):213–227.

Kelley, H.H. 1972. *Causal Schemata and the Attribution Process*. Morristown, N.J.: General Learning Press.

Kelley, H.H., and J. Michela. 1980. Attribution theory and research. *Annual Review of Psychology* 31:457–501.

Kelley, H.H., and A.J. Stahelski. 1970. Social interaction basis of cooperators' and competitors' beliefs about others. *Journal of Personality and Social Psychology* 16:66–91.

Kelley, H.H., and J.W. Thibaut. 1978. *Interpersonal Relations: A Theory of Interdependence*. New York: Wiley.

Keohane, R.O. 1984. *After Hegemony*. Princeton, N.J.: Princeton University Press.

———. 1986. Reciprocity in international relations. *International Organization* 40:1–28.

Keohane, R.O., and J.S. Nye. 1977. *Power and Interdependence: World Politics in Transition*. Boston: Little, Brown.

Kissinger, H. 1979. *The White House Years*. Boston: Little, Brown.

Komorita, S.S. 1973. Concession-making and conflict resolution. *Journal of Conflict Resolution* 17:745–762.

Krachtowil, F., and J.G. Ruggie. 1986. International organization: A state of the art or an art of the state. *International Organization* 40:753–776.

Krasner, S., ed., 1982*a*. International Regimes. *International Organization* (Special Issue) 36:2.

———. 1982*b*. Structural causes and regime consequences: Regimes as intervening variables. *International Organization* 36:185–205.

Kuhlman, D.M., and A.F.J. Marshello. 1975. Individual differences in game motivation as moderators of preprogrammed strategy effects in prisoner's dilemma. *Journal of Personality and Social Psychology* 32:922–931.

Kuhlman, D.M., and D.L. Wimberley. 1976. Expectations of choice behavior held by cooperators, competitors and individualists across four classes of experimental game. *Journal of Personality and Social Psychology* 34:69–81.

Larson, D.W. 1985. *Origins of Containment: A Psychological Explanation*. Princeton, N.J.: Princeton University Press.

———. 1986. Game theory and the psychology of reciprocity. Paper presented to the annual meeting of the American Political Science Association, Washington, D.C.

———. 1987. The Austrian state treaty. *International Organization* 41:27–60.

———. 1988. The psychology of reciprocity in international negotiation. In J.G. Stein, ed., International negotiation: A multidisciplinary perspective. *Negotiation Journal* 4:281–302.

Lau, R.R., and D.O. Sears. 1986. Social cognition and political cognition: The past, present, and the future. In R. Lau and D.O. Sears, eds., *Political Cognition*, pp. 347–366. Hillsdale, N.J.: Erlbaum.

Lazarus, R.S. 1982. Thoughts on the relations between emotion and cognition. *American Psychologist* 37:1019–1024.

Lebow, R.N. 1981. *Between Peace and War*. Baltimore, Md.: Johns Hopkins University Press.

———. 1985a. Conclusions. In R. Jervis, R.N. Lebow, and J.G. Stein, *Psychology and Deterrence*, pp. 203–232. Baltimore, Md.: Johns Hopkins University Press.

———. 1985b. Miscalculation in the South Atlantic: The origins of the Falklands War. In R. Jervis, R.N. Lebow, and J.G. Stein, *Psychology and Deterrence*, pp. 89–124. Baltimore, Md.: The Johns Hopkins University Press.

———. 1987. Deterrence failures revisited. *International Security* 12(Summer):197–213.

———. 1989. Deterrence: A political and psychological critique. In P. Stern, R. Axelrod, R. Jervis, and R. Radner, eds., *Perspectives on Deterrence*. New York: Oxford University Press.

Lebow, R.N., and J.G. Stein, 1987a. Beyond deterrence: Alternative strategies of conflict management: *Journal of Social Issues* 43(4):5–71.

———. 1987b. Beyond deterrence: Building better theory. *Theory of Social Issues*. 43(4):155–170.

———. 1989a. Rational deterrence theory: I think, therefore I deter. *World Politics* 41:208–224.

———. 1989b. The limits of cognitive models: Carter, Afghanistan and foreign policy change. Paper presented to the International Society of Political Psychology, Tel Aviv, Israel.

———. 1989c. *When Does Deterrence Succeed and How Do We Know?* Ottawa: Canadian Institute for International Peace and Security.

———. 1990. Deterrence: The elusive dependent variable. *World Politics* 42(forthcoming April 1990).

Leng, R.J., and S.G. Walker. 1982. Comparing two studies of crisis bargaining: Confrontation, coercion, and reciprocity. *Journal of Conflict Resolution* 26:571–591.

Levy, J.S. 1983. Misperception and the causes of war: Theoretical Linkages and Analytical Problems. *World Politics* 36:76–99.

———. 1987. Declining Power and the Preventative Motivation for War. *World Politics* 40(October):82–107.

———. 1989. Quantitative studies of deterrence success and failure. In P. Stern, R. Axelrod, R. Jervis, and R. Radner, eds., *Perspectives on Deterrence*. New York: Oxford University Press.

Lindskold, S. 1978. Trust development, the GRIT proposal, and effects of conciliatory acts on conflict and cooperation. *Psychological Bulletin* 85:772–793.

Lindskold, S., and J.R. Aronoff. 1980. Conciliatory strategies and relative power. *Journal of Experimental Social Psychology* 16:187–198.

Lindskold, S., and M.G. Collins. 1978. Inducing cooperation by groups and individuals. *Journal of Conflict Resolution* 22:679–690.

Lindskold, S., P.S. Walters, and H. Koutsourais. 1983. Cooperators, competitors, and response to GRIT. *Journal of Conflict Resolution* 27:521–532.

Linville, P.W. 1982a. Affective consequences of complexity regarding the self and others. In M.S. Clark and S.T. Fiske, eds., *Affect and Cognition: The 17th Annual Carnegie Symposium on Cognition.* 79–110. Hillsdale, N.J.: Erlbaum.

———. 1982b. The complexity-extremity effect and age-based stereotyping. *Journal of Personality and Social Psychology* 42:193–211.

Lipson, C. 1984. International cooperation in economic and security affairs. *World Politics* 37:1–23.

Lynn-Jones, S. 1985. A quiet success for arms control: preventing incidents at sea. *International Security* 9:154–184.

Mandler, G. 1975. *Mind and Emotion.* New York: Wiley.

Maoz, Z., and D.S. Felsenthal. 1987. Self-binding commitments, the inducement of trust, social choice, and the theory of international cooperation. *International Studies Quarterly* 31:177–200.

Marwell, G., K. Ratcliff, and D.R. Schmitt. 1969. Minimizing Differences in a Maximizing Difference Game. *Journal of Personality and Social Psychology* 12:158–163.

MccGwire, M. 1987. Drain the Bath but Spare the Child. *Journal of Social Issues* 43(4):135–142.

McClintock, C.G. 1972. Social motivation: A set of propositions. *Behavioral Science* 17:438–454.

McClintock, C.G., and S.P. McNeel. 1966a. Reward and score feedback as determinants of cooperative game behavior. *Journal of Personality and Social Psychology* 4:606–613.

McClintock, C.G., and S.P. McNeel. 1966b. Reward level and game playing behavior. *Journal of Conflict Resolution* 10:98–102.

Mearsheimer, J. 1983. *Conventional Deterrence.* Ithaca, N.Y.: Cornell University Press.

Messick, D.M., and C.G. McClintock. 1968. Motivational bases of choice in experimental games. *Journal of Experimental Social Psychology* 4:1–25.

Messick, D.M., and W. Thorngate. 1967. Relative gain maximization in experimental games. *Journal of Experimental Social Psychology* 3:85–101.

Morgan, P. 1983. *Deterrence: A Conceptual Analysis.* Revised edition. Beverly Hills, Calif.: Sage.

Mueller, J. 1973. *War, Presidents, and Public Opinion.* New York: Wiley.

Nemeth, C. 1970. Bargaining and reciprocity. *Psychological Bulletin* 74:297–308.

Nielson, S.L., and S.G. Sarason. 1981. Emotion, personality, and selective attention. *Journal of Personality and Social Psychology* 41:945–960.

Nisbett, R.E., and L. Ross. 1980. *Human Inference: Strategies and Shortcomings of Social Judgment.* Englewood Cliffs, N.J.: Prentice-Hall.

Nye, J.S. 1987. Nuclear learning and U.S.–Soviet security regimes. *International Organization* 41(Summer):371–402.

———. 1988. Neorealism and neoliberalism. *World Politics* 40(January):235–251.

Orme, J. 1987. Deterrence failures: A second look. *International Security* 11:3–40.

Osgood, C. 1962. *An Alternative to War or Surrender*. Urbana: University of Illinois Press.

———. 1980. The GRIT strategy. *Bulletin of Atomic Scientists* (May):58–60.

Oskamp, S. 1971. Effects of programmed strategies on cooperation in the prisoner's dilemma and other mixed-motive games. *Journal of Conflict Resolution* 15:225–259.

Ostrom, C., and B. Job. 1986. The president and the political use of force. *American Political Science Review* 80:541–566.

Ostrom, C., and D. Simon. 1985. Promise and performance: A dynamic model of presidential popularity. *American Political Science Review* 79:334–358.

Oye, K. 1985. Explaining cooperation under anarchy: Hypotheses and strategies. *World Politics* 38:1–24.

Patchen, M. 1987. Strategies for eliciting cooperation from an adversary. *Journal of Conflict Resolution* 31:164–185.

Pilisuk, M., and P. Skolnick. 1968. Inducing trust: A test of the Osgood proposal. *Journal of Personality and Social Psychology* 8:121–133.

Pruitt, D.G. 1981. *Negotiation Behavior*. New York: Academic Press.

Pruitt, D.G., and M.J. Kimmel. 1977. Twenty years of experimental gaming. *Annual Review of Psychology* 28:363–392.

Pruitt, D.G., and J.Z. Rubin. 1986. *Social conflict: Escalation, Stalemate, and Settlement*. New York: Random House.

Quester, G.H. 1989. Some thoughts on deterrence failures. In P. Stern, R. Axelrod, R. Jervis, and R. Radner, eds., *Perspectives on Deterrence*. New York: Oxford University Press.

Rapoport, A., and A.M. Chammah. 1965. *Prisoner's Dilemma*. Ann Arbor: University of Michigan Press.

Reder, L.M., and J. R. Anderson. 1980. A partial resolution of the paradox of inference: the role of integrating knowledge. *Cognitive Psychology* 12:447–472.

Rosenau, J. 1986. Before cooperation: Hegemons, regimes, and habit-driven actors. *International Organization* 40:849–894.

Ross, L. 1977. The intuitive psychologist and his shortcomings: distortions in the attribution process. In L. Berkowitz, ed., *Advances in Experimental Social Psychology* 10:174–241. New York: Academic Press.

Ross, M., and F. Sicoly, Fiore. 1979. Egocentric bias in availability and attribution. *Journal of Personality and Social Psychology* 37:322–326.

Russett, B. 1967. Pearl Harbor: Deterrence theory and decision theory. *Journal of Peace Research* 4:89–105.

Sadat, A. 1977. *In Search of Identity: An Autobiography*. New York: Harper and Row.

Schank, R., and Abelson, R. 1977. *Scripts, Plans, Goals and Understanding: An Inquiry into Human Knowledge Structures* Hillsdale, N.J.: Lawrence Elbaum.

Schelling, Thomas. 1960. *The Strategy of Conflict.* Cambridge, Mass.: Harvard University Press.

————. 1966. *Arms and Influence.* New Haven, Conn.: Yale University Press.

————. 1980. The intimate struggle for self-command. *The Public Interest* 60(2):94–118.

Schoemaker, P.J.H. 1982. The expected utility model: Its variants, purposes, evidence, and limitations. *Journal of Economic Literature* 20:529–563.

Schopler, J., and V.D. Thompson. 1968. Role of attribution processes in mediating amount of reciprocity for a favor. *Journal of Personality and Social Psychology* 2:243–250.

Sermat, V. 1964. Cooperative behavior in a mixed-motive game. *Journal of Social Psychology* 62:217–239.

Sermat, V. 1967. The effect of an initial cooperative or competitive treatment upon a subject's response to conditional cooperation. *Behavioral Science* 12:301–313.

Shubik, M. 1971. Games of status. *Behavioral Science* 16:117–129.

Shure, G.H., R.J. Meeker, and E.A. Hansford. 1965. The effectiveness of pacifist strategies in bargaining games. *Journal of Conflict Resolution* 9:106–116.

Slovic, P., and S. Lichtenstein. 1968. Relative importance of probabilities and payoffs in risk taking. *Journal of Experimental Psychology* 78:1–18.

Smith, R.K. 1987. The non-proliferation regime and international relations. *International Organization* 41:253–281.

Snidal, D. 1985. The game *theory* of international politics. *World Politics* 38(October):25–57.

Snyder, G.H. 1961. *Deterrence and Defense: Toward a Theory of National Security.* Princeton, N.J.: Princeton University Press.

————. 1972. Crisis bargaining. In C.F. Hermann, ed., *International Crises: Insights from Behavioral Research,* pp. 217–256. New York: The Free Press.

Snyder, G.H., and P. Diesing. 1977. *Conflict Among Nations: Bargaining, Decision Making and System Structure in International Crisis.* Princeton, N.J.: Princeton University Press.

Snyder, J. 1984. *The Ideology of the Offensive: Military Decision Making and the Disasters of 1914.* Ithaca, N.Y.: Cornell University Press.

————. 1985. Perceptions of the Security Dilemma in 1914. In R. Jervis, R.N. Lebow, and J.G. Stein. *Psychology and Deterrence,* pp. 153–179. Baltimore, Md.: Johns Hopkins University Press.

Stein, A. 1982. Coordination and collaboration: Regimes in an anarchic world. *International Organization* 36:299–324.

Stein, J.G. 1983. The alchemy of peacemaking: The prerequisites and co-requisites of progress in the Arab-Israel conflict. *International Journal* 38:531–555.

————. 1985a. Calculation, miscalculation, and conventional deterrence I: The view from Cairo. In R. Jervis, R.N. Lebow, and J.G. Stein. *Psychology and Deterrence,* pp. 34–59. Baltimore, Md.: Johns Hopkins University Press.

————. 1985*b*. Calculation, miscalculation, and conventional deterrence II: The view from Jerusalem. In R. Jervis, R.N. Lebow, and J.G. Stein. *Psychology and Deterrence*, pp. 60–88. Baltimore, Md.: Johns Hopkins University Press.

————. 1985*c*. Detection and defection: Security regimes and the management of international conflict. *International Journal* 40:599–627.

————. 1987*a*. Extended deterrence in the Middle East: American strategy reconsidered. *World Politics* 39:326–352.

————. 1987*b*. Managing the managers: Crisis prevention in the Middle East. 171–198. In G. Winham, ed., *New Issues in Crisis Management*. Boulder, Colo.: Westview Press.

————. 1988*a*. International negotiation: A multidisciplinary perspective. *Negotiation Journal* 4:221–231.

————. 1988*b*. Building psychology into politics: The misperception of threat. *Political Psychology* 9:245–272.

Stein, J.G., ed., 1989. *Getting to the Table: Processes of International Prenegotiation.* Baltimore, Md.: Johns Hopkins University Press.

Stern, P.C. 1986. Blind spots in policy analysis: What economics doesn't say about energy use. *Journal of Policy Analysis and Management* 5(2):200–227.

Stern, P.C., R. Axelrod, R. Jervis, and R. Radner, eds., 1989*a*. Introduction. In *Perspectives on Deterrence*. New York: Oxford University Press.

Stern, P.C., R. Axelrod, R. Jervis, and R. Radner, eds., 1989*b*. Conclusions. In *Perspectives on Deterrence*. New York: Oxford University Press.

Strongman, K.T. 1978. *The Psychology of Emotion*. New York: Wiley.

Stuart, D., and H. Starr. 1982. Inherent bad-faith reconsidered: Dulles, Kennedy, and Kissinger. *Political Psychology* 3:1–33.

Tetlock, P.E., and A. Levi. 1982. Attribution bias: On the inconclusiveness of the cognitive-motivation debate. *Journal of Experimental and Social Psychology* 18:68–88.

Tesser, A. 1978. Self-generated attitude change. In L. Berkowitz, ed., *Advances in Experimental Social Psychology* 11, pp. 289–338. New York: Academic Press.

Thorndyke, P.W., and B. Hayes-Roth. 1979. The use of schemata in the acquisition and transfer of knowledge. *Cognitive Psychology* 11:82–105.

Tripp, C. 1986. Iraq: Ambitions checked. *Survival* 28:495–508.

Tversky, A., and D. Kahneman. 1973. Availability: A heuristic for judging frequency and probability. *Cognitive Psychology* 5:207–232.

Van Evera, S. 1984. The cult of the offensive and the origins of the First World War. *International Security* 9:58–107.

von Winterfeldt, D., and E. Edwards. 1986. *Decision Analysis and Behavioral Research*. New York: Cambridge University Press.

Weiner, B. 1980. A cognitive (attribution-) emotion action model of motivated behavior: An analysis of judgment of help-giving. *Journal of Personality and Social Psychology* 39:186–200.

————. 1982. The emotional consequences of causal attributions. In M.S. Clark and

S.T. Fiske, eds., *Affect and Cognition: The 17th Annual Carnegie Symposium on Cognition,* pp. 185–210. Hillsdale, N.J.: Erlbaum.

Wilson, W. 1971. Reciprocation and other techniques for inducing cooperation in the prisoner's dilemma game. *Journal of Conflict Resolution* 15:196–198.

Wohlstetter, A. 1959. The delicate balance of terror. *Foreign Affairs* 31(2):211–234.

Young, O.R. 1986. International regimes: Toward a new theory of institutions. *World Politics* 39:104–122.

Zagare, F.C. 1987. *The Dynamics of Deterrence.* Chicago: University of Chicago Press.

Zajonc, R.B. 1980. Feeling and thinking: Preferences need no inferences. *American Psychologist* 35:151–175.

Zajonc, R.B., P. Pietromonaco, and J. Bargh. 1982. Independence and interaction of affect and cognition. In M.S. Clark and S.T. Fiske, eds., *Affect and cognition: The 17th annual Carnegie symposium on cognition,* pp. 211–228. Hillsdale, N.J.: Erlbaum.

Zartman, W. 1985. *Ripe for resolution.* Oxford: Oxford University Press.

2

Arms Races and War

GEORGE W. DOWNS

Introduction

After decades of systematic study, the relationship between arms races and war remains a contentious issue. While there is a general recognition that there are exceptions to both Sir Edward Grey's melancholy dictum that "arms races lead inevitably to war" and the Roman general Vegetius's adage, "*Si vis pacem, para bellum*" (if you wish peace, prepare for war), there is little consensus beyond this, Intellectual descendants of Grey—spiral theorists and those who stress the importance of the security dilemma—emphasize the role of arms races in increasing perceptions of hostility. Deterrence theorists in the tradition of Vegetius stress the stability that arms races can produce by increasing the cost of aggression. Empiricists, seeking to arbitrate the debate using case studies and aggregate data analysis, appear to have only confused matters by discovering that arms races have little independent effect on the outbreak of war.

This chapter examines current views about the relationship between arms races and war and discusses the theoretical and methodological roots from which they emerge. Rather than survey the vast arms race literature, I will describe the source of present controversies and the fragileness of the arguments that support the dominant positions. Relatively little attention will be devoted to classic questions, such as "What is an arms race?" and "Are arms races inspired by international or domestic politics?" As interesting as these questions might be, they are not the source of the basic disagreements about the arms race–war link. There is a surprising consensus about what constitutes the population of arms races that have been carried out during the nineteenth and twentieth centuries (see Huntington, 1958 and Kennedy, 1983), and it is difficult to find an account of any single arms race—much less two—where both international and domestic politics did not operate and where their relative impacts did not fluctuate over time (Gray, 1974).

I will begin by arguing that the most robust—if poorly understood— discovery of the past 25 years of both case study and theoretical research is that the quest for an estimate of the "global" impact of arms races on war is ill-conceived. Whether a given arms race leads to war or whether a decision maker committed to peace should aggressively match the arms policies of a rival state (or ignore them as a gesture of cooperation) depends on a host of factors. These include national goals, strategic choices, the current technology of war, and the level of uncertainty and misperception that exist. Because these factors vary dramatically from case to case, the likelihood that an arms race will lead to war and the optimal arms policy that a nation should follow vary as well. This is the reason why adherents of both the spiral and deterrence perspectives are each able to marshal an impressive amount of confirmatory evidence and to offer aggressive critiques of the opposing school. It is also the reason why the conclusions of aggregate data analysis are so problematic. Any estimate of the "average" likelihood that an arms race will lead to war can be expected to vary from decade to decade as technologies and the distribution of other key factors, such as goals and resources, change. This ever changing figure may possess intrinsic historical interest, but to use it to infer something about the effect of arms races in general, or the U.S.–Soviet or Israeli–Arab arms races, is unwise. For a policymaker to use this estimate as the basis for choosing the optimal response to a rival nation's stepped-up arms acquisitions would be sheer folly.

After attempting to show that the preoccupation with historical accounting and the search for a summary measure of the effect of arms races on the likelihood of war has been counterproductive for those employing aggregate data analysis, I survey progress made by two more theoretically oriented research traditions. The first is closely related to rational deterrence theory.[1] Researchers in this tradition present increasingly sophisticated pictures of the conditions under which arms races will and will not promote stability. In their recent work, they have begun to consider the problems posed by uncertainty about actions and intentions. Critics of the rational deterrence approach, who have been sensitive to uncertainty from the outset, use case studies to document the destabilizing effect of the biased heuristics used to resolve it.[2]

Yet as significant as these advances have been, there is still no well-developed theory that describes the circumstances under which arms races will and will not lead to war. Nor is there a theory that provides a reliable guide for policymakers. This is largely a function of both traditions' tendency to ignore the insights and methods of its rival. Historically, the deterrence perspective has emphasized the effect of arms races on increasing the cost of conflict while ignoring their effect on perceptions of intent. In true Hegelian fashion, critics of this approach proceeded to emphasize perceived intent and ignore the role of cost. I argue that this theoretical schizophrenia constitutes a major stumbling block. The issue is not whether the development of a new weapon system will increase the price that a rival perceives it must pay for initiating conflict, or whether it will increase the rival's perception of the offensive threat that it poses—it will do both, except in rare cases where the weapon is purely defensive. What matters is the trade-off between the security induced by increasing the cost of aggression and the insecurity induced by increasing the perception of hostile intent. Obviously, this trade-off varies across contexts. A nation in a situation of highly redundant, mutually assured destruction (MAD) is unlikely to have its security threatened (policy influence is another matter) by a modest increase in the countervalue capabilities of its rival. On the other hand, a nonnuclear power with a significant arms advantage over its rival might be tempted to initiate a preventive war to stave off the impact of an arms race that it feels it would lose. The question is how much the intent-cost trade-off varies and the relative effect of different contextual variables.

After discussing some of research tactics that may help in getting a grasp on the intent-cost issue, I consider some of the key tasks that remain within the present domain of each approach. Formal modelers must take the steps necessary to integrate deterrence and arms race models. As it stands, there is no satisfactory model that links the individual decisions of two strategy-generating rivals locked in an arms race "game" with the probability of war. They must also investigate the consequences of variation in controversial auxiliary assumptions about risk and the nature of learning that too frequently go unacknowledged. The research mandate for the rival school involves giving more serious attention to its own assumptions, such as that regarding the inability of institutions to compensate for or overcome the biases that lead to misperception.

Empirical Research

The inductive, empirical literature on the relationship between arms races and war can be divided into three categories: individual case studies, multiple case studies, and aggregate data analysis. I will devote little attention to individual case studies because their cumulative message is different, and more notable, than that of any single study. Taken together, the studies of nineteenth-century arms races and of those preceding the two world wars convinced most scholars (and should have convinced others) that three things were true: (1) arms races do not always lead to war; (2) some wars take place in the absence of an arms race; and (3) an aggressive policy of arms accumulation for deterrence purposes does not always prevent war.

These results set the intellectual context and to some degree the research agenda for the multiple case study and aggregate data approaches to the arms race–war question. Was it variation in the type of arms race that lead to the finding that arms races sometimes lead to war and sometimes do not? If arms races were not the only cause of war (wars occurred without them), how did they fit in with all of the other causes, and what could be said about their relative importance?

Multiple Case Studies

Huntington's classic essay, "Arms Races: Prerequisites and Results" (1958), contains some of the earliest reflections on the significance of variation in the type of arms race that is being conducted. Although most often noted for its contention that arms races reduce the likelihood of war by providing an alternative medium for nations to compete to establish a new balance of power, this observation was not intended to be a historical generalization. It is an interesting deduction about the impact of qualitative arms races (those that focused on technological advances in weaponry) as compared with quantitative arms races (those that involved increases in the numbers of weapons already developed).

When a nation initiates an arms race, it sets up a challenge to the status quo that can be accepted, resisted with violence, or met by a corresponding arms increase. Huntington did not venture to describe the decision calculus that would drive the choice between war and peace, but he argued that it involved a "window" logic of preemption. The nation that is currently the most powerful is the one most likely to resort to war and will do so near the beginning of an arms race if it fears that it cannot maintain its relative advantage. Huntington believes that qualitative arms races are safer because they put less pressure on a state's economy. This reduces the chances that decision makers will come to view war as less costly than a continued arms race. In answer to the potential objection that qualitative arms races might be destabilizing because they produce a transient technological advantage that could be exploited, Huntington responds that the technology diffuses too quickly. The situation from 1945 to 1949, when the United States enjoyed qualitative superiority by virtue of the atomic bomb, is unusual. Far more commonly, the technology diffuses to the second nation before the first can capitalize on its lead (Huntington, 1958:73).[3]

Apart from the fact that few arms races can be classified as purely quantitative or purely qualitative, there are at least two problems with this theory. First, the intervening 30 years have thrown considerable doubt on the contention that qualitative arms races are necessarily cheaper than quantitative races. Advocates of an aggressive arms race with the Soviet Union, for example, inevitably stress the economic pressure created by Soviet efforts to keep up expensive U.S. weapons programs.

Second, if policymakers were permitted any role in choosing the type of race they would like to engage in, there is no reason to believe that the more resources-rich nation would ever refrain from a quantitative arms race. The wealthier nation will realize that it has to cope with qualitative improvements in its rival's arm stocks, but it will also realize that continued quantitative increases will be a reliable source of superiority. For its part, the nation aspiring to an advantageous balance of power should eventually realize that any stable reversal of positions must be the product of a quantitative race. Looked at in this light, Huntington's analysis provides us with little reason to be optimistic about the implications of arms races. Instead of peacefully harnessing competition over the balance of power, an arms race will often lead to preemption by the dominant power or to a situation where the tensions and costs of the race eventually become greater than the costs of war. Only by departing from the structure of Huntington's analysis and considering the relationship between arms races and deterrence does the situation brighten somewhat. Perhaps because Huntington wrote his article in a pre-MAD world, he pays very little attention to the role that an arms race might play in convincing a prospective opponent that war would be too costly. Yet this has almost certainly been the effect of the U.S.–Soviet race and arguably of those connected with Great Britain's efforts to maintain its "two-power standard" in naval forces. Moreover, the deterrent effect of arms races can easily be obscured by selection bias. Because the focus is on arms races, no attention is paid to the possibility that some part of the wars that occurred without an arms race might not have taken place had an arms race occurred. Whether World War II would have been prevented by more aggressive arms policies on the part of France, the Soviet Union, and Great Britain is difficult to establish; but it seems improbable that such behavior would have increased Hitler's enthusiasm for war.

The most influential recent treatment of the arms race and war connection through the use of multiple-case study data is that by Paul Kennedy (1983). Written 25 years after Huntington's essay, it stresses many of the same themes and possesses the same limitations. Kennedy, like Huntington, emphasizes that the historical record reveals no inexorable link between arms races and war. Unlike his predecessor, however, Kennedy believes that the importance of this fact is that it provides evidence that "political will" is paramount and that the independent effect of arms races is modest.

> What, ultimately, this argument is saying is that arms increases—and arms-races—are the reflection of complex political/ideological/racial/economic/ territorial differences rather than phenomena which exists, as it were, of themselves. . . . Such differences and tensions between states (or at least, between elites of states) have often produced feelings of insecurity, which are manifested in increased armaments, and in some cases eventually manifested in war. (Kennedy 1983:174)

In short, arms races are consequences of aspirations and fears. They do not cause war but rather are themselves caused by its true causes.

Beyond the redemonstration that arms races do not always lead to war, the chief virtue of Kennedy's essay is his evidence that historical arms races have been motivated by different patterns and intensities of preferences. The statesmen in Whitehall, Washington, and Tokyo who overruled their military advisors to create the Washington Naval Treaty in 1921 had different priorities than their successors, who failed to conclude any comparable agreement in the 1930s (Kennedy, 1983:172–173). As we shall see, this simple observation has two important implications. It raises the possibility that the game theorist will be unable to represent all arms races by a single game and that the data analyst will have to control for preferences in order to estimate the effect of arms races on war.

Kennedy's argument that arms races do not have an independent effect on the likelihood of war because they are initially a product of political and economic differences is provocative but unconvincing. It bears a resemblance to the contention of the gun lobby that the attention on handgun availability is misplaced, because a person bent on murder would simply find another instrument to accomplish that goal. Yet the existence of "first" causes do not make subsequent links in a causal chain irrelevant. The ease by which murder can be committed affects the homicide rate. Similarly, much of modern medicine is aimed at reducing mortality by treating ailments that are themselves caused by conditions that cannot be treated directly.

Kennedy's inferences about the controllable nature of arms races and the supremacy of political will are also suspect. The fact that arms races only sometimes lead to war does not by itself mean they can always be peacefully resolved—especially if we believe Kennedy's claim that arms races are inspired by varying degrees of economic and social differences. The lack of a perfect connection between arms races and the initiation of conflict may signify a threshold effect. Differences between nations may have to attain some threshold in order to cause war. When they are modest, they are not powerful enough to inspire attempts to gain policy leverage through arms advantage. When the differences become great, however, war is inevitable.

The "political will" argument is just as shaky. Political will is just one factor that effects the expected value of conflict, and Kennedy has presented no evidence that it is the most manipulable. In fact, the majority of arms races cited by Kennedy that were peacefully concluded were influenced by outside events not directly connected to their development or conduct. The principal cause of their resolution has been the activity of a third power. Consider the series of Anglo–French naval races that took place during the last half of the nineteenth century. The race of 1852–1853 was resolved when the two nations joined forces to fight the Russians in the Crimean War; that of 1859–1861 gradually dissipated as Napoleon III turned his attention and resources to coping with Mexico and the rising power of Prussia; and that of 1884–1890 ended in the face of increased German power and aggressiveness (Cobden, 1868; Kennedy, 1983; Marder, 1976). Although each of these arms races came to a halt without the rivals going to war with each other, they do not provide much assurance that the arms race would have stabilized or disappeared in the absence of other international challenges. They tell us even less about the ameliorative powers of political leadership and political will.

Finally, the emphasis on underlying political differences tends to obscure the questions of whether and how much arms races increase the probability of war. Kennedy acknowledges that arms races increase alarm and insecurity. By acting in this way, they exacerbate the fears and hatreds that cause them in the first place. But he says nothing about the magnitude of this effect or its policy implications. Have arms races exacerbated state differences to the point that a war took place that would not have existed otherwise? Are there wars that would have been prevented if nations had the wisdom to control their arms competition? Given the preeminence of "underlying differences," is it even possible to talk about arms control without there having been a prior change in political preferences? None of these questions receives attention.

In general, one emerges from multiple-case study literature with a refined historical sense that simple generalizations about the arms race–war relationship will not be easy to come by. Huntington drives home the point that the likelihood that arms races will lead to war depends on the technology that drives the race and each nation's resources and expectations. Kennedy's emphasis on the variation of national objectives adds an additional layer of complexity. It is important to keep the character and degree of this complexity in mind as we turn to more systematic attempts to explore the relationship between arms races and war.

The Statistical Analysis of Aggregate Data

The component of the empirical tradition that relies on the analysis of aggregate focuses on what appears to be a precise and tractable question: To what extent do arms races increase the likelihood that rival nations will go to war? Approaching the matter statistically rather than through a handful of case studies encourages the use of a larger sample and will, I hope, lead to a more precise conclusion. The use of multivariate statistics also holds out the possibility of investigating the impact of variables that might be responsible for exacerbating or moderating the influence of arms races: the type of arms race, the intensity with which it is conducted, the resources available to each nation, and so forth. As we shall see, however, the problems associated with this kind of analysis are far greater than they might first appear.

There is a strong temptation to assume that if a certain percentage of arms races lead to war, then there is roughly the same chance that a current arms race will end in the same manner, and that a policymaker contemplating how to respond to a rival nation's aggressive behavior should keep this fact in mind. This is the driving force behind many of the early studies that employed aggregate data analysis. Wallace (1979, 1982), one of the pioneers in this tradition, found modest support for the hypothesis that arms races increase the chances that a crisis will ignite into war. While the implications of an arms race for crisis escalation is a narrower question than the relationship between arms races and war, it is clearly related to the issue of whether arms races create a more dangerous international environment. If there is a strong relationship between arms races and escalation, the inference that arms races are related to war seems inescapable.

Critics argued, however, that there were serious methodological problems with Wallace's work. One difficulty involved the independence of the "dyadic disputes" that constituted his sample. Despite the role of alliances and the importance of diffusion effects, the two world wars were each coded as multiple arms races that resulted in multiple wars (Weede, 1980). Moreover, as Altfeld (1983) notes, some of the coded races were not only not independent, they did not even exist (for example, Great Britain and Japan on the eve of World War II). Another problem stemmed from Wallace's decision to construct his arms race index by multiplying the arms growth rates of the two nations in the dyad together (Diehl, 1983). This procedure can obviously lead to equating a strong unilateral buildup with a more modest bilateral race. This problem is more than a technical triviality, because any theory of deterrence would predict that the two situations are incommensurate. Ceteris paribus, the cost of aggression in the first instance will be much lower than in the second.

The skepticism of the critics was reinforced by subsequent reanalysis by Diehl (1983). The conditional probability of a dispute preceded by an arms race turning into war appeared to be somewhat greater than one that was not preceded by an arms race, but the difference was quite small. A more elaborate treatment of the question failed to discover any difference (Diehl, 1985). When Diehl and Kingston (1987) examined the more basic question of whether a military buildup increases the chances that a militarized dispute would occur in the first place, they found no evidence to support a relationship: "Arms competition apparently does not increase the chances of a confrontation between the superpowers in Western Europe or Central America" (1987:812).

Any empirical work that addresses the arms race and war connection is vulnerable to a variety of criticisms. As all of the analysts realize, military expenditures or any other measure of arms race "effort" is an imperfect surrogate for a rival nation's perception of military power. It does not capture the effect of the development of a specific weapon like the iron-hulled ship or an antiballistic missile (ABM) system, which can foster far more insecurity than a mere spending gap. Since such innovations are rare and their relationship to year-to-year spending uncertain, the impact of these weapons may be concealed by a preoccupation with fiscal measures. The possibility of entering alliances as a spending surrogate and the potential disequilibrium brought about by a change in force structure or strategic doctrine also increases skepticism about the integrity of a unidimensional measure (see Mearsheimer, 1983; Walt, 1987). Nonetheless, the findings that suggest that arms races (as measured by expenditures) and war are unrelated are interesting, because the logic expressed by Paul Kennedy would lead us to expect the opposite. If whatever causes war also increases the intensity of arms races, then there should be a strong positive relationship between the probability of war and the degree of arms competition. The absence of such a relationship is provocative—even in the presence of measurement problems.

Yet the case studies suggest that any attempt to estimate the impact of arms races on war through the analysis of aggregate data must cope with more formidable challenges. Except in situations where the arms policies of both nations are driven entirely by domestic forces, case studies make it clear that the decision to build arms is a strategic move inextricably bound to each state's goals, resources, dissatisfaction with the status quo, and expectations about the future. Unless we can assume that these are all the same—something that no historian or diplomat would ever encourage—the wisdom of a given strategy will vary. In terms of preserving peace, an arms race will be a praiseworthy joint strategy when it leads both sides to appreciate the commitment of the rival to defend itself and the high costs of conflict, and it will be a foolish strategy when it convinces each side that the other is committed to aggression. Those who engage in aggregate data analysis are attempting to evaluate the strategy of arms racing, but what they are actually accessing is the outcome of a mixture of different strategies, games (some internal as well as external), and perceptions. While it is interesting from a historical point of view to know whether arms races have generally led to war or not, the implication that the answer to this question has theoretical or strategic value depends on whether there is any reason (1) to believe that the past mixture of strategies, games, and perceptions is likely to characterize the future; and (2) to assume that a real-life strategic situation is likely to take place in an environment where the players have no information about utilities and perceptions beyond that which can be inferred from historical patterns.

Both propositions are almost certainly wrong. While the future blend of strategies, games, and perceptions may be the same as that in the past, there is good reason to believe that it will not be. The arms race contexts that characterized the first half of the twentieth century could not have been extrapolated from the last half of the nineteenth century, much less from the previous 200 years. Even if we make the heroic assumption that the distribution of preferences for expansion, resources, and misperception is the same, the technology of war has changed in such a way that the costs associated with great-power wars have risen dramatically. Regardless of one's regard for expected utility models, it is hard to envision a world where this fact has no implication for the likelihood that arms races will lead to war. Data analysis based on data from the entire set of arms races that have taken place since 1850 (or 1900) does not take this into consideration. It is as if someone proposed to make a general statement about the impact of a college education on expected lifetime earnings by using an average figure calculated over the period from 1900 to 1988. The average earnings figure may be of some use to a social historian—especially when compared with those found in other nations—but the changes in the economy and the percentage of people with a college education would mean that the "average" figure would have no enduring stability. The likelihood that arms races will lead to war will keep changing for a variety of similar reasons and the "average" likelihood is no more meaningful.

The more critical point concerns the relationship between strategy and context. Relying on aggregate historical information to infer the wisdom (or danger) of the strategy to engage in an arms race is no more sensible than relying on aggregate information to select football plays. A far higher percentage of quarterback sneaks result in touchdowns each year than do long-pass plays. If one knew nothing about the game of football and was not permitted to see the field, choosing the former would be quite defensible. However, it turns out that the efficacy of the quarterback sneak as a scoring device depends a great deal on field position. Outside the opponent's 10-yard line, it does very poorly; indeed, almost any alternative is better. Coaches are not forced to make decisions in the absence of information about where the ball is and how the other team's defense has played up to that point. Similarly, states engaged in arms races and contemplating war do not make this decision in the absence of information about their rival state's objectives, resources, and strategies that they have used in the past. To infer something from aggregate data about the wisdom of engaging in an arms race at a particular moment in history suggests that decision makers ignore factors like whether the arms race is nuclear or nonnuclear and whether a rival leader's objectives are similar to those of Hitler or Charles de Gaulle.

Alluding to the importance of variables such as objectives and resources may lead the reader to wonder if all of this is simply an elaboration of Kennedy's point about the paramount importance of the complex differences and tensions that he argues underlie every arms race. It is not. It does not follow that because arms races are themselves the product of political and economic differences, arms race behavior and its consequences are completely determined by these differences. Arms behavior is a strategy, and strategies are frequently not determined by utilities alone. If they were, both chess and football would be less interesting games than they are, and every contestant in Axelrod's famous computer tournaments would have submitted the same entry (Axelrod, 1984). Indeed, one would be hard pressed to demonstrate that arms behavior in any arms race was a simple function of the level of initial differences.

The fact that in many situations preferences do not inexorably lead to the selection of a particular strategy leads us to expect that the arms strategy used to express an interstate antipathy will have an independent impact on the probability that war will break out. It also suggests one approach to evaluating the impact of arms races: learn how the interaction of different arms race strategies—given utilities and uncertainties—increase or decrease the likelihood of war.

There are two ways of carrying out this general approach. The first would be to continue along the correlates of war path used by Wallace and Diehl, but would involve more complicated data gathering and analysis. The second would exploit formal methods and simulation to explore in a theoretical way the consequences of different arms strategies under different assumptions.

The many problems associated with this more complicated version of the data analytic approach help explain why it has never been attempted. Even the most gifted team of contemporary historians would have a difficult time estimating U.S. and Soviet priorities during the past 40 years, the perception each had of the other's priorities, the arms strategy each was employing and how it was perceived, and so forth. To compile similar data about the arms race between Argentina and Chile (1890–1902) or between Great Britain and France (1840–1866) would be an even more formidable task.

Rational Deterrence Models

Realist theorists from Vegetius to the present have assessed the impact of arms races on war from an implicitly deterrence perspective. If an arms race increased the cost of conflict for both parties, it was believed to contribute to the cause of peace by deterring each; if it increased the power of one of the rivals relative to the other, it would increase the likelihood of war. A natural step in the evolution of this perspective was that it be refined through the use of formal models rooted in economics and decision theory. The deceptively simple idea of cost of conflict could be understood more deeply by recasting it as expected value and breaking it down into its constituent elements: perceived benefits as well as costs, the probability of success, the stability and utility of the status quo, attitudes about risk, and expectations about the future. The fact that some of these elements depended on the behavior of the rival nation and the likelihood that the rival nation was in much the same position suggested the relevance of game theory.

Formal modeling in the rational deterrence tradition is used to represent the deterrence perspective, but no claim is made that all deterrence-oriented theorists have a taste for formal modeling.[4] It is emphasized here because it contains the most complete and systematic explication of the deterrence point of view, and because its systematic character brings the strengths and weaknesses of deterrence theory into relief. The choice is further reinforced by the fact that since Schelling (1960), the formal approach has dominated the evolution of deterrence theory.

One immediate payoff from considering the rational deterrence perspective lies in the insight that it provides about the difficulties associated with the empirical approach. Because it suggests that arms races will reduce as well as increase the chance that war will occur, it tells us that any attempt to characterize "the" effect of an arms race must be based on a demonstration that every race will have the same effect on the dimensions of the expected value of conflict. Simple inspection of the factors that characterize the expected value of conflict suggests that no such demonstration will be possible. Whether an arms race teaches an aggressive state that the probability of success is higher or lower than it initially estimated will depend at a minimum on variables such as the resources of its rival and the preemptory potential of weapons developed during the arms race.

Just as many deterrence theorists do not engage in formal modeling, there are formal modelers who do not adopt a rational deterrence perspective. In fact, there are few models that possess the three minimal attributes that one would expect of a satisfactory formal theory dealing with the relationship of arms races to war. These attributes are: (1) the existence of two reacting, strategy-generating opponents; (2) specification of the conditions under which deterrence is sustainable; and (3) the explicit incorporation of arms increases (and decreases) as a decision variable that is tied to the probability of war.

Arms race models in the Richardsonian tradition are a good example of formal models that have little to do with deterrence and possess none of the necessary attributes. Here the rate of growth of one nation's arms stock is a linear function of the arms stocks of the two participating sides. For certain values of the parameters, this system of equations is stable, meaning that any trajectory tends toward a point where the rates of change are both zero. For other values, trajectories diverge and arms stocks increase without bound at an increasing rate (Richardson, 1960). Implicitly, Richardson and those who have followed his approach have identified this second situation as leading inevitably to war.

Although it is possible to reexpress a Richardson-like arms race as a differential game (see Simaan and Cruz, 1975), it is basically a deterministic process that involves no strategic choices on the part of either participant. The outcome is strictly a function of initial conditions. While Richardson hoped that nations would come to their senses and act in such a way as to overcome the model's implications, the decisions that they would need to make are not included in the model. This specification means that the Richardson model has little to offer from the standpoint of prescription. No mitigating strategies are possible. It also embodies the a priori assumption that an arms race has no independent impact on the probability that war will occur. War may or may not occur, but whether it does or not is wholly a function of the initial conditions. The model leaves no room for a counterfactual.

Richardson's model also lacks an explicit theory of deterrence. He simply assumes that war will eventually occur whenever a trajectory fails to converge to a point where the rate of change is zero. War is not so much predicted as anticipated to be the most likely outcome when the enormous rate of weapons production predicted by the model becomes absurd or impossible. Yet there is another possibility. The justification for the use of a linear differential equations model lies in its simplicity and the fact that other nonlinear models can be approximated over a small region by a linear one. When an arms race leaves this region, as would be implied by an unstable model, it might be more realistic to assume that the character of the arms race might change. For example, it is quite plausible that the coefficients in the model might vary depending on the arms levels. The relative significance of the addition of one missile is greater when both sides have 10 than when both sides have 1,000. In a similar vein, it is easy—especially after 40 years of U.S.–Soviet arms racing—to imagine a perfectly stable, dynamic equilibrium that is based on a diminishing but still nonzero rate of increase.

Faith in the Richardsonian formulation is not increased by examining historical arms races. Majeski and Jones (1981) looked at 12 arms races that have commonly been used by researchers. In most cases, changes in expenditures of one nation were only marginally related to those of its opponent and, when they were related, the Richardsonian specification was not supported. Even allowing for the fact that expenditure levels is an imperfect surrogate for arms levels, this is not encouraging support.

Intriligator and Brito (1976; 1984; Brito and Intriligator, 1974) have investigated the relationship between armament levels and war initiation using an approach that is more sensitive to the contingent effect of arms races and more closely tied to deterrence. While the details of this work varies somewhat, it centers around the construction of a model of a missile war that begins with a counterforce first strike followed by a countervalue retaliation. They postulate conditions under which a potential attacking side will be deterred and use these conditions to investigate the effect of changes in armaments levels that might be brought about by any arms race or arms control agreement.

Overall, they reach three conclusions that have a strong deterrence flavor and appear to solve the problem of tying arms decisions to the likelihood of war:

1. An equal arms race from an equal base increases stability. The quantitative, nuclear arms race between the United States and the Soviet Union has reduced the chances that war will occur and provided insurance against the destabilizing potential of qualitative improvement in weapons.

2. The minimum level of stable disarmament that is possible is a function of the potential for technological innovation and treaty verification.

3. Unilateral reductions and unbalanced arms increases can lead to instability and a reduction in deterrence.

This formalizes the contingent effect of arms races on the probability of war that many classical deterrence theorists intuited. Arms races that are balanced decrease the chances that war will occur; arms races that are characterized by differential rates of arms growth will increase the chances of war.

As helpful as their formulation is in explaining why some arms races end in war and others do not, the Brito and Intriligator treatment does not meet all of the requirements that we would like in a formal theory linking arms races to war. It succeeds in specifying the conditions under which deterrence is sustainable, but it has little to say about the role of strategy and does not treat arms increases (or decreases) as a decision variable. The last characteristic is more important than it seems. It may be somewhat helpful to tell a nation's decision makers what part of a decision plane is unstable (that is, what level and relative balance of arms stocks is dangerous). However, a point on a plane is not the same as a decision. The arms levels of two nations and relative balance are the product of the decisions of both nations, not just one. If an unbalanced situation exists, decision makers of either nation must cope with the dilemma of how to get both nations to a more stable point without precipitating war, and whether any strategy they might come up with is worth the costs. Estimations of what the other side will do in response to their actions is critical to either decision.

One prescription might be that a nation interested in decreasing the chances of war would do well to follow a tit-for-tat strategy in which the arms balance is preserved by mimicking the arms behavior of its rival. This is very helpful, but problems arise even when there is *already* balance between the two nations. Two that will be discussed later involve information uncertainty and interpretation. Decision makers must not react to nonexistent moves and the rival nation must not overestimate the magnitude or misinterpret the significance of the response. Another problem is that the ability to engage in a tit-for-tat strategy is a function of resources. One consequence of the incomplete integration of arms races and deterrence theory is that Intriligator and Brito do not deal with whether or not a nation having fewer resources than its rival is likely to launch a preemptive attack before the arms ratio becomes unbalanced.

When an unbalanced situation exists, the strategies that the two nations can be expected to pursue are not clear. The Intriligator and Brito model makes use of a second threshold that represents the maximum acceptable loss. Although it plays only a small role in their analysis, the idea that there is a level of expected damage that makes even certain victory unattractive is compelling. Historically, it is the key to Swiss deterrence. In terms of arms races, such a threshold is important because it places a limit on the effect of resource advantage. Unfortunately, it may have a strategic effect as well.

Suppose one nation possesses more resources than its rival and presently enjoys an arms advantage. What strategy should the weaker nation follow in this situation? Should it attempt to gradually expand its arm stocks in an effort to reach this more stable threshold where the weapons and resource advantage of the stronger nation become irrelevant? What will the more powerful nation do? The expectation that this threshold will be reached creates another kind of "window." In this case it is an offensive rather than a defensive window, a last opportunity to expand or to maintain the same level of policy influence as opposed to a last chance to avoid capitulation or defeat. Instead of preempting inevitable defeat, the nation is preempting increased independence and security for its rival. With this in mind, does a decision on the part of the weaker nation to step up arms production increase or decrease the likelihood of war?

Brams and Kilgour (1988) are more explicit about the game-theoretic aspects of arms races and deterrence and in this way meet the requirement of dealing with two strategy-generating opponents. They refrain, however, from directly linking arms race decisions (and arms races) with deterrence and the probability of war. In fact, the topics are treated in separate chapters and tied to separate underlying games. Brams and Kilgour are clearly more interested in exploring the circumstances under which arms races can be stabilized and reversed than in connecting them to the outbreak of war, and quite correctly believe that arms races represent only a part of the problem of deterrence.

Their discussion of the two issues is useful for our purposes because unlike most formal modelers they recognize the significance of assuming that policymakers know what game they are playing. This may be reasonable in the nuclear case—at least if we avoid the fuzzy case of extended deterrence—but it is far less so in cases where nonnuclear weapons are involved and neither side has the luxury of assuming that the other shares its belief that war is the worst possible outcome. Similarly, they acknowledge that in the presence of uncertainty about intentions and the underlying game, threats—including arms increases—become the evidence that each side uses as a basis for action. ". . . [w]hen threats themselves become provocative and severely undermine trust, one must ask whether their deterrent value outweighs the cost of creating an inflammatory situation" (Brams and Kilgour, 1988:53). Thus, although Brams and Kilgour do not resolve the many questions about the impact of arms decisions on uncertainty about intentions and its effect relative to increasing the expected cost of conflict, they implicitly place them within the domain of the deterrence model.

Approaches such as that of Bruce Bueno de Mesquita (1981; 1985), which focuses on expected utility, have not used arms level as a decision variable that is explicitly tied to the probability of war, or treated the interaction of nations as a game where the success of one state's strategy depends on the strategic behavior of the other. This is not to say that the expected utility school has been silent on the relationship between arms races and war. Morrow (1984) employs time series data and indirect measures of risk acceptance and risk aversion to test a number of hypotheses relating the impact of risk attitudes and swings in military superiority to the initiation of conflict. These results are important because they corroborate the importance of transient advantage or "windows."[5] However, further work is still needed to explain the expected utility justification for permitting the existence of such windows. It is not clear why a government or population of voters would be rational in its consideration of the domestic impact of military expenditures but ignore their impact on the propensity of a rival to initiate hostilities. Is it because the cost of war is underestimated? Or is it because the expected value of satisfying domestic interests is greater than the expected cost of conflict?

The three minimal attributes that one expects of a formal model dealing with the relationship of arms races and war listed near the beginning of this section are very general and were logically derived. They must be met before formal theory will be capable of generating a prediction about the consequences of an arms decision on the likelihood of war. Yet their existence alone does not guarantee that the output of the formal model will have any correspondence with reality. In this case, as in many others, the degree of that correspondence will be strongly affected by the appropriateness of certain auxiliary assumptions that are necessary to specify a model but about which choice is possible. For example, a well-specified formal model must implicitly make some assumption about the nature of the decision maker in each state. The modeler is not logically compelled to choose between the convention of a unitary actor and a more complicated choice process, but a well-specified model will embody *some* choice. Sometimes the modeler will decide to slide by with an assumption of convenience and the hope that the world behaves *as if* it were true. At other times it will be based on more solid formal or empirical grounds.

In any formal model that links arms decisions to deterrence, three of the most important auxiliary assumptions concern national objectives (for example, utility functions), risk attitudes, and the accuracy of intelligence estimates about relative capabilities. While it may be convenient to assume that national objectives are homogenous or, at a minimum, correctly estimated by a rival, that nations are risk neutral, and that intelligence estimates are unbiased and accurate, case study evidence provides scant justification for any of these assumptions. Indeed, it has helped inspire the "spiral model" and "security dilemma" literature and constitutes the most salient theoretical challenge to the deterrence view of how arm races are related to war. Before discussing the ways that rational deterrence modelers are beginning to deal with these issues, it is necessary to examine the nature of that challenge.

The Security Dilemma, Spiral Theory, and Other Critiques of Rational Deterrence Theory

Most critics of the rational deterrence and formal modeling approach to understanding the relationship between arms races and war base their critique on the bias induced by individual and institutional-level misperceptions about the intentions of rivals and their vision of national goals. A state confident of its own benign intentions, but believing in the potential aggressiveness of the states around it, takes steps to improve its security. The rival, motivated by an equivalent desire for security and wary of the implications of its rival's behavior, responds in kind. An arms race ensues in which the probability of war increases because each infers that the other is growing increasingly hostile. The temptation to engage in preemptive or preventive war mounts as the intensity of weapons acquisition spirals ever upward (hence the term *spiral model*). This process has traditionally been viewed as one of the principal causes of World War I and has been extended to other conflicts such as the Seven Years' War (Smoke, 1977). It supplies the logic behind Sir Edward Grey's fear of arms races and reflects the effects of the security dilemma that Butterfield believed supplied the "very geometry of human conflict" (Jervis, 1976:65–66).

Where traditional deterrence theory emphasized the effect of arms race behavior on demonstrating capabilities, resolve, and the cost of aggression, the security dilemma perspective emphasizes its effect on goal perceptions and, implicitly, expectations about the ability of national resources to absorb the continued cost of peace. The difference in emphasis leads to different predictions about the consequences of arms races and how they should be conducted. An equal arms race is nonthreatening from a deterrence standpoint because it demonstrates mutual resolve and increases the cost of initiating conflict for both parties. Deterrence theory recognizes the temptation to engage in preventive war that will occur if one side begins to run out of resources, but holds out the possibility that the arms buildup will have made the cost of conflict so great that the impact of superior resources will be attenuated. This is why Brito and Intriligator (1974) speak of "maximum acceptable," and it is the basis for Glaser's (forthcoming) argument that MAD creates a situation that is enormously stable. From a security dilemma standpoint things look very different. Even an equal arms race is dangerous because it convinces each side of the other's aggressive intent. As the pace of the race continues to escalate in a vain attempt to increase security, war is viewed as increasingly inevitable. The side with less resources faces a choice of fighting sooner at equal odds, fighting later at a great disadvantage, or surrendering.

The prescriptive divergence of the two perspectives follows from this. Where deterrence theory prescribes increasing the cost of aggression, those who focus on the security dilemma concentrate on minimizing the inference of hostile intention. The first perspective emphasizes massive retaliation and uses the aggressive defense of peripheral issues to avoid any incursion on basic interests. The second perspective believes that any actions other than unambiguously defensive ones is provocative and stresses the power of unilateral, conciliatory gestures to provide the opponent with the opportunity to achieve its security goals at lower cost.

Misperception of behavior and intentions is the bedrock of the security dilemma and the spiral model (see, for example, Jervis, 1976; Lebow, 1981; Stein, 1982; Snyder, 1984), and the case for their validity is strengthened by evidence that misperception is a basic characteristic of decision making. Apart from case material, most of this evidence has come from psychology. One of the most commonly cited examples is the heuristic referred to as the "fundamental attribution bias" (Nisbett and Ross, 1980). This refers to the tendency of individuals to view their own actions as a consequence of circumstance, while viewing the actions of others as a consequence of choice. In the context of arms races this (1) prevents each state from appreciating its role in provoking the arms increases of the other and (2) leads it to undervalue the extent to which its rival's arms policies were the consequence of domestic concerns unrelated to the objective of arms advantage. The fundamental attribution bias thus increases the propensity to interpret arms behavior as indicative of a rival nation's growing hostility and discontent with the status quo. This, in turn, increases the incentive to engage in preemptive or preventive war.

The incentive to engage in preventive war may be further increased by another characteristic of individual decision making identified by cognitive psychologists. This involves the propensity of individuals to exhibit risk aversion in seeking gains, to exhibit risk seeking when attempting to avoid losses, and to be more sensitive to losses than to gain. Taken together the tendencies constitute the background of what psychologists refer to as "prospect theory" and has most recently been applied to decisions such as voting (for example, Quattrone and Tversky, 1988). These tendencies suggest that the motivation for initiating an arms race or aggressively pursuing arms advantage once a race has commenced is likely to be either defensive (a conclusion that is quite consistent with the spiral model) or the prospect of substantial political or military leverage at relatively little risk. They also suggest that the impact of an arms race on the likelihood of war will have a great deal to do with how it is conducted. A state that is slightly ahead in a relatively even arms race should underestimate the advantage that this provides.

This is encouraging because it provides some assurance that a transient advantage of the type that would result from a weapons innovation or different rates of economic growth might not be exploited. The only catch lies in preemption and prevention. A state will be tempted to choose an option that is potentially costly but has some probability of success in place of an option that is somewhat less costly but makes defeat or capitulation inevitable. This means that relatively equal arms races might be safer than is normally assumed and that the cumulative effect they exert by increasing the expected cost of aggression could be greater than would be anticipated by expected value calculations alone. The negative side is that the use of these heuristics would increase the possibility that an arms race will lead to war during the "window" that exists when one state discovers it is falling behind (or anticipates that it will), but before either the costs of conflict or the probability of defeat have increased dramatically. This logic can be argued to have played a major role in the Israeli decision to initiate the Suez War in 1956. Israel believed that it was important to act before the ever-growing Soviet arms program in Egypt brought about a decisive shift in the balance of power in the Middle East.

Cognitive biases and heuristics do not exhaust the possible sources of misperception. The judgments made by decisions makers about the intentions, capabilities, and resources of both their own state and their rival—the basis for the decision to choose war or peace—are colored by organizational and political processes as well as individual cognition. To the extent that arms races affect the way key organizations operate or the distribution of power within a government, they can affect the likelihood that war or peace will result.

It is important that the superficial attractiveness of this argument not seduce us into confusing cause and effect. For example, one of the least controversial consequences of an arms race is its tendency to increase the budget of the military. Because it is safe to assume that (1) the impact of a government official is related in some way to the size of the budget he or she administers, and (2) officials connected with the defense establishment often have different perceptions and priorities than those connected with the typical domestic agency, it might seem reasonable to conclude that an arms race will always act to increase the probability that war will take place. A somewhat less compelling but equally popular corollary is that this process will be exacerbated by the fact that in most political systems, success breeds success. That is, the interest groups that support the military will be able to exploit every political victory to increase the chances of future victories. In the case of the United States, for example, it is common to assume that a Political Action Committee that is successful in promoting its candidate for election will receive economic benefits that permit it to expand its range of influence in the next election.

These arguments do not have the a priori power that they seem to possess. A proponent of a pure public-choice approach to budgetary allocations could argue that the growth in the military establishment was nothing more than a new equilibrium outcome that need have no implications for future changes. From this perspective, the increased prominence of a political lobby with bellicose views or the difference in the ideology of a defense official and someone from a domestic agency simply reflects the underlying distribution of power, preferences, perceptions, and expectations among the voting public or the governing elite. It is this distribution of power and preferences that will determine what will occur next, and there is no reason to believe that the present distribution effects the future distribution.

Yet the belief that the military bureaucracy and the interests that support it constitute something more than passive instruments of an underlying distribution of voter preferences is not so easily extinguished. While deduction assures us that the mere existence of an arms race and an expanded military need exert no independent effect on decision maker preferences and perceptions, induction suggests that such an effect exists. Scholars who have studied the role of bureaucracies in policy formation have consistently been struck by their ability to manipulate information and mold preferences in ways that further agency ambitions. Rourke (1972), George (1980), Enthoven and Smith (1971), and Van Evera (1984) are just a few of those who provide a wealth of cases where the military shaped the perspectives of their overseers.

Policymakers are not ignorant of the efforts to manipulate them. President

Kennedy was well aware of the fact that the military's account of Vietnam was distorted (Halberstam, 1973:345), and today the majority of those in Congress know that the defense budget contains a great deal of slack. But policymakers are involved in a game where their information disadvantage is great. This makes it difficult for them to compensate for biases that they know exist. They realize that the Department of Defense has an incentive to inflate threat assessments and weapons requirements, but the *magnitude* of the inflation is difficult to estimate. This is exacerbated by the problems associated with evaluating the financial and force requirements connected with successful deterrence. It is far more difficult for a domestic agency to obscure the failure or waste associated with an education or farm program than for the Navy to do the same with a major weapons system. Policymakers are further prevented from reducing the biases induced by the military by their membership in "iron triangles" and the fact that the "cost" of failed deterrence is inestimably greater than the cost of an error in judgment about a domestic program.

Most of the work referred to in the previous paragraph has focused on the general question of how the military establishment effects policymaker perceptions rather than the issue of how arms races increase (or decrease) the likelihood of war. The two are not necessarily connected. Every nation-state has a military, but only a subset are involved wars. What reason is there to believe that distorting effects that are always present *increase* as an arms race progresses or are *more likely* to lead to war as an arms race unfolds?

A reasonable place to begin is with the tendency of the military establishment to overemphasize the strategic value of the offensive forces relative to defensive forces, or what has become known as the "cult of the offensive." Although reference to this tendency can be found in much of the national security literature (for example, Brodie, 1973; Waltz, 1979; Posen, 1984), the most systematic exposition of the bias is Jack Snyder's *The Ideology of the Offensive* (1984). This exploration of the determinants of strategic policymaking in France, Russia, and Germany prior to World War I puts together a formidable argument that the adoption of offensive strategies by these states cannot be determined by any rational calculus. Ignoring the lesson of the Boer and Russo–Japanese wars that the technological and logistical balance had tipped in favor of the defender, the military of all three nations pressed offensive initiatives that reduced the chances of victory. Germany's aggressiveness managed to provoke Great Britain into joining the war, France conducted an inept offensive that led to the surrender of a significant part of northeastern France, and Russia weakened itself by attacking too quickly and in the wrong place.

When it comes to generalizing from the World War I experience, Snyder is cautious. He notes that although some of the sources of offensive bias were common to all three states, the decisive sources "were peculiar to each case, rooted in specific interests, preconceptions and circumstances" (Snyder, 1984:16). He further emphasizes the importance of transient and idiosyncratic factors by pointing out that if war had broken out 3 years earlier, two of the three powers would have employed more defensive strategies. Overall, Snyder argues that there is a bias toward the offensive that can interact with other contextual variables to produce war but that its operation is more subtle than the term "cult of the offensive" implies.

The list of generic sources of offensive bias that Snyder enumerates is formidable. Offensive as opposed to defensive strategies (1) are expensive and provide a justification for the large budgets sought by all institutions; (2) produce a more demonstrable return on investment; (3) increase the prestige of the military more than defensive strategies; (4) permit more organizational autonomy; (5) reduce uncertainty in planning; and (6) are more consistent with the Hobbesian view of international relations that is a foundation of military ideology.

Snyder's analysis would suggest that the offensive bias of the military is not increased by an arms race, but its impact increases because the objective base that it operates on is larger. It is in this sense that his analysis suggests that arms races cause wars. Where a bias of 20 percent may convince a nation that it can take a small piece of enemy territory when its army is small, it may convince it that total victory is possible when its army is large. This difference in potential benefit can be a critical motivation.

Offensive bias not only leads decision makers to overestimate the likelihood that they will be victorious, it leads them to overestimate the probability of their state being attacked. In the case of World War I, Snyder's account makes it clear that in many cases an inflated fear of other nations' forces dominated a confidence in the offensive capabilities of one's own military. Belief in the importance of preemption was everywhere in evidence and pessimism about the long-term security offered by defense against the inflated perception of a rival's strength seems to be a more powerful motivation than the faith in easy victory. In Germany, the nation had the most justification for believing that an offensive might prove successful and whose aspiration to world power might seem most to necessitate it, there was a real concern about the need for preventive war against the growing power of the Entente. Indeed, this concern had been a consistent theme of German strategists for four decades. When war did come, the Russians launched a campaign that was driven more by the fear of a quick French collapse than by the prospects of sure victory (Snyder, 1984:23). The thinking of World War II strategists—like those in Japan—was dominated by the vision of a "window of opportunity" that would not only be closed in the near future but would be inexorably followed by a new window that could and would be exploited by its rival. Carried to an extreme, caution can produce war as easily as a faith in manifest destiny or excessive zeal.

Note how the fundamental attribution bias, prospect theory, and offensive bias all operate to increase the incentive for preemption and preventive war as an arms race evolves. The fundamental attribution bias leads decision makers to believe that the other state's arms behavior is motivated by political or territorial ambitions rather than self-defense. The offensive bias leads them to overestimate the danger that the added arms represent. Any prospect theory leads them to be risk-seeking in trying to neutralize the inflated danger. This preemptive orientation explains the apparent contradiction between the argument that military establishments promote a cult of the offensive and the findings of Huntington (1958) and Betts (1977) that military attitudes toward conflict are no more aggressive than civilian attitudes. The tendency to initiate a conflict that might be generated by a faith in the offense versus the defense will usually be offset—at least partly—by prospect theory's risk averseness in seeking gains and the implied aggressiveness of the enemy suggested by the fundamental attribution theory.

The Research Agenda

There is much to be gained by integrating the findings and methods of the rational deterrence approach to the arms race war question and that of its critics. Even the preceding brief summary of the security dilemma and spiral model reveals their value as a corrective to crude deterrence theory. By ignoring variation in the motivations of states and the fact that arms races convey signals about the propensity to attack as well as the commitment to defend, early deterrence theorists were being both theoretically naive and ahistorical. On the other hand, there is the suspicion that the critique of the deterrence approach may also have lacked balance and perspective. Instead of supplementing the insights of deterrence theory about the role of arms increases in raising the cost of conflict, it focused on an equally narrow (and incomplete) set of factors that influences arms race and conflict decisions. From a historical standpoint, salient examples of nations driven by security interests do not eliminate the significance of other nations that have been driven by expansionary aspirations. It would be difficult to argue that more wars have resulted from mutual misinterpretation than from aggressive national objectives. From a psychological or logical standpoint, the importance of increases in perceived aggressiveness that an arms race can produce does not diminish completely the importance of expectations about cost of aggression as a determinant of behavior. Hitler may have been committed to war in the West, but even he demanded to be convinced that victory was achievable at an acceptable cost (Mearsheimer, 1983:chap. 4).

This is not to argue that every scholar has been victim of the theoretically driven selective perception that leads deterrence theorists to focus on World War II and the nuclear arms race and critics to focus on World War I and conventional weapons races. Jervis's *Perception and Misperception in International Politics* (1976) emphasized the wealth of examples that support both theories. Going well beyond the contradictory lessons of the two world wars, Jervis first notes many cases where the conciliatory prescriptions of the security dilemma model have encouraged the aggressive response predicted by deterrence theory. French conciliation toward Germany before the outbreak of the Franco–Prussian War and during the first Moroccan crisis only produced a new set of demands, as did Japanese concessions to the United States in 1941. He then cites examples such as the Balkan crisis of 1885–1887, where demonstrations of strength damped the aggressive instincts of opponents. An equally impressive body of evidence is then presented that supports the spiral model. Although many of Jervis's examples involve alliance rather than arms activity, two implications were inescapable: (1) the goals of nations vary such that neither naive deterrence theory nor its rival is always true; and (2) nations are uncertain about the goals of their rivals.

Fortunately, the theoretical division between the deterrence theorists and their critics that took place in spite of Jervis has begun to erode in recent years. Although the methodological predilections remain, there is an increased appreciation for the ways that the two approaches complement each other and the necessity of attending to aspects of the arms race that each formerly relegated to the other. This new synthesis is most apparent in the works of the formal modelers. Given the inspiration, the benefit-cost logic of deterrence and the strategic depth of game theory had always been broad enough to cope with most of the criticisms directed toward it. Early theorists like Schelling (1960) were sensitive to issues such as the ambiguity of intention, uncertainty, and misperception. What was needed was a recognition by the field in general that auxiliary assumptions, like homogeneous goals and perfect information, had to be relaxed and the development of a body of theory capable of investigating the implications of those changed assumptions.

Although formal modelers have yet to produce a well-developed theory linking arms race decisions to war, some modest progress has been made while separately exploring the impact of uncertainty on arms races and on deterrence. For example, it turns out that effectiveness of tit-for-tat as a strategy for maintaining arms stability or for inducing two states to deescalate their arms race depends on an absence of misperception about the rival nations activities. With a 1 percent chance of misperception, two tit-for-tat states that begin with mutual cooperation will eventually degenerate into an arms race, with one or the other side defecting (building arms) 75 percent of the time (Downs, Rocke, and Siverson, 1985). The fact that tit-for-tat is "too ready" to defect arms increases that have not taken place causes arms spirals. One obvious solution is consistent with the message of the spiral theorists: states should be more forgiving, they should not be provoked by a single defection, and they should respond at a level less than the supposed provocation.

The problem is more complicated if one admits the possibility that one is uncertain about a rival's intentions as well as its arms behavior. At a crude level, how much a state should back away from a strict tit-for-tat response is determined by its assessment of the probability that the rival is motivated by security concerns versus aggressive intent. This can be seen by considering the two archetypical cases. If all opponents are equally aggressive, as naive deterrence theory would have us believe, the cost of departing too greatly from tit-for-tat will be the suggestion of appeasement and the gradual loss of policy influence and, ultimately, security. On the other hand, if states are motivated by the security considerations that lie at the heart of the spiral model, then a modest response can defuse a mutually undesirable arms race before it gets started or initiate a process that will end an existing race.

Recent work on deterrence by Nalebuff (1989) and Powell (1989) that is inspired by economic research on games with incomplete information is also helpful in illuminating the effects of uncertainty. One of the important functions of arms behavior is to establish a reputation for strength that will deter and grant policy influence. Shifted to an arms race setting, Nalebuff's discussion of the impact of intervention on reputation suggests that uncertainty can produce a higher rate of building than would exist under perfect information. This higher rate is not sustained because risk averseness inspires an attitude of "better safe than sorry," but because uncertainty provides a state with the opportunity to inflate a rival's perception of capability.

Powell's research on crisis stability also has implications for the arms race–war connection. Although the analogy between crisis escalation and an arms race is imperfect, they have certain characteristics in common: both are driven by a desire for greater policy influence, both involve communicating commitment and capability in a world of uncertainty, and both run the risk of provoking war if one of the participants is convinced that war is inevitable. Using sequential equilibrium models, Powell shows that under very broad assumptions, the chance of a crisis escalating to nuclear war is zero (Powell,

1989:chaps. 5 and 6). This is true even when there is an advantage to striking first. For our purposes this suggests that in a MAD world the risk of an arms race resulting in war is similarly small, even if there is a first strike advantage or cult of the offensive.

Part of Powell's result stems from the fact that under MAD, a first-strike advantage is worth very little. It basically involves the unenviable opportunity of dying several minutes after a rival. Striking first dominates the outcome of being struck first, but it is inferior to *any* other outcome. Not surprisingly, in Powell's model nations always choose to do neither. The more interesting logic driving the finding lies in the argument that no behavior will take place in the escalation bargaining game that is sufficiently aggressive to convince either side that the probability of war exceeds the critical threshold. Because this phenomena is also a consequence of the costs incurred from a retaliatory strike, this too may seem unremarkable. However, Powell's idea of creating a model that treats the estimate of the probability that the enemy will attack as endogenous is an important innovation. Not only is it responsive to the criticism of the spiral theorists that deterrence models overlook the effect of arms behavior on assessments of intention, but it shows how the cost of aggression (in this case represented by nuclear retaliation) places a limit on what will (or at least should) be inferred. In this way it takes an important step toward uniting the essence of the naive deterrence model and the security dilemma model. What remains to be done is to capitalize on this unification and see what can be said about arms races in which first strike advantages are *not* made irrelevant by retaliatory capacity. Once this assumption is dropped, we can better understand how and why the likelihood that an arms race will end in war varies with defensive capability, uncertainty, and first-strike advantage.

The work of Nalebuff and Powell is a beginning, but they each make assumptions about the structure of the game that mask the difficulty of the intentions versus cost question. National policymakers often do not have this luxury. They are not sure whether their counterparts have initiated a weapons program because they are committed to aggression or increasing their policy influence, because they simply wish to be more secure, or because a domestic constituency demanded it for economic reasons. They do suspect that the motives of their rivals makes a difference in what their response should be. A situation of MAD makes this problem somewhat simpler because it can ameliorate the effect of modest arms advantages on the probability of total war. Yet there are still difficulties at the level of extended deterrence—will an arms advantage promote military adventurism at the margin—and the lurking problem of a breakout from MAD.

Formal theory is likely to move forward in two ways. One will involve a kind of sensitivity analysis based on decision theory, which would tell the decision maker what move would be optimal *given* different motives on the part of the rival nation. It would then be up to the decision maker to use intelligence data and other information to assess the probability attached to each motive. The other approach is more closely tied to game theory and would rest on complicated equilibrium calculations. Here, the starting point would be the work in oligopoly theory that was the inspiration for Powell's work (for example, Kreps and Wilson, 1982*a*, 1982*b;* Milgrom and Roberts, 1982). Instead of using intelligence information that might come from informed sources within the rival nation or documents, the intentions of the rival state would be estimated directly on the basis of its arms behavior. For example, what does rational deterrence theory tell us about the inferences to be drawn from the fact that a state has initiated a new weapons program in a condition of MAD—assuming that it is rational and knows that its rival will make inferences from its behavior?

It is possible that relatively little can be inferred, because such behavior is consistent with a wide range of preferences. It also possible that any inference is treacherous, because it is unreasonable to assume that decision makers will behave in a fashion consistent with elaborate equilibrium calculations (this would no doubt be the position of critics of rational choice). Yet rational deterrence theory is almost certainly an exercise that is worth undertaking. One of its advantages over the decision analysis perspective is that it is inherently reciprocal. Not only is it concerned with the implications of a rival's behavior, it suggests what inferences a rational rival will make from the nation's own arms policies. In this way it holds out the promise of uniting the concerns of both classic deterrence and spiral theorists.

There are a variety of other issues that also remain unresolved. Sequential equilibrium models are useful tools, but they require some assumptions of convenience about belief systems, stopping points, and updating rules that may be playing a large role in some of their more provocative implications. Similarly, the present knowledge of reputation effects and the impact of utility uncertainty are based on binary choice rather than discrete choice models. The general message of a model in which a state chooses between acting tough or weak may not change when there is a continuum of choices from which to pick. It may always be wise to choose a given role and act in a consistent fashion. However, it is possible that the precise character of that role (that is, how tough or weak) may be quite different when there is a continuum of choices from which to choose. In particular, the frequency with which extremal solutions (for example, announce that you will build at the maximum rate for the rest of time if the other side increases beyond a certain threshold) are found dominant may lead to doubts about the soundness of the whole approach. If the rival state believes such an extreme threat, then the threats provide a powerful disincentive against building new arms, but the issue of credibility arises. It is another variant of the "paradox of deterrence:" Why should the rival state believe in the likelihood of a punishment that will hurt the punisher as much (or almost as much) as the transgressor?

Examining the implications of risk functions that are consistent with prospect theory is another reasonable next step. Once this is done, the only dimension of the security dilemma approach that will remain outside the rational deterrence perspective will be biased perceptions. Formal modelers are reluctant to examine the effect of bias for a very good reason. If you know its consequences, you can correct for its effects; once this is done, there is no reason to include it in the model. Nonetheless, because it may not be eradicated instantly, formal modelers may want to learn more about its consequences. These can be explored through simulation. Early indications are that they are little short of devastating (Downs and Rocke, 1987:311).

Researchers in the psychological and institutional school who focus on the security dilemma and the spiral model face a different research agenda. Perhaps because an inductive methodology tends to be more tolerant of unrelated findings than a deductive methodology, these scholars have not yet begun to deal with integrative issues such as the relationship between perceptions of intention, the cost of aggression, and offensive advantage. Faced with the undeniable fact that case study evidence can be produced to support the importance of all of these factors, they must explore their interrelationship and how this affects the likelihood that arms races will end in war. It is much easier to ignore the cost of war when deciding whether to build arms than when actually contemplating the decision to initiate conflict. In this sense the security dilemma provides a much better basis for predicting a spiral arms race than it does for the onset of war—at least in the absence of a belief in a dramatic offensive advantage. The degree of redundancy in the environment of MAD between the United States and the Soviet Union may reveal the tell tale signs of the overbuilding that the spiral model would predict (even if that pattern was obtained through a process that has little in common with either a spiral or a Richardsonian process of exponential growth). However, the high degree of stability in the relations between the two nations and relatively constant (or declining) percentage of the gross national product (GNP) going to strategic weapons development has little in common with the spiral model. These aspects of the arms race between the two states are far better predicted by a cost-of-war deterrence model.

Other key questions involve the stability of the heuristics associated with misperception and the ability of institutions to overcome their ill effects. One of the findings of the heuristics and bias literature that is rarely emphasized is that none are universally employed. The susceptibility to the fundamental attribution bias varies across individuals for reasons that are not well understood. What implications does this have for arms race strategies? If individuals can learn to overcome it, will this serve to place a limit on the arms spiral and inferences of hostile intentions that accompany arms races?[6] Are there any actions a nation can take to make a rival self-conscious about this bias? One of the things that suggests that progress is possible in coping with this bias is that most arms races do not escalate at the ever-increasing pace that a simple interpretation of the spiral model and the fundamental attribution bias might imply. The races between Great Britain and its European naval rivals did not escalate uniformly, and the U.S.–Soviet race, at least up to this point, has certainly not done so. This might be attributed to the intermittent operation of economic constraints, but this ignores the no-less confounding fact that these races did not consume—even at their height—a part of national income that was as large as a spiral theorist might predict.

The capacity of institutions to cope with misperception is also an area that requires more research. While it is undeniably true that institutions are made up of individuals, it is no less true that institutions can create procedures and incentive systems to overcome biases that are organizationally dysfunctional. Overestimating the probability of rare events is an example of one such heuristic (Kahneman, Slovic, and Tversky, 1982). It can lead to inefficient decisions on the individual level, but it can easily be compensated for at the organizational level. The success of brokerage and insurance firms depend on it. Should we expect less of the decision making arm of government in relation to attribution bias? Those who write articles advocating that decision makers understand the way that this heuristic will lead a security motivated arms increase to be interpreted as indicating hostile intent obviously believe that such compensation is possible. They are simultaneously asking their leaders to refrain from making an incorrect attribution and to consider the possibility that rival decision makers may not be so wise. Even if this is good advice in the short run, the psychologist must address the formal modeler's question as to why the rival nation's decision makers cannot be expected to act similarly once their psychologists have made the same observation. Where does this leave us? How much should the United States cede to the Soviet Union on the grounds that their leaders may be less insightful? Can we expect decision making institutions to overcome dysfunctional heuristics so that arms races all evolve according to the tenets of formal theory? Or are some heuristics—for reasons not well understood—resistant to change or compensation? Such questions have barely begun to be addressed.

Conclusion

A discussion of the questions that remain unanswered can lead us to under-estimate how far we have come. In this case, the contradictory findings of empiricists combined with the conceptual disjointedness of formal and misperception-oriented approaches can easily give the impression that the arms race–war literature has yielded little. This is not true. The flaws that are visible have been made apparent by real, if still unintegrated, insights.

The problems associated with the statistical analysis of aggregate data are a good example. Although it may be dismaying to realize that simple statistical assessments of the relationship between arms races and war are of little value, this judgment follows from progress in both case study research and axiomatic research. It is progress to learn—or recognize the implications of the fact— that nations are motivated by different objectives and expectations, possess different resources, employ different arms strategies that can alternatively deter or invite aggression, and are involved in races that are dominated by disparate technologies. This mixture of initial conditions and arms strategies produces the expectation that some arms races will be a prelude to war and others will not. The low correlation between arms races and war is consistent with this; it does not signify that arms races have no impact on the probability of war, simply that they have a highly contingent impact. From a strictly historical point of view, it may be interesting to learn whether Sir Edward Grey's distaste for the provocative component of arms races appears more or less justified than General Vegetius' appreciation for the deterrent effect, but the task of social scientists lies elsewhere. As generalizations both statements are incorrect; as observations about specific arms races both observations can be supported. The theoretical challenge lies in explicating the contingencies that make the generalizations break down and in understanding the implica-tions. The strategic challenge lies in exploiting this knowledge in an uncertain environment.

The present understanding of the role that context plays in determining the wisdom or folly of the decision to engage in an arms race represents a real advance over Richardsonian determinism and the belief that arms races sim-ply reflect underlying differences between states. Despite their differences, contemporary rational deterrence theorists and their critics both suggest that the fundamentally strategic character of arms decisions means that initial conditions alone rarely determine outcomes. While doubtless there have been states that would not have been deterred or provoked by any arms strategy available to its rival, the behavior of the other nation is usually important. What makes this point something more than a banal homily are its game theoretic implications that equivalent environments can lead to different kinds of arms races and may or may not result in war.

The unresolved issues surrounding the tension between the provocative impact of an arms increase and its deterrent effect should also not detract from an emerging consensus about how the chances that an arms race will lead to war can be minimized. Each reinforces traditional ideas about the importance of balance and prescribes that the response be of somewhat less magnitude than the perceived provocation. Predictably, the rationales behind this prescription are different. The motivation of the formal school lies in the knowledge that even reasonably good intelligence (that is, intelligence with a low-error rate) coupled with a response rule based on reciprocity will produce a never-ending arms race. This presents no great problem if both sides possess nuclear arms and are in MAD. In such a situation, rational opponents would be unprovokable, and most arms increases would be a mixture of a job program for defense workers and efforts to demonstrate resolve for the purpose of extended deterrence. However, if the cost of conflict threshold that defines MAD is not exceeded, the nation with the least resources may be tempted to engage in preventive war. The urgency of this prescription is greater for the misperception school. It argues that bias will lead attempted reciprocity to degenerate into an even swifter escalation of the arms race and that attribution bias coupled with the cult of the offensive can lead both nations to view preventive war or preemption as necessary.

This is not to say that either approach advocates that a rival nation's arms increases be greeted with indifference. Both agree that a response that is too much less than that required by reciprocity is dangerous, although again they each have a different rationale for their prescription. A formal modeler would stress the counterproductive inference that an aggressive and uncertain opponent would make about a rival's capability, resources, and willingness to stand behind its commitments. A security dilemma theorist familiar with prospect theory would worry about the ability of a state that has fallen behind to avoid risk-seeking behavior as it seeks to reestablish parity or avoid the specter of sacrificing vital interests.

While differences in assumptions about the goals of states and the deterrent value of increasing the cost of aggression can lead to disagreements about the impact of offensive weapons, both approaches also stress the virtues of defense and, by extension, the virtues of countervalue weapons over counterforce weapons. Formal modelers have long argued that defense can increase the cost of aggression to a point where it is irrational—even in the presence of a substantial first strike advantage or offensive bias. Now as they stand on the threshold of doing serious research on the impact of utility uncertainty, formal modelers have begun to appreciate the fact that defense and countervalue weapons can do so while minimizing the perception of aggressive intent. For researchers in the psychological tradition, defense not only helps solve the structural dimension of the security dilemma but the misperception dimension as well. Defense may be—and doubtless often is—misperceived as indicative of aggressive intent and countervalue weapons can have offensive implications; however, the probability that they will set off an arms spiral is less than that associated with an increase in offensive or counterforce weapons. If mutual security is the objective and the arms policies of a rival state are thought to demand some response, developing weaponry that reduces rather than increases the probability that the rival will attribute the action to aggressiveness is a wise policy.[7]

These complementary policy recommendations are helpful, but they should not obscure the fact that continued progress in understanding the relationship between arms races and war rests on the willingness of scholars from each intellectual tradition to examine the same questions. The most important prerequisite for this is the admission that, at present, the only sensible way to organize trying to answer these questions is to acknowledge the existence of a single—if loosely defined—theoretical framework. This framework speaks to the futility of trying to investigate the deterrent impact of raising the cost of conflict in isolation from the potentially provocative implications of arms increases or vice versa. It also tells any researcher that he or she must recognize the distinction between the decision to increase arms and the decision to go to war, the wide variation in national objectives and consequently the games that arms races represent, the utility and information uncertainty, the estimates of the cost of conflict, and the expectations about the rival's intentions.

This does not mean that the scholars from the various traditions must put aside every difference. Issues about how arms races are conducted; the amount, character, and stability of bias in policymaking; and the relative impact that each factor has on the decision to go to war all remain fertile ground for disagreement. But there is everything to be gained by recognizing that the real battle is over these issues, not a battle between to distinct paradigms.

Notes

A part of this research was supported by the Pew Charitable Trust. This chapter benefited from the comments of Steve Walt, Robert Gilpin, Steve Van Evera, Jack Levy, Charles Glaser, Robert Jervis, Edward Kolodziej, and Philip Tetlock.

1. This close relationship to deterrence theory (whether in its formal or more qualitative manifestation) is to be expected. Although deterrence consists of more than

arms stocks, the link between arms races and war is subsumed under deterrence in its broadest sense. The fundamental question is whether an arms race leads to a situation where the parties are more or less deterred from initiating conflict than they would have been had there been no race.

2. Those in the rational deterrence tradition (for example, Steven Brams, Marc Kilgour, Dagobrit Brito, Michael Intriligator, Bruce Bueno de Mesquita, Dina Zinnes, and Robert Powell) form a much more homogeneous group than their critics. Some like Robert Jervis, Alexander George, and Ned Lebow draw much of their inspiration from psychology. Others, like Steve Van Evera and Jack Snyder, draw from primary historical sources and research on organizations. What these scholars share in common is the belief that the rational deterrence model is undermined (or made irrelevant) by misperceptions and biases that are commonly found in arms races and that provide the critical link between arms races and war.

3. Recent treatments of the connection between technological innovation and the arms race include Evangelista (1988) and Wells and Litwak (1987).

4. For other recent studies in the formal tradition, see Avenhaus, Huber, and Kettell (1986), Isard and Anderton (1985), Kugler and Zagare (1987), Leidy (1985), Mayer (1986), Luterbacher and Ward (1985), Majeski (1984), Wagner (1983), and Zagare (1987).

5. An impressive counterargument about the importance of "windows of opportunity" is presented by Lebow (1984).

6. Tetlock (1985a, 1985b) has shown that accountability alone can provide a check on the fundamental attribution bias.

7. This enthusiasm for defense is not unqualified, particularly on the part of deterrence theorists. Even the crudest formal model would suggest that unbalanced defense can be as dangerous as unbalanced offense because it reduces the retaliatory cost that the defense-rich nation must pay for its aggressiveness. This forms the core of the argument that Star Wars will have a destabilizing effect on the U.S.—Soviet arms race. A very revealing discussion of a different set of offense-defense issues can be found in Van Evera (1987).

References

Altfeld, M. 1983. Arms races—and escalation? *International Studies Quarterly,* 27:225–231.

Avenhaus, R., R.K. Huber, and J.D. Kettelle. 1986. *Modelling Analysis in Arms Control.* Berlin: Springer-Verlag.

Axelrod, R. 1984. *The Evolution of Cooperation.* New York: Basic Books.

Betts, R.K. 1977. *Soldiers, Statesman, and Cold War Crises.* Cambridge: Harvard University Press.

Brams, S.J., and D.M. Kilgour. 1988. *Game Theory and National Security.* New York: Basil Blackwell.

Brito, D., and M. Intriligator. 1974. Uncertainty and the stability of the armaments race. *Annals of Economic and Social Measurement* 3:279–292.

Brodie, B. 1973. *War and Politics.* New York: Macmillan.

Bueno de Mesquita, B. 1981. *The War Trap.* New Haven, Conn.: Yale University Press.

————. 1985. The war trap revisited: A revised expected utility model. *American Political Science Review* 79:157–176.

Cobden, R. 1868. *The Political Writings of Richard Cobden.* London: William Ridgway.

Diehl, P. 1983. Arms races and escalation: A closer look. *Journal of Peace Research* 22:249–259.

————. 1985. Arms races to war: Testing some empirical linkages. *Sociological Quarterly* 26:331–349.

Diehl, P., and J. Kingston. 1987. Messenger or message?: Military buildups and the initiation of conflict. *Journal of Politics.* 49:801–813.

Downs, G.W., D.M. Rocke, and R. Siverson. 1985. Arms races and cooperation. *World Politics* 38:118–147.

Downs, G.W., and D.M. Rocke. 1987. Tacit bargaining and arms control. *World Politics* 39:297–326.

Enthoven, A., and K. Smith, 1971. *How Much Is Enough?* New York: Harper and Row.

Evangelista, M. 1988. *Innovation and the Arms Race.* Ithaca, N.Y.: Cornell University Press.

George, A.L. 1980. *Presidential Decisionmaking in Foreign Policy.* Boulder: Westview.

Glaser, C. in press. *Analyzing Nuclear Weapons Policy.* Princeton, N.J.: Princeton University Press.

Gray, C.S. 1974. The urge to compete. *World Politics* 36:207–233.

Halberstam, D. 1973. *The Best and the Brightest.* Greenwich, Conn.: Fawcett Crest.

Huntington, S. 1958. Arms races: Prerequisites and results. *Public Policy* 8:41–86.

Intriligator, M., and D. Brito. 1976. Formal models of arms races. *Journal of Peace Research* 2:77–88.

————. 1984. Can arms races lead to the outbreak of war? *Journal of Conflict Resolution* 28:63–84.

Isard, W., and C.H. Anderton. 1985. Arms race models: A survey and synthesis. *Conflict Management and Peace Science,* 8:27–98.

Jervis, R. 1976. *Perception and Misperception in International Politics.* Princeton, N.J.: Princeton University Press.

Kahneman, D.P., P. Slovic, and A. Tversky. 1982. *Judgement Under Uncertainty: Heuristics and Biases.* Cambridge, England: Cambridge University Press.

Kennedy, P.M. 1983. *Strategy and Diplomacy.* Aylesbury, England: Fontana.

Kreps, D.M., and R. Wilson. 1982*a*. Reputation and imperfect information. *Journal of Economic Theory* 27:253–279.

Kreps, D.M., and R. Wilson. 1982*b*. Sequential equilibria. *Econometrica* 50:862–887.

Kugler, J., and F. Zagare, eds. 1987. *Exploring the Stability of Deterrence*. Boulder, Colo.: Lynne Rienner.

Lebow, R.N. 1981. *Between Peace and War*. Baltimore: Johns Hopkins University Press.

————. 1984. Windows of opportunity: Do states jump through them? *International Security* 9:171–186.

Leidy, M.P. 1985. Economic issues and methodology in arms race analysis. *Journal of Conflict Resolution*. 29:503–530.

Luterbacher, U., and M.D. Ward. 1985. *Dynamic Models of International Conflict*. Boulder, Colo.: Lynne Rienner.

Majeski, S.J. 1984. Arms races as iterated prisoner's dilemma games. *Mathematical Social Sciences* 7:254–266.

Majeski, S.J., and D.L. Jones. 1981. Arms race modeling. *Journal of Conflict Resolution* 25:259–288.

Marder, A.J. 1976. *Anatomy of British Seapower*. New York: Octagon Books.

Mayer, T.F. 1986. Arms races and war initiation. *Journal of Conflict Resolution* 30:3–28.

Mearsheimer, J.J. 1983. *Conventional Deterrence*. Ithaca, N.Y.: Cornell University Press.

Milgrom, P., and J. Roberts. 1982. Limit pricing and entry under incomplete information: An equilibrium analysis. *Econometrica* 50:443–449.

Morrow, J. 1984. A twist of truth: A reexamination of the effects of arms races on the occurrence of war. Paper presented at the annual meeting of the American Political Science Association, Chicago, Ill.

Nalebuff, B. 1989. Rational deterrence in an imperfect world. Center of International Affairs Discussion Paper, Princeton University.

Nisbett, R.E., and L. Ross. 1980. *Human Inference: Strategies and Shortcomings of Social Judgment*. Englewood Cliffs, N.J.: Prentice-Hall.

Posen, B.R. 1984. *The Sources of Military Doctrine*. Ithaca, N.Y.: Cornell University Press.

Powell, R. 1989. *Deterrence and Credibility*. New York: Cambridge University Press.

Quattrone, G., and A. Tversky. 1988. Contrasting rationale and psychological analyses of political choice. *American Political Science Review* 82:719–736.

Richardson, L.F. 1960. *The Statistics of Deadly Quarrels*. Chicago: Quadrangle.

Rourke, F.E. 1972. *Bureaucracy and Foreign Policy*. Baltimore: Johns Hopkins University Press.

Schelling, T.C. 1960. *The Strategy of Conflict*. Cambridge, Mass.: Harvard University Press.

Simaan, M., and J. Cruz. 1975. Formulation of Richardson's model of arms race from a differential games viewpoint. *Review of Economic Studies* 42:63–77.

Smoke, R. 1977. *War: Controlling Escalation*. Cambridge, Mass.: Harvard University Press.

Snyder, J. 1984. *The Ideology of the Offensive: Military Decision Making and the Disasters of 1914*. Ithaca, N.Y.: Cornell University Press.

Stein, A.A. 1982. When misperception matters. *World Politics* 34:505–526.

Tetlock, P.E. 1985a. Accountability: A social check on the fundamental attribution error. *Social Psychology Quarterly* 48:227–236.

———. 1985b. Accountability. *Research in Organizational Behavior* 7:297–332.

Van Evera, S. 1984. *Causes of War*. Ph.D. Dissertation, University of California, Berkeley.

———. 1987. Offense, defense, and strategy: When is offense best? Paper delivered at the annual meeting of the American Political Science Association. Chicago, Ill.

Wagner, R.H. 1983. Theory of games and the problem of international cooperation. *American Political Science Review* 77:330–346.

Wallace, M.D. 1979. Arms races and escalation: Some new evidence. *Journal of Conflict Resolution* 24:289–292.

———. 1982. Arms races and escalation. *International Studies Quarterly* 26:37–56.

Walt, S.M. 1987. *The Origins of Alliances*. Ithaca, N.Y.: Cornell University Press.

Waltz, K. 1979. *Theory of International Politics*. Reading, Mass.: Addison-Wesley.

Weede, E. 1980. Arms races and escalation: Some persisting doubts. *Journal of Conflict Resolution* 24:285–288.

Wells, S.F., and R. Litwak, eds. 1987. *Strategic Defenses and Soviet–American Relations*. Cambridge, Mass.: Ballinger.

Zagare, F.C. 1987. *The Dynamics of Deterrence*. Chicago: The University of Chicago Press.

3

Nuclear Decisions: Cognitive Limits to the Thinkable

BARUCH FISCHHOFF

Historically, the requirements for successfully prosecuting a war have been physical prowess and personal courage. The requirements for successfully setting the terms of a war have been wisdom (needed to identify the best courses of action) and leadership (needed to convince others of the rectitude of those actions). The advent of nuclear weapons has dramatically changed the physical demands of war. Strength is much less important, except perhaps for the stamina needed to stay with a task through the long hours of a crisis. Courage, of a sort, is needed to send and receive nuclear weapons, but it is a more ascetic courage than that of a foxhole or cavalry charge. Changes in technology have made fighting easier. Having the "right staff" is more a question of research and development and less a question of character and personality.

The new technology has not, however, reduced the need for thinking clearly and getting along with others (friend and foe). On the contrary, it has probably increased the importance of those skills dramatically. The complexity of modern technology means much longer time lines for research and development (R&D), as well as for training people to operate the equipment (not to mention training the scientists needed to perform the R&D). As a result, leaders need to be very foresightful (and forceful), in order to have the pieces in place for creating effective deterrents or for responding if deterrence fails. Crash programs cannot compensate for inappropriate strategic planning. The speed and lethality of the new weapons preclude relying on trial and error for responding to a threat.

The need to "get it right the first time" means further that the development of weapons and defense plans is ever more an intellectual enterprise. Legions of planners attempt to imagine future contingencies and to anticipate how people and machine will behave in them. Yet, the conditions of any next war will be unique, making those predictions a matter of judgment, however many theoretical analyses and field exercises are conducted. When long periods separate conflicts, generations of soldiers and weapon systems can come and go without anyone ever knowing how they would have performed if put to the test. As a result, decision makers (presidents, diplomats, senior and junior commanders) must still exercise judgment when the time comes to act. They must still diagnose their situation, decide what contingency plan best fits it, adapt that plan to the specifics of their concrete situation, and improvise if the plan they are supposed to implement makes no intuitive sense or if the situation is unexpected.

Modern technologies often reduce dramatically the time available for thought and consultation. Assaults can be launched more quickly. Diplomatic proposals arrive electronically rather than by courier. Although the new technologies can also increase the availability of information on which to reflect, that information load poses a further strain. The technological response to these challenges is often to automate the processing of information and even the execution of responses to it. Yet even here, human decision makers must stay "in the loop," ready to override the automated system when it seems out of its depths. Each automated system, in turn, reflects the product of human judgment. Its designers must have incorporated in it their understanding of how ambiguous situations are to be interpreted and what objectives should be sought.

People bring two sets of intellectual abilities to a problem: substantive knowledge about the specific situation, and general decision-making skills. These skills are the focus of this chapter. Although *what* people think about must be unique to the problems of peace and war, *how* people think about them may not be that different from how people think when making the other, more mundane decisions in their lives. These thought processes include recognizing that a decision must be made, setting goals for that decision, thinking of creative ways to respond to it, accessing existing knowledge about the situation, spotting the holes in that knowledge, seeking help (and evaluating it), keeping emotion from coloring thinking, coping with painful value conflicts, integrating a welter of considerations under varying degrees of time pressure and mental overload, and communicating one's thinking to others. It is the belief in the generality of these cognitive processes that leads investigators to study the psychology of decision making per se. That belief underlies the present attempt to extrapolate from the literature to predict how nuclear decisions will be made and what interventions might enable them to be made better.

The first half of the chapter provides an introduction to that literature. It begins by describing a conceptual scheme that underlies much of the research and then showing how that scheme applies to typical "nuclear decisions." It continues with a review of representative research findings, some of them empirical results, others "mere" observations that emerge from worrying about decision making in general. To provide a critical perspective on this research, the generality of its results are then discussed at length, considering how they can be extrapolated responsibly from the settings where they were obtained to other settings, including those of nuclear decisions. The second half of the chapter speculatively extracts the implications of this behavioral research for several intellectual activities related to nuclear war and its prevention. These are: the command and control of nuclear weapons, managing a distributed diplomatic corps, crisis decision making, contingency planning, evaluating and creating arms control proposals, and public debate. Rather than append "if the behavioral research applies" to each statement in these sections, I have written the statements as though the research has some applicability. The final section repeats and reflects on the consequences of taking the behavioral research too seriously or too casually.

Work in this or any other field should carry strong caveats regarding the quality of the help that it is capable of providing and the degree of residual uncertainty surrounding even its best advice. Such warnings are essential because it is hard for the buyer to beware. People have enough experience to evaluate quality in toothpaste and politicians. However, it is hard to evaluate advice, especially when the source is unfamiliar and the nature of the difficulties that it is meant to overcome is unclear. A first principle of decision theory is that advice is useless without an assessment of how good it is.

The Decision-Making Perspective

Decisions

Decisions are choices among alternative courses of action (including, perhaps, inaction). They are characterized qualitatively by:

- A set of possible alternative actions (or options)—describing what one can do;
- A set of possible consequences of those actions—describing what might happen (in terms of desirable and undesirable effects); and
- A set of sources of uncertainty—describing the obstacles to predicting the connection between actions and consequences.

Decisions are characterized quantitatively by:

- Trade-offs among consequences—describing their relative importance; and
- Probabilities of consequences—describing the chances that they will actually be obtained.

This basic conceptual scheme has been used by investigators to characterize a very wide variety of decisions, from having children (Beach et al., 1976), to operating on the basis of x-rays (Eddy, 1982), to siting energy facilities (Keeney, 1980), to testing houses for radon (Svenson and Fischhoff, 1985), to seeing which of two simultaneously presented lights is brighter (Coombs, Dawes, and Tversky, 1970). In some cases, the usage has been *descriptive,* attempting to show how people actually make decisions in these situations. In other cases, the usage has been *normative,* attempting to show how decisions ought to be made, if decision makers are to choose the actions in their own best interests. In some cases, both approaches are used, in order to show the difference between how well people do make decisions and how well they might. In some of these cases, there is an additional, *prescriptive* purpose, attempting to tell people how to go about making decisions in a way that will bring them closer to the normative ideal than if they were left to their own devices (Watson and Buede, 1987; von Winterfeldt and Edwards, 1986). Because it is concerned with how decisions are actually made, this approach is called *behavioral decision theory*, in order to distinguish it from approaches that assume people to be fully rational (or optimizing) in all situations.

Nuclear Decisions

A country with nuclear capability faces, in theory or in practice, a great variety of decisions. They include:

- How much to spend for defense;
- Whether conventional or strategic weapons provide a better investment for additional expenditures;
- Whether civil defense is better served by building shelters or by investing in programs designed to reduce the probability of war;
- What institutional arrangements best ensure civilian control over the military without unduly imperiling military effectiveness;
- How to formulate and present arms control proposals;
- How to treat an anomaly detected by an imperfect early-warning system; and
- When to report such anomalies to allies and enemies.

These decisions vary in many ways: who is making them, how much time is available, what the possibilities are for recovering from mistakes, what computational aids exist for deciding what to do, how bounded is the set of alternative actions, and where the greatest uncertainties lie (in evaluating the importance of the consequences or in evaluating the possibilities for achieving them). What these decisions have in common is that some human judgment is needed before an action is consummated, if only to let things take their course.

Judgment is needed most obviously in the qualitative components of the decision-making process: creating options, identifying relevant consequences, and spotting sources of uncertainty. There may be routine ways of defining these fundamental aspects of decision problems, such as relying on standard operating procedures or checklists. However, even then, judgment is needed to determine the relevance of these procedures and to adapt them to novel circumstances.

There are more likely to be standard procedures for the quantitative aspects of decision making. For example, cost-benefit analysts have elaborate procedures for determining the value of different consequences (Bentkover, Covello, and Mumpower, 1985); risk analysts can develop complex models for the reliability of technical systems or the feasibility of people's plans (Armstrong, 1985; McCormick, 1981). Yet, despite the formal appearance of these models, they, too, require substantial doses of human judgment (for example, for specifying particular models, estimating uncertain component parameters, and determining the adequacy of each application) (Bentkover, Covello, and Mumpower, 1985; Lehner and Adelman, 1989; Merkhofer and Covello, in press).

Table 3.1 characterizes several nuclear decisions in terms of this overall scheme. The first decision is to choose a level of defense spending. The decision options here are different levels of such spending, represented as L_i. One obvious consequence of this decision is some degree of actual military strength. What that turns out to be will depend on such uncertainties as the particular military systems chosen (including materiel, training, development, and maintenance), the eventual effectiveness of those systems, and the responses of military adversaries (and allies). For example, increased spending ought to increase military readiness; however, it might backfire if the money is not spent wisely (for example, if it is spread over too many systems, or if it promotes dependence on untried new systems to the detriment of maintaining existing systems, or if it overloads the administrative capacity for monitoring the efficiency—and honesty—of defense contractors).

Even greater uncertainties are associated with the other two consequences in the incomplete list of Table 3.1. Money spent on defense might produce spinoffs for the domestic economy. It might also soak up resources (money, personnel) that could otherwise strengthen the general economy. It is fairly straightforward to identify these *opportunity costs* in principle, but very difficult to estimate their magnitude in practice. As a result, they are convenient arguments to cite in opposition to military spending, just as ill-defined contri-

TABLE 3.1 Some Nuclear Decisions

Decisions	Options	Selected Consequences	Selected Uncertainties
Defense spending level	Alternative spending levels (L_i , . . . L_n)	Actual strength Domestic spinoffs Opportunity costs	System chosen System effectiveness Other's responses
Spending on SDI	Spend X	As above	As above
Voting for L_i in Congress	Yes/No on various proposals	As above Voter popularity Collegial relations Self-respect	As above Public response
Voting for candidates supporting L_i	Yes/No/Abstain	As above Satisfaction Other issues	As above Political process Understandability

butions to national science and engineering are convenient benefits to cite in support of military spending.

These uncertainties may be reduced somewhat by detailed analysis of the military and international systems in which the money will be spent (How wisely has the defense department spent past increases? How coherently has it responded to past cuts? What are allies and opponents currently expecting?) These uncertainties might also be reduced by generic research, like that show-cased in this series of volumes on *Behavior, Society, and Nuclear War.* (How inevitable is escalation? How do countries respond to unilateral reductions in spending?) Even if these general processes were much better understood than they are today, some uncertainty would remain regarding their expression in particular circumstances.

The second decision in Table 3.1 is considerably more specific: how much to spend on the strategic defense initiative (SDI). The options again are spending levels, from $0 to whatever $X seems possible. The consequences associated with overall military spending also recur here. SDI might produce domestic spinoffs, say, general techniques for engineering the software of complex systems. On the other hand, it might also divert scarce computer scientists from projects that would do much more to enhance U.S. economic competitiveness. It should be easier to analyze these impacts for SDI than for defense spending in general because one can ask more specific questions: What kind of computer skills are needed? How many people have those skills? What domestic engineering problems resemble SDI in their complexity, and hence might benefit from its breakthroughs? Nonetheless, variants of the same sources of uncertainty remain. For example, what becomes of SDI will depend on exactly which systems are chosen for development, how well they end up working, and how other nations respond to U.S. initiatives (for in-stance, will allies participate in SDI but hold back their best scientists?) The greater specificity of this decision would, in effect, allow each of the conse-quence dimensions to be broken down into more specific elements.

The first two decisions in Table 3.1 are couched in terms of their conse-quences for the country as a whole. The choices will be made directly by congressional representatives and indirectly by the voters who choose them. Their decisions appear next in the table. The former act by choosing to support different spending levels; the latter act by choosing to support different candi-dates, one of whose features is their defense policy. Both sets of voters ought to consider the effects of defense policies on the country as a whole when deciding how to vote. As a result, their decision problems include the same conse-quences and their associated uncertainties. Given the limits to their expertise and the time available for pondering these issues, the uncertainties facing lay voters must be very large—a fact that they may or may not realize.

Both kinds of decision makers face additional consequences as well. For the representative, these will include popularity with voters, relations with colleagues, and self-respect. The chances of incurring these consequences might be clarified by such measures as polling public opinion, conferring with colleagues, and consulting one's conscience. For the citizen, the personal consequences of a single secret vote are fewer. They might include satisfaction with getting one's way (which depends on the outcome of congressional votes held some time hence), reducing support for candidates strong on other issues, and the *transaction costs* of trying to understand the issues. What sometimes looks like voter apathy can reflect an inability of the voter to understand what to do despite a concerted effort; it might even reflect a thoughtful decision not even to try.

The structure of each of these decisions could be elaborated in much greater detail. Doing so would, among other things, lead to elaborating their interdependencies. The prescriptive objective of such elaboration would attempt to characterize the decisions sharply enough to apply a proper *decision rule,* identifying the course of action in the nation's, representative's, or citizen's best interest (at least insofar as the problem can be modeled in the language of decision theory). The descriptive objective would be to see which aspects of the overall decision appear in individuals' subjective representation.

The value of using a formal framework for conceptualizing decision making is that it offers a coherent set of basic concepts for describing decision situations and a standard for evaluating the optimality of the decisions made in them. Thus, even at this rudimentary level of elaboration, the scheme affords some, possibly nontrivial, observations about decision-making processes. For example, it shows that decision making involves a choice among alternatives. Thus, it makes little sense to consider a defense policy in isolation without considering the alternatives. Choosing one option means rejecting others. Or, once a choice has been made, that need not mean that the risks associated with it are "acceptable" in any absolute sense. Whenever other consequences (for example, monetary costs, political repercussions) have been considered, the most acceptable policy need not be the one with the least risk. Defense policy decisions are not just about defense.

Having incomplete definitions of a decision problem can lead to ineffective deliberations, as can be seen in the interminable debates over what constitutes an "acceptable level of risk" for hazardous technologies or an acceptable level of deterrence. Those questions have no absolute answers. The acceptable level of risk depends on the alternatives to a technology, the cost of control options for reducing its risk, the benefits to be gained by incurring greater risks, and the distribution of risks and benefits (that is, who gets what). The acceptable level of deterrence depends on the price paid for additional weapons, the savings possible with reduced spending, the response evoked by different spending levels, the international initiatives foreclosed or facilitated by various defense postures, and so on.

Conversely, a decision-making perspective can held provide a comprehensive guide to diagnosing the sources of disagreements about defense policies. People may have different preferences because they disagree about what alternative policies merit consideration (perhaps excluding different ones as being "unthinkable"), or about what consequences are relevant at all (Need one be concerned about the impact of military spending on civil liberties or on income distributions—or should those issues be addressed separately?), or about the relative importance of those consequences that are pertinent (How large an increase in defense spending can be justified for the sake of a weapons system that promises an XX percent decrease in the chances of war, or a YY percent decrease in expected casualties, should war begin?). People may also disagree about the chances of those consequences being realized (Will SDI increase or decrease the chances of a preemptive strike during its development stage?), or about how all those considerations are to be combined (Should we plan for the worst or attempt to take reasonable gambles?). Because people have different desires and beliefs, they may have legitimate grounds for preferring different defense policies, even if they are strict adherents to the principles of rational decision making.

In evaluating people's choices, decision theory focuses on how those beliefs and desires are integrated, rather than on how pleasant are the outcomes that follow. In some cases, the rational choice means taking the best of several unattractive options (for example, different ways of backing off from a failed policy, different possibilities for diverting economic resources to defense programs). In other cases, the outcomes of the best option may not be certain, so that a wise choice can be followed by a disappointing result. For example, wearing a seat belt is much more likely to save one's life after a collision than to threaten one's life after going off a bridge; however, one might be one of those rare rational people trapped under water. Another example would be responding positively to a peace offer, which may seem the best gamble, but then weaken one's position when those who made the offer are unexpectedly swept from office. Just like the randomness of a sample, the rationality of a decision is determined by the process that produces it. Following the rules is the best one can do. After that, one must live with the result, even if it means drawing 10 successive clubs from a well-shuffled deck, interviewing 75 percent white males in a supposedly representative survey of U.S. adults, being one of the responsible unfortunates who drive off bridges, or meeting an unpredictable rebuff. For those who followed the correct procedure, knowing that one has made the best possible choice might help keep the insult of regret from compounding the injury of whatever misfortune has occurred.

Studying Decision Making

Giving advice on decision making is an old profession. Today, its practitioners include a variety of consultants, analytical techniques, and computerized support systems. Its combination of descriptive, normative, and prescriptive research attempts to build from people's strengths while compensating for their weaknesses (Abelson and Levi, 1985; Arkes and Hammond, 1986; Dawes, 1988; Einhorn and Hogarth, 1981; Fischhoff, 1988*b;* Kahneman, Slovic, and Tversky, 1982; Pitz and Sachs, 1984).

Initially, this research took its marching orders from mainstream U.S. economics, which rests on the metatheoretic assumption that people always optimize when they make decisions, in the sense of identifying the best possible course of action (Schoemaker, 1983). Although plausible in some circumstances and essential for using economics' sophisticated mathematical tools, the assumption of optimization severely constrains the kinds of behavior that can be considered. It restricts descriptive research to the limited (if difficult) goal of discerning what desires people have succeeded in optimizing in their behavior. It leaves little role at all for prescriptive research, because people can already fend quite well for themselves. By contrast, behavioral decision research is concerned with identifying the conditions conducive to optimizing, the kinds of behavior that come in its stead, and, especially, the measures that can be taken to improve people's performance.

Overview

The desire to aid decision makers makes investigators extremely interested in identifying situations where aid is needed. The resulting search for problems has been well rewarded. Behavioral decision researchers have identified a long list of judgmental foibles, pointing to things that can go wrong at every stage of the decision-making process (Fischhoff and Beyth-Marom, 1983). The sheer length of this list has sometimes created the impression that researchers here have shown (or at least claimed to have shown) that people's decision making is uniformly woeful. As might be expected, the further one gets from the basic research literature, the broader and the less discriminating such generalizations tend to become (Berkeley and Humphreys, 1982).

Many items on this list of potential woes will be described in the first half of this chapter. The usefulness of this research for illuminating nuclear decisions depends on how well its strengths and weaknesses are understood. As a result, the description of results that follows is embedded in a methodological discussion of how judgment can be studied and how empirical findings can be extrapolated to practical settings (that is, their external validity).

The next section, "Clinical Judgment," recounts the roots of behavioral decision-making research. It reveals some fundamental findings regarding the limits both to studying how people make decisions and to developing ways to help them.

The following section, "Intuitive Statistics," takes as an example a single judgmental task for which studies have found both very good and very bad performance: estimating the relative frequency of events. It points to the need for understanding the psychological properties of tasks if one is to predict performance in them.

"Living with Bias" discusses the importance of analyzing the opportunities that people have to acquire better judgment skills.

"Prejudices about Bias" recounts the controversy among behavioral decision researchers over the generality of judgmental biases. Some of these claims (and counterclaims) have a distinctly ideological character, whereas others raise testable hypotheses regarding the boundary conditions for observing bias.

One such set of hypotheses, which is critical to making informed speculations regarding nuclear decisions, concerns the extent to which technical experts are subject to the judgmental problems observed with lay people. The moderate body of evidence on this question is reviewed in the section entitled "Experts."

Less evidence is available regarding how individuals' decision making is affected by the organizational settings within which they do their work. Given the importance of such settings for nuclear decisions, an extended theoretical discussion considers how to characterize the psychological properties of specific settings ("Organizational Settings"). Having laid this groundwork, the following section, "Judgmental Skills," can then responsibly present a list of research results regarding people's ability to execute each element of the decision-making process.

Finally, a "Summary" recaps the opportunities for using this research to illuminate or improve nuclear decisions. It leads into an analysis of the psychology of six different classes of nuclear decisions.

Clinical Judgment

Ironically, perhaps, the research whose relevance to nuclear decisions is discussed here received much of its initial impetus in World War II. The war provided an important turning point in the development of American psychology. When put to the test, psychologists proved able to handle large numbers of people in a relatively efficient way, using either their clinical skills to diagnose and treat psychological problems or their psychometric tests to assign soldiers to different jobs. After the war, interest grew in just how effective those efficient decisions were.

One focus of this interest was the efficacy of *clinical judgment*. Initially, these studies looked at the judgments of psychologists making decisions such as whether clients were "psychotic" or "neurotic." In time, the research expanded to include other kinds of diagnoses with diverse content but similar structure. These included radiologists sorting x-rays of ulcers into "benign" or "malignant," personnel officers choosing the best applicants from a set of candidates, crisis-center counselors assessing whether callers are serious about suicide threats, auditors pondering which loans to classify as "nonperforming," and brokers weighing which stocks to recommend (Dawes, 1979; Goldberg, 1968, 1970; Kelly and Fiske, 1951; Meehl, 1954). The methods used in these studies could be applied to any well-characterized set of repeated decisions. In the nuclear domain, that might include decisions about the stability of personnel assigned to missile silos, the readiness of combat forces, the genuineness of other countries' diplomatic overtures, the interpretation of ambiguous signals on radar screens, and the attractiveness of alternative arms reduction proposals.

In a typical study, a large set of judgments is collected, each characterized by those *cues* that the judge might have considered. In a well-known example, Dawes (1971) examined how the graduate admissions committee of the University of Oregon psychology department evaluated 384 applicants for the 1969–1970 academic year. Although the committee looked at many cues (for example, letters of recommendation, full transcripts), their decisions could be predicted very well from just three variables: total Graduate Record Exam score (GRE), overall undergraduate grade-point average (GPA), and a crude index of the quality of undergraduate institution (QI). The specific equation for predicting the average admissions committee rating was

$$.0032 \text{ GRE} + 1.02 \text{ GPA} + 0.0791 \text{ QI}$$

Dawes suggested that, if the department really endorsed this implicit policy, then much time and money could be saved (by all parties) if prospective applicants were given the formula and told not to bother applying if their score was very low. Alternatively, the study provided the department with vital feedback, offering it an opportunity to revise its selection procedures to reflect a more suitable policy.

In addition to illuminating a specific practical problem, Dawes's study demonstrated some patterns that have been replicated in many other studies. One is that a rather simple model was able to predict what would seem to be a rather complex process (that is, the results of experts' case-by-case deliberations). A second pattern is that the judgmental strategy described by that model did not at all match what the judges involved thought they were doing. Not only did admissions committee members feel that they were considering more variables, but they reported considering even these three variables in more complex ways than simply weighing and adding. A commonly asserted form of complexity is called *configural judgment,* in which the diagnostic meaning of one cue depends on the meaning of other cues (for example, "that tone of voice makes me think 'nonsuicide' unless the call comes at midday").

At least three major reasons have emerged for this difference between the descriptions provided by the models and by the judges themselves. One is that people have difficulty introspecting into their own complex cognitive processes. Particularly when asked to summarize a set of judgments some time after those have been completed, people tend to confuse what they did do with what they intended to do and with what they believe is done in such situations (Ericsson and Simon, 1980; Herrmann, 1982; Nisbett and Wilson, 1977; Smith and Miller, 1978). A second reason for the discrepancy is the realization that combining enormous amounts of information in one's head overwhelms the computational capacity of anyone but an idiot savant. A judge trying to implement a complex strategy would have difficulty doing so consistently. Unless they were implemented consistently, more complex strategies would just wash out when many judgments are studied.

The third reason for the discrepancy was discovered independently by psychologists playing around with specific data (Dawes and Corrigan, 1974; Yntema and Torgerson, 1961) and statisticians thinking about the properties of data in general (Wilks, 1938). It is that a simple linear equation, like the one given earlier, is an extraordinarily powerful predictor. If one can identify and measure the cues that judges consider, then one can mimic their summary judgments quite well with simple models that combine those cues in ways bearing no resemblance to the underlying cognitive processes. Indeed, one can often predict well with a model, assuming that people just count the number of factors favoring and opposing a particular judgment or decision, giving equal weight to each; then they go with the alternative having the best overall tally.

The predictive power and inconclusiveness of these simple models is discouraging for those who want to know how people really think. They are, however, encouraging for those with more applied purposes. If all one wants is to predict people's decisions, then a rough model may work quite well.

Indeed, the models are so powerful that the cause of effective prediction can be served by replacing judges with equations modeling their own behavior. Such a *bootstrapped model* can make better predictions than the judges themselves because it is more mechanical and, therefore, more reliable than they are. Equations never have off days or suffer fatigue, nor are they distracted by irrelevant cues (for example, a student's teeth, clothes, accent, or hobbies). Clearly, people know more than what is included in such mechanical models of their behavior. However, the research indicates that they often cannot convert this sensitivity to the richness of life's situations into superior predictions.

Applied, for example, to the evaluation of arms control proposals, these findings suggest practical conclusions, such as the following: (1) negotiators will have difficulty explaining their decision-making processes accurately, even when they attempt to do so candidly (for example, when training aides); (2) it should be possible to predict their evaluations reasonably well with simple models, if one can identify the considerations that they usually attend to; (3) complex, novel proposals will be hard to evaluate thoroughly without some computational assistance; and (4) a country might benefit from automatic evaluation of proposals (forcing it to consider why its customary evaluation policy should not just be applied to each new proposal). Additional possible implications of behavioral decision research results are discussed in the section below on "Evaluating (and Creating) Arms Control Proposals."

Intuitive Statistics

The observation that intelligent, motivated individuals with extensive experience (for example, clinical psychologists and bank auditors) could be outperformed by a relatively unsophisticated statistical procedure was disturbing to many, including some of those intelligent, motivated individuals. It prompted the desire for a more detailed understanding of judgmental processes than was possible with formal modeling, focused on the question of "How good are people as *intuitive statisticians,* attempting to discern—and then use—the statistical relationships that they observe in the world around them?"

Two seemingly contradictory trends have emerged in studies of how people intuitively process statistical information, one suggesting that people do quite well, the other suggesting that they do quite poorly. The difference seems traceable to whether their task requires counting or inference.

A typical counting study exposes subjects to a series of stimuli drawn randomly from a fixed but unknown population. The subjects' task is to estimate some summary statistic based on what they observe and remember of the sample. The population might be a hidden urn full of red and blue marbles, while the sampling procedure is drawing out one marble at a time and the summary statistic is the proportion of red marbles in the urn. One counting task relevant to nuclear decisions might be reporting the frequency of different events during one's overnight watch at a radar screen or crisis-management center. Another might be summarizing the weapons one noted while touring enemy bases or observing enemy exercises.

Although there are many interesting nuances to the research on such judgments (Estes, 1964, 1976; Hintzman, 1976), it generally shows that people do a pretty good job of assessing common measures of the central tendency (for example, mean and mode) of what they have just seen (Hasher and Zacks, 1979; Peterson and Beach, 1967). Performance deteriorates when people's cognitive load increases, as when there are many colors of marble to monitor, many observations, long time intervals between observations, time pressure, emotional strain, or concurrent tasks demanding attention. In such cases, one can no longer count everything, but must make inferences about what has occurred on the basis of what has been noticed and remembered. In some cases, such cognitive overload typically adds unsystematic error (or "noise") to people's frequency estimates, making them less reliable but not biased in any particular way. One exception might occur with estimates of very small proportions (for example, 0.1 percent blue). Because people tend not to give fractional values, it is easier for the estimates to get larger than smaller, resulting in an artifactual tendency to overestimate small values and a comparable tendency to underestimate large ones (Poulton, 1977, 1982). Failure to see a rare event in a limited sample may create an unjustified feeling that it is impossible, even when one would not expect to see a single example in a sample that size.

More interesting problems can arise when more interesting stimuli are used, ones that allow active involvement with their meaning, which is difficult with a series of marbles. The result is often systematic biases in inferred frequencies. In a seemingly trivial but illustrative example, Tversky and Kahneman (1973) played two recordings that read aloud the names of some famous people (for example, Richard Nixon and Elizabeth Taylor) and some not-so-famous ones (for example, William Fulbright and Lana Turner). One recording had 19 famous men and 20 less-famous women; the other had 19 famous women and 20 less-famous men. When asked, 80 percent of the subjects thought that there were more men in the first list and more women in the second, even though the opposite was (marginally) the case. When asked, subjects remembered about 50 percent more famous names than unfamous ones. Thus, it could be that these subjects kept (in their minds) a rough, running tally of the number of names of each sex that they had heard, but paid more attention to the more famous names. Or, it could be that they did no counting while listening, but used the number of names they could remember as an indicator of each sex's frequency. By either of these interpretations, subjects went astray because they attached meaning to the stimuli. What they knew prior to entering the experiment affected either what attracted their attention or what activated their memories. The idea of relying on memory to estimate frequency was labeled the *availability heuristic* by Tversky and Kahneman (1973).

The contrast between these flawed frequency judgments and the fine ones observed in studies using artificial stimuli suggests that people can count what they see, but what they see is not necessarily exactly what they are shown. Rather, they interpret what they see, whenever that is even remotely possible. By some accounts, such interpretation is an automatic and almost unstoppable process. Once they are perceived, stimuli may immediately begin to activate associations with a wide network of related events (for example, Collins and Loftus, 1975).

Simple extrapolation of these results to nuclear decisions might lead to predictions like the following: (1) observers can be trusted to summarize what has occurred on a short watch with relatively unambiguous events; (2) they might overestimate the frequency of events that particularly capture their attention (for example, those that are unfamiliar or make a good story); and (3) rare events that have not occurred recently will tend to drop from consciousness (even though one would not expect them in a brief period of time). Obviously, a more careful task analysis is needed to determine the likelihood of particular biases under particular conditions (Combs and Slovic, 1978; Lichtenstein et al., 1978).

Living with Bias

Availability bias would not occur if people did not have a natural tendency to interpret the events that they see and, as a result, overestimate the frequency of more interpretable events. Conceivably, such an insistence on finding meaning has some broad evolutionary utility, in the sense that a thinking organism has a better chance of survival if it always generates some meaningful hypothesis about what is happening in its environment (even if that means interpreting situations where nothing discernible is happening). Speculations about the evolutionary value of behavior are often intriguing, but always difficult to test. A behavioral pattern that seems useful for some situations may be useless for others. A strategy that complicates life in the short run may simplify it in the intermediate run and complicate it in new ways over a longer period of time. Behavior patterns that produce big biases may be less dangerous than behavior patterns that produce modest biases: if big biases lead to sharp, unpleasant feedback, then people may learn the error of their ways. Behaviors that mildly mess things up may go undetected for a long time until, perhaps, they become critical to some decision. The overall toll exacted by a judgmental bias depends on the overall kinds of decisions that people are forced to make. Estimating that toll means making impossibly sweeping generalizations regarding what life is like and how much margin it leaves for error.

A more reasonable aspiration is to identify the local effects of particular biases. For example, people judge randomness differently than statisticians, often seeing patterns (or "signals") where there is just randomness (or "noise") (Gilovich, Vallone, and Tversky, 1985; Tune, 1964; Wagenaar, 1970). The most familiar example may be the "gambler's fallacy," the belief that random sequences (for example, coin flips) should even out in the short run as well as in the long run. This belief keeps people alert and focused, always searching for patterns (Lopes, 1982). Often, they may suffer little from occasionally seeing illusory patterns. The same strategy has disastrous results in serious decisions (for example, birth planning) or in environments where this foible could be exploited. For example, couples ought not to expect four girl babies to be followed by a boy; Feller (1968) found that the citizens of London exposed themselves to unrecognized risk by reading patterns into the largely random distribution of bomb hits during the Blitz, encouraging them to believe that they could predict where the Germans were aiming.

A second example of the need for careful task analysis if one is to predict the impact of behavior patterns on decisions comes from the effect of prior beliefs on judgment. Some reliance on prior knowledge is essential to the efficient processing of experiences. However, it can also distort people's perceptions of what they see. For example, a popular diagnostic technique in psychotherapy requires clients to draw a picture of a person. In a survey of practicing therapists, Chapman and Chapman (1969) found that the great majority reported seeing correlations between clinical symptoms and features of the drawings that systematic research had shown did not exist, such as a tendency for clients worried about manliness to draw figures with broad, muscular shoulders or a tendency for suspicious people to draw figures with atypical eyes. One possible source of the clinicians' biased perceptions is that when these symptoms and features do occur together, they create a highly coherent and memorable package. As a result, when clinicians review their experience, these tidy pairs stand out. A second possible source of this *illusory correlation* is that knowing (or suspecting) a client's diagnosis may increase a clinician's chance of seeing, say, strange eyes if they are there or, perhaps, even if they are not (or if their "strangeness" is borderline) (Hamilton and Rose, 1980; Spears, van der Pligt, and Eiser, 1986). A comparable phenomenon in the strategic arena would be misestimating the effectiveness of deterrence because of the disproportionate memorability of a few cases in which deferrence apparently did or did not work—or allowing one's belief (or disbelief) in the theory to affect one's judgment regarding just how much of a deterrence a country had mounted before it was attacked or left alone (Jervis, 1976; Lebow and Stein, 1987).

As with gambler's fallacy, there is no simple summary of the net impact on decision making of the tendency for expectations to guide perceptions. It may emerge as expertise, when expectations allow people to characterize emerging situations quickly. Or, it may emerge as an inability to see evidence contrary to one's beliefs. In some cases, biased judgments will lead to egregious decisions. In other cases, those judgments will be good enough for the decision at hand, perhaps because there is insufficient time for a more refined analysis, or perhaps because both biased and better judgments lead to the same conclusion (that is, the decision is *insensitive* to differences in those judgments). Theoretical analysis of decisions is needed to determine their sensitivity to particular biases. Empirical study of actual judgments is needed to determine the robustness of biases. Both are detailed pursuits that can be treated only briefly here (Raiffa, 1968; von Winterfeldt and Edwards, 1982). In a sense, however, the most important message of research on judgmental biases may be to recognize the possibility of their existence. Such awareness allows, indeed requires, being ready for bias when designing decision-making procedures, when anticipating an opponent's actions, or when making one's own plans.

Understanding the limits to one's own knowledge is a critical aspect of assessing the possibility for judgmental problems. A common measure of the appropriateness of people's confidence is their degree of *calibration*. Over a large set of judgments, it should be the case that probabilities of *.XX* are associated with true beliefs *XX* percent of the time. A typical study of calibration might present subjects with 100 two-alternative questions, such as: absinthe is (1) a liqueur; (2) a precious stone. The subject's task is to pick the more likely answer and give the probability that it is correct. Figure 3.1 shows some typical results. People's confidence in their answers (the abscissa) is related to the truth of those answers (the ordinate), but only moderately so. Overall, there is a tendency to *overconfidence*. For example, when subjects in Figure 3.1 were 100 percent confident, they had chosen the correct answer only 80 percent of the time (Lichtenstein, Fischhoff, and Phillips, 1982). It is not hard to imagine the impact of overconfidence on nuclear decisions. The result would be inadequate caution, insufficient collection of evidence, and incomplete attention to hints that a plan has gone astray.

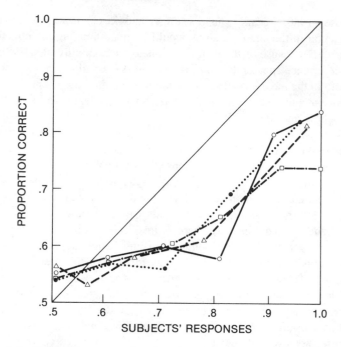

FIGURE 3.1. Calibration curve, showing the appropriateness of confidence levels. "Subjects' responses" are their judgments of the probability that the answers they have chosen to two-alternative questions are correct. These are contrasted with the proportions of answers that were actually correct. △---- data from Hazard and Peterson (1973); ●---- data from Hazard and Peterson (1973), judgments expressed as odds; □---- data from Phillips and Wright (1977); ○---- data from Lichtenstein (unpublished).

The basic pattern of results portrayed in Figure 3.1 has proven so robust that it has been hard to get much insight into the psychological processes producing it (Wallsten and Budescu, 1983). One of the few manipulations that has made a difference is forcing subjects to give reasons why their chosen answers might be wrong (Koriat, Lichtenstein, and Fischhoff, 1980). That simple instruction seems to prompt recall of contrary reasons that would not normally come to mind, given people's natural thought processes, which seem to focus on retrieving reasons supporting chosen answers.

A second "successful" manipulation has been to use very easy tasks. In such cases, people's overall insensitivity emerges as a tendency to underconfidence. Unfortunately, in practical situations, one must work with the tasks that life provides, with whatever difficulty levels they have. Because calibration depends on task difficulty, one cannot mechanically adjust people's confidence judgments to more realistic values. Thus, treating 100 percent confidence as 80 percent knowledge would help with the judgments in Figure 3.1, but would make matters worse in cases where people are underconfident.

Prejudices About Biases

Like other empirical results, these findings are not without controversy. This section provides a brief overview of the internal debates of behavioral decision making. Some of these arguments accompany all debates among psychologists; others are special to research claiming to show limits to people's performance (Cohen, 1981; Edwards and von Winterfeldt, 1986; Hogarth, 1981; Kahneman and Tversky, 1982; Lopes, 1982). Together, they provide a conceptual structure for extrapolation to nuclear decisions.

IT'S NOT TRUE

Psychologists are adept at picking holes in the design and analysis of experiments. The number of possible criticisms is, however, very large. As a result, it is tempting to answer skepticism with counterskepticism, producing a stalemate between attackers and defenders. One possible way to avoid checking every possible alternative explanation for every empirical result is to see whether any general statements can be made about the impact of particular manipulations on the quality of performance. The top section of Table 3.2 ("unfair tasks") describes some common methodological criticisms, such as the fact that the biases would vanish if one only raised the stakes or clarified the instructions. A review of all studies that varied these factors in attempts to eliminate two biases (overconfidence and hindsight bias) found no evidence of improvement (Fischhoff, 1982*a*). If this pattern of results were sustained with further studies considering additional biases, then the burden of proof might shift to those who raise such routine criticisms.

IT'S TRUE, BUT YOU SHOULDN'T SAY IT

Demonstrations of bias could be construed as an exercise in which one very small group of people, the investigators, makes a very large group of people, everybody else, look stupid. This juxtaposition is not only distasteful, but also dangerous if it unduly lowers people's self-esteem or the legitimacy of their decision making. What right do the psychologists have to undermine people's faith in themselves, or in their leaders? How can they publicize results that help leaders to discount public opinion as incompetent? (Fischhoff, 1990).

A combative response to these charges is that an investigator's responsibility is to tell it like it is, reporting the data accurately, integrating them with extant theory, and surrounding them with appropriate qualifications. Doing

Table 3.2   Debiasing Methods According to Underlying Assumption

Assumption	Strategies
Faulty tasks	
Unfair tasks	Raise states
	Clarify instructions
	Dispel doubts
	Use better response modes
	Discourage second guessing
	Ask fewer questions
Misunderstood tasks	Demonstrate alternative goal
	Demonstrate semantic disagreement
	Demonstrate impossibility of task
	Demonstrate overlooked distinction
Faulty judges	
Perfectible individuals	Warn of problem
	Describe problem
	Provide personalized feedback
	Train extensively
Incorrigible individuals	Replace them
	Recalibrate their responses
	Plan on error
Mismatch between judges and task	
Restructuring	Make knowledge explicit
	Search for discrepant information
	Decompose problem
	Consider alternative situations
	Offer alternative formulations
Reeducation	Rely on experts
	Educate from childhood

Source: Fischhoff (1982b).

otherwise is not only dishonest, but also unfair to the people whose behavior is being described. Giving people too much credit for decision-making prowess can deny them access to needed help, just as giving them too little credit can deny them access to power.

A more conciliatory response is that it is hard to create a balanced summary of such research. Even the clearest demonstration of a bias says little about its prevalence in life. As mentioned, making such sweeping generalizations requires a comprehensive theory of what life is like and how the situations that it poses resemble those in the laboratory—hardly work for the timid. Moreover, even if one reports studies accurately, biases make such a good story that they easily become a "figure" overshadowing the "ground" created by people's psychological processes in routine (and reasonably successful) operation. The danger of such misinterpretation increases as results are reported in secondary and tertiary sources (Berkeley and Humphreys, 1982).

IT'S TRUE, BUT IT DOESN'T MATTER

Many interesting psychological problems have few direct consequences for everyday life. For example, optical illusions reveal important properties of vision without often being a major hindrance. A casual way of dismissing judgmental biases as trivial is to argue that somehow or other, experience would have taught people to avoid behavior that is frequently bad for them. A more rigorous way is to show, analytically, the insensitivity of particular decisions to particular errors. For example, in an analysis that focused originally on the effect of perceptual imperfections on motor behavior, von Winterfeldt and Edwards (1982) showed that under certain general conditions, the expected value of a decision with continuous options (for example, invest X) changes little if one of its component probability or value estimates is moderately inaccurate. A less optimistic result is Einhorn and Hogarth's (1978) demonstration of how actions based on overconfident judgments can have consequences that misleadingly reinforce that overconfidence. Their classic example is that of a grant review committee, which evaluates the quality of its (overconfident) decisions by comparing the productivity of its grantees with that of the applicants it has rejected—without realizing that its funds alone will increase productivity even if it has very little ability to discern quality.

Such analyses help clarify the relationship between people and their environment. In situations where the analysis shows that decisions are insensitive to biases in judgment, it also shows that people have little chance to learn more optimal behaviors. That is, if biases do not affect most decisions, then there will not be the kind of sharp feedback needed to get people to change. As a result, people may be particularly vulnerable to the effects of suboptimal judgment and decision making in those, perhaps few, situations where accuracy really matters. Indeed, any difficulties that people have in thinking their way through to good decisions might be attributed to their great ability to reach good decisions through trial and error. Unfortunately, this combination leaves them very exposed when they need to get things right the first time.

PEOPLE ARE DOING SOMETHING QUITE DIFFERENT—
AND DOING IT QUITE WELL

Describing behavior as suboptimal presumes knowledge of what is optimal. Within decision theory, optimality is defined in terms of what the decision maker knows and wants. It would, therefore, be wrong to claim suboptimality if people act overconfidently in a world that rewards bravado, if a good decision is followed (unfortunately) by a bad outcome, or if they fail to do as well as we might have done in their stead given the "wisdom" of hindsight. The second of the six sections in Table 3.2 shows some generic ways in which one might eliminate an apparent bias by demonstrating that subject and experimenter have misunderstood one another's perspective on a task. In avoiding such problems, the study of decision making has retreated to the laboratory where, in principle, all details can be specified and all extraneous beliefs and distractions can be eliminated. Yet, no investigator conducts manipulation checks to ensure that each feature is understood exactly as intended. Nor could many subjects absorb a detailed explication of how they should think about every such detail.

Where subjects do seem to have understood the task as the experimenter intended, they might still be defended against charges of bias by arguing that they subscribe to alternative theories of optimality. Even though the basic definition of rationality underlying these studies is widely accepted, some theorists have proposed alternative accounts that seem more consistent with observed behavior (see, for example, Cohen, 1981; Shafer, 1976). Time will tell whether this is a case of psychology stimulating philosophy or of throwing out the baby (time-honored models of rationality) with the bath water (a few apparently discrepant psychological results).

Analogous arguments surround pundits' criticisms of the decisions made by political leaders. A critic who wishes to charge incompetence must judge leaders in terms of what goals they were pursuing, what information they had at the time of decision, and how well they exploited that information. If the goals seem wrong, then the problem is one of values rather than competence. If leaders are expected to know more than was possible at a given time, then they are victims of hindsight bias (Fischhoff, 1975). If they are faulted for how things turned out, rather than how sensibly they acted, then they are subject to unrealistic demands. We may choose to turn out leaders who have bad luck or face unpleasant alternatives; however, that means avoiding reality.

BUT LOOK AT HOW WELL PEOPLE DO OTHER THINGS

The psychological evidence of bias seems strikingly at odds with the fact that planes fly, meals get on the table, and games of enormous complexity (for example, chess and handball) are played. One quick way to reconcile this conflict is to dismiss biases as laboratory curiosities. The converse is to claim that the world is not working all that well and that we would be better off if we made better decisions. A more involved response is to admit the reality of laboratory results, but search for environmental conditions that induce more effective thinking.

The fifth section of Table 3.2 shows some conditions that have proven to be effective. One might be fortunate enough to find such conditions in life or have to restructure tasks deliberately in ways that facilitate using one's mind more effectively. One such possibility described earlier is the Koriat, Lichtenstein, and Fischhoff (1980) procedure of having people generate reasons why they might be wrong before assessing their confidence. One aspect of scientific training is to make this a natural way of thinking. Scholars are taught to generate alternative explanations of their results before publishing, and then to share those reasons when they do. The length and rigors of graduate training, as well as the rejection rates for submitted articles, reflect, in part, the difficulties of mastering these turns of mind. A detailed analysis would be needed to determine if specific nuclear decisions were fortuitously presented in ways that enable people to use their minds to best advantage. Pressures to decide quickly, to defend one's decisions, and to present a confident exterior, for example, would create conditions opposite of those of Koriat and his colleagues.

FACING THE PROBLEMS

Taking judgmental problems seriously opens a number of lines of inquiry. One is understanding why people are so good at some tasks and so poor at others. The ambient account among behavioral decision researchers is that there are no fundamental psychological limitations, beyond information-processing capacity, that prevent people from acquiring the skills needed to make better judgments. The barriers are environmental: people receive little training in decision making per se and live in a world whose ecology of information does not provide conditions for learning.

If the problems are real, then one can seriously begin doing something about them. The third section of Table 3.2 lists approaches to training better judgment, which might also incorporate the restructuring options of the fifth section. Such programs have shown some promise (Beyth-Marom et al., 1985; Lichtenstein and Fischhoff, 1980; Nickerson, Perkins, and Smith, 1985; Nisbett et al., 1983). Ironically, the very robustness of biases complicates demonstrating improvement. Often, any intervention that destabilizes the dominant response pattern will tend to reduce the extent of bias, making confusion look like wisdom (Fischhoff and Bar-Hillel, 1984). Although confusion is often an intermediate state between holding erroneous beliefs and holding appropriate ones, it can also be an intermediate state between two erroneous beliefs.

The fourth section of the table lists approaches to living with incorrigible fallibility. An example of the second entry, recalibration, was the (U.K.) Central Electricity Generating Board's doubling of engineers' chronic underestimates of the time needed to return units to production before using those estimates in forecasts of power availability (Kidd, 1970). In the defense area, Tihansky (1976) has documented the persistent overconfidence in cost estimates for military air frames. Unfortunately for research purposes, this result could reflect inadvertent overconfidence or deliberate misstatement. In either case, more realistic estimates could be produced by adjusting those that are offered.

Finally, accepting the reality of judgmental biases pushes one to develop better theories for predicting how and when they will arise. One current need is for theories regarding how people choose and apply judgment and decision-making strategies in specific situations (see, for example, Payne, 1982). People show such great ingenuity in construing situations that even such apparently straightforward rules as availability could often be interpreted in a variety of ways (How long does one produce examples? Just how are categories defined? What attributes guide the search?). A second need is for theories predicting when people actually make deliberate, analytical decisions, synthesizing available facts. When do laziness, inattention, or confusion lead people to rely on habit, tradition, or some other rule of thumb to guide their behavior—rather than trying to figure out what to do?

Expert Judgment

Except for nuclear decisions made by the general public, the obvious generalization question regarding the behavioral decision-making literature is whether it applies to the judgmental processes of experts working in their areas of expertise.

Figures 3.2 and 3.3 present two faces of the evidentiary record with experts. Figure 3.2 shows the performance of weather forecasters working for the U.S. National Weather Service, which requires them to attach probabilities to precipitation forecasts and reinforces them for accuracy and candor. They are, in a word, outstanding. It rains almost exactly XX percent of the time when they say that there is an XX percent chance of rain. The only (mild) problem is saying 1.00 too often when it does not rain. In terms of psychological learning theory, these forecasters enjoy near-perfect conditions for acquiring this skill. They receive large quantities of prompt, unambiguous feedback with a clear-cut criterion event (that is, rain/no rain).

Such opportunities for learning would seem to be rare in the lives of most people for most kinds of analytic judgments about uncertain events. In that light, it should not be too surprising if people—even experts—do not learn how to make such judgments optimally (Murphy and Winkler, 1984). Unfortunately, such ideal conditions for learning are rare in the experience of many

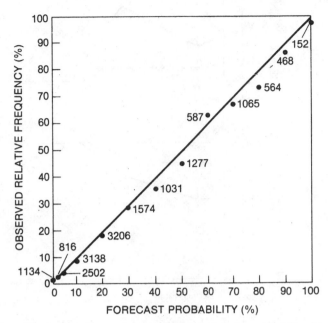

FIGURE 3.2. Reliability diagram for subjective precipitation probability forecasts formulated by U.S. National Weather Service offices. The number at each point indicates the number of forecasts with that forecast probability. *Source:* Murphy and Winkler (1977).

experts. Politicians, for example, seldom make sufficiently precise judgments such that anyone could evaluate their performance. This protects them from criticism, but also from feedback. They are rewarded for exuding confidence, which may obscure how much they actually think they know from themselves as well as from the public. They make judgments about long-term processes, so that feedback is long delayed, until perhaps they have forgotten what they predicted and why. Under these conditions, it is would be hard to learn about the quality of one's judgment, even if one were conscientious enough to attempt a systematic review.

Figure 3.3 describes one aspect of the judgments of a group of esteemed experts, performing in their field of expertise, but without the benefit of good learning conditions. In it, particle physicists' best estimates of the value of several physical constants are bracketed by what might be called "confidence intervals," showing the range of likely values, within which the true value should fall, once it is known. Narrower intervals indicate greater confidence. These intervals have shrunk over time, as knowledge of physics has increased. However, at most points in time, they seem to have been too narrow.

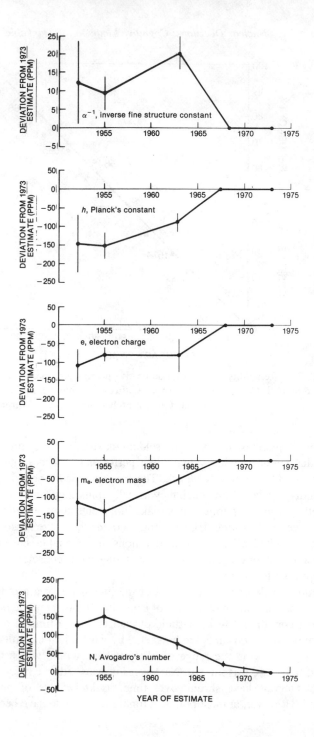

Otherwise, subsequent best estimates should not have fallen outside the range of what previously seemed plausible so frequently. In an absolute sense, the level of knowledge represented here is extremely high and the successive best estimates lie extremely close to one another. However, the confidence intervals define what constitute surprises in terms of current physical theory. Unless the possibility of overconfident judgment is considered, values falling outside the intervals suggest problems with the theory. Indeed, the surprising estimates of the speed of light generated in the 1920s and 1930s evoked serious suggestions that it might be increasing or varying sinusoidally over time. These last results reflect a general principle of decision theory, namely, that the kind and quality of judgment needed depends on the task at hand (Henrion, 1980; Krzysztofowicz, 1983; Raiffa, 1968).

In some cases, one cares primarily about getting the best available estimate; in others, it is crucial to know how good that best guess is. One might even be willing to sacrifice some knowledge (in the sense of having more information) for some greater wisdom (in the sense of knowing the limits to the information). This is also one reason for the cautiousness of the present approach to expert judgment compared, say, to the enthusiasm found among developers of expert systems (see, for example, Buchanan and Shurtliffe, 1984; Coombs, 1984; Hollnagel, Mancini, and Woods, 1986). Those developers are typically more concerned with making the best current knowledge more widely available than with determining its limits. Additional reasons for caution include concern over the ability of experts to provide valid introspections regarding their own thought processes (the building blocks of expert systems), concern over the difficulties of pooling judgments from diverse sources (so that one expert may be expected to understand all of a complex problem), concern over the reliability of expert knowledge for novel situations (for which no "experts" have had the benefit of trial and error to educate their intuitions), and concern over the extent to which the values of experts may be embedded in their judgments and recommendations (rather than separated, as required by decision theory, so that opinions about facts and values can be scrutinized independently). The contrast between these perspectives promises to be an important area of future research (Cohen, 1985; Kanal & Lemmer, 1986; Mumpower et al., 1987; National Research Council, 1987; Olson, 1990; Oskamp, 1965). Although this is not the place for a detailed discussion, these

←———————————————————————————————

FIGURE 3.3. Recommended values for fundamental physical constants, 1952–1973. The uncertainties associated with these estimates are expressed by error bars representing one standard error. *Source:* Henrion and Fischhoff (1986).

concerns suggest the need for great caution in relying on expert systems for any nuclear decision.

Organizational Setting

Many nuclear decisions involve not only experts, but experts functioning in organizational settings. As a result, extrapolating from studies of individual decision making requires sensitivity to how organizational factors affect individuals' behavior and to how those psychological processes accumulate to shape organizational actions and policies. Such sensitivity is inherently difficult for psychology with its focus on individuals. For historical reasons, this particular area in psychology might be somewhat less vulnerable than most. Some of its basic orientation comes from studies of imperfect decision making in organizations (Cyert and March, 1963; Simon, 1957); many investigators are located outside of psychology departments (for example, business schools and consulting firms). Many are not even psychologists; those that are often come from social psychology. Many studies have been conducted in institutional settings with expert decision makers (for example, Equation 3.1; Figure 3.2). Nonetheless, most studies use convenience samples of young adults working alone on static problems.

There are two generic strategies for embedding individual behavior in organizational contexts. The "top-down approach" defines the organization with an eye to locating individuals in it, as they respond to its challenges and constraints. The "bottom-up approach" begins with the individuals populating an organization and considers how their performance is encumbered and facilitated by increasing levels of organizational complexity. For either approach to be sensible, it must aim at making contact with analyses coming from the other direction. There are, at present, only pieces of such integrative theories (see, for example, March and Weissinger-Baylon, 1985; Ungson and Braunstein, 1983; Weick, 1979). The following discussion of possible organizational influences on individual judgment and decision making is culled from such accounts and other sources. It is necessarily speculative, but may provide a point of departure for extrapolating research results to specific settings.

This account is a bottom-up analysis, beginning with the image of individual performance extracted (as already noted) from the behavioral decision research literature, asking how it might be affected by various complications. It might be thought of as a *task analysis,* the standard point of entry for human factors engineers, specialists in how people perform in technical systems (Perrow, 1984; Wickens, 1984). Such analyses characterize systems in terms of their behaviorally significant dimensions, those that need to be considered when designing a system or predicting its performance. Given the variety of nuclear decisions, no simple statement can be offered regarding whether organizational settings per se improve or frustrate decision making. A detailed analysis is needed regarding what features an organization has and how they matter. (George [1980] provides a classic example of a bottom-up analysis of a specific setting—presidential decision making on foreign policy.)

SINGLE-PERSON SYSTEMS

The simplest situation faced by an individual decision maker involves a static world about which everything can be known and no formal representation of knowledge is required. The threats to performance in this "basic" situation include any individual psychological limitations in identifying relevant options, assembling and reviewing relevant knowledge, identifying and weighing relevant values, and integrating these pieces in an effective way. The experimental research on static, familiar tasks can be extrapolated most readily to these situations.

A first complication is the addition of *uncertainty*. With it, research on intuitive statistics becomes relevant—with its concern about biases such as illusory correlation, overconfidence, and availability-induced misjudgments. Also relevant are the solutions that have been found effective in improving judgment (for example, Table 3.2), such as training in judgmental skills, restructuring tasks to overcome bad habits, and keeping a statistical record of experience to reduce reliance on memory. Many nuclear decisions are dauntingly difficult even without uncertainty, given the wrenching trade-offs (for example, money versus lives) that they require. Adding uncertainty opens the possibility of bias in the judgments needed to reduce it and the possibility of the associated remedial interventions.

As second complication is going from a static to a dynamic external world. With it come new difficulties, such as undue adherence to current beliefs and reliance on habitual behaviors. "Fighting the last war" is the classic allegation for treating a dynamic world as though it were static.

A third complication is using a "modeling language" to organize knowledge and decision making. It could be as simple as storing information in computerized spreadsheets or as complex as cost-benefit analyses and risk analyses of alternative actions. Complexity alone requires some such formalization. Undue faith in the power of formal analysis can push it far beyond its domain of usefulness. One psychological problem with modeling is the inability of technical experts to express their knowledge in terms that the modeling language can accommodate. For example, the operators of a weapons system may not be able to assess the probability that they will give various responses to crisis situations—at least not with the precision needed to calculate system reliability. Another associated problem is ignoring problems that cannot be readily modeled, such as allies' responses to arms control proposals or the effect of defense spending on innovation in the civilian economy. All of these complicating conditions might face individuals in their private lives as well. Being in an organizational setting can raise the stakes riding on the decisions for which they are individually responsible. It can also provide the resources needed to address such problems seriously. For example, intelligence research can reduce some uncertainties; human factors research can make computerized models more manageable.

TWO-PERSON SYSTEMS

The simplest organization involves two people making decisions in some interdependent way. Clearly, adding a second person raises additional issues for decision-making processes. However, before addressing them, it is important to ask what happens to the old issues. That is, are they eliminated, exacerbated, or left unchanged by the complications of various kinds of two-person systems?

In behavioral terms, the simplest two-person system involves individuals with *common goals, common experience,* and *hardened communication links.* Such individuals should have highly compatible "mental models" of their situation and the opportunity to keep those models consistent. Having a colleague can reduce some difficulties experienced by individuals. For example, information overload might be reduced by dividing information-processing responsibilities; mistakes might be avoided by having a partner available to check one's work. On the other hand, having someone who thinks similarly in the system may just mean having two people prone to the same judgmental difficulties. It might even make matters worse if both drew confidence from the convergence of their (similarly flawed) judgmental processes.

More generally, agreement on any erroneous belief is likely to increase confidence without a corresponding increase in accuracy, perhaps encouraging more drastic (and more disastrous) actions. "Group polarization" is a term for groups' tendency to adopt more extreme positions than would their individual members (Myers and Lamm, 1976); "groupthink" is a term for the social processes that promote continued adherence to shared, but faulty, beliefs (Janis, 1972). Restricting communication would be one way to blunt these tendencies; however, it would come at the price of allowing the partners' mental models to drift apart, perhaps without their realizing it. Even with unrestricted communication, discrepant views can last quite a while without being recognized. "False consensus" refers to the erroneous belief that others share one's views (Dawes, in press; Nisbett and Ross, 1980); "pluralistic ignorance" refers to the erroneous belief that one is the odd person out (Fiske and Taylor, 1984). Both have been documented repeatedly; both can be treated if the threat is recognized and facing the discrepancy is not too painful (both are typically studied in larger groups, but can arise whenever incomplete communication is possible).

Such problems arise because frequent interaction can create a perception of completely shared models, whereas sharing is inevitably incomplete. Thus, an obvious complication in two-person decision-making systems is created by inherent *limits to the sharing of prior experience*, such as when people with different backgrounds must work together (Meshkati, in press). People who see the world differently should, at times, reach different conclusions and decisions. In addition to disagreements about the facts of a decision, parties may use key terms differently, yet not recognize, say, that "risk," "threat," "likely," or "destructive power" have different meanings (Beyth-Marom, 1982a; Bunn and Tsipis, 1983; Fischhoff, Watson, and Hope, 1984; Kess and Hoppe, 1985). One possible device for coordinating perceptions is to provide efficient checking procedures, so that partners can detect and diagnose discrepancies in their mental models. An understanding of how to alleviate such problems should also help one to predict their prevalence and intensity.

A further complication of decision making in two-person systems is *incomplete fidelity* of those communications that are made. Problems might come from the communication technology (for example, telephone, telex, or mail) or from institutionalized procedures, such as restricted vocabularies, time- or event-related reporting requirements, or interaction protocols. Any restriction on normal communication may suppress the cues that people depend on to understand others and make themselves understood. It is unclear what substitutes people will find (or even find necessary) when deprived of facial expression, body language, or intonation as indicators of just what others believe (Hirokawa and Poole, 1987; Kiesler, Siegel, and McGuire, 1984). In such cases, social relations may be restricted along with social understanding (Kiesler et al., 1985). Communication systems that cannot transmit levels of confidence probably cannot generate confidence; it may be hard to lead through electronic mail.

The final complication with two-person decision-making systems is *inconsistent goals*. Two dependent parties may have similar goals, but differ over which are relevant to a particular decision; they may have a common opponent, yet stand to share differently from the spoils of victory; they may strive for power within the system, while still being concerned about its ability to meet external challenges. Like other complications, these can be useful or detrimental. For example, disagreement over goals can uncover imprecise thinking that an average decision maker might overlook; internal competition might sharpen the wits of the competitors. By some accounts, conflict itself is part of what binds social units together (Coser, 1954).

MULTIPLE-PERSON SYSTEMS

By itself, increasing the size of a system adds some new wrinkles to participants' decision-making process. As the number of parties multiplies, so does the number of messages (and perhaps information) that must be managed. If everyone hears everything, then there may be too much going on to ensure that anyone hears anything or keeps track of who knows what. Thus, size alone reduces the opportunities to share experiences. Maximum sharing might be found in a hierarchical organization whose leaders had progressed through the ranks from the very bottom, so that they have a deep understanding of the reality of their subordinates' worlds. In such situations, less needs to be said to people and more can be predicted about their behavior, making the organization more intimate than it might otherwise seem. On the other hand, when the world is changing rapidly, then the experience of having been at every level in the organization may give an illusory feeling of understanding its reality. For example, the education, equipment, and challenges of foot soldiers (or sales representatives) may be quite different now than when their senior officers were in the trenches. An indicator of these threats might be the *degree of technological change* in the organization and its environment. One possible solution would be periodic rotation through the ranks; a second would be to provide opportunities to cut through the normal lines of communication in order to find out what is really happening at different levels. Problems might be reduced by resisting opportunities to change the organization, unless the improvements would be so great as to compensate for the likely decrease in internal understanding.

A complicating factor with multiple-person systems, for which the two-person version exists but is relatively uninteresting, concerns the *heterogeneity* of its parts. At one extreme is a homogeneous organization whose parts interact in an "additive" fashion, with each performing roughly the same functions and the system's strength depending on the sum of such parts. At the other extreme is a heterogeneous organization having specialized parts dependent on one another for vital services, with its strength coming from the sophistication of its design and the effectiveness of its dedicated components. A relatively undifferentiated infantry group might anchor one end of this continuum and an integrated carrier strike force the other.

The operational benefits of a homogeneous system are its ability to use individuals and materials interchangeably, the opportunities to create widely applicable policies, and relative insensitivity to the loss of any particular units (insofar as their effect is additive). An inherent limitation of having homogeneous perspectives and skills is the vulnerability to shared misconceptions (what might be called "intellectual common-mode failure") and the accompanying ability to initiate or detect significant changes.

The operational benefits of a heterogeneous system include its ability to provide precise responses to the variety of the challenges posed by a complex environment. One inherent psychological disadvantage is the difficulty of bearing in mind or modeling the operations of a complex interactive system, so that it is hard to know who is doing what when, and how their actions affect one another. Thus, backlash and friendly fire may be more likely across diverse units than across similar ones. Even if they do have a clear picture of the whole, the managers of such a system may find it difficult to formulate an organizational philosophy that is meaningful in all the diverse contexts it faces. Heterogeneity also threatens interoperability problems, hampering communication and cooperation.

Both kinds of systems may be most vulnerable to the threats against which the other is most strongly defended. The additive character of homogeneous systems means that it is numbers that count. A system adapted to this reality may be relatively inattentive to those few ways in which individual units are indispensable, such as their ability to reveal vital organizational intelligence or to embarrass the organization on the whole. Conversely, the command structure that has evolved to orchestrate the pieces of a heterogeneous system may be severely challenged by situations in which mainly numbers matter. An inevitable byproduct of specialization is having fewer of every specialty and less ability to transcend specialty boundaries. There may, therefore, be less staying power in protracted engagements.

Perhaps the best treatment for these limitations is incorporating some properties of each system in the other. Thus, for example, homogeneous organizations could actively recruit individuals with diverse prior experience in order to ensure some heterogeneity of views; they might also develop specialist positions for dealing with nonadditive issues wherever those appear in the organization (for example, intelligence officers, publishers' libel monitors). Heterogeneous organizations might promote generalists with the aim of mediating and attenuating the differences among their parts; they might also transfer specialists across branches to encourage the sharing of perspectives (at the price of their being less well equipped to do the particular tasks to which they have been assigned).

GOALS OF THE ANALYSIS

This task analysis began with the problems faced in designing the simplest of decision-making systems—those involving single individuals grappling with their fate under conditions of certainty—with no attempt at formalization. It proceeded to complicate the lives of those single individuals, forcing them to make decisions in consort with others, and then to consider several levels of complication within two-person and multiple-person organizations.

Predicting or aiding decision making in any concrete organizational context would require a detailed analysis of how such issues emerge there, shaping the reality of the individuals in it. In some cases, that analysis will illuminate the reality faced by individual decision makers, enhancing or exacerbating their inherent intellectual strengths and weaknesses. In other cases, such analysis will reveal individuals with so little autonomy that an understanding of their psychology sheds little light on organizational functioning. Thus, here as elsewhere, there are few simple statements that will take one from the general study of behavior to predictions or prescriptions for specific individuals and settings. Rather, what behavioral research can give is a heightened awareness of phenomena that might be observed, and their robustness—that is, the extent to which they have been observed under diverse circumstances.

Other Aspects of Decision Making

It is impossible to provide a comprehensive guide to anticipating and addressing all potential obstacles to effective decision making. This section describes some representative research results relating to each stage of decision making. Extrapolating them to specific settings faces the issues just raised regarding the results described earlier.

DEFINE PROBLEM

The critical test for the problem definition used in making a decision is that it be complete, in the sense of encompassing all alternatives and consequences that decision makers would consider relevant if those were placed before them. The two obstacles to developing such a definition might be divided into "failures of imagination" and "failures of motivation:" not thinking hard enough to raise all relevant possibilities and choosing to ignore possibilities whose treatment is awkward or unpleasant. For example, flood-plain residents may fail to insure their homes because they forget that insurance is an option or because they dislike thinking about unpleasant eventualities (Kunreuther et al., 1978); cost-benefit analysts may ignore a factory's impact on landscape aesthetics because that consequence never occurred to them or because they do not know how to put a dollar value on it (Cummings, Brookshire, and Schulze, 1986); strategic analysts may neglect confidence-building measures because those are outside their usual repertoire of considerations or because they want to avoid tough decisions like trading off concrete weapons systems for nebulous changes in the climate of relations. These cognitive constraints are in addition to the political constraints that might lead decision makers to knowingly ignore awkward considerations.

Such omissions are made particularly dangerous by another reported judgmental difficulty: insensitivity to incompleteness in problem descriptions.

Elements that are out of sight also tend to be out of mind (Fischhoff, Slovic, and Lichtenstein, 1978; Pitz, Sachs, and Heerboth, 1980); people who have undue faith in the thoroughness of their problem definitions may also have undue faith in the definitiveness of the decisions derived from them.

This bias complicates the insensitivity to systematic biases that gives the availability heuristic its power to bias judgments (Tversky and Kahneman, 1973). Thus, readers of a strategic analysis might not only have an exaggerated feeling of its completeness, but also fail to notice that the omissions are, say, predominantly confidence-building options, consequences for the civilian economy (or for relations with allies), or uncertainties due to the fallibility of people (operators, leaders) in times of stress. The producers and consumers of analyses may forget the cumulative impact of omitting various hard-to-model actions, consequences, and uncertainties.

It is an abuse of an analytical process to impose it where it does not fit. It is an abuse of the policymaking process to deny the reality of the unanalyzed. The stakes riding on strategic analyses make it especially important to get them right. Those stakes also make it especially difficult. Not only are the issues often novel and complex, but their classified nature may reduce the opportunities for peer review from diverse perspectives.

Once the elements of a decision problem have been identified, they must be defined operationally. Imprecision makes it difficult to evaluate them, communicate them, follow them if they are adopted, and know to abandon them when conditions have changed enough to justify rethinking the decision. Imprecision also complicates learning from experience, insofar as it is hard to reconstruct exactly what one was trying to do and why (Brehmer, 1980; Shanteau and Phelps, 1977). That reconstruction is further complicated by hindsight bias, the tendency to exaggerate in hindsight the extent to which one knew all along what was going to happen (Fischhoff, 1982b). That bias leads one to be unduly harsh on past decisions (if it was obvious what was going to happen, then failure to select the best option must mean incompetence) and to be unduly optimistic about future decisions (by encouraging the feeling that things are generally well understood—even if they are not working out that well).

Some of the clearest evidence of imprecision comes from seemingly unresolvable conflicts between groups (or individuals) that do not realize that they are solving different problems. Classic examples can be found in the conflicts over technological hazards facing the Western democracies (Fischhoff, 1985; Freudenberg and Rosa, 1984; Williams and Mills, 1986). Even if opponents and proponents hold similar views on the facts of, say, nuclear power (for example, how risky, costly, and efficient it is), they can still be poles apart regarding its desirability if they disagree on what alternatives and consequences are relevant to decisions about the technology. Often proponents of nuclear power insist on smaller sets of considerations in both respects. For them, the viable energy options are coal and oil, compared to which the risks of nuclear power seem reasonable. Opponents, however, often add options, such as radical energy conservation programs or massive investment in renewable energy resources; in this light, nuclear power's risks loom larger and its benefits smaller. Regarding consequences, many opponents are concerned about the increased centralization of power and the inequitable distribution of risks and benefits that they believe accompany nuclear energy. For many proponents, these consequences are simply not relevant to managing energy technologies.

Although such conflicts can be acrimonious, the interplay between the parties at least has some chance of revealing the imprecision of their individual thinking. Where individuals interact only with their own kind, they are left to their own devices for sharpening their definitions. For example, groups of technological risk analysts working in different communities have routinely used different and inconsistent definitions of "risk," without realizing the existence or consequences of those differences. Thus, some use "lost days of life expectancy," where others use "increased probability of premature death." The former measure puts extra weight on deaths among young people; for the latter, a death is a death. Or, some analysts measure coal safety in casualties per worker and others in casualties per ton mined. By the latter measure, mines are getting much safer; by the former measure, the risks are more constant. It is hard to trade off risks effectively without a clear definition of what they are (Crouch and Wilson, 1983; Fischhoff, Watson, and Hope, 1984).

Parallel analyses might show comparable incompatibilities in the definitions of defense policy decisions held by opposing countries, allied countries, competing candidates, or leaders and citizens. A shared definition might reveal shared values and focus debates on legitimate conflicts.

EVALUATE CONSEQUENCES

Determining the relative importance of potential consequences might seem to be the easy part of decision making, insofar as people should know what they want and like. Although this is doubtless true for familiar and simple consequences, many "interesting" decisions present novel consequences and unusual juxtapositions. For example, two potential consequences that may arise when deciding whether to dye one's graying hair are reconciling oneself to aging and increasing the risk of cancer 10 to 20 years hence. The stereotypical trade-off in U.S. defense debates, "better dead than Red," involves similar incommensurables. Who knows what either event is *really* like, particularly with the precision needed to make trade-offs between the two? In such cases, one must go back to some set of basic values (for example, those concerned with pain, prestige, or vanity), decide which are pertinent, and determine what role to assign to each. As a result, evaluation becomes an inferential activity (Rokeach, 1973).

The evidence suggests that people often have trouble making such inferences. They may fail to identify all relevant values, to recognize the conflicts among them, or to reconcile those conflicts that they do confront. As a result, the values that they express may be highly (and unwittingly) sensitive to the exact way in which evaluation questions are posed, whether by survey researchers, decision aids, politicians, merchants, or themselves. Formally equivalent versions of the same question can evoke quite different considerations and, hence, lead to quite different decisions (Fischhoff, Slovic, and Lichtenstein, 1980; Hogarth, 1982; Kahneman and Tversky, 1984; National Research Council, 1982; Turner and Martin, 1984). Here are four examples from survey-type questions:

1. The act of answering six items concerning their political alienation reduced people's expressed confidence in national institutions (Turner and Krauss, 1978).

2. People judged the risks of technologies to be more acceptable after answering questions about their risks (Fischhoff, Slovic, and Lichtenstein, 1980).

3. Insurance became less attractive when its premium was described as a "sure loss" (Hershey and Schoemaker, 1980).

4. A public health program's attractiveness dropped precipitously when described in terms of the lives that would be lost, rather than in terms of the lives that would be saved (Tversky and Kahneman, 1981).

The occasional ability of politicians to put a new spin on defense issues, while the underlying facts remain relatively stable, may reflect such "framing" effects.

The low rates of "no opinion" reported by surveys that superficially address diverse, obscure, and even fictitious topics suggest that the values that respondents report may not be their own, or at least not what they would report after more thoughtful deliberation. Producing some opinion on every topic may reflect the desire to be counted, to feel involved, to have a pleasant interaction with an interviewer, or to be represented by one's gut level response to a general issue. Having some opinion on every topic means having considered opinions on none (Ellul, 1969; Smith, 1984).

These difficulties, as others, arise from routine judgmental processes, but can be amplified by external factors. Advertisers make a living from highlighting particular evaluative perspectives. Publicists try to alleviate or skirt value conflicts by offering simple perspectives, catchily formulated. Successful political candidates attempt to describe their election as a mandate for all parts of their platform. Such manipulations can work, in part, because it is hard to reformulate a problem spontaneously unless one has substantive familiarity with a topic (Hogarth, 1982). With unfamiliar topics, the observers of a debate can feel like spectators at center court of tennis match. The limited validity of people's introspections abut the factors motivating their past actions means that even consideration of one's own past decisions does not provide a stable point of reference (Ericsson and Simon, 1980; Nisbett & Wilson, 1977). Thus, uncertainty about values can be as serious a problem as uncertainty about facts.

ASSESS THE LIKELIHOOD OF CONSEQUENCES

Although people are often ready to recognize uncertainty about what will happen, they are not always well prepared to judge the likelihood of those future events. This is the overall message of the research into intuitive statistics. In addition to the problems discussed earlier, 25 years of research into intuitive judgment under conditions of uncertainty has documented a panoply of problems in gathering, interpreting, and integrating information (Kahneman, Slovic, and Tversky, 1982; Nisbett and Ross, 1980). For example, people may know what usually happens in a situation and recognize how a particular instance is special, yet they may be unable to integrate those two facts appropriately; the most common bias here is focusing on the specific information and undervaluing experience (for example, letting a neighbor's bad time with a particular car outweigh the accumulated reports of *Consumer Reports* readers) (Bar-Hillel, 1980; Tversky and Kahneman, 1974). One reason for this particular bias has been termed reliance on the *representativeness heuristic* (Bar-Hillel, 1984; Kahneman and Tversky, 1972). Namely, people can tell how similar a specific instance (a job candidate) is to a prototypical case (the successful employee), but not how important similarity is for making predictions, usually relying on it too much (Bar-Hillel, 1984; Kahneman and Tversky, 1972). Matching instances to prototypes is such a natural process (Murphy and Medin, 1985) that an international situation might quickly evoke a feeling for how well it seems to embody the central features of "Munich," "Pearl Harbor," "1914," "Yom Kippur," or whatever other cases come to mind. The "trick" is integrating this case-specific matching with knowledge of what typically happens in such situations (Kahneman and Tversky, 1979a).

Yet another bias reflecting the difference between counting and inference is that people can tell how many times they have seen an effect follow a potential cause, yet not infer what that says about causality, often perceiving correlations where none really exist (Beyth-Marom, 1982b; Langer, 1975; Shaklee and Tucker, 1980). A speculative extrapolation to defense matters might be mistaken inferences about the effectiveness of deterrence despite accurate memory for cases in which one is quite convinced that it worked (or failed). Other systematic biases include unfair dismissal of information that threatens favored beliefs (Mahoney, 1979), exaggeration of personal immunity to various threats (Weinstein, 1980), insensitivity to the rate at which exponential processes accelerate (Wagenaar and Timmers, 1979), and oversimplification of other people's behavior (Ross, 1977).

By analogy, for example, one would wonder whether political leaders turn a more critical eye to opponents' arguments than to their own (when trying to understand competing policies, not just in trying to defend them); whether generals believe that they can routinely beat the law of averages (when analyzing situations, not just when trying to inspire soldiers); whether congressional representatives understand the cumulative impact of an annual increase (or decrease) of a few percentage points in the defense budget; or whether our leaders really understand the complex pressures on Soviet leaders or the historical experiences that shape their deliberations.

DECIDE

Decision theory is quite clear about the sort of rule that people should use to integrate their beliefs and values when choosing a best alternative. It should be an *expectation rule,* whereby an option is evaluated according to the attractiveness of its consequences, weighted by their likelihood of being obtained.

Since it has become acceptable to question the descriptive validity of this rule, voluminous research has looked at how well it predicts behavior. Its conclusions parallel those from research in clinical judgment, which ignores questions of value and focuses on questions of diagnosis:

1. The expectation rule often predicts people's choices fairly well—if one knows how they evaluate the probability and attractiveness of consequences. This is more likely to be the case in a structured setting with experimenter-supplied stimuli than in an unconstrained real-world setting, where people's values and beliefs are hard to determine (Lebow and Stein, 1987; Tetlock, 1987, 1989). However, the predictive power of linear models means that rough approximations of people's perceptions will produce reasonable approximations of their choices. Given the noisiness of many decision-making processes and the limits to introspections even when people attempt to describe their thoughts candidly, it may be hard to predict decisions much more accurately.

2. With enough ingenuity, one can usually find some set of subjective evaluations for which the rule would dictate choosing the selected option—meaning that it is hard to demonstrate that the rule has not been used. Some of the more imaginative "fudge factors" fall into the categories of *transaction costs:* decision making itself is seen as incurring costs and the process is managed to keep

them down. Thus, a decision that seems to select a suboptimal alternative can be reinterpreted as the result of having worked with a simplified view of the world to minimize transaction costs. Although such speculations can be disciplined (see, for example, Simon, 1957; Williamson, 1981), that requires considerable effort.

3. Expectation rules often predict the outcome of decision-making processes well, even when they do not capture the thought processes involved, so that predicting behavior is not sufficient for understanding or aiding it (Abelson and Levi, 1985; Dawes, 1979; Fischhoff, 1988b; Schoemaker, 1983). More process-oriented approaches reveal a more complicated situation. People are unlikely to report attempting anything as computationally demanding as an expectation rule or to feel comfortable using it when it is proposed to them (Lichtenstein, Slovic, and Zink, 1969). To the extent that they do compute, they often seem to use quite different rules. Indeed, they even seem unimpressed by the assumptions used to justify the expectation rule. To the extent that they do not compute, people use a variety of simple rules whose dictates may be roughly similar to those of the expectation rule, or very different. These range from such simple ones as "do as we've always done, unless it got us into big trouble last time" to fairly sophisticated techniques for efficiently screening large sets of options. One common feature of these competing rules is that they can be expressed in simple terms that provide a ready justification for the chosen option. A second feature is a reluctance to deal explicitly with uncertainty. The extra weight given a certainty can make it possible to change the attractiveness of options simply by changing their presentations to highlight their certain consequences. For example, an insurance policy that covers fire rather but not flood is more attractive when viewed as full protection against the specific loss of fire than as a reduction in the overall probability of property loss (Abelson and Levi, 1985; Janis and Mann, 1977; Kahneman and Tversky, 1979b; Payne, 1982; Simon, 1957; Slovic and Tversky, 1974).

An extreme, but not uncommon way to circumvent these expectation and computation problems is to avoid analytic decision making altogether, relying on trial-and-error learning. Instead of trying to think one's way through to a right answer, one hopes to shape that answer gradually by responding to flaws that appear in one's initial attempts (Hogarth, 1981). This hands-on experience might be particularly useful for discovering the high-order consequences of particular options (by seeing what really happens when they are tried). As mentioned earlier, the effectiveness of learning by doing may account, in part, for people's failure to develop fully the analytical skills needed when one must get a decision right the first time.[1]

Summary

The significance of these results from experimental studies depends on how common they are outside the laboratory, how much insight they provide into improving decision making, and how adversely the problems that they reveal can affect the optimality of decisions. As might be expected, there is no simple answer to any of these questions. Life poses a variety of decisions, some of which are sensitive to even modest imprecision in their formulation or in the estimation of their parameters, some of which yield an optimal choice with almost any sensible procedure, and some of which can tolerate occasional inaccuracies, but not recurrent biases, such as persistently exaggerating how much one knows (Henrion, 1980; Krzysztofowicz, 1983; von Winterfeldt and Edwards, 1982). Placing decisions within a group or organizational context may ameliorate or exacerbate problems, depending on how carefully members scrutinize one another's decisions, how independent the perspectives are that they bring to that scrutiny, and whether that social context has an incentive structure that rewards effective decision making, as opposed to rewarding posturing or affirmation of common misconceptions (Davis, 1982; Lanir, 1982; Myers and Lamm, 1976).

The robustness of laboratory results is an empirical question. Where evidence is available, it generally suggests that these judgmental problems are more than experimental artifacts, of the sort that can be removed by such "routine" measures as encouraging people to work harder, raising the stakes contingent on their performance, clarifying the instructions, varying the subject matter of the tasks used in experiments, or using better educated subjects (Abelson and Levi, 1985; Fischhoff, 1982a).[2] There are many fewer studies than one would like regarding the judgmental performance of experts working in their own areas of expertise. What studies there are suggest reason for concern, indicating that experts have cognitive process like those of everyone else, unless they have had the conditions needed to master a particular kind of judgment as a learned skill (Abelson and Levi, 1985; Fischhoff, 1982a; von Winterfeldt and Edwards, 1986).

The litany of problems in this literature paints quite a dismal picture of people's ability to make novel, or analytic, decisions—so much so that the investigators doing this work have been accused of being problem mongers (Berkeley and Humphreys, 1982; Jungermann, 1983). Of course, if one hopes to help people, then the problems are what matter, for they provide a point of entry and leverage. In addition to meaning well, investigators in this area have also had a basically respectful attitude toward the object of their studies. It is not people, but their performance that is shown in a negative light. Where that performance is found lacking, the absence of an opportunity to learn is invoked. Indeed, in the history of the behavioral sciences, interest in judgmental biases came as part of a "cognitive" backlash to psychoanalysis, with its often dark interpretation of human foibles. The cognitive perspective showed how biases could (also) emerge from honest, unemotional thought processes.

Typically, these minitheories show people processing information in reasonable ways that often work well, but that can lead to predictable trouble. A simple example would be relying on habit or tradition as a guide to decision making. That might be an efficient way of making relatively good decisions, but it would lead one astray if conditions had changed or if those past decisions reflected values that were no longer applicable. A slightly more sophisticated example is reliance on the "availability heuristic" for estimating the likelihood of events for which adequate statistical information is lacking (Tversky and Kahneman, 1973). As mentioned earlier, this is a rule of thumb by which events are judged likely if it is easy to imagine them happening or remember them having occurred in the past. Although it is generally true that more likely events are more available, use of the rule would lead to exaggerating the likelihood of events that have been overreported in the media or are the topic of personal worry.

The list of problems suggests some procedures that might be incorporated in on-line decision aids, as well as in their low-technology human counterparts. To counteract the tendency to neglect significant options or consequences, an aid could provide checklists with generic possibilities (Beach et al., 1976; Hammer, 1980; Janis, 1982). To reduce the tendency for overconfidence, an aid could force users to list reasons why they might be wrong before assessing the likelihood that they are right (Koriat, Lichtenstein, and Fischhoff, 1980). To discourage hindsight bias, an aid could preserve the decision makers' rationale by showing how things looked at the time the decision was made (Fischhoff, 1982b). To avoid incomplete value elicitation, an aid could force users to consider alternative perspectives and to reconcile the differences among them (Behn and Vaupel, 1983; Fischhoff, Slovic, and Lichtenstein, 1980), or, at least those seem like plausible procedures. Whether they work is an empirical question. For each intervention, one could think of reasons why it might not work, at least if done crudely; for example, long checklists might reduce the attention paid to individual options, leading to broad but superficial analyses.

More comprehensive interventions would include intensive training, to confer the general intuitions needed for effective judgments of all kinds, and intensive aiding, to step decision makers through the solutions of specific problems. One threat to the former strategy is that the training will be ineffective, leaving people more confident in their judgment but no more accurate.

For example, like many statistics classes, the training may succeed in teaching the formal rules of inference, but not the ability to diagnose real-world situations in those terms (Alpert and Raiffa, 1982). One threat to the latter strategy is that sound advice may involve inferential processes so different from decision makers' natural thought processes that they are left uncertain about how far the advice is to be trusted and whose problem is really being solved.

These are the kinds of interventions that will be considered in the following sections, each of which considers one class of nuclear decisions and the threats to its validity. That discussion will assume the accuracy of the preceding descriptive account of judgmental processes and the possibility of the preceding list of potential interventions. However, all the accompanying caveats apply and will be summarized in a concluding section.

The Command and Control of Nuclear Weapons

The first line of offense and defense for a nuclear power is the organization managing its nuclear weapons (Ball, 1981; Bracken, 1983; Brewer and Bracken, 1984; Carter, 1985; Tucker, 1983; Zraket, 1984). Typically, that organization is intended to have "merely" an executive function, namely, following the orders of political leaders. Nonetheless, the individuals within such organizations make numerous decisions that shape the perceptions and, hence, the decisions of those leaders. The most obvious of these decisions are responses to immediate events. Operators must decide, for example, whether the observations that prompted a Missile Display Conference (MDC) merit "escalation" to a Threat Assessment Conference (TAC); how recent political events should affect the interpretation of reports from electronic sensors; or, whether to assume that the president is still part of the National Command Authority, rather than being dead or just out of communication (Steinbruner, 1981–1982). Ways to aid these decisions are discussed, in part, in the sections below on crisis decision making and contingency planning.

Less obvious, and potentially more critical, are decisions made in the design of these command-and-control systems that shape their subsequent operational decisions. For example, what are the conditions calling for a MDC or TAC, and how should those general conditions be translated into concrete directives (Hwang et al., 1982)? How should political and electronic data be displayed to facilitate their integration (Wohl, 1981)? What trade-off between false alarms and false positives should the system strive to attain (Pate-Cornell and Neu, 1985)? Some of these decisions are made overtly and are expressed in a system's design philosophy or in the instructions to its technical operators. Other design decisions are made indirectly, as the product of decisions about the promotion and training of operators or about the choice and maintenance of equipment. For example, many fail-safe systems "work" as well as they do only because the people in them have learned, by trial and error, to manage problems that are not supposed to happen (Perrow, 1984; Rasmussen, Duncan, and Leplat, 1987; Rochlin, LaPorte, and Roberts, 1987). If the existence of such unofficial organizational intelligence has no place in the system's formal design, then it may have to be hidden, may be unable to get needed resources (for example, for record keeping or realistic exercises), and may be destroyed by any changes in the system. These changes can invalidate operators' understanding of those intricacies of the system's operation that do not appear in plans or training manuals (Tushman and Anderson, 1986).

From this perspective, the quest for perfection can threaten system performance (by denying operators the opportunity to learn the system's quirks), as can rapid changes in technology (by changing the character of those quirks). The quest can also lead to "deskilling," whereby critical intellectual skills are allowed to atrophy in a largely automated system (Sheridan et al., 1984). In such systems, operators assume a largely supervisory role, being forced "back into the loop" only for the most difficult and nonroutine decisions, at times when the system's state may be most difficult to discern, especially for those who have not had their "hands on the controls" continuously (Fischhoff and Johnson, 1990; Hollnagel, Mancini, and Woods, 1986; Moray, 1987; Rasmussen and Rouse, 1982). Thus, ironically, concern for protecting operators from information overload during routine operations can produce unmanageable cognitive tasks during a time of crisis. Furthermore, the system only "works" routinely because experienced operators have mastered its quirks. In that case, great efforts should be made to retain experienced operators and avoid the regular turnover found, for example, at U.S. North American Air Defense Command Committee (NORAD) (Committee on Government Operations, 1981).

These problems, and the jargon used to describe them, are those of "human factors engineering," the application of behavioral science research to the design, operation, and staffing of technical systems (Bailey, 1982; Broadbent, 1971; Fitts and Posner, 1965; Salvendy, 1987; Warm and Parasuraman, 1987). Initially, human factors specialists focused on "knobology," the physical interface connecting operator and system (for example, ensuring that pilots can read displays under low-light and high-stress conditions, or that manual controls function similarly in simulators and in the various configurations of the planes they are meant to simulate). Even though these basic lessons are still often unheeded even in advanced technical systems (see, for example, Kirwan, 1987; Perrow, 1984; Sheridan, 1980), human factors research has in-

creasingly focused on the design of more intellectual interfaces, those intended to support decision making (Brown, 1988; Helander, 1987; Rasmussen,
1986; Sage, 1981). Indeed, much of the funding for basic research in decision
making (and decision aiding) has come from sources concerned about people's performance in technologically saturated military environments—the
Office of Naval Research, Army Research Institute, Air Force Office of Scientific Research, and Defense Advanced Projects Research Agency. But that is,
of course, no guarantee that the research has affected the operational systems
in any way. The lament of most human factors practitioners is that their craft
is either unknown or invoked at such a late stage in the design process that it
can amount to little more than the development of warning labels or training
programs for coping with inhuman systems (Meister, 1987; Perrow, 1983).
Investigations of the inadvertent U.S. downing of an Iranian civilian airliner
in 1988 have focused on how well the decision support systems actually
supported its operators (Fogarty, 1988; Helmrich, 1988; Pew, 1988).

One reason that designers ignore the research literature is that it is so easy
to speculate about human behavior (and perhaps provide a little supporting
anecdotal evidence) that systematic empirical research hardly seems necessary. A second reason is that the qualitative advice provided by human factors
research may seem quite vague alongside the quantitative prescriptions coming from, say, electronics or materials science. In the absence of direct human
factors input, insensitive design is particularly likely when the designers have
never been operators, are physically removed from actual operations (so that
they cannot observe problems), or have higher social status than operators (so
that they need not attend to problems). A common sign of insensitivity is
using the term "operator error" to describe problems arising from the interaction of operator and system. A rule of thumb might be that human problems
seldom have purely technical solutions, while technical solutions typically
create human problems (Perrow, 1983; Seminara and Parson, 1982; Sheridan,
1980).

Anticipating how operators will make the decisions required by command-
and-control systems for nuclear weapons requires a detailed task analysis,
first, of what the decisions are and, second, of the cognitive demands that
they impose (Andriole and Hopple, 1982). Where the design process has been
relatively insensitive to the needs of operators, there is little reason to expect
the system to ameliorate, instead of exacerbate, human limitations. Thus, one
may find people's general discomfort in dealing with uncertainty emerging in
telecommunications protocols that discourage the expression of uncertainty
by others and reduce the opportunities for nonverbal expressions of confidence; the system may increase the amount of information generated and

transmitted, without addressing the problem of determining what is relevant; fancy electronic displays may enhance people's inability to detect omissions or to integrate off-display information; or, the interoperability of equipment may suddenly bring into contact decision makers at distributed sites who lack the shared understanding needed for effective communication (Coulam and Fischer, 1985; Kiesler, Siegel, and McGuire, 1984; March and Weissinger-Baylon, 1985).

Where the design process is sensitive to operators' needs, behavioral decision-making researchers could attempt solutions such as special displays for representing uncertain information, protocols for communication among friendly strangers, training programs for making do with "unfriendly" systems, contingency plans for coping with predictable system failures, and systems that lend themselves to trouble-shooting even at the risk of accepting a higher rate of troubles. Such solutions should be grounded in existing research and subjected to rigorous testing that will, in part, establish the generalizability of that research.

Although these solutions might make systems better, they are unlikely to make them whole. As a result, the design of a system is incomplete without an assessment of its reliability. That assessment is essential for giving those who depend on a system realistic expectations of its performance (Britten, 1983; Bunn and Tsipis, 1983; Cimbala, 1987; Fischhoff, 1988a; Frei, 1983; Wallace, Crissey, and Sennott, 1986; Zraket, 1984). Without such expectations, the nuclear power operating a fallible command-and-control system cannot responsibly evaluate strategic policies, determine the risk of accidental nuclear war, or estimate the effect of changes in technology or policy on that risk. Overestimating the operability of command-and-control systems means underestimating closeness to the brink.

It is equally important to understand the reliability of opponents' command-and-control systems. That assessment might provide valuable cautionary messages regarding the kinds of challenges that the opponent is least likely to handle effectively. Indeed, each power might unilaterally issue recommendations to the effect, "Don't test us in this way unless you really mean it. We're not equipped to respond flexibly." Of course, such warnings might not seem possible, because they would reveal critical technical information, and they might not be trusted, because they could be used for strategic purposes. In such cases, the unreliability of the command-and-control system would introduce a seemingly irreducible uncertainty into the international system.

Even attempting such reliability assessments requires the leadership needed to be candid about one's own limitations. That leadership may be particularly difficult in a political climate where the proficiency of weapons systems must be exaggerated in order for them to secure financial support. Being committed to assessing system reliability is a necessary, but not sufficient, condition to securing such assessments. Over the last 30 years, sophisticated analytical techniques have been developed, capable of studying the reliability of systems whose complexity defies intuitive comprehension (General Accounting Office, 1986; McCormick, 1981; Suokas, 1988; U.S. Nuclear Regulatory Commission, 1983). However, even these techniques are sorely stretched when critical system components (for example, interlinked equipment, computer software) have never experienced the actual conditions under which they will eventually be tested, making their performance the object of that educated guesswork called "expert judgment" (Turner, 1978). There has been relatively little systematic study of the particular judgments entering strategic analyses (Fischer, 1983; Holdren, 1976; Rosenau, 1974; Tihansky, 1976). However, the studies seem to be exercised under conditions providing little of the

TABLE 3.3   Some Problems in Structuring Risk Assessments

Failure to consider the ways in which human errors can affect technological systems.
>Example: Owing to inadequate training and control room design, operators at Three Mile Island, Pennsylvania, repeatedly misdiagnosed the problems of the reactor and took inappropriate actions (Sheridan, 1980; U.S. Government, 1979).

Overconfidence in current scientific knowledge.
>Example: DDT came into widespread and uncontrolled use before scientists had even considered the possibility of the side effects that today make it look like a mixed blessing (Dunlap, 1978).

Failure to appreciate how technological systems function as a whole.
>Example: The DC-10 failed in several early flights because its designers had not realized that decompression of the cargo compartment would destroy vital control systems (Hohenemser, 1975).

Slowness in detecting chronic, cumulative effects.
>Example: Although accidents to coal miners have long been recognized as one cost of operating fossil-fueled plants, people were slow to discover the effects of acid rain on ecosystems (Rosencranz and Wetstone, 1980).

Failure to anticipate human response to safety measures.
>Example: The partial protection afforded by dams and levees gives people a false sense of security and promotes development of floodplains. Thus, although floods are rarer, damage per flood is much greater than the average yearly loss in dollars before the dams were built (Burton, Kates, and White, 1978).

Failure to anticipate common-mode failures, which simultaneously afflict systems that are designed to be independent.
>Example: Because electrical cables controlling the multiple safety systems of the reactor at Browns Ferry, Alabama, were not spatially separated, all five emergency core-cooling systems were damaged by a single fire (Jennergren and Keeney, 1983; U.S. Government, 1975).

Source: Fischhoff et al. (1981).

feedback needed for skilled performance. Table 3.3 offers one collection of judgmental oversights in professional analyses.

The human aspect of system performance is particularly resistant to formal analysis. Although considerable progress has been made in predicting functions such as vision or motor performance (National Research Council, 1988; Swain and Guttman, 1982), there is little in the way of proven methods for modeling features like shared misperceptions among operators (Adams, 1982; Embry, 1986; Pidgeon, Blockley, and Turner, 1987; Woods, Roth, and Pople, 1987). Inevitably, such "analyses" rely heavily on human judgment, as designers and operators attempt to guess how various components of the system will perform in (more and less) unique circumstances. As discussed earlier, such judgments are not only fallible, but they also force substantive experts to express themselves in a somewhat unfamiliar modeling language. If the experts cannot translate what they know into the terms of the modeling language, then the model may miss or even misrepresent their beliefs (Fischhoff, 1989; Poulton, 1982; Turner and Martin, 1984).

Thus, potentially fallible judgment and decision making is an inevitable part of military command-and-control. Without an appreciation of these limits, strategic policies will be but fictions, producing systems whose actual operations are quite different from what they were intended to be. Appreciating this vulnerability allows one to perform a task analysis of how it affects system design and operation. A minimal result would be a more realistic expectation. A more ambitious one would be to improve the system's reliability and controllability by making its design more sensitive to its operators' need to make judgments and decisions.

Managing a Distributed Diplomatic Corps

Partly to avoid testing their military forces, countries maintain diplomatic corps. When the home governments' efforts to preserve understanding fail, then these corps may serve as agents for keeping crises from escalating into conflicts, for fighting those conflicts more effectively, or for bringing them to an end. Historically, the challenge in managing a diplomatic corps has been to achieve an appropriate balance between centralization and autonomy in decision making. Representatives must have enough freedom to be able to solve problems in ways that exploit their local knowledge and contacts, but enough constraints to ensure that those solutions represent national policy.

For diplomats, performing this role has required the full range of intellectual skills involved in judgment and decision making. They have had to generate options, gather information, assess the implications of general policies for specific circumstances, communicate the rationales for their choices, learn from historical instances, and so on. Typically, their choices have been made by raw intuition, buttressed perhaps by technical analyses of particular points of information (for example, the economic consequences of an action or the speed with which funds or troops could be transferred).

One ambitious exploitation of behavioral research would be to identify cases in which those intuitive processes are not to be trusted—meaning that one should increase reliance on formal analysis. For example, analysis might be required in cases where decision makers must extrapolate the future state of exponentially growing processes (for example, the spread of a new weapons system), estimate the cumulative uncertainty surrounding a decision with many unclear components, estimate the absolute number of violations to be expected from a cease-fire where each side has incomplete control over its forces, or evaluate the accuracy of intelligence sources—all tasks related to ones for which judgmental problems have been demonstrated in more benign circumstances. Formal analyses can capture only a portion of any interesting problem. However, they can provide a check on intuition, particularly when their results are counterintuitive—and somehow must be reconciled with intuitions.

An even more ambitious exploitation of this research would be to try to train better intuitions. Unfortunately, there are few proven techniques for doing so. Indeed, it is hard to point to any validated courses dedicated to teaching judgment and decision making (or other aspects of "thinking") as general cognitive skills (Beyth-Marom et al., in press; Resnick, 1987). There are courses that teach specific analytical skills (for example, statistics, operations research, or economics). However, it is unclear that they change *how* graduates think. Of particular concern is whether coursework enables graduates to diagnose messy real-world situations in ways that allow application of textbook methods, or whether it even prompts the search for such solutions. Training (like any other kind of aiding) can even be deleterious if it leaves performance untouched, but increases confidence.

There are also numerous courses of study that attempt, through an apprenticeship process, to inculcate the ability to perform some specialized judgment, such as that involved in medical diagnosis (Elstein, Shulman, and Sprafka, 1978). These courses presumably achieve the best performance currently possible. However, it may be unclear just how good that performance is or how readily it generalizes from the cases studied to the cases encountered. Weather forecasters, as shown in Figure 3.2, achieve quite excellent performance in at least one of the judgments that they make repeatedly. It seems unlikely that diplomats would have similar circumstances or similar achievements (Brecher, 1974). They see too few cases, receive too poor feedback on what was really happening (or on what they really should have done), and live in too unstable a world to rely on proven solutions (O'Leary et al., 1974).

Much of the research in judgment and decision making has been conducted with an eye to "debiasing" (Fischhoff, 1982a), namely, the development of general procedures for helping people to use their minds more effectively— both within analyses and without the benefit of analysis. Some suggestions, supported by varying amounts of evidence,

1. explicitly list reasons why a favored belief might be wrong, before relying on it (Koriat, Lichtenstein, and Fischhoff, 1980);

2. explicitly imagine how an event might have otherwise turned out before judging its inevitability in hindsight (Slovic and Fischhoff, 1977);

3. create some simple models to check the accuracy of quantitative estimates (Singer, 1971);

4. rely on explicit calculation, rather than on mental arithmetic (Armstrong, Dennison, and Gordon, 1975);

5. record the reasons for decisions, to facilitate evaluating them in the light of subsequent experience (Fischhoff, 1982b);

6. explicitly review past experiences, rather than rely on memory for reviewing them (Kahneman and Tiversky, 1979a);

7. find out how other people conceptualize a problem (but without plying them for recommendations), in order to gain alternative perspectives without incurring additional social pressures (Janis and Mann, 1977);

8. sample a few concrete examples, in order to check generalizations (Evans, 1982);

9. consider what usually happens in a particular situation, to avoid placing too much weight on case-specific information (Bar-Hillel, 1980);

10. model other actors' situations in detail, to gain perspective on one's own (Svenson and Fischhoff, 1985);

11. specify in advance what conditions could show a belief to be wrong (O'Leary et al., 1974);

12. use a list of objectives as an aid to generating options (Pitz, Sachs, and Heerboth, 1980);

13. learn to identify and walk away from "sunk costs," judging actions solely by the expected return from future investments (Dawes, 1988; Thaler, 1980);

14. express uncertainties in numerical probabilities, rather than verbal quantifiers—for example, "likely" (Beyth-Marom, 1982a).

It is an empirical question whether these techniques work at all, whether they can be embedded in substantively meaningful training exercises, and whether the "enlightened" judgments that they produce can weather debates with less enlightened colleagues.

Analogous manipulations can be seen in some of the procedures that organizations institute in order to overcome the cognitive limitations of their individual members. For example, they use brainstorming sessions to generate alternative perspectives. They routinize performance reviews in order to look systematically at how well people are doing. They solicit proposal reviews in order to elicit reasons why favored beliefs might be wrong. These processes can fail, as when groupthink stifles alternative perspectives (Janis, 1972; Tetlock, 1979), when group polarization processes (once called "risky shift") lead a group to a position that few of its members would adopt independently (Myers and Lamm, 1976), or when "pluralistic ignorance" keeps members from realizing their areas of disagreement (Fiske and Taylor, 1984; Nisbett and Ross, 1980). Such failures can be encouraged by faulty institutional design (for example, restricting communication among individuals with differing experiences or inhibiting the sharing of uncertainties) (March and Simon, 1958; Wilensky, 1967). However, even the best design probably can do no more than make success possible. The people in the organization must still make it happen, by adjusting the official organizational structure and policies to their circumstances and personalities.

That adjustment process can, however, be threatened by any changes in the organization's internal or external environment. For a diplomatic corps, the greatest contemporary changes are probably due to modern technology (Harris, 1986). It increases the speed with which decisions must be made and the degree of supervision that central governments can exert over their representatives. In time, an organization could adjust to such differences, through a combination of formal and informal changes in procedures. That is, through trial and error, it could develop rules that ensured local diplomats the latitude needed to do their job—despite the presence of telecommunications systems that allow (or perhaps compel) them to report instantaneously on their activities. A corps could also try to facilitate the personal relations needed to "fine tune" the balance between autonomy and central control (for example, through its transfer and promotion policies). However, until an organization has had the time to recognize and remediate an imbalance, its performance will be affected. For diplomatic corps, one result of better telecommunications might be greater involvement of central government figures in situations formerly managed by diplomats on site. This might produce more coordinated policies or ineffective meddling by newcomers who are out of their depths (for example, because they lack local knowledge or negotiation skills) (Chain, Dixon, & Weissinger-Baylon, 1986; Lanir, Fischhoff, and Johnson, 1988; Metcalf, 1986).

Crisis Decision Making

Nuclear crises arise after diplomatic (or perhaps command-and-control) processes have failed (Holsti, 1989). These situations threaten not only the deliberate use of nuclear weapons, but also the increased chance of their accidental use—if only because the operators of command-and-control systems will be thrust into novel situations, for which the systems' quirks are poorly understood. As a result, crises must not only be managed, but they must be managed quickly, before they take on a life of their own (George, 1984).

Dr. Johnson was doubtless right in claiming that the threat of impending doom marvelously focuses the mind. Unfortunately, a focused mind need not be an effective one. In crisis situations, leaders may "need to analyze large amounts of ambiguous and inconsistent evidence under severe time pressure, always with the knowledge that miscalculations may have serious consequences for their own careers and vital national interests" (Tetlock and McGuire, 1986:270). Converging behavioral evidence suggests that the "disruptive stress" of such situations can "reduce the complexity and quality of information processing. The [attending] impairment includes a lessened likelihood of accurately identifying and discriminating among unfamiliar stimuli; rigid reliance on old, now inappropriate problem-solving strategies; reduced search for new information; and heightened intolerance for inconsistent evidence" (Tetlock and McGuire, 1986:270–271). There is little reason to think that high stress and high stakes alone would be conducive to the particular skills involved in nuclear decisions (Fischhoff, 1982a; Holsti, 1989; Janis and Mann, 1977; Wright and Barbour, 1977).

Although it seems possible to train people in the skills needed for crisis decision making, as discussed in the previous section, no proven method exists. Any such training would have to be quite intense if decision makers were not to "regress," under stress, to earlier and more deeply learned skills. Given the other peacetime demands on the senior officials who would be involved in crisis management, they are unlikely to subject themselves to such training (even if a more convincing case could be made for its efficacy). Leaders who attributed their current posts to their decision-making ability should be particularly uninterested (Holsti, 1989).

Those who control resources can often affect the outcomes of their decisions in ways that lend apparent confirmation to overconfident judgments (Einhorn and Hogarth, 1978). Conceivably, those who have the ability to survive bureaucratic and political wars may adversely select individuals relative to their ability to manage crises that might lead to nuclear wars.

Leaders' confidence in their own abilities is likely to shape the sort of staff work they request in crisis (or other) situations (Schelling, 1984). The perennial challenge for staff is to be heard when they feel that they are needed. With its suggestion of overconfident leaders, whose thought processes are overfocused in time of stress, the research literature on cognitive processes merely suggests further obstacles to staff being heard (perhaps just confirming what staff know all too well). The complementary research literature on group dynamics shows the social psychological barriers facing attempts to implement such apparently sensible solutions as having staff (1) play the role of "devil's advocate" for alternative perspectives, (2) routinely suggest reasons why leaders' favored beliefs might be wrong, or (3) present analyses made precrisis of something like the current contingency (George, 1972; Janis, 1972).

Plying the cognitive literature produces suggestions such as the following for making the best of such difficult situations: if staff have messages that they feel need to be heard, then those should be expressed in ways that conform to recipients' intuitive thought processes. For example, if the likelihood of scenarios is determined by their imaginability, then imaginability should be manipulated in proposals and briefings. If people think better by analogy with known instances than by abstract principles, then it would pay to have a repertoire of concrete historical examples with which to illustrate messages (Neustadt and May, 1986; Resnick, 1987). If people tend to neglect base rates (Bar-Hillel, 1980), then one should be ready to remind them of what has usually happened in similar situations. If people exaggerate the degree to which they have the initiative and ability to shape situations (Ross and Sicoly, 1979), then staff must explicate opponents' options.

Quite a different strategy for staff to become effective in stressful situations is to become masters of stress (Cook, 1987; Goldberger and Breznitz, 1982; Suedfeld and Tetlock, 1977). Within the military, the career path for combat leaders begins with arduous training in maintaining their wits under acute stresses (Koranyi, 1977). Officers lead by their demeanor, as well as by their knowledge (Keegan, 1987); staff who seem in control of themselves are more likely to influence others. Similarly, leaders who lack such experiences might benefit from training in acute-stress management. Its most likely vehicle would be simulation exercises of potential nuclear crises. If leaders can be persuaded to participate in them, then attention should be paid to the simulations' visceral, as well as factual, verisimilitude (Bredemeier and Greenblat, 1981; Norris and Snyder, 1982).

Simulations are often used for training purposes, to convey information, to show how to use equipment, and to test operators' mastery of accepted solutions (Flexman and Stark, 1987). There are, however, cognitive reasons to worry about the validity of simulator experiences (Caro, 1988; Thompson, 1983). For example, do those who develop the exercises and evaluate participants' performance share some deep misconceptions about the world, so that critical crises and solutions are never considered? Do people interpret cues of evolving crises differently in the simulator than in the corresponding reality, where they are not necessarily primed to expect problems or held accountable in the same ways? Are simulator responses overlearned so that they come to dominate future thinking, in the way that a salient historical example might (May, 1973; Vertzberger, 1986)? Do simulators create an expectation of crisis, leading to much different responses than everyday life with its expectation of tedium (Broadbent, 1971; Warm and Parasuraman, 1987)?

In crisis management, as elsewhere, technology will shape the decision-making process. Key internal factors may be the deluge of information and unfamiliar communication protocols. Leaders may have too much information coming at them, too little experience in managing its flow, and inadequate time to discover who knows and assumes what among those in the command structure (Allison, 1971; Coulam and Fischer, 1985; March and Weissinger-Baylon, 1985). Externally, there is the risk of ineffective communication when unfamiliar channels are used. For example, there are many possible lessons to take from the Reykjavik summit meetings of 1986. One is that a meeting "in four eyes" provides no assurance of understanding, even between leaders who to some extent desire it, if they are unaccustomed to direct interaction. A recurrent proposal for crisis management is to upgrade the fidelity of the "hot line" connecting U.S. and Soviet leaders. Yet, one must wonder how well they will be able to exploit this unconventional medium, especially if it is used first under the direst of circumstances. It is all too easy to assume that one's verbal and nonverbal communications have achieved just the intended effect, even when the recipient is from another culture and under intense stress (Neale and Bazerman, 1985). By the same token, any suggestion of a joint crisis-management center should consider seriously the "human factors" details of the environment that it creates, both for the joint crisis managers and for those who must communicate with them (Allison, Nye, and Carnesale, 1985; Ury and Smoke, 1984; Woods, Roth, and Pople, 1987).

Contingency Planning

In order to improve coping with potential and actual crises, countries (as well as organizations, groups, and individuals) engage in contingency planning. Possible problems are anticipated, the best response to each is identified, and then those responses are incorporated in the training of the individuals who will be at the helm when the contingencies arise. These preemptive decisions are expected to benefit from reduced time pressure and emotional stress, as well as from the opportunity to recruit experts and conduct research.

Achieving this potential requires a number of variants on the basic intellectual skills involved in all decision making. At the planning stage, these skills include imagining the relevant contingencies, elaborating their details, generating alternative responses for evaluation, evaluating those responses critically in a hypothetical mode, and communicating the resultant decisions to those who must execute them. At the execution stage, these skills include recognizing that some contingency has arisen quickly enough to access the set of plans, matching the concrete contingency with the appropriate hypothetical one, and adjusting the plan to the nuances of the specific situation. Failure at either stage can result in inappropriate plans, perhaps even worse than the plans produced in spontaneous responses to crises. Subordinates required to implement poor plans may feel deep distress. Leaders faced with seemingly inappropriate plans may just cut the telephone lines to the plan repository and go with their intuitions.

Thus, contingency planners face the dual challenge of first getting the analysis right and then making it seem right to its ultimate consumers. Potential contributions of behavioral decision research to contingency planning are analogous to those for the analysis of command-and-control systems: identifying where judgment enters the planning process, characterizing threats to the quality of that judgment, offering ways to improve its quality, and assessing the overall trustworthiness of plans, considering the cumulative role of fallible judgment in them. Where the fallibility of plans has been acknowledged, policymakers still need help in improvising alternatives.

Uncovering the full range of uncertainty surrounding an analysis requires a deliberate effort to solicit competing schools of thought. The institutional barriers to such openness may be considerable (McCormick, 1983). On the one hand, it means involving more people in shaping the analysis. Diverse material scientists are needed to elicit the range of possible opinions regarding the precise magnitude of the failure rate for a valve in a weapons system; diverse Soviet specialists are needed to uncover the possible ways in which a particular U.S. move will be interpreted (Cohen, 1986; Jervis, Lebow and Stein, 1985). Even where the numbers are manageable, political or interpersonal pressures may still drive opposing views from an analytical organization or keep them from ever being hired (Herken, 1985; Markey, 1985). Social pressures may restrict the kinds of people who acquire specialized knowledge in an area. For example, one legacy of the Vietnam War has been the relative paucity of technically informed comment about defense systems from individuals on the political left in the United States. As a result, analytical errors that are more visible from that perspective have probably gone systematically uncorrected. Indeed, the sort of controversy that is essential to understanding complex defense issues may be forthcoming only when the interests of the different armed services clash. Social processes may also restrict the supply of "experts" to individuals with an axe to grind. For example, Middle East "studies" seem to be populated heavily by individuals whose analyses are driven by their conclusions, rather than vice versa. Incorporating such individuals in an orderly analytical process may strain any organization. Even when experts are committed to separating their appraisal of political facts from their political values, it may be hard to do so. Such separation requires not only an unusual degree of self-reflection, but also a deep understanding of the epistemology of one's field. For example, whenever resources are needed to create evidence (for example, by sponsoring research), those who control the purse strings may impose their values on the debate by failing to create facts that would make competitors' options into credible alternatives (Bazelon, 1979; Campen, 1986; Levine, 1974; Mazur, Marino, and Becker, 1979). The behavioral-decision research literature suggests that asking about such hidden assumptions is an unlikely question that is hard to answer. One sign of how vulnerable particular experts' judgments are to such problems might be the extent to which epistemological reflections are part of routine empirical research, instead of being relegated to low-circulation specialty journals.

A further intellectual barrier to recruiting alternative perspectives is that experts from competing schools may question not only particular assumptions of one another's analyses (for example, the Soviet interpretation of a U.S. move), but also their entire conceptualization (Jervis, 1984; Krepon, 1984; Kull, 1988; Rosenau and Holsti, 1983). Even with a strong commitment to openmindedness, it may be very difficult to express strongly divergent views within a single analysis. The only viable alternative may be conducting and presenting competing analyses in parallel. If the operative conclusions of these analyses converge, despite their diverging assumptions, then confidence should increase. If not, the decision makers must somehow integrate these incompatible views and recommendations. The very fact that the experts cannot agree should offer a valuable cautionary message, namely, that the situation is relatively unpredictable. However, it might be interpreted as meaning that "my guess is as good as theirs." Dismissing the experts may be particularly attractive when it is realized that their competing perspectives lay a firm foundation for second guessing leaders' eventual decisions, whatever they do. The competition guarantees that it can be said in hindsight that "some of your own advisors warned you that. . . ." The procedures suggested earlier offer some hope of protecting oneself from exercising hindsight bias. Keeping oneself from becoming the victim of someone else's biased judgment means taking debiasing procedures a step further than they have been taken in the laboratory.

Being judged harshly is a common experience for the analysts of social systems. In hindsight, it is typically easy to see signs that they overlooked, "despite their purported expertise" (Wohlstetter, 1962). Given the choice between blaming leaders and their advisors for miscues, many people will prefer to conclude that the leaders did the right thing given what they were told, thereby deflecting responsibility to the experts who were doing the telling (Betts, 1978; Chan, 1979). A risky form of preemptive defense against such criticism is to stress the limited predictability of complex phenomena, thereby emphasizing just how much (or little) certainty has been promised (Shlaim, 1976). One risk of this strategy is to be ignored altogether by leaders content to rely on their own best guesses; a second is to be upstaged by competing experts with more bravado. In some ways, the role of responsible contingency planners resembles that of responsible investment counselors—who claim only to do a little better than just betting the market, but view that as sufficient grounds for seeking their advice (Dreman, 1982).

One way to substantiate and regulate claims to expertise would be to create an explicit track record. Following U.S. National Weather Service forecasters (Murphy and Winkler, 1984), strategic analysts could attach numerical probabilities to their forecasts and see how appropriate their levels of confidence are (Beyth-Marom, 1982a; Heuer, 1978). The very commitment to evaluation should also create conditions more conducive to learning how to make such judgments (for example, ensuring that predictions are sufficiently precise to allow evaluation, and basing evaluations on records rather than on memory). Here, too, there might be institutional resistance. All analyses are fallible; all decisions are gambles. Credit, rather than approbation, should accrue to those who check their own performance. Unfortunately, the politicized atmosphere surrounding many strategic analyses may discourage expressing uncertainty at all. Winning the battle for candor should be a primary responsibility for the agency commissioning an analysis (Armstrong, 1985). Without explicit performance criteria, leaders face a difficult task in evaluating their advisors fairly. The intuitive reasonableness of an analysis is neither necessary nor sufficient for its validity.

Experts would not be needed if they did not sometimes reach surprising conclusions. Understanding the world might not ensure being able to explain it—or at least not in an engaging way. A more legitimate test is to judge the process by which an analysis was produced. Like other forms of applied science, such as survey research, cost-benefit analysis, or evaluation research, strategic analyses may assume more of the rights than the responsibilities of a science. They should, therefore, be judged by how fully they have followed scientific norms. Explicitly acknowledging judgmental assumptions is one such norm. Actively soliciting peer review is another. Identifying omissions is a third. Involving all relevant disciplines on a continuing basis is a fourth. Relying on proven methods, rather than on untested fads with poorly understood frailties, is a fifth.

However much leaders decide to rely on contingency plans, they must be able to access them. For a nuclear power hoping to respond flexibly to challenges, the number of contingency-response combinations may be very large. Some cognitive engineering is needed to make retrieval feasible, especially under time pressure. The structures of the data base and of the leaders' mental representation of the problem must fit one another, changing whichever is more malleable (Fischhoff, MacGregor, and Blackshaw, 1987; Furnas et al., 1983). Once retrieved, plans must be readily comprehended. Information about each plan should follow some common format, sensitive to what leaders want and need to know. Thus, its initial material should include information on its key assumptions, its trustworthiness, and the image it will create for leaders who follow it (that is, will it be good for them, as well as for the nation and world?).

Evaluating (and Creating) Arms Control Proposals

In many cases, time pressure is no threat at all to the formulation and evaluation of arms control proposals. Rather, the pace of negotiations is painstakingly slow, so that all involved have plenty of time to ruminate over proposals and counterproposals. Indeed, it is often considered poor form to raise radically new proposals in circumstances that do not allow deliberate evaluation. Why, with all that time, is it often so difficult for individuals in a single country to agree on the attractiveness of proposals and for the negotiators of different countries to identify proposals that will be mutually acceptable? And what might the study of individual decision making contribute to the discovery of latent agreements?

Perhaps the greatest contribution might come from a sharpened understanding of the reasons for disagreement. From a decision theory perspective, evaluating options requires a factual assessment of the consequences likely to follow from adopting each option and an evaluative assessment of the relative importance of each consequence (Judd and Weisenberger, 1980; Tetlock, 1983). In principle, people could disagree either about the facts or about the values. Knowing which is the case could help focus the political debate over proposals on the most sensitive areas of disagreement. It might even improve the tenor of the debate. For example, it may be reassuring to know that opponents are actually well informed, but have different (although legitimate) goals for national policy. Or, it may be reassuring to know that opponents share the same goals, but disagree about the facts in ways that might be resolved by research. Either case might encourage a political debate that was conducted in cold blood and with mutual respect (Bazerman and Lewicki, 1988).

One vehicle for such clarification is explicitly modeling the decision-making problems that the different parties to a debate believe that their country is facing (Tetlock, 1983). Those models would include the probability and importance attributed to each consequence of each option. If one assumed the decision-making rule used by each party, it might even be possible to perform *sensitivity analyses,* in order to identify the probabilities and importance weights with the greatest impact on the attractiveness of the options. These would be the logical foci of further debate and research.

These descriptions might also help structure the search for new options, by indicating places where one side could give the other a lot without sacrificing very much of importance. If the models were accurate, they could help predict opponents' responses to new proposals. Inappropriate proposals not only fail to achieve agreement but leave a negative affective residue, by showing how little the sides understand one another.

Using the framework of decision theory to organize one's perceptions of others' perceptions need not imply that any of the parties are paragons of rational thinking, say, in the manner of some accounts of deference theory (Lebow and Stein, 1987; Schelling, 1970). Rather, it would provide a disciplined and respectful way of ensuring that all aspects of an opponent's problem are considered, somewhat reducing the threat of ethnocentrism (Raiffa, 1982; Svenson and Fischhoff, 1985). Indeed, dropping the assumption of rationality allows one to exploit such explicit descriptions in order to identify possible areas of suboptimality in each party's model and, hence, the limits to rationalist accounts. For example, options, consequences, or sources of uncertainty might be missing entirely (Cimbala, 1987; Lau and Sears, 1986; White, 1986). Identifying major omissions might contribute more to the debate than arguing the details of those issues that are included (Fraser and Marsh, n.d.; Prins, 1983, 1984). A National Research Council (1975) study of the effects of thermonuclear war was criticized for deliberately failing to consider options for avoiding war and inadvertently neglecting secondary consequences that followed directly from the primary consequences that it had discussed. It observed that the growth of tubers would be relatively unaffected by the increased ultraviolet radiation due to disruption of the earth's ozone shield, but not that the radiation would hamper survivors attempting to work in the fields (Boffey, 1975). In Great Britain, a citizens' group, Scientists Against Nuclear Arms (Quasrawi, 1983), has attempted to undermine official civil defense analyses by showing their neglect of basic aspects of how a nuclear attack might transpire and how citizens might respond to it (for example, would they follow instructions?). U.S. strategic proposals routinely seem to catch its North Atlantic Treaty Organization (NATO) allies by surprise, suggesting that their response is not routinely considered as a consequence in analyses of U.S. options. Adding this consequence to analyses might avoid routine embarrassment and backtracking. Tactfully informing opponents of their own oversights might be interpreted as an act of good faith and increase the chances of lasting agreements, by avoiding problems that would be realized eventually.

A more ambitious—and more common—use of decision-making models is to identify the choices that the parties *should* make, assuming that they want to follow the principles of rational decision making, but need some computational help. That help might be especially useful where there is time pressure (for example, during a nuclear crisis, when new proposals arise during negotiations). Then, plugging the particulars of a specific option into a general evaluative model would be one way of achieving a quick, comprehensive appraisal of its strengths, weaknesses, and overall attractiveness. Indeed, fortunes are spent on defense contracts for assessing the lethality of the arms allowed by different arms control agreements, or for developing online decision aids to help commanders analyze emerging situations.

One risk with such quantitative models is that they are often best suited to readily quantified concerns. That could augment any tendency for defense debates to be dominated by technical considerations (for example, throw weights), with their relatively hard facts, to the detriment of qualitative (for example, political) considerations. On the other hand, it might counterbalance any tendency for background statistical information to be neglected in favor of more concrete case-specific information (Nisbett and Borgida, 1975). Here, as elsewhere, the challenge is first to get the formal thinking straight and then to convey that understanding to the informal setting in which decisions are actually made.

Computational analyses attempt to address two problems identified by behavioral research, people's relative insensitivity to omissions in problem representations (when relying on judgment rather than on systematic analysis), and their limited capacity for mental arithmetic (Krzysztofowicz, 1983; Raiffa, 1968). A third behavioral problem, which analyses cannot escape, is the sensitivity of people's evaluations to the precise way in which proposals are formulated, or "framed" (Fischhoff, Slovic, and Lichtenstein, 1980; Hogarth, 1982; Tversky and Kahneman, 1981). That is, formally equivalent ways of presenting a decision problem can lead to quite different conclusions. One possible way to achieve more rounded intuitive evaluations is to present alternative formulations. For example:

> Because losses loom larger than equivalent gains (Kahneman and Tversky, 1979b), it is important to describe proposals in terms of both the lives expected to be lost and the lives expected to be saved (or in terms of the increased chances of peace and the decreased chances of war).

Because it is hard to maintain a long-term perspective (Thaler and Shefrin, 1981; Wagenaar and Timmers, 1979), the cumulative consequences of proposals should be computed explicitly. For example, the benefit from any reduction in the probability of war increases with the period of aggregation, in ways that will not be intuitively apparent.

Because people place added weight on consequences that will be obtained with certainty (Kahneman and Tversky, 1979b), it is essential to ensure that at least a shadow of doubt be cast on the consequences of all proposals, lest they benefit from the undeserved status of "sure things." Similarly, it should be shown how programs that promise certain solutions to narrow problems (for example, weapons systems designed to counter a specific form of attack) may have uncertain effects when viewed in a larger context (for example, their effect on international trust or on the reliability of civilian command of complex military systems) (Slovic, Fischhoff, and Lichtenstein, 1982).

Because statistical abstractions using unfamiliar units are hard to grasp, they should be personalized (for example, into the effects of war or defense programs on individual citizens). Conversely, where people's thinking is dominated by sharp images, then one should emphasize statistics, rendered into some comprehensible form (for example, risk analyses of SDI or probabilities that lurid worst-case scenarios will come to pass).

These psychological processes might also be exploited in the design of arms control proposals, so as to make them intuitively appealing. For example:

Disarmament or "peace" proposals often require people to give up something tangible (arms, territory) in return for something intangible (reduced probability of war). In order to satisfy the desire for tangible outcomes, such proposals would be more attractive if they included concrete returns, such as increased trade, reduced defense spending, and reduced status for the military establishment in other countries—assuming that these features can be added without reducing a proposal's "analyzed" attractiveness.

The piecemeal character of military proposals provides many "small" accomplishments, achieved whenever a new weapons system is approved. Nonmilitary proposals might attract more adherents if they offered more opportunities for positive reinforcement, by including intermediate goals such as reducing arms spending, demonstrating the existence of a meaningful "peace block" in other countries, and increasing or just sustaining the pace of arms control talks.

An unsatisfying aspect of many armaments proposals is that it is hard to verify their validity. For example, one must take it on faith that new weapons systems will work if they are ever really needed and that they will deter the Soviets from military adventures. Those proposals would be made psychologically, and perhaps analytically, more attractive if they offered some verification.

Public Debate

In a nuclear crisis, the public will have little input, beyond perhaps the effects on leaders of the thought of how history, if any, will judge the decisions that they make. Indeed, in sufficiently intense crises, it is unclear that even the civilian leadership (for example, the president) will have very much input into those decisions (Bracken, 1983; MacLean, 1986).

In times of peace or before, however, citizens can hope to shape nuclear policy through the ballot box, lobbying, or public opinion (Fiske, 1987; Fiske, Fischhoff, and Milburn, 1983; Lau and Sears, 1986; Meuller, 1979; White, 1986). One problem facing citizens is just following the debate over defense issues when, paradoxically, public opinion seems highly volatile, changing dramatically over relatively short periods of time, yet quite confident and polarized at any point in time (Kramer, Kalick, and Milburn, 1983; Markey, 1985; Polyson, Hillmar, and Kriek, 1986; U.S. Department of Commerce, 1980). One contributor to this apparent confusion and malleability might be the polarized character of political debate over defense issues. It is hard for the public to learn to synthesize integrated positions when all it hears is leaders and pundits confidently espousing strong, simple positions, despite the complexity of the issues involved.

Here, the same modest contribution that simple applications of decision theory might make to leaders' thinking might also be found if its tools were made available to the public. Even a simple decision-making framework could help show, for example, where leaders disagree simply because they are talking past one another (that is, addressing different parts of their country's nuclear decision problem or neglecting issues that would undermine their proposals).

Citizens committed to defense issues might hope to spot consequences absent from arms control proposals, just as citizens committed to auto mechanics might be able to catch the features that a manufacturer fails to mention in its sales pitches. However, structuring complex decisions is an uncertain and laborious process at any level of sophistication. Public energies might be invested more efficiently if they were guided by trusted, neutral sources that laid out the issues in a format-facilitating comparisons (for example, as *Consumer Reports* does for purchases). Even more helpful would be analyses providing conditional recommendations, showing which choices would follow from using various importance weightings and various interpretations of uncertain facts. The simplest form of such advice would be "Best (and Worst)

Buys in Arms Policy," in the sense of options that dominate (or are dominated by) the alternatives, whatever one's perspective on the issues.

In recent years, there have been a number of thoughtful expositions of the reasons for disagreement over particular defense issues, as well as advocacy documents that attempt to set forth particular positions in a nonpolemic way (Allison, Nye, and Carnesale, 1985; Freedman, 1981; Prins, 1983, 1984). Few of these guides, however, have taken the next step of structuring readers' decision-making process. Without imposing any external perspectives, a guide could work through the details, reaching conclusions of the form, "if you believe X and value Y, here is a rough ordering of defense policies by how attractive they should seem to you" or, even more basically, "here are the possible consequences of nuclear decisions whose relative importance needs to be weighed before creating or evaluating options." Without such a framework, it is hard to organize one's work and focus on the issues that matter. Indeed, thoughtful expositions that just list facts can backfire if they encourage the feeling that nuclear decisions are hopelessly complex, hence best left to the experts.

Clearly, the greatest effort in communicating about nuclear decisions should be invested in conveying the information that people need the most. The only orderly way to identify such information is to know what those decisions are in sufficient detail to perform sensitivity analyses (showing how sensitive conclusions are to variations in estimates of facts and values). That requires, in turn, an understanding of what various members of the public currently know and want. Surveying what people know should be relatively straightforward, drawing on established methodologies (see, however, Turner and Martin, 1984). Surveying what they want may be complicated by the lack of well-articulated values for the difficult trade-offs underlying many nuclear decisions (for example, how much national pride [or annual income] would you be willing to relinquish in return for an XX percent decrease in the annual chances of nuclear war?). Only after knowing what they want can people start thinking seriously about what they can get. If people cannot figure out what they want, then they may need (and even invite) some exploration of value issues. Why not philosophy for the masses? Such messages are hard to communicate or unlikely to garner large audiences. However, their very production may change the tenor of the debate (MacLean, 1986; U.S. Catholic Conference, 1983).

Having decided the "what" of communication, attention can move to the "how." This clearly requires a detailed analysis of the particular information that needs to be communicated, focusing on those concepts that the behavioral research points to as being most problematic. Some of these problems were discussed in the preceding sections, which asked how nuclear decisions could be made more comprehensible to technical experts and political decision makers. To the extent that the intuitive judgmental processes of experts and lay people are similar, the same advice would apply here. Making certain that important issues are mentioned explicitly and that alternative formulations are displayed is especially important. Things that are out of sight tend to be out of mind. Other problems include making very small probabilities comprehensible, keeping well-described scenarios from being unduly persuasive, blocking the biasing effects of hindsight when evaluating leaders' performance, and ensuring awareness of the situational constraints that leaders (in each country) perceive as circumscribing their options. No attempt should be made here to give simple solutions. Rather, the implications of the behavioral principles found in the literature must be articulated for particular applications. Moreover, any application should have an evaluation component, to ensure that a message has the intended effect. It is too easy, especially for technical experts, to communicate badly and then hold the public responsible for failing to understand them (Fischhoff, 1985; National Research Council, 1989).

An assessment of what various publics need to know is also essential for evaluating their "competence" to participate in nuclear decisions. A common response of technical experts to public skepticism about their proposals is to doubt that lay people know enough to comment sensibly (Fraser and Marsh, n.d.; Starr and Whipple, 1980). As evidence, experts often point to some factual mistake that they have heard a lay person make. Yet, not all mistakes are equally important. The proper measure of importance is whether having the right information would lead to a different position on some nuclear decision. To take an example from another domain, the Institute of Medicine's (1986) fine report, *Confronting AIDS*, criticizes the public because only 41 percent of respondents to a survey knew that acquired immune deficiency syndrome (AIDS) was caused by a virus. That fact is obvious to technical experts, yet it is hard to think of a lay person's decision that would depend on it.

Moreover, in some cases, the crucial information has to do with the experts themselves. Most nuclear decisions depend to some extent on one's confidence in the experts' ability to manage their own affairs. In part, this is a political question: Will the experts act in the public's best interest, or are they captives of some faction or pursuing their own agenda (Zuckerman, 1982)? Judging other people's integrity or loyalty may be one domain in which lay people are relatively expert (DePaulo and Rosenthal, 1979; Ekman, 1985; Knapp, Cody, and Reardon, 1987). However, trust is also a judgmental question, depending on how well experts understand the systems that they are directing. In some domains (for example, auto mechanics), the ranking experts know about all there is to know. In others, those who know the most still do not know very much, in absolute terms. Whatever the overlay of technical analysis and jargon on nuclear policies, the people making nuclear decisions are just people, doing the best they can with the intellectual skills at their disposal. Understanding the limits of those skills can help citizens follow policy debates, identify lacunae in political analyses, and evaluate their leaders' wisdom (Fischer, 1983).

Conclusion

Living in a nuclear age is largely an intellectual activity. We can only imagine the precedents and consequences of nuclear crises and wars (Fiske, Fischhoff, and Milburn, 1983; Kozielecki, 1985). The vicarious experience of Hiroshima and Nagasaki provides some indirect feeling for what an attack is like, as do recent television shows and books. However, those consequences are still something of an abstraction, must like the experience of a serious disease is to those who have not suffered from it. Other possible outcomes may be equally unfamiliar. For example, do Americans really know what it would be like to experience the national humiliation of "backing down" before the Soviets (or Iranians), the exaltation of having a dramatic peace proposal accepted, the lasting terror of having weathered another Cuban missile crisis, the national decline that would follow if too much scientific talent were invested in military R&D, or the social turmoil of reinstituting the draft to strengthen conventional forces? Wherever the imagination fails, then, on some basic level, we do not know what we are getting ourselves into with nuclear decisions.

Equally abstract at present are the concrete events that might precede a nuclear war or lasting peace. Even events happening today (or yesterday) are subject to alternative interpretations. Is it a provocation, an act of desperation, a step taken for internal consumption, a measure to appease allies, a power move by a warring faction, a tough-sounding prologue to a conciliatory act, an ill-considered gesture, or a simple mistake? Knowing what is happening in the nuclear arena requires knowledge not just of events, but also of interpretations by leaders from various countries and cultures. As a result, it is difficult to establish even simple causal relations ("why they did X in response to our Y"), much less to test and use such multiply-defined theories as deterrence (Jervis, Lebow, and Stein, 1985). Thus, any move is a gamble, whose consequences can only be guessed.

That uncertainty surrounds even what might seem like the most predictable part of nuclear decisions—the operation of military sytems. Yet, they, too, are abstractions, tested only in the semireality of theoretical analyses and field exercises. The current debate over whether any SDI-like system could ever work is an extreme example of this uncertainty. However, there must be doubts about the performance of every weapons and command-and-control system under the unprecedented conditions of a nuclear crisis or war (Barnaby, 1987; Bracken, 1983; Cushman, 1983; Wallace, Crissey, and Sennott, 1986).

It would be nice to believe that the human mind had developed the facility to take such gambles wisely (Holsti, 1989). For those who harbor doubts about those abilities on the basis of anecdotal observation, the research literature suggests further reason for concern. Given the stakes involved, it would not take much confidence in that literature or observation to take that concern seriously. Nor would improvements in the quality of nuclear decisions have to be very large to justify a substantial investment in them.

To that end, the present analysis attempted initially to identify the role of judgmental processes in various nuclear decisions. That task analysis was done with some confidence. The next two steps, diagnosing potential weaknesses in those judgments and suggesting ameliorative procedures, were done with increasing timidity. The empirical research base is not (ever) as large as one would like. It is particularly weak with regard to studies of experts forced to go beyond hard data and rely on intuitive judgments within their field of expertise. Further evidence is needed to substantiate the claim that experts think like everyone else unless they have had the opportunity to master a particular kind of judgment as a learned skill. Although there is both theoretical and empirical reason to believe that various forms of decision aiding are possible, the high stakes involved mandate caution before proposing any intervention. Ineffective steps may make matters worse if they raise confidence without improving performance, or if they disrupt the "cognitive ecology" within which decision makers are accustomed to functioning, so that they lose touch with their own imperfect intuitions without acquiring viable alternatives.

A final reason for caution is to protect the investigators (Fischhoff, Pidgeon, and Fiske, 1983). A common experience for the behavioral sciences is to be ignored as irrelevant until a social problem becomes so obviously "behavioral" that some help from this direction seems essential. Behavioral scientists are then expected to produce solutions in short order and with few resources. They might be asked to write a paper, give a seminar, suggest prcedural changes, sit on an advisory board, or quickly make a decision aid or training program. Often there will be little opportunity to learn how key players conceptualize their problem, field test proposals, conduct needed supplementary research, adapt an initial solution to the problems it encounters, or build institutional support for it. When their intervention fails, they will be discredited. The behavioral problems will then be viewed either as intractable or as anybody's guess. Any attempt to use this, or any other, research needs realistic expectations, a reasonable institutional setting, and an extended commitment to seeing what can be gotten out of it.

Notes

Support for the preparation of this chapter was provided by the National Science Foundation under grants SES-8213452 and SES-8715564, which are very much appreciated. I have benefited greatly from comments to earlier drafts provided by Robyn Dawes (Carnegie Mellon University), Lita Furby (Eugene Research Institute), Alex George (Stanford University), Michael Herman (Oxford University and Chatham House), Zvi Lanir (Jaffe Center for Strategic Studies), Philip Tetlock (University of California), and Paul Stern (National Research Council).
    1. These issues, in some ways, parallel those raised by the debate over incrementalism versus planning in organizational contexts (Lindblom, 1959; Steinbruner, 1974).
    2. These "debiasing" studies might be seen as an empirical response to Tetlock's (1989) challenge to clarify the boundary conditions on behavioral phenomena observed at any level.

References

Abelson, R.P., and A. Levi. 1985. Decision-making and decision theory. In G. Lindzey and E. Aronson, eds., *Handbook of Social Psychology*, Vol. I, pp. 231–309. New York: Random House.

Adams, J. 1982. Issues in human reliability. *Human Factors* 29:1–15.

Allison, G.T. 1971. *Essence of Decision: Explaining the Cuban Missile Crisis.* Boston: Little, Brown.

Allison, G.T., J. Nye, and A. Carnesale, eds. 1985. *Hawks, Doves, and Owls.* New York: Norton.

Alpert, M., and H. Raiffa. 1982. A progress report on the training of probability assessors. In D. Kahneman, P. Slovic, and A. Tversky, eds., *Judgment under Uncertainty: Heuristics and Biases,* pp. 294–305. New York: Cambridge University Press.

Andriole, S.J., and G.W. Hopple. 1982. They're only human: Decision makers in command and control. *Signal* 36(7):45–49.

Arkes, H.R., and K.R. Hammond, eds. 1986. *Judgment and Decision Making: An Interdisciplinary Reader.* New York: Cambridge University Press.

Armstrong, J.S. 1985. *Long-Range Forecasting.* New York: Wiley.

Armstrong, J.S., W.B. Denniston, and M.M. Gordon, 1975. The use of the decomposition principle in making judgments. *Organizational Behavior and Human Performance* 14:257–263.

Bailey, R.W. 1982. *Human Performance in Engineering.* Englewood Cliffs, N.J.: Prentice Hall.

Ball, D. 1981. Can nuclear war be controlled? Adelphi Paper No. 169. London: International Institute for Strategic Studies.

Bar-Hillel, M. 1980. The base-rate fallacy in probability judgments. *Acta Psychologica* 44:211–233.

————. 1984. Representativeness and fallacies of probability judgment. *Acta Psychologica* 55:91–107.

Barnaby, F. 1987. *The Automated Battlefield.* Oxford: Oxford University Press.

Bazelon, D.L. 1979. Risk and responsibility. *Science* 205:277–280.

Bazerman, M.H., and R. S. Lewicki, eds. 1988. *Research in Negotiations in Organizations.* New York: JAI Press.

Beach, L.R., B.D. Townes, F.L. Campbell, and G.W. Keating. 1976. Developing and testing a decision aid for birth planning decisions. *Organizational Behavior and Human Performance* 15:99–116.

Behn, R.D., and J.W. Vaupel. 1983. *Quick Analysis for Busy Decision Makers.* New York: Basic Books.

Bentkover, V.T., V.T. Covello, and J. Mumpower, eds. 1985. *Benefits Assessment: The State of the Art.* Dordrecht, the Netherlands: D. Reidel.

Berkeley, D., and P. Humphreys. 1982. Structuring decision problems and the "bias heuristic." *Acta Psychologica* 50:201–252.

Betts, R.K. 1978. Analysis, war, and decision: Why intelligence failures are inevitable. *World Politics* 31:61–90.

Beyth-Marom, R. 1982*a*. How probable is "probable"?: Numerical translation of verbal probability expressions. *Journal of Forecasting* 1:257–269.

————. 1982*b*. Perception of correlation reexamined. *Memory and Cognition* 10:511–519.

Beyth-Marom, R., S. Dekel, R. Gomdo, and M. Shaked. 1985. *An Elementary Approach to Thinking under Uncertainty.* Hillsdale, N.J.: Erlbaum.

Beyth-Maron, R., B. Fischhoff, M. Jacobs, and L. Furby. In press. Teaching adolescents decision making. In J. Baron and R. Brown, eds., *Teaching Decision Making.* Hillsdale, N.J.: Lawrence Erlbaum Assoc.

Boffey, P.M. 1975. Nuclear war: Federation disputes Academy on how bad effects would be. *Science* 190:248–250.

Bracken, P. 1983. *Command and Control of Nuclear Weapons.* New Haven, Conn.: Yale University Press.

Brecher, M. 1974. Inputs and decisions for war and peace. *International Studies Quarterly* 18(2):131–178.

Bredemeier, M.E., and C.S. Greenblat. 1981. The educational effectiveness of simulation games: A synthesis of findings. *Simulation and Games* 12:307–332.

Brehmer, B. 1980. In a word: Not from experience. *Acta Psychologica* 45:223–241.

Brewer, G.D., and P. Bracken. 1984. Some missing pieces of the C³1 puzzle. *Journal of Conflict Resolution* 28:451–469.

Britten, S. 1983. *The Invisible Event: An Assessment of the Risk of Accidental or Unauthorized Detonation of Nuclear Weapons and of War by Miscalculation.* London: Menard.

Broadbent, D.E. 1971. *Decision and Stress.* London: Academic Press.

Brown, C.M. 1988. *Human-Computer Interface Design Guidelines.* Norwood, N.J.: Ablex.

Buchanan, B.G., and E. Shurtliffe, eds. 1984. *Rule-Based Expert Systems.* Reading, MA: Addison Wesley.

Bunn, M., and K. Tsipis. 1983. The uncertainties of preemptive nuclear attack. *Scientific American* 249(5):38–47.

Burton, I., Kates, R.W., & White, G.F. 1978. *Environment as Hazard.* New York: Oxford University Press.

Campen, J.T. 1986. *Benefits, Cost and Beyond.* Cambridge, Mass.: Ballinger.

Caro, P.W. 1988. Flight training and simulation. In E. L. Wiener and D.C. Nagel, eds. *Human Factors in Aviation.* San Diego, Calif.: Academic Press.

Carter, A. 1985. The command and control of nuclear war. *Scientific American* 252:32–39.

Chain, J.T., R. Dixon, and R. Weissinger-Baylon. 1986. *Decision Making in the Atlantic Alliance: The Management of Political Military Crises.* Menlo Park, Calif.: Strategic Decisions Press.

Chan, S. 1979. The intelligence of stupidity: Understanding failures in strategic warning. *American Journal of Political Science* 73(1):171–180.

Chapman, L.J., and J. Chapman. 1969. Illusory correlation as an obstacle to the use of valid diagnostic signs. *Journal of Abnormal Psychology* 74:271–280.

Cimbala, S.J. 1987. Intelligence deterrence and uncertainty. In S.J. Cimbala, ed., *Intelligence and Intelligence Policy in a Democratic Society.* Dobbs Ferry, N.Y.: Transnational.

Cohen, J. 1981. Can human irrationality be experimentally demonstrated? *The Behavioral and Brain Sciences* 4:317–331.

Cohen, P.R. 1985. *Heuristic Reasoning about Uncertainty: An AI Approach.* Boston: Pitman.

Cohen, S.F. 1986. *Sovieticus: American Perceptions of Soviet Realities.* New York: Norton.

Collins, A.M., and A.F. Loftus. 1975. A spreading activation theory of semantic processing. *Psychological Review* 82:407–428.

Combs, B., and P. Slovic. 1978. Causes of death: Biased newspaper coverage and biased judgments. *Journalism Quarterly* 56:837–843, 849.

Committee on Government Operations. 1981. *Failures of the North American Aerospace Defense Command's (NORAD) Attack Warning System.* Washington, D.C.: U.S. Government Printing Office.

Cook, K.S. 1987. Social stress in computer-mediated communication systems and human productivity in space stations. In T.B. Sheridan, D.S. Kruser, and S. Deutsch, eds., *Human Factors in Automated and Robotic Space Stations.* Washington, D.C.: National Academy Press.

Coombs, C.H., R.M. Dawes, and A. Tversky. 1970. *Mathematical Psychology.* Englewood Cliffs, N.J.: Prentice Hall.

Coombs, M.J., ed. 1984. *Development in Expert Systems.* London: Academic Press.

Coser, L.A. 1954. *The Social Functions of Conflict.* Glencoe, Ill.: The Free Press.

Coulam, R.F., and G.W. Fischer. 1985. Problems of command and control in a major European war. In R.F. Coulam and R.A. Smith, eds., *Advances in Information Processing in Organizations,* Vol. 2. Greenwich, Conn.: JAI Press.

Crouch, E., and R. Wilson. 1983. *Risk/Benefit Analysis.* Cambridge, Mass.: Ballinger.

Cummings, R.R., D.S. Brookshire, and W.D. Schulze, eds. 1986. *Valuing Environmental Goods.* Totowa, N.J.: Rowman and Allenheld.

Cushman, J.H. 1983. *Command and Control of Theater Forces: Adequacy.* Washington, D.C.: AFCEA International Press.

Cyert, R.M., and J.G. March. 1963. *A Behavioral Theory of the Firm.* Englewood Cliffs, N.J.: Prentice Hall.

Davis, J.H. 1982. *Group Performance.* Reading, MA: Addison-Wesley.

Dawes, R.M. 1971. A case study of graduate admissions: Applications of three principles of human decision making. *American Psychologist* 26:180–188.

———. 1979. The robust beauty of improper linear models in decision making. *American Psychologist* 34:571–582.

———. 1988. *Rational Choice in an Uncertain World.* New York: Harcourt Brace Jovanovich.

———. In press. The potential non-falsifiability of the false consensus effect. In R. Hogarth, ed., *Insights in Decision Making: A Tribute to Hillel J. Einhorn.* Chicago: University of Chicago Press.

Dawes, R.M., and B. Corrigan. 1974. Linear models in decision making. *Psychological Bulletin* 34:571–582.

DePaulo, B.M., and R. Rosenthal. 1979. Telling lies. *Journal of Personality and Social Psychology* 37:1713–1722.

Dreman, D. 1982. *A New Contrarian Investment Strategy.* New York: Random House.

Dunlap, T.R. 1978. Science as a guide in regulating technology: The case of DDT in the United States. *Social Studies of Science* 8:265–285.

Eddy, D.M. 1982. Probabilistic reasoning in clinical medicine: Problems and opportunities. In D. Kahneman, P. Slovic, and A. Tversky, eds., *Judgment under Uncertainty: Heuristics and Biases,* pp. 249–267. New York: Cambridge University Press.

Edwards, W., and D. von Winterfeldt. 1986. On cognitive illusions and their implications. *Southern California Law Review* 59:401–451.

Einhorn, H., and R.M. Hogarth. 1978. Confidence in judgment: Persistence in the illusion of validity. *Psychological Review* 85:395–416.

———. 1981. Behavioral decision theory: Processes of judgment and choice. *Annual Review of Psychology* 32:53–88.

Ekman, P. 1985. *Telling Lies.* New York: Norton.

Ellul, J. 1969. *Propaganda.* New York: Knopf.

Elstein, A.S., L.S. Shulman, and S.A. Sprafka. 1978. *Medical Problem Solving: An Analysis of Clinical Reasoning.* Cambridge, Mass.: Harvard University Press.

Embrey, D.E. 1986. Human reliability. In A. Serra and R. E. Barlow, eds., *Theory of Reliability.* Amsterdam: North Holland.

Ericsson, A., and H. Simon. 1980. Verbal reports as data. *Psychological Review* 87:215–251.

Estes, W.K. 1964. Probability learning. In A.W. Melton, ed., *Categories of Human Learning.* New York: Academic Press.

———. 1976. The cognitive side of probability learning. *Psychological Review* 83:37–64.

Evans, J. St. B. 1982. *Deductive Reasoning.* London: Routledge & Kegan Paul.

Feller, W. 1968. *An Introduction to Probability Theory and Its Applications,* 3d ed., Vol. 1. New York: Wiley.

Fischer, G.W. 1983. Conceptual models and military threat assessment. *Journal of Social Issues* 39(1):87–116.

Fischhoff, B. 1975. Hindsight≠foresight: The effect of outcome knowledge on judgment under uncertainty. *Journal of Experimental Psychology: Human Perception and Performance* 1:288–299.

———. 1982a. Debiasing. In D. Kahneman, P. Slovic, and A. Tversky, eds., *Judgment under Uncertainty: Heuristics and Biases.* New York: Cambridge University Press.

———. 1982b. For those condemned to study the past: Heuristics and biases in hindsight. In D. Kahneman, P. Slovic, and A. Tversky, eds., *Judgment under Uncertainty: Heuristics and Biases.* New York: Cambridge University Press.

———. 1985. Managing risk perceptions. *Issues in Science and Technology* 2:83–96.

———. 1988a. Human factors in national defense. Testimony before the U.S. House of Representatives Armed Services Committee, 6 October 1988.

———. 1988b. Judgment and decision making. In R.J. Steinberg and E.E. Smith, eds., *The Psychology of Human Thought,* pp. 153–187. New York: Cambridge University Press.

———. 1989. Eliciting expert judgment. *IEEE Transactions on Systems, Man and Cybernetics.* 19(3):448–461.

———. 1990. Psychology and public policy: Tool or tool maker. *American Psychologist.*

Fischhoff, B., and Bar-Hillel, M. 1984. Focusing techniques: A shortcut to improving probability judgments? *Organizational Behavior and Human Perfomrance* 34:175–191.

Fischhoff, B., and Beyth-Marom, R. 1983. Hypothesis evaluation from a Bayesian perspective. *Psychological Review* 90:239–260.

Fischhoff, B., and S. Johnson. (1990). The possibility of distributed decision making. Appendix to *Distributed Decision Making.* Washington, D.C.: National Academy Press.

Fischhoff, B., S. Lichtenstein, P. Slovic, S. Derby, and R. Keeney. 1981. *Acceptable Risk,* p. 18. New York: Cambridge University Press.

Fischhoff, B., D. MacGregor, and L. Blackshaw. 1987. Creating categories for databases. *International Journal of Man-Machine Systems* 27:33–67.

Fischhoff, B., N. Pidgeon, and S. Fiske. 1983. Social science and the politics of the arms race. *Journal of Social Issues* 39:161–180.

Fischhoff, B., P. Slovic, and S. Lichtenstein. 1978. Fault trees: Sensitivity of assessed failure probabilities to problem representation. *Journal of Experimental Psychology: Human Perception and Performance* 4:330–344.

————. 1980. Knowing what you want: Measuring labile values. In T. Wallsten, ed., *Cognitive Processes in Choice and Decision Behavior*. Hillsdale, N.J.: Erlbaum.

Fischhoff, B., S. Watson, and C. Hope. 1984. Defining risk. *Policy Sciences* 17:123–139.

Fiske, S. T. 1987. People's reactions to nuclear war: Implications for psychologists. *American Psychologist* 42(3):207–217.

Fiske, S., and S. Taylor. 1984. *Social Cognition*. Reading, Mass.: Addison-Wesley.

Fiske, S.T., B. Fischhoff, and M. Milburn, eds. 1983. Images of nuclear war. *Journal of Social Issues* 39(1).

Fitts, P., and M. Posner. 1965. *Human Performance*. Belmont, Calif.: Brooks/Cole.

Flexman, R.F., and E.A. Stark. 1987. Training simulators. In G. Salvendy, ed., *The Handbook of Human Factors*. New York: Wiley.

Fogarty, R. 1988. *Formal Investigation into the Circumstances Surrounding the Downing of Iran Air Flight 655 on 3 July 1988*. Washington, D.C.: Department of Defense.

Fraser, C., and C. Marsh, eds. n.d. *Public Opinion and Nuclear Defense*. Cambridge: Cambridge University Press.

Freedman, L. 1981. *The Evolution of Nuclear Strategy*. London: Macmillan.

Frei, D. 1983. *Risks of Unintentional Nuclear War*. Beckenham, England: Croom Helm.

Freudenberg, W.R., and E.A. Rosa, eds. 1984. *Public Reaction to Nuclear Power: Are There Critical Masses?* Boulder, Colo.: Westview.

Furnas, G.W., T.K. Landauer, L.M. Gomez, and S.T. Dumais. 1983. Statistical semantics: Analysis of the potential performance of key-word information systems. *Bell System Technical Journal* 62:1752–1806.

General Accounting Office. 1986. *Technical Risk Assessment: The Status of Current DoD Efforts* (PEHD86-5). Washington, D.C.: General Accounting Office.

George, A.L. 1980. *Presidential Decision Making in Foreign Policy*. Boulder, Colo.: Westview.

George, A.L. 1972. The case for multiple advocacy in making foreign policy. *American Political Science Review* 66:751–785, 791–795.

George, A.L. 1984. Crisis management: The interaction of political and military considerations. *Survival* (Sept./Oct.):223–234.

Gilovich, T., R. Vallone, and A. Tversky, A. 1985. The hot hand in basketball: On the misperception of random sequences. *Cognitive Psychology* 17:295–314.

Hohenemser, K.H. 1975. The failsafe risk. *Environment* 17(1):6–10.

Holdren, J.P. 1976. The nuclear controversy and the limitation of decision-making by experts. *Bulletin of the Atomic Scientists* 32:20–22.

Holsti, O.R. 1989. Crisis decision making. In P.E. Tetlock, J.L. Husbands, R. Jervis, P.C. Stern, and C. Tilly, eds., *Behavior, Society and Nuclear War*, Vol. 1. New York: Oxford.

Hollnagel, E., G. Mancini, and D. Woods, eds. 1986. *Intelligent Decision Support in Process Environments*. Heidelberg, Federal Republic of Germany: Springer-Verlag.

Hwang, J., D. Schutzer, K. Shere, and P. Vena, eds. 1982. *Selected Analytical Concepts in Command and Control*. New York: Gordon and Breach.

Institute of Medicine. 1986. *Confronting AIDS*. Washington, D.C. National Academy Press.

Janis, I.L. 1972. *Victims of Groupthink: A Psychological Study of Foreign Policy Decisions and Fiascos*. Boston: Houghton Mifflin.

Janis, I.L. 1982. *Counseling on Personal Decisions*. New Haven, Conn.: Yale University Press.

Janis, I.L., and L. Mann. 1977. *Decision Making*. New York: Free Press.

Jennergren, L.P., and R.L. Keeney. 1983. In *Handbook of Applied Systems Analsyis*. Laxenberg, Austria: International Institute of Applied Systems Analysis.

Jervis, R. 1976. *Perception and Misperception: International Politics*. Princeton, N.J.: Princeton University Press.

———. 1984. *The Illogic of American Nuclear Strategy*. Ithaca, N.Y.: Cornell University Press.

Jervis, R., R.N. Lebow, and J.G. Stein. 1985. *Psychology and deterrence*. Baltimore, Md.: Johns Hopkins University Press.

Judd, B.R., and S. Weisenberger. 1980. A systematic approach to safeguard decision-making. *Management Science* 28:289–302.

Jungermann, H. 1983. The two camps on rationality. In R. W. Scholz, ed., *Decision Making under Uncertainty* pp. 63–86. Amsterdam: Elsevier.

Kahneman, D., P. Slovic, and A. Tversky, eds. 1982. *Judgment under Uncertainty: Heuristics and Biases*. New York: Cambridge University Press.

Kahneman, D., and A. Tversky. 1972. Subjective probability: A judgment of representativeness. *Cognitive Psychology* 3:430–454.

———. 1979a. Intuitive prediction: Biases and corrective procedures. *TIMS Studies in Management Science* 12:313–327.

———. 1979b. Prospect theory. *Econometrica* 47:263–292.

———. 1982. On the study of statistical intuitions. *Cognition* 11:123–141.

———. 1984. Choices, values, and frames. *American Psychologist* 39:341–350.

Kanal, L.N., and J. Lemmer. 1986. *Uncertainty in Artificial Intelligence*. Amsterdam: North Holland.

Keegan, J. 1987. *The Image of Command*. New York: Viking.

Keeney, R. 1980. *Siting Energy Facilities*. New York: Wiley.

Kelly, E.L., and D.W. Fiske. 1951. *The Prediction of Performance in Clinical Psychology*. Ann Arbor: University of Michigan Press.

Kess, J.E., and R.A. Hoppe. 1985. Bias, individual difference and "shared differences" in ambiguity. *Journal of Pragmatics* 9:21–39.

Kidd, J.B. 1970. The utilization of subjective probabilities in production planning. *Acta Psychologica* 34:338–347.

Kiesler, S., J. Siegel, and T.W. McGuire. 1984. Social and psychological aspects of computer-mediated communication. *American Psychologist* 39:1123–1134.

Kiesler, S., D. Zubrow, A.M. Moses, and V. Geller. 1985. Affect in computer-mediated communication: An experiment in synchronous terminal-to-terminal discussion. *Human-Computer Interaction* 1:77–104.

Kirwan, B. 1987. Human reliability analysis of an offshore emergency blowdown system. *Applied Ergonomics* 18:23–33.

Knapp, M.L., M.J. Cody, and K.K. Reardon. 1987. Nonverbal signals. In C.R. Berger and S.H. Chaffee, eds., *Handbook of Communication Science*. Newbury Park, Calif.: Sage.

Koranyi, E.K. 1977. Psychobiological correlates of battlefield psychiatry. *Psychiatric Journal of the University of Ottawa* 2(1):3–19.

Koriat, A., S. Lichtenstein, and B. Fischhoff. 1980. Reasons for confidence. *Journal of Experimental Psychology: Human Learning and Memory* 6:107–118.

Kozielecki, J. 1985. The specter of Armageddon. *Dialectics and Humanism* 3–4:139–152.

Kramer, B.M., S. Kalick, and M. Milburn. 1983. Continuity and change in nuclear attitudes: 1945–1982. *Journal of Social Issues* 39(1):7–24.

Krepon, M. 1984. *Strategic Stalemate: Nuclear Weapons and Arms Control in American Politics*. London: Macmillan.

Krzysztofowicz, R. 1983. Why should a forecaster and a decision maker use Bayes Theorem. *Water Resources Journal* 19:327–336.

Kull, S. 1988. *Minds at War*. New York: Basic Books.

Kunreuther, H., R. Ginsberg, L. Miller, P. Sagi, P. Slovic, B. Borkin, and N. Katz. 1978. *Disaster Insurance Protection: Public Policy Lessons*. New York: Wiley.

Langer, E.J. 1975. The illusion of control. *Journal of Personality and Social Psychology* 32:311–328.

Lanir, Z. 1982. *Strategic Surprises*. Ramat Aviv, Israel: Tel Aviv University Press.

Lanir, Z., B. Fischhoff, and S. Johnson. 1988. Military risk taking: C³I and the cognitive functions of boldness in war. *Journal of Strategic Studies* 11(1):96–114.

Lau, R.R., and D.O. Sears, eds. 1986. *Political Cognition*. Hillsdale, N.J.: Erlbaum.

Lebow, N., and J.G. Stein. 1987. Beyond deterrence. *Journal of Social Issues* 43:5–71.

Lehner, P., and L. Adelman, eds. 1989. Knowledge elicitation. *IEEE Transactions on Systems, Man and Cybernetics* 19(3).

Levine, M. 1974. Scientific method and the adversary method. *American Psychologist* 29:661–716.

Lichtenstein, S., and B. Fischhoff. 1980. Training for calibration. *Organizational Behavior and Human Performance* 26:149–171.

Lichtenstein, S., B. Fischhoff, and L.D. Phillips. 1982. Calibration of probabilities: State of the art to 1980. In D. Kahneman, P. Slovic, and A. Tversky, eds., *Judgment Under Uncertainty: Heuristics and Biases.* New York: Cambridge University Press.

Lichtenstein, S., P. Slovic, B. Fischhoff, M. Layman, and B. Combs. 1978. Judged frequency of lethal events. *Journal of Experimental Psychology: Human Learning and Memory* 4:551–578.

Lichtenstein, S., P. Slovic, and D. Zink. 1969. Effect of instruction in expected value on optimality of gambling decisions. *Journal of Experimental Psychology* 79:236–240.

Lindblom, C. 1959. The science of muddling through. *Public Administration Review* 29:79–88.

Lopes, L. 1982. Doing the impossible: A note on induction and the experience of randomness. *Journal of Experimental Psychology: Human Learning and Memory* 8:626–636.

MacLean, D., ed. 1986. *The Security Gamble: Deterrence Gambles in the Nuclear Age.* Totowa, N.J.: Rowman and Allenheld.

Mahoney, M.J. 1979. Psychology of the scientist: An evaluative review. *Social Studies of Science* 9:349–375.

March, J.G., and H. Simon. 1958. *Organizations.* New York: Wiley.

March, J.G., and R. Weissinger-Baylon, eds. 1985. *Ambiguity and Command.* Marshfield, Mass.: Pitman.

Markey, E.J. 1985. The politics of arms control: A matter of perception. *American Psychologist* 40:557–560.

May, E.R. 1973. *"Lessons" of the Past: The Use and Misuse of History in American Foreign Policy.* New York: Oxford University Press.

Mazur, A., A.A. Marino, and R.O. Becker. 1979. Separating factual disputes from value disputes in controversies over technologies. *Technology in Society* 1:229–237.

McCormick, G.H. 1983. The dynamics of doctrinal change. *Orbis* 27:266–274.

McCormick, N.J. 1981. *Reliability and Risk Analysis.* New York: Academic Press.

Meehl, P.E. 1954. *Clinical Versus Statistical Prediction: A Theoretical Analysis and a Review of the Evidence.* Minneapolis: University of Minnesota Press.

Meister, D. 1987. Systems design and testing. In G. Salvendy, ed., *The Handbook of Human Factors.* New York: Wiley.

Merkhofer, M.W., and Covello, V., eds. In press. *Risk Assessment and Risk Assessment Methods.* New York: Plenum.

Meshkati, N. In press. An integrative model for designing reliable technological organizations: The role of cultural variables. In J. Rasmussen and R. Batstone, eds., *Safety Control and Risk Management.* Washington, D.C.: World Bank.

Metcalf, J. III. 1986. Decision making and the Grenada rescue operation. In J. G.

March and R. Weissinger-Baylon, eds., *Ambiguity and Command*. Marshfield, Mass.: Pitman.

Meuller, J.E. 1979. Public expectations of war during the cold war. *American Journal of Political Science* 23(2):301–329.

Moray, N. 1987. Monitoring behavior and supervisory control. In K. Boff, L. Kaufmann, and J. Thomas, eds., *Handbook of Perception and Human Performance*. New York: Wiley.

Mumpower, J.L., L.D. Phillips, O. Renn, and V.R.R. Uppuluri, eds. 1987. *Expert Judgment and Expert Systems*. Berlin: Springer.

Murphy, A.H., and R.L. Winkler. 1977. Can weather forecasters formulate reliable probability forecasts of precipitation and temperature? *National Weather Digest* 2:2–9.

———. 1984. Probability of precipitation forecasts. *Journal of the American Statistical Association* 79:391–400.

Murphy, G.L., and D.L. Medin. 1985. The role of theories in conceptual coherence. *Psychological Review* 92:289–316.

Myers, D.G., and H. Lamm. 1976. The group polarization phenomenon. *Psychological Bulletin* 83:602–627.

National Research Council. 1975. *The Effects of Thermonuclear War*. Washington, D.C.: National Academy Press.

———. 1982. *Survey Measure of Subjective Phenomena*. Washington, D.C.: National Academy Press.

———. 1987. *Research Needs in Automated and Robotic Space Systems*. Washington, D.C.: National Academy Press.

———. 1988. *Human Performance Models*. Washington, D.C.: National Academy Press.

———. 1989. *Improving Risk Communication*. Washington, D.C.: National Academy Press.

Neale, M.A., and M.H. Bazerman. 1985. Perspectives for understanding negotiations: Viewing negotiation as a judgmental process. *Journal of Conflict Resolution* 29:33–55.

Neustadt, R.E., and E.R. May. 1986. *Thinking in Time*. New York: Free Press.

Nickerson, R.S., D.N. Perkins and E.E. Smith. 1985. *The Teaching of Thinking*. Hillside, N.J.: Erlbaum.

Nisbett, R.E., and E. Borgida. 1975. Attribution and the psychology of prediction. *Journal of Personality and Social Psychology* 32:932–943.

Nisbett, R.E., D.H. Krantz, C. Jepson, and Z. Kunda. 1983. The use of statistical heuristics in everyday inductive reasoning. *Psychological Review* 90:339–363.

Nisbett, R.E., and L. Ross. 1980. *Human Inference: Strategies and Shortcomings of Social Judgment*. Englewood Cliffs, N.J.: Prentice-Hall.

Nisbett, R.E., and T.D. Wilson. 1977. Telling more than we know: Verbal reports on mental processes. *Psychological Review* 84(3):231–259.

Norris, D.R., and C.A. Snyder. 1982. External validation of simulation games. *Simulation and Games* 13:73–85.

O'Leary, M.K., W.D. Caplan, H.B. Shapiro, and D. Dean. 1974. The quest for relevance. *International Studies Quarterly* 18:211–237.

Olson, J.R., ed. 1990. *Human Factors Issues in Expert Systems Development and Use.* Washington,D.C.: National Academy Press.

Oskamp, S. 1965. Overconfidence in case-study judgments. *Journal of Consulting Psychology* 29:261–265.

Pate-Cornell, M.E., and J.E. Neu. 1985. Warning systems and defense policy: A reliability model for the command and control of U.S. nuclear forces. *Risk Analysis* 5:121–138.

Payne, J. 1982. Contingent decision behavior. *Psychological Bulletin* 92:382–401.

Perrow, C. 1983. The organizational context of human factors engineering. *Administrative Science Quarterly* 28:521–541.

———. 1984. *Normal Accidents.* New York: Basic Books.

Peterson, C., and L. Beach. 1967. Man as an intuitive statistician. *Psychological Bulletin* 63:29–46.

Pew, R. 1988. Testimony before the U.S. House of Representatives Armed Services Committee, 6 October 1988.

Phillips, L.D., and G.N. Wright. 1977. Cultural differences in viewing uncertainty and assessing probabilities. In H. Jungermann and G. de Zeeuw, eds., *Decision Making and Change in Human Affairs.* Amsterdam: D. Reidel.

Pidgeon, N.F., D.I. Blockley, and B.A. Turner. 1987. Design practice and snow loading: Lessons from a roof collapse. *The Structural Engineer* 65A(6):236–240.

Pitz, G.F., and N.J. Sachs. 1984. Judgment and decision: Theory and application. *Annual Review of Psychology* 35.

Pitz, G.F., N.J. Sachs, and J. Heerboth. 1980. Procedure for eliciting choices in the analysis of individual decisions. *Organizational Behavior and Human Performance* 26:396–408.

Polyson, J., J. Hillmar, and D. Kriek. 1986. Levels of public interest in nuclear war: 1945–1985. *Journal of Social Behavior and Personality,* 1(3):397–401.

Poulton, E.C. 1977. Quantitative subjective assessments are almost always biased, sometimes completely misleading. *British Journal of Psychology* 68:409–425.

———. 1982. Biases in quantitative judgments. *Applied Ergonomics* 13:31–41.

Prins, G., ed. 1983. *Defended to Death: A Study of the Nuclear Arms Race from the Cambridge University Disarmament Seminar.* Harmondsworth, England: Penguin.

———. 1984. *The Choice: Nuclear Weapons Versus Security.* London: Chatto and Windus.

Quasrawi, A. 1983. *Civil defense, Nuclear-free Zones, and Local Advisory Service.* London: SANA.

Raiffa, H. 1968. *Decision Analysis.* Reading, Mass.: Addison-Wesley.

———. 1982. *The Art and Science of Negotiation.* Cambridge, Mass.: Harvard University Press.

Rasmussen, J. 1986. *Information Processes and Human-Machine Interface: An Approach to Cognitive Engineering.* Chichester, England: J. Wiley and Sons.

Rasmussen, J., K. Duncan, and J. Leplat. 1987. *New Technology and Human Error.* Chichester, England: Wiley.

Rasmussen, J., and W.B. Rouse. 1982. *Human Detection and Diagnosis of Detection Failure.* New York: Plenum.

Resnick, L.B. 1987. *Education and Learning to Think.* Washington, D.C.: National Academy Press.

Rochlin, G.I., T.R. LaPorte, and K.H. Roberts. 1987. The self-designing high-reliability organization: Aircraft carrier flight operations at sea. *Naval War College Review* Autumn:76–90.

Rokeach, M. 1973. *The Nature of Human Values.* New York: Free Press.

Rosenau, J.N. 1974. Assessment in international studies: Ego trip or feedback? *International Studies Quarterly* 18(3):339–367.

Rosenau, J.N., and O.R. Holsti. 1983. U.S. leadership in a shrinking world: The breakdown of consensus and the emergence of conflicting belief systems. *World Politics* 35:368–392.

Rosencraz, A., and G.S. Wetstone. 1980. Acid precipitation: National and international responses. *Environment* 22(5):6–20, 40–41.

Ross, L. 1977. The intuitive psychologist and his shortcomings: Distortions in the attribution process. In L. Berkowitz, ed., *Advances in Experimental Social Psychology* 10. New York: Academic Press.

Ross, M., and F. Sicoly. 1979. Egocentric biases in availability and attribution. *Journal of Personality and Social Psychology* 37:322–336.

Sage, A.P. 1981. Behavior and organizational considerations in the design of information systems and processes for planning and decision support. *IEEE Transactions on Systems, Man and Cybernetics* SMC-11(9):640–678.

Salvendy, G., ed. 1987. *The Handbook of Human Factors.* New York: Wiley

Schelling, T.C. 1970. *The Strategy of Conflict.* Cambridge, Mass.: Harvard University Press.

Schelling, T.C. 1984. Confidence in crisis. *International Security* 8:55–66.

Schoemaker, P.J. 1983. The expected utility model: Its variants, purposes, evidence, and limitations. *Journal of Economic Literature* 20:528–563.

Seminara, J.L., and S.O. Parson. 1982. Nuclear power plant maintainability. *Applied Ergonomics* 13:177–189.

Shafer, G. 1976. *A Mathematical Theory of Evidence.* Princeton, N.J.: Princeton University Press.

Shaklee, H., and D. Tucker. 1980. A rule analysis of judgments of covariation events. *Memory and Cognition* 8:459–467.

Shanteau, J., and R.H. Phelps. 1977. Judgment and swine: Approaches and issues in applied judgment analysis. In M.F. Kaplan and S. Schwartz, eds., *Human Judgment and Decision Processes in Applied Settings* pp. 255–272. New York: Academic Press.

Sheridan, T.B. 1980. Human error in nuclear power plants. *Technology Review* 82(4):23–33.

Sheridan, T., B. Fischhoff, R. Pew, and M. Posner. 1984. *Supervisory Control Systems*. Washington, D.C.: National Academy Press.

Shlaim, A. 1976. Failures in national intelligence estimates: The case of the Yom Kippur War. *World Politics* 28(3):348–380.

Simon, H. 1957. *Models of Man: Social and Rational*. New York: Wiley.

Singer, M. 1971. The vitality of mythical numbers. *The Public Interest* 23:3–9.

Slovic, P., and B. Fischhoff. 1977. On the psychology of experimental surprises. *Journal of Experimental Psychology: Human Perception and Performance* 3:544–551.

Slovic, P., B. Fischhoff, and S. Lichtenstein. 1982. Response mode, framing, and information processing effects in risk assessment. In R. Hogarth, ed., *New Directions for Methodology of Social and Behavioral Science: Question Framing and Response Consistency* pp. 21–36. San Francisco: Jossey-Bass.

Slovic, P., and A. Tversky. 1974. Who accepts Savage's axiom? *Behavioral Science* 19:368–373.

Smith, E.R., and R.S. Miller. 1978. Limits on perception of cognitive processes. *Psychological Review* 85:355–362.

Smith, T.W. 1984. Nonattitudes: A review and evaluation. In C. F. Turner and E. Martin, eds., *Surveying Subjective Phenomena*, Vol. 2. New York: Russell Sage.

Spears, R., J. van der Pligt, and J. R. Eiser. 1986. Generalizing the illusory correlation effect. *Journal of Personality and Social Psychology* 51:1127–1134.

Starr, C., and C. Whipple. 1980. The risks of risk decisions. *Science* 208:114–119.

Steinbruner, J. 1974. *The Cybernetic Theory of Decision*. Princeton, N.J.: Princeton University Press.

———. 1981–1982. Nuclear decapitation. *Foreign Policy* 45:16–28.

Suefeld, P., and P.E. Tetlock. 1977. Interpretive complexity of communication with international crises. *Journal of Conflict Resolution* 21:427–442.

Suokas, J. 1988. The role of safety analysis in accident prevention. *Accident Analysis and Prevention* 20(1):67–85.

Svenson, O., and B. Fischhoff. 1985. Levels of environmental decisions. *Journal of Environmental Psychology* 5:55–68.

Swain, A.D., and H.E. Guttman. 1982. *A Handbook of Human Reliability Analysis with Emphasis on Nuclear Power Plant Applications* NUREG/CR-1278. Washington, D.C.: Nuclear Regulatory Commission.

Tetlock, P.E. 1979. Identifying victims of groupthink from public statements of decision makers. *Journal of Personality and Social Psychology* 37:1314–1324.

———. 1983. Policy makers' images of international conflict. *Journal of Social Issues* 39:67–86.

———. 1987. Testing deterrence theory: Some conceptual and methodological issues. *Journal of Social Issues* 43(4):85–92.

————. 1989. *Methodological Themes and Variations.* In P.E. Tetlock, J.L. Husbands, R. Jervis, P.C. Stern, and C. Tilly, eds., *Behavior, Society and Nuclear War,* Vol. 1. New York: Oxford.

Tetlock, P.E., and C.B. McGuire. 1986. Cognitive perspective on foreign policy. In R. White, ed., *Psychology and the Prevention of Nuclear War.* New York: New York University Press.

Thaler, R. 1980. Towards a positive theory of consumer choice. *Journal of Economic Behavior and Organization* 1:38–60.

Thaler, R., and H.M. Shefrin. 1981. An economic theory of self-control. *Journal of Political Economy* 89:392–406.

Thompson, F. 1983. Beyond the war game mystique. *Proceedings of the United States Naval Institute.* October: 82–87.

Tihansky, D. 1976. Confidence assessment of military airframe cost predictions. *Operations Research* 24:26–43.

Tucker, J.B. 1983. Strategic command and control vulnerabilities: Dangers and remedies. *Orbis* 26(4):941–963.

Tune, G.S. 1964. Response preferences: A review of some relevant literature. *Psychological Bulletin* 61:286–302.

Turner, B.A. 1978. *Man-Made Disasters.* London: Wykeham.

Turner, C.F., and E. Krauss. 1978. Fallible indicators of the subjective state of the nation. *American Psychologist* 33:456–470.

Turner, C.F., and E. Martin. 1984. *Surveying Subjective Phenomena,* Vol. 2. New York: Russell Sage.

Tushman, M.L., and P. Anderson. 1986. Technological discontinuities and organizational environments. *Administrative Science Quarterly* 31:439–465.

Tversky, A., and Kahneman, D. 1973. Availability: A heuristic for judging frequency and probability. *Cognitive Psychology* 5:207–232.

————. 1974. Judgment under uncertainty: Heuristics and biases. *Science* 185:1124–1131.

————. 1981. The framing of decisions and the psychology of choice. *Science* 211:453–458.

Ungson, G.R., and D.N. Braunstein, eds. 1983. *Decision Making: An Interdisciplinary Perspective.* New York: Kent.

U.S. Catholic Conference. 1983. *The Challenge of Peace: God's Promise and Our Response.* Washington, D.C.: U.S. Catholic Conference.

U.S. Government. 1979. Report of the President's Commission on the Accident at Three Mile Island. Washington, D.C.: U.S. Government Printing Office.

U.S. Department of Commerce. 1980. *Social Indicators.* Washington, D.C.: U.S. Department of Commerce.

U.S. Nuclear Regulatory Commission. 1983. *PRA Procedures Guide.* NUREG/CR-2300. Washington, D.C.: U.S. Nuclear Regulatory Commission.

Ury, W.L., and R. Smoke. 1984. *Beyond the Hotline: Controlling a Nuclear Crisis.* Cambridge, Mass.: Harvard Law School.

Vertzberger, Y.Y.I. 1986. Foreign policy decision makers as practical intuitive historians: Applied history and its shortcomings. *International Studies Quarterly* 30:223–247.

von Winterfeldt, D., and W. Edwards. 1982. Costs and payoffs in perceptual research. *Psychological Bulletin* 93:609–622.

———. 1986. *Decision Analysis and Behavioral Research*. New York: Cambridge University Press.

Wagenaar, W.A. 1970. Subjective randomness and the capacity to generate information. *Acta Psychologica* 33:233–242.

Wagenaar, W.A., and H. Timmers. 1979. The pond-and-duckweed problem: Three experiments on the misperception of exponential growth. *Acta Psychologica* 43:239–251.

Wallace, M.D., B.L. Crissey, and L.W. Sennott. 1986. Accidental muclear war: A risk assessment. *Journal of Peace Research* 23:9–27.

Wallsten, T., and D. Budescu. 1983. Encoding subjective probabilities: A psychological and psychometric review. *Management Science* 29:151–173.

Warm, J.S., and R. Parasuraman, eds. 1987. Vigilance: Basic and applied research. *Human Factors* 29:6.

Watson, S., and D. Buede. 1987. *Decision Synthesis*. Cambridge, England: Cambridge University Press.

Weick, K.E. 1979. *The Social Psychology of Organizing*. New York: Random House.

Weinstein, N.D. 1980. Unrealistic optimism about future life events. *Journal of Personality and Social Psychology* 39:806–820.

White, R.K., ed. 1986. *Psychology and the Prevention of Nuclear War*. New York: New York University Press.

Wickens, C.D. 1984. *Engineering Psychology and Human Performance*. Columbus, Ohio: Merrill.

Wilensky, H. 1967. *Organizational Intelligence: Knowledge and Policy in Government and Industry*. New York: Basic Books.

Wilks, S.S. 1938. Weighting systems for linear functions of correlated variables when there is no dependent variable. *Psychometrica* 8:23–40.

Williams, R., and R. Mills, eds. 1986. *Public Acceptance of New Technologies*. London: Croom Helm.

Williamson, O. 1981. The economics of organization. The transaction cost approach. *American Journal of Sociology* 87(3):548–574.

Wohl, J.G. 1981. Force management decision requirements for Air Force tactical command and control. *IEEE Transactions on Systems, Man and Cybernetics* SMC-11:618–639.

Wohlstetter, R. 1962. *Pearl Harbor: Warning and Decision*. Stanford, Calif.: Stanford University Press.

Woods, D.D., E.M. Roth, and E.H. Pople, Jr. 1987. *Cognitive Environment Simulation: An Artificial Intelligence System for Human Performance Assessment*. Washngton, D.C.: U.S. Nuclear Regulatory Commission.

Wright, P., and F. Barbour. 1977. Phased decision strategies: Sequels to an initial screening. In M.K. Starr and M. Zeleny, eds., *Studies in the Management Sciences*, Vol. 6. Amsterdam: North Holland.

Yntema, D.B., and W.S. Torgerson. 1961. Man-computer cooperation in decisions requiring common sense. *IRE Transactions of the Professional Group in Human Factors in Electronics* 2:20–26.

Zracket, C.A. 1984. Strategic command, control, communication, and intelligence. *Science* 224:1306–1311.

Zuckerman, S. 1982. *Nuclear Illusion and Reality.* London: Collins.

4

Is There a Role for Third Parties in the Prevention of Nuclear War

PETER WALLENSTEEN

Introduction

D o third parties have a role in the relations between major powers? In which conflicts can third parties be of significance? Can they contribute to moderating issues of contention to help avoid a major war or a nuclear war? These are the questions raised in this chapter by a review of the theoretical and empirical literature on mediation and conflict resolution. Ultimately the answers depend on an evaluation of the peace-promoting role third parties *could have*—that is, the potential of this opinion, not only the role they possibly *have had* in recent history.

Escalation and the Outbreak of Nuclear War

Nuclear war among major powers is, in most scenarios, seen as a result of contention and escalation of conflict. It is rarely a bolt from blue sky. For example, most scenarios assume that in an East–West setting, military confrontation grows into a conventional war, followed eventually by a limited nuclear and then a total nuclear war. In scenarios involving relations between other nuclear powers (for example, the Soviet Union and China, or countries in the Middle East), the patterns are similar: disputes leading to local military actions and escalation. Thus, the analysis of locally initiated conflicts and their dynamics might yield important insight into ways of preventing escalation. In such dynamics, third parties may play a role in reducing escalation potential. This makes scholarly studies of mediation and conflict resolution in local conflicts of great relevance.

A major war between the United States and the Soviet Union, although specified by the leaders of the two countries at the 1985 summit meeting in Geneva as something that cannot be won and must never be fought (Weihmiller, 1986:202), remains a possibility. It involves issues of conflict and conflict resolution in at least two ways.

First, such a global war could be the outcome of a local confrontation that pits the two superpowers directly against each other. Due to commitments, internal pressures, power calculations, and actions and reactions, such a local dispute could escalate to a major war. This is what we might call the *Sarajevo scenario*. World War I broke out following the assassination of the heir of Austria–Hungary by a "terrorist" (in today's language) supported by a revisionist country, Serbia. Russia in turn was allied to Serbia, while Germany stood behind Austria–Hungary. France and Great Britain in turn were allied to Russia. This delicate fabric of alliances and counteralliances was intended to ensure balance and peace. In the crisis of 1914 it suddenly worked the other way around: the ties pulled the opposing alliances into war with one another. The lessons for today points to the danger of the escalation of local wars, as well as the importance of negotiation.

Could the crisis in 1914 have been dealt with differently? After World War I, there was a strong sentiment in this direction. Direct negotiations were seen as a way of avoiding repetition. The 1920s and 1930s became a time of constant contact, agreement, and verbal support for international governance and agreed procedures (partly, but not exclusively, within the framework of the League of Nations). The Sarajevo scenario colored thinking, particularly among the Western powers, only to be proved wrong by Nazi Germany. The policies of Adolf Hitler suggested another way in which major wars could break out between major powers—as deliberate attempts to gain advantage. By fooling the others with lofty promises and impressive agreements that were not serious but deceptive, an advantageous opportunity was created and exploited. This is the legacy of the Munich Conference—the *Munich syndrome,* which has haunted Western statesmen ever since. It is remarkable that this agreement has left such an imprint in the West, whereas the agreement of the following year between Stalin and Hitler, which divided Eastern Europe, but also led to a direct attack on the Soviet Union in less than 2 years, has not. However, as deception this agreement has all the same traits, albeit in a magnified way. Let us also include this experience under the Munich syndrome.

The Munich syndrome gives us a second model for how war could break out between major powers, also in the nuclear age. For the United States and the Soviet Union, the conclusion from Munich is that there is to be no error in understanding the power calculus of the opponent. Instead, one assumes that the worst possible, the "worst case," is probable enough to be taken seriously. For each side it is obvious or likely that the other is bent on "world domination." In fact, each would argue that if the other side gains the "upper hand," this equals "world domination." This means that if "we" are "weak" in a confrontation, "we" might "lose" initially or completely. Thus, be on your guard! The Munich lesson is that whatever the other side does, it is assumed that this is only to the benefit of the other, not to both. This interpretation leaves very little room for discussion or compromise.

The lessons from the Sarajevo scenario are, "Do not judge the other side unheard" and "Find out by listening!," whereas the Munich syndrome teaches, "Do not trust your opponent!" and "Make your own critical judgment!"

It may sound as if the two lessons cancel each other, or, alternatively, as if we are today back in 1914. Neither is necessarily true. The combination might be the optimum: listen first, judge later, but in any case listen! In the case of

Sarajevo, decision makers felt that they were firmly in control of events, and, thus, underestimated the potentially fatal links that existed between a local issue and the great-power relations. They did not see the need to listen. In the case of Munich, leaders, at least in the West, felt that they were not going to make the Sarajevo mistake once more, so they worked to contain the conflict from the beginning, to avoid its escalation. They were prepared to listen but not to take a firm stand. Thus, instead of defending Czechoslovakia in 1938, as Russia had defended Serbia in 1914, Czechoslovakia was allowed to disappear. In retrospect, we know that neither action nor inaction prevented the escalation of the conflict from engulfing the major powers themselves.

The inopportune handling of conflict was essential for the outbreak of both world wars. In both cases, measures were taken that in fact brought about what was to be avoided. The actions neither resolved the issue at hand nor reduced the intensity of the conflict. And, most important from our perspective, in neither case was a third party outside the alliance frameworks involved in the attempts to find a solution.

The Sarajevo scenario and the Munich syndrome both tell us that relations involving smaller countries are important for the major powers. In both these situations, the problems of a small country gradually involved one major power (ambitious neighbors in both cases), and, as a consequence, other major powers also became entangled. The history of conflicts in the nuclear age shows that much conflict involving major powers actually focuses on smaller countries. The repeated crises in the Middle East, Southwest Asia, Indochina, and Korea all testify to this. The major nuclear powers become actors through their alliances and commitments.

However, not all major power conflicts arise this way. Conflicts in Europe have directly and immediately involved the victors of World War II, so there also has been fear of more direct escalatory processes. Chains of escalation and the strength of the linkages in these chains are important, even though the chains may look somewhat different. It is in terms of these linkages that the role of the third parties becomes interesting. Is there a role third parties can play for the prevention of escalation and the finding of equitable solutions without resort to war?

The Dilemmas of Third Parties

In historical writings on the outbreaks of the two world wars, little attention is given to third parties working for mediation, conflict resolution, or both. Even if one examines the scholarly literature searching for a larger role of third parties, one will find little material on the actual or potential uses of third parties in these developments. History suggests that major powers do not normally allow third parties to become engaged: they want to deal with other major powers themselves. Although this may be historically true, is this also true today? Does it mean that there is always a very restricted space available to the third parties in major-power relations? Would major powers find intermediaries of more significance in relations between small countries? The nuclear age gives every state and every people a stake in major-power conflicts. The number of actors have increased, including states as well as nongovernmental actors. This might enlarge the role of third parties. Pertinent questions can be asked about the potential role of third-party involvement in conflicts by drawing on an empirical literature on mediation in conflicts that builds on psychological approaches and modern case studies.

Third parties face different issues depending on the conflict. Some situations actually cause serious dilemmas for the third parties and jeopardize their efficacy in contributing to an equitable solution of a conflict. The literature of interest in this chapter is that which can help us find the answers to these dilemmas.

First, we need to consider the role of third parties in different situations of power relations between the primary parties. These variations, it can be assumed, will expose third parties to different challenges. Situations of power relations are represented across the top of Figure 4.1.

Second, we need to consider whether a conflict is in an acute crisis phase at the time a third party becomes involved. It might be argued that third parties

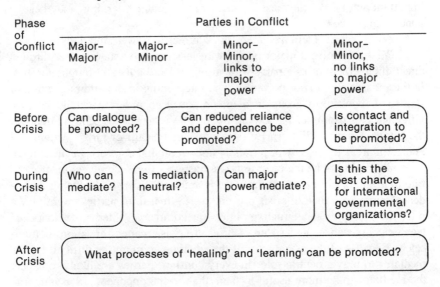

FIGURE 4.1. Some dilemmas for third parties in conflict resolution.

can play more important roles in a long-term, less dramatic situation. Thus, attention has to be given to activities before a crisis appears, as well as what happens after a crisis. This gives us a second dimension to consider, as shown in Figure 4.1. Different relations of power between the opponents expose prospective third parties to different challenges, and these challenges vary depending on the degree of tension in the relations. Figure 4.1 illustrates these challenges. For example, in relations between two parties of similar status and influence, (for example, two major powers), third parties may be very important in promoting dialogue *before a crisis* in low tension situations, notably in multilateral negotiation fora. Such interventions are preventive and ultimately can be helpful in avoiding the emergence of crisis between the major powers. Problems take on another dimension *during a crisis,* when it might be unacceptable for major powers to consent to mediation. From the perspective of the major powers, mediation at this stage could appear as unwarranted interference in "their" affairs, even if "their" actions threaten the survival of the world. Thus, it might be difficult to have the principle established that nonmajor states or nongovernmental actors have the right to interfere peacefully, even though simply having such a principle agreed would achieve something meaningful for the moderation of major-power relations. Finally, there are the *postcrisis* situations. After a crisis, direct relations between the participants have been affected, the crisis has had an impact on other major powers, and lessons from the crisis have to be drawn. Here again, third parties could be important actors, not the least because "healing" and "learning" may best be done in dialogue.

A second set of dilemmas arises in asymmetric power situations—that is, conflicts that involve a major power with less powerful states either through direct engagement or as a party with strong links to a locally fought conflict. In these cases, the major power may be intervening in the affairs of a minor state or supporting a group in a minor power in order to extend its own influence (for example, the United States in Vietnam and Central America, the Soviet Union in Eastern Europe and Afghanistan, or Great Britain and France in areas previously or presently under colonial control). In such cases, dialogue might not be the most important aspect of *crisis prevention.* If, as is true in a number of cases, dependence is among the causes, reducing dependence might be a road to crisis prevention. In this, third parties might play a role, for example, as alternative outlets for commerce, alternative donors of technical assistance, and so on. During a crisis, matters are more complicated. Because of the asymmetry of the situation, it might be difficult for the mediator to play a neutral role. In every conflict, parties are likely to expect the mediator to be more useful to them than to the opponent. In asymmetric situations, however, these expectations might be even stronger. The underdog (the weaker, often rebellious side) may expect support (and demands support, because it is so important to legitimize its struggle), while the dominant expects support because it is upholding an established order (and demands support, because rebellions are "illegitimate" and "criminal"). The neutrality of the mediator becomes a serious issue. There is a parallel between third parties involved in international intervention cases (a major state invading a smaller one) and in internal rebellion (the government fighting a rebel movement).

In the *aftermath of a crisis,* third parties may take on new roles. They might be particularly useful in promoting a common analysis and understanding of the situation. It appears that this role, which has rarely been explored or used, is a potentially useful one. For example, U.S.–Vietnamese relations remain very contentious even 15 years after a peace treaty was signed. The crisis has still not been healed and the lessons for the relations between the two parties have still to be drawn. The necessary healing process might be furthered by parties outside this relationship.

Finally, there is a set of conflicts in which the links to major powers, or to any outsiders for that matter, might be very limited. Outsiders sometimes leave conflicting parties to themselves because they see the conflict as "tribal" or "ethnic" and therefore local and of little general interest. Here, international governmental organizations (IGOs) have a special role to play. Their specific normative systems might help in bringing about mediation. The main problem in such cases concerns the perceived relevance or irrelevance of the conflict to the international community.

The Aim of This Chapter

The literature on conflict resolution gives insights into many of the problems facing third parties. This chapter asks whether the intervention of a third party might influence a particular dispute and prevent its escalation. The questions being raised concern the role of third parties in conflict resolution in general and in conflicts affecting the major nuclear powers in particular. First, what possibilities are available for third parties in mediating or resolving conflicts in which they themselves are not directly involved? The general literature gives some clues to this (see the section on "The Study of Third Parties") and also attempts to establish the likelihood of third-party activity in different types of conflicts. This effort requires an analysis of all conflicts at a given moment in time. The section on "Third Parties in Armed Conflicts of the 1980s" gives some results in this respect.

Second, what role can major powers play in contributing to the resolution of conflict? This question is of significance concerning the prevention of a nuclear war between the major powers. This question is approached in the section on "Power Relations and Third-Party Activity." The role of major powers in conflict is emphasized, relating to the Sarajevo scenario and the Munich syndrome.

In general, the focus is on the contextual determinants of third party activity for conflict resolution. Under what conditions can it take place? What forms could be conceived to further its applicability? In the last section, some general conclusions on third parties in the prevention of nuclear war are advanced.

Although the focus is on conflict and crisis, literature relevant to the analysis of conflict phases before or after a crisis is also examined. But because the primary concern is with manifest conflict behavior, where parties have been, or actively are, pressing each other to change positions, this chapter does not examine the role of third parties in permanent or semipermanent negotiation settings, such as test ban treaties, European security, the Law of the Seas, or the General Agreement on Tariffs and Trade (GATT). In many instances, third parties can play a considerable, useful, and effective role in such situations, but the conditions are less immediately relevant for the possibilities of the outbreak of a nuclear war.

A major focus is on armed conflict—that is, the use of force or the threat of force (wars, civil wars, military confrontations, and other armed struggles), based on an assumption that there is a critical difference between armed and nonarmed conflicts. Weapons, in all likelihood, transform conflicts and make them more deadly, more irreversible. This feature also makes the role of the third parties different. Third parties may have a more obvious role in non-armed conflicts than in situations in which the primary parties are directly confronting each other militarily. In permanent or semipermanent negotiations, the outcome is determined by the capacity of the negotiators as well as by the internal policies of the parties. In the war-related negotiations, however, the resort to arms is always a distinct possibility and makes negotiations different.

This chapter is mainly concerned with third-party activities conducted "in the open." That is, the parties to a conflict have officially invited or accepted the appointment by others of a third party to contribute to an agreement concerning the conflict between the two sides. The third parties are either states or international governmental organizations. In this respect, the present study of the potential uses of third parties is severely limited, as informal, nongovernmental activity might also be very important. The literature on third-party consultation is included in this review, because it suggests approaches in which parties accept an ongoing intervention, and can benefit from it, without committing themselves openly and fully.

Third parties are differentiated from the primary parties, which are the ones involved in direct conflict with one another. Although the third party is not necessarily a disinterested observer, it cannot actively send troops into the situation. This chapter uses the concept of "mediation" as synonymous to conflict resolution activity and does not apply the legally important distinction between conciliation, good offices, and mediation (Merrills, 1983). Parties that act as intermediaries are also of interest, even though they can be distinguished from mediators (Pruitt, 1971:227; Young, 1967). These concepts refer to a wide range of activities aimed at resolving a conflict. All of them point to the third party placing him or herself "between" the parties, by contributing to communication between fighting parties, or by presenting proposals (formally or informally). Thus, no particular distinction is made between the concepts in this context. Issues of arbitration are left untouched because, despite its importance, such third-party activity is infrequent.

Some literature on mediation examines settings on an interpersonal level, while some deals with interstate relations. To what extent, one may ask, is knowledge gained about interpersonal conflicts (for example, in a school setting) relevant for the rivalries between two contending societies? Certainly, personal matters will play a role, but at the same time, other factors might reduce their significance. Among such considerations are a state leader's feelings of responsibility, historical chances, and concern about upcoming elections. Thus, some knowledge gained on interpersonal relations might be relevant, while other knowledge might be more of an heuristic nature. Third-party mediation among warring parties places certain extreme pressures on individuals, and they are not necessarily easily replicable in experimental form.

On the other hand, historical and biographical data are not entirely reliable. People giving the accounts might not be trained to perceive, for example, psychological or social dimensions. Also, there is much information lost, because accounts will be based only on a fraction of the evidence. Additional evidence is lost or never recorded. The insights from interpersonal relations might, under these circumstances, be highly important to help filling the gaps.

We need to recall that we are dealing with some highly complex social, political, and psychological webs of interaction when addressing the question of third-party mediation in armed conflicts.

The Study of Third Parties

Overview

The literature on third parties in conflict resolution has attracted inquiries of many different fields and thus is rich in approaches. However, very few studies explicitly treat the question of third parties and the prevention of nuclear war. This means that the literature has to be seen as a body of knowledge with implications for the present purpose, rather than as something raising more direct propositions applicable to the nuclear war situation. Some studies contain very clear policy implications, because the focus often is to "be practical." In fact, studies fall along an axis of practical involvement, from largely academic studies with implications for third-party activity to studies suggesting that academics themselves should be involved as third parties, in third-part consultation or workshops. Most of the work is primarily academic. A second dimension, relevant for most of the work, relates to a difference in focus on development of maxims, theory, or descriptions. According to Pruitt (1986), maxims are rules of thumb, statements about what to do and what not to do. Theoretical propositions, by contrast, are specifying conditions under which certain matters are true or false and are given in a form that makes them empirically testable (Pruitt, 1986). An additional category of studies, not relating directly to these dimensions, describes the legal and other tools available to third parties. Most of the work providing conclusions for third parties falls clearly into these categories, whereas the third-party consultation approach actually combines several of them. Thus, the work on third-party activity is found in four broad methodological groups:

1. development of maxims for negotiations and third-party activity;
2. development of theoretical and empirical propositions on third-party activity;
3. development of resource descriptions on third-party work;
4. development of forms of academic third-party involvement.

The first group of negotiation studies is devoted to development of maxims. Some studies offer maxims in a form that is scientifically testable, while others leave the test to real-life experience. These studies place mediation or third-party activity within the general field of negotiation and bargaining. Thus, propositions are formulated on the basis of what is a good bargaining strategy. The studies drew on the approach of the practitioner (Cancio, 1959) or the theoretician (Fisher and Ury, 1981), and often generate how to act as a negotiator or as a mediator.

The second set of studies are theoretical ones based on empirical research. These aim at generalization, but with maximal empirical support. Depending on the methodology as well as the level of analysis used, these studies in turn fall into two categories, namely, those based on social-psychological analysis, and those based on case analysis of historical (recent or modern) cases of mediation. In the former category we find the work of Pruitt (1971) and Druckman (1977). Most notable among the latter are the works of Touval and

Zartman, which enrich the mediation literature with considerable historical material (Touval, 1982; Zartman and Berman, 1982; Touval and Zartman, 1985). Also in the latter group are studies focusing on the operation of international organizations (Young, 1967, 1971; Claude, 1971; Ott, 1972; Haas, 1983) and studies of negotiations and mediations in the Middle East, either explicitly relating to mediation theory or not (Rubin, 1981; Quandt, 1986). Both these types of study give strong arguments for the uses of mediation. Some carefully formulated propositions have been forwarded. Some studies based on quantitative methods have also emerged, focusing links between norms and third-party activity for conflict resolution (Raymond and Kegley, 1985 on mediation; Raymond, 1980, on arbitration).

The third set of studies is of a legalistic orientation, not aiming at generalization, but nevertheless providing useful tools for the would-be third parties (Bailey, 1982; Curle, 1971). In this line of inquiry, propositions on institutionalization of mediation are among those raised.

Finally, the fourth group of studies combine the development of maxims and theory in real-world applications with conflict participation, either to test the maxims to develop theory or to contribute to the solution of the conflict. Workshops using different techniques have been suggested or reported (Burton, 1969; Doob, 1970; Walton, 1970; Kelman, 1972; Fisher, 1980, 1983; Mitchell, 1981; Kelman, 1982; Azar and Burton, 1986). The workshop approach is an interesting development, because it balances on the border between a scientific experiment and political action. Workshop approaches raise some severe ethical issues that, in the pioneering spirit typical of this work, seem largely to be undiscussed.

Considerable insight can be generated from these sources. Many propositions can be raised, some fairly self-evident, others more counterintuitive. Some of them carry considerable empirical support. The basic problem is to estimate their relevance for major-power relations and the prevention of nuclear war. Such extrapolation faces the problems of level of analysis (to what extent are conclusions from one level, such as the laboratory, applicable to another, such as the international) and analogy transfer (are conclusions from a nonarmed situation applicable to armed conflict, where the use of weapons and even nuclear weapons is a real option?).

The literature includes interesting and divergent approaches to mediation and third-party activity. Some of it draws conclusions relevant for the mediation in a strict sense, that is, for third-party explicitly appointed by the primary parties to find a solution to their conflict. This classical interpretation of the role of third parties is the focus of the three first groups of work. In such work, the analysis of the primary parties and their ambitions and behavior is important. The role of third parties is seen largely as a reflection of what transpired between the primary parties. This literature differs markedly from work of the fourth category, which reports instances of third parties who, on their own initiative, present themselves to the parties in conflict with some proposals or procedures for conflict resolution. Such initiatives rely on the acceptance by the primary parties, who, however, remain detached from the process, although prepared to use it whenever suitable.

This fourth research approach is an alternative form of conflict resolution activity, similar to what some term *track II* diplomacy (Bendahmane and McDonald, 1986). It works under very different conditions than conventional mediation, because it does not involve the direct explicit negotiation between appointed representatives of the conflicting parties. The ambition is often to explore basic issues, generate ideas, and, in this way, help break impasses. This work builds on a body of psychological literature other than those drawn on within conventional mediation studies.

The different approaches can be said to contrast with each other. It is *not*, however, unreasonable to conclude that they in fact may complement each other. Conflict resolution can most fruitfully be viewed as a process into which all these approaches can provide useful insights and may be relevant under different conditions or at different phases of a reconciliation process. Although the strict mediation approaches have so far received more attention, the workshop approaches are also relevant to the present purpose.

Research Questions

A serious problem in the literature on mediation is that many highly pertinent questions have received little attention. For example, there is surprisingly little information available on the frequency of uses of mediation and other forms of third-party involvement for conflict resolution. Are they used often? When are they used? Such information may appear rather trivial, but it is almost nonexistent. The case study or experimental approaches, almost by definition, cannot answer these questions. They can point to the existence of the phenomenon and indicate some of its intricacies. A full answer requires access to all conflicts of a particular type, making possible the comparison of cases with and without third-party conflict resolution activity. Thus, there is no response available, as yet, to the provocative remarks by Clark Kerr from 1954 when discussing mediation in industrial conflict:

> . . . mediation appears always to be successful . . . all disputes end at some point, and all strikes are concluded. . . . Contrariwise, mediation might be said to make little or no contribution in the sense that all disputes would be settled sometime without outside intervention. In fact, there is no accurate quantifiable

test of its efficiency . . . much mediation, where relations are well established, is quite ceremonial . . . ." (Kerr, 1954:236).

This means that one cannot, at this time, evaluate what would happen if there were no mediation or other conflict resolution activities. From Kerr's provocative statements it follows that one needs to know not just what mediators do, but what they do better than the primary parties themselves. Although this is implied in much research, there is no body of literature trying to compare mediator activity to the principal parties' activities in a given conflict. Third-party studies tend to focus on the mediator's contribution, and a full assessment of all the actors' roles in a particular settlement is rarely attempted. In some sense, it is obvious that the mediator cannot, and perhaps should not, impose an agreement on the primary parties. From the point of view of a durable settlement, it has to be something the primary parties can live with: the substance of the agreement has to be made by them. Thus, Kerr's challenge should not be overstated. Conflict resolution has to be seen as a process, and the contribution of the third-party might be of another kind. It is visible more in its ability to shorten the time to reach an agreement, its impact on particular elements of an agreement, and its help in legitimizing an agreement. A mediator can do the last by showing that both sides have pushed their point as far as possible, even to the point where a mediator had to be invited. The third party, then, takes on a role of a conflict resolution mechanism (Galtung, 1965).

The significance of mediation and other methods of conflict resolution can probably be more easily analyzed with respect to industrial conflict than to international relations. This is because considerable statistical and historical information has been accumulated on industrial mediation. For labor as well as for management, it has been important to learn about the particular conflict being faced, and to be able to generalize from one type of conflict to another. The literature on mediation in armed conflicts, however, lacks such resources. Remarkably, the parties to armed conflict have seldom been interested in an objective analysis of the conflict phenomenon in general. Instead, there is a preference for reports on particular issues, without generalizing ambition. The difference could well be that armed conflicts rarely are seen to involve a repetition of a similar conflict between the same primary parties. Primary parties to one conflict often see their conflict as a result of special circumstances. Thus, their interest in generalization becomes limited. Scholarly literature may well reflect this. However, there is a set of protracted conflicts that could support efforts at generalization, where comparison would be policy relevant, as well as theoretically warranted (for example, the conflicts between Israelis and Palestinians, the superpowers, India and Pakistan, and

Greece and Turkey), where the protraction of the conflict may itself be the most distinguishing feature of the conflict (Brecher and James, 1988:453). The internationally accepted scientific data bank on conflicts and conflict resolution remains to be created.

This means that fairly little systematic evidence is available on the circumstances that give rise to mediation or other conflict resolution activity. Some data have been generated, however, describing the historical uses of international organizations (Butterworth, 1976; Haas, 1983). Because the issue is important, the third section of this chapter concerns an initial analysis of a set of ongoing wars in order to understand how third-party activity for conflict resolution emerges.

Considerably more attention has been given to the functions of third-party activity. What do mediators do that is seen as useful to the primary parties of the conflict? The answers are deduced from theory or emerge from observations of what mediators have actually done in a large number of conflicts. In general, the mediator's job is "to try to persuade each party to accept the largest concession the other is willing to make" (Pruitt, 1971:230). Presumably, a successful mediator has some special qualifications for this that the parties in conflict do not have. The functions different analysts identify for mediators are remarkably similar. This suggests that there are some aspects common to many conflicts that mediators can attend to with particular emphasis.

Wall, in an extensive review of the literature, enumerates 107 different functions that mediators can provide (Wall, 1981). Many of these are of the "providing service" type—that is, helping, guiding, and supporting the primary parties in identifying, understanding, and explaining issues, and so forth. Wall differentiates several relationships involving the mediator, such as internegotiator relations and mediator-negotiator relations (Wall, 1981:171–175). There are many lists of the functions mediators may carry out. An illustrative presentation is given by Pruitt (1971:229) below.

- Educate an inexperienced negotiator.
- Arrange a meeting.
- Give strategic advice.
- Aid in reality testing.
- Urge that a concession be made.
- Recommend a known option.
- Devise a new integrative option.
- Guarantee compliance to an agreement.
- Help undo a commitment.
- Be a channel for communication.
- Facilitate the coordination of mutual concessions.

A special function of mediators arises from the fact that "a negotiator who concedes on his own feels personally weaker than one who concedes in response to a mediator's suggestion" (Pruitt, 1971:230). From the point of view of the primary parties, "image loss in the eyes of outsiders or constituents is minimized with a mediator, to the extent he respects the norm of keeping these dealings secret" (Pruitt, 1971:231).

The strength of the mediator would, thus, lie in informal bargaining. Much work on this topic has concerned norms of behavior that would improve the chances for the mediator's success.

Although the mediator is normally seen as having little power or influence beyond the intellectual (finding the apparent and mutually satisfactory solution) and diplomatic (presenting solutions in a nonoffending way), the importance of other forms of power still emerges from this research. Thus, Pruitt presents the following hypothesis on making agreements as unusually well supported: "A negotiator will be more likely to initiate such efforts, the greater the apparent authority of his opponent. By 'authority' is meant a negotiator's influence over substantive decisions made by his own side . . ." (Pruitt, 1971:234).

This suggests that negotiations on higher levels in a decision hierarchy are more important. In international affairs, this implies that summit diplomacy is more successful than other types of negotiation. It might also imply that powerful mediators are more successful. This is a reason for us to consider the role of major powers as third parties (see "Power Relations and Third-Party Activity").

Pruitt also finds support for the hypothesis that the overall relations between the primary parties is important, and that the mediator could play a role when relations are less well established between the parties:

> Intermediaries and mediators are more likely to be employed, the more hostile and suspicious each party is of the other . . . because people who are hostile and suspicious of each other tend to avoid face-to-face meetings and are often unable to deal productively with each other in such meetings if they arise. (Pruitt, 1971:236).

The literature focusing on case studies emphasizes the significance of the timing of mediation for success. Mediation may come in at the right moment, sometimes described as the "ripe" moment. Success may come only when the primary parties and their relations have reached a particular situation, sometimes described as a "hurting stalemate" or as "maturity" (Zartman, 1986; Claude, 1971:239). The observation seems to cover much of the practitioners' notion: when there is a realization among the primary parties that a particular war can no longer be won (however, "victory" is defined by the primary parties), finding a solution with the help of intermediaries becomes a way out. To objectively define such situations seems more difficult, and some retrospective analysts suggest that other factors may be more important, for example, changes in regime in one of the fighting parties (Ott, 1972:612).

The issue of the mediator's motives emerges more strongly in historical and modern political case studies than in the psychological literature. An example is Touval's study of peacemaking efforts in the Middle East, *The Peace Brokers* (Touval, 1982). The title addresses motivation, alluding to the American expression "honest broker." Touval writes: "Mediators, like brokers, are in it for profit. It is, of course, a profit that can be earned in the pursuit of a praiseworthy cause. Whether they should be called 'honest brokers' is another matter; the question of their honesty arises only insofar as the term is applicable to power politics" (Touval, 1982:321). Although doubting the mediator's honesty may seem to run counter to much of the thinking on mediation, this need not necessarily be so. Touval sees, for example, an institutional self-interest in the work of some of the international and regional organizations engaged in mediation. Successful mediation would strengthen the organization. This analysis relates to the proposals and activities of the mediator. It leaves open the question of whether the mediator's self-interest will affect the mediation attempt. The role of a generalized self-interest will be considered in the discussion of the circumstances under which mediation takes place (see the next section, "Third Parties in Armed Conflicts of the 1980s").

The question of self-interest becomes particularly important when considering the role of major powers in mediation. Obviously, they have interests that could run counter to those of the parties in conflict. Also, major powers do not need to be motivated by a desire to *settle* a conflict. A mediation effort might spring from other considerations, notably the establishment of relations in general (Touval, 1982:324). Within both a Sarajevo scenario and a Munich syndrome, the potential mediating role of major powers might suggest policies to avoid or prevent escalation of armed conflicts. However, the literature is seldom rich on such suggestions, except on a very general level.

Finally, the literature raises a question about the selection of mediator. Again to quote Touval (1982:325): "It is not necessary for mediators to be perceived as impartial." Rather, Touval argues, "the mediator's ability to induce the parties to make concessions and accept compromise proposals did not derive from his impartiality but from the material resources at his disposal. These enabled the mediator to exert pressure on the parties" (Touval, 1982:326). This comment emphasizes the extramediation powers of the mediator. The primary parties can turn to a mediator who they expect to be able to deliver something nobody else is capable of. In many cases, an appropriate mediator might consequently be a very interested party with ties to one of the fighting parties, rather than one completely disinterested and unrelated to the situation. The mediator might, under certain circumstances, be more successful by being involved in the situation, rather than distant from it. Whether this is generally true, or only derives from one particular situation (the Arab–Israel conflict) is something Touval leaves unanswered. The dilemma, then, is to select mediators that are at the same time relevant (that is, have some interest in the situation, understand it, even relate to the situation) and impartial (that is, do not pursue particular interests of their own and have equidistance to the primary parties). A close study of mediators actually selected for particular conflicts would yield more insight on this. How do parties select mediators if there is a conflict between relevance and impartiality? Again, there is a lack of available systematic information on the basics of the problem.

The limited literature on independent third-party consultation or work-shops, the fourth approach, raises issues of great interest. The third party is often termed a consultant or a facilitator, drawing on social science knowl-edge of conflict processes at large or on specialization area knowledge. Usu-ally there is a team of persons with different sets of expertise. The format is a workshop in which participants leave the actual scene of conflict for a new surrounding and keep largely to themselves for a period of time. The most extensively reported workshop is for the Horn of Africa conflict, which met in Italy in 1969. This so-called Fermeda workshop was reported on by the organizers and the participants themselves (Doob, 1970; Walton, 1970). The workshop approach draws on work on international relations (Burton, 1969), as well as conflict resolution, and has been employed in different settings (Northern Ireland: Doob and Foltz, 1973, 1974; Cyprus: Doob, 1974; more general: Azar and Burton, 1986). Most of these workshops have not been as extensively documented as the Fermeda workshop. A slightly different ap-proach within this category, although perhaps more directly geared to the political problem, is the problem-solving workshops carried out by Kelman concerning the Israeli–Palestinian conflict and advanced as a way toward direct negotiations between the conflict parties (Kelman, 1982:68–74). The same issues that were discussed concerning the strict mediation approach arise in these workshop approaches.

The question of frequency is less relevant in this context. The initiative does not rest with the primary parties themselves. Rather, it stems from knowledge and ability of the independent scholars. This fact may make this category of third-party involvement less easy to define. There are obviously many forms of such activity, including not only explicit workshops, but also general discussions on a particular conflict with participation from all sides, such as scholarly and political conferences, or exchanges and dialogues with-in national and international frameworks. The possibilities of third-party intervention are many and an impact can be expected on many different levels. The frequency of such informal exchanges in a particular conflict is hard to estimate, but again might be a most worthwhile analysis. All the workshops reported to have taken place were initiated by groups coming from an Anglo–Saxon culture, and they typically concerned conflicts particularly interesting to certain Western audiences. This is to suggest that there might, in fact, be a number of initiatives in other contexts (that is, nonacademic settings) and other conflicts (that is, with less direct Western involvement) that are not equally well documented and thus less easily analyzed.

The approach taken in the strict workshop design is to bring out the real problems, by making the participants from each side listen to the opposite side, and even formulate the adversaries' position themselves. In that sense, workshops involve nonpartisan communication. This value of the workshops is also acknowledged by very critical participants (Doob, 1970:38–56). Workshops, like other forms of exchanges, can help clarify issues, even making it possible to formulate incompatibilities in ways that may make compatibility obvious to the participants. Kelman (1982:73–74; Kelman and Cohen, 1976) describes the workshops as useful as they are "conducive to new learning" and specifies that they:

- provide opportunity to listen to and learn from the other side;
- explore a range of possible solutions;
- give and receive signals; and
- identify necessary and possible steps.

Comparing this to the lists on mediator's usefulness quoted earlier, the functions performed are fairly similar: there is again a provision of services. The workshop approach, however, has a more educational content, probably comes in at an earlier stage conflict resolution process (for example, Kelman [1982] mentions their significance in a prenegotiation period), and is less directly tied to the political-governmental negotiations process. The two approaches can be seen as contradictory, the workshop being "softer" and the mediation "harder" in their relations to politics. However, realities consist of both hard and soft elements, and it is thus more reasonable to note their complimentarity.

The experience reported from some of the workshops shows that clarification of issues also makes the conflict more transparent to the primary parties, so that the incompatibility becomes more strongly formulated (for example, the Fermeda workshop). This, however, is not unique to only this form of conflict resolution activity. In conventional mediation work, such consequences can also be expected. From the perspective of the conflict resolution process, clarification of issues can be a step forward. It could help eliminate misunderstandings and, thus, redirect attention of the primary parties to the real issues.

Some of the special problems encountered by the workshop approach are found elsewhere. The intervenor enters on his or her own initiative. Will the intervenor's independence and integrity, obvious to the intervenor, be accepted by the primary parties? Probably not. The Fermeda workshop report shows considerable suspicion on the part of the African participants toward the U.S. organizers. This could be due partly to the novelty of the approach, and partly to the fact that the arrangement was expensive. But one should also consider the fact that nationality is important. The questions of relevance and impartiality with respect to the selection of a mediator apply equally well to the third-party intervenor. The nasty questions raised by Touval on the motives of "peace brokers" are also relevant here and will be seen as significant by the participants.

Furthermore, and unlike the strict mediator, the participants come in their own personal capacity and are not appointed by their governments. In one way this is positive because the discussions can be freer, which is largely the intention of the arrangement. In another way, however, the workshops differ from "normal" academic conferences by having an ambition to contribute to a solution of a particular conflict, where the participants might in fact feel very constrained. They will have to live with the agreement, if any, when they return home. If the agreement is sanctioned by the home government, as is the case in a conventional mediation situation, there is no personal problem. If, however, the workshop has gone beyond what is acceptable to the home government, the participants might face problems on their return. In anticipation of this, participants may restrict their participation in the workshop so that the "free" discussion will not be as free as hoped for. Obviously, the severity of this problem will depend on the type of regimes and milieus involved. By contrast, the problems facing a conventionally mediated agreement are political. The questions raised are: Has the government achieved as much as was possible? Has it compromised important elements?

What this review suggests is that independent third-party consultation approaches will face some of the same problems as conventional mediation. It might circumvent some problems, but it introduces its own. The approach, however, is novel and could carry considerable potential if further developed (Fisher, 1983:330). For example, carried out in an international framework, rather than in a major-power setting as has often been the case, some of the problems may be remedied.

Conclusions

Some of the dilemmas of third parties were described in Figure 4.1. What light does the literature on mediation and independent third-party consultation for conflict resolution throw on these dilemmas? We have already observed that the literature is weak on analysis of structural properties of different parties and their relations. This is surprising in view of the significance this aspect plays in some of the conclusions. In particular, it is disturbing that there is so little literature on major-power relations, especially in the nuclear age. In historical accounts of the outbreaks of the two world wars as well, very little is said about actions of third parties in any form. There are several possible reasons for this lack. It could be that there is, in fact, very little third-party activity to analyze scientifically. It could be true that the relations between the United States and the Soviet Union often have been formed on a direct bilateral level, avoiding the involvement of other parties. Their periods of détente are distinctly theirs, as are their periods of confrontation. Similarly, major powers in crisis in 1914 and 1939 probably preferred to deal directly with each other, rather than rely on third parties. Major-power conflict presents a real dilemma: How can third parties make themselves relevant to those powers that are on the top of the international hierarchy of power? Perhaps the emergence of more actors in today's world (corporations, political parties, religious bodies, trade unions, professional organizations, peace movements, environmental organizations, and so on) could make a difference in major-power conflict. In this sense, the possibilities for third parties should have increased tremendously. There is, however, very little reflection on this in the available literature.

The most challenging question could be put in this way: Could the courses of the Sarajevo and Munich crises have been altered through third-party activity? The literature does not claim a strong impact of mediation, preferring rather to illustrate the potentialities. The empirical literature on historical cases tends to emphasize the constraints, rather than the successes. There is no answer to the challenges raised by Kerr in 1954: Does third-party activity matter? But perhaps the question is wrongly put. Conflicts, even major conflicts or conflicts with the danger of nuclear war, concern more parties than the superpowers. Third parties might be part of the conflict, whether effective or not. A nuclear war has no outsiders and no third parties.

However, the apparent lack of studies on third parties in major power relations does not rule out the possibility that there is more activity to scrutinize. Obviously there are attempts at mediating conflicts that involve major powers. Some, to be discussed later, even involve political leaders of other countries as go-betweens. There are initiatives from nonaligned countries at times of tension, which might yield interesting insights. Indeed, there are whole sets of negotiation frameworks where third-party activities might be usefully analyzed, for example, with the United Nations (U.N.) and in European Security Conference settings. In addition, there are some nongovernmental links that also would need closer scrutiny—for example, in the arms control field, the Pugwash Conferences. The conflict resolution literature, in other words, seems to have a rich field of inquiry to plow.

In the literature on historical cases and conflict resolution experiments, there is a preference for studying third parties in particular situations. Prominent are conflicts between nonmajor states, where third parties, often drawn from a major power, are active (for example, the Palestine and Horn of Africa situations). There is also some justification for this emphasis in terms of our interest, because such conflicts have considerable escalatory potential. However, a full understanding of the phenomenon of third-party activity would have to fill out more cells in the conflict matrix given in Figure 4.1.

The conflict matrix gives an additional dimension to consider for the conflict resolution literature: What phase of a conflict does a particular approach relate to? A general summary suggests that it is heavily directed to the less acute phases of a conflict, (that is, before and after), rather than during a crisis. Thus, there are a number of studies, for example, on negotiations and proposals for settlement relating to postwar conditions, obviously with the intention of preventing a new war. Such mediation activities relate to situations of military tension, albeit of varying degree, rather than military crisis or nonmilitarized settings. The third-party workshop approach definitely falls into this category, as do many studies of mediation and negotiation. Again, we face the problem of representativeness. Does the frequency of studies of noncrisis mediation mean only that such third-party attempts are more often observed and better documented, or that they are the most frequent and most significant? The fact that the literature shows a low success rate suggests that the studies show no bias in favor of third-party successes. Still, for relevance to nuclear confrontation, there would also be a need to analyze situations of a higher level of crisis and even of war termination. The literature on crisis management in the nuclear age, however, seldom explicitly occupies itself with the question of third-party activity.

The fact that the literature is focused on noncrisis situations still does not preclude some interesting findings. The conclusions tend to point in the direction of the significance of dialogue itself, rather than the actual finding of solutions. The interesting workshop on the Horn of Africa in 1969 (Doob, 1970; Walton, 1970) has given rise to a number of reflections. From the point of view of the participants, the significant conclusion is that the parties learned more about the other side and probably also about themselves, and thus came to understand the conflict more accurately. Although this might have been disappointing to the organizers, it is very important from the point of view of conflict resolution. An accurate understanding of the adversary can be—indeed, must be—the basis for successful conflict resolution. This point seems to be missed in many evaluations of the workshop approach (Fisher, 1983).

Third parties can contribute to an educational process, rather than just directly to conflict resolution. Looking at the third-party activity in this light would suggest that the measure of evaluation should not be in the degree of success or failure in finding commonly agreed solutions, but in the impact on the participants and their perceptions of the situation. Such an impact can sometimes lead to solutions, but it is more reasonable to expect some changes of conflict actions, reconsideration of what postconflict situations could be like, and so on. These are significant contributions as well and should not be discarded. This reflection suggests that a range of educational approaches may contribute to such changes in the parties. In the direct relations between nuclear weapon states, educational contacts can be brought about either directly or by third parties. Their long-term impact is difficult to assess.

Third Parties in Armed Conflicts of the 1980s

Scope of Analysis

A common assumption underlying much of the study of mediation is that there is a lack of mediation, or third-party involvement, in conflict resolution, and furthermore that this is a significant, contributing factor to the absence of conflict settlement. The research on mediation and third-party involvement presented in the previous section does not address these assumptions, because it is not devoted to a comparative analysis of conflicts with and without third-party activity. This research pays considerable attention to cases where mediation has taken place or successfully has contributed to the resolution of a conflict, in order to make clear that mediation is a realistic alternative for decision makers. However, if the interest is to promote the use of third-party activity, this does not suffice. One would also need to know under what circumstances third-party involvement does take place. This would provide information on changes needed to stimulate nonarmed methods of treating conflict.

This section attempts such an analysis. It compares conflicts with and without mediation, using a list of contemporary armed conflicts. It analyzes the extent of third-party activity for conflict resolution in a set of conflicts. The term "mediation" refers to several types of actions undertaken by third parties to promote conflict resolution, sometimes more appropriately labeled "good offices," indirect contact, conciliation, or facilitation of communication. Largely it refers to situations of third-party activity involving the presentation of ideas for solution of the conflict to the parties, where the parties are willing to entertain a dialogue on such issues.

Several studies of these questions focus on the role of international organization and emphasize conflicts between states (Holsti, 1966; Butterworth, 1976; Haas, 1983; Bercovitch, 1986; Sherman, 1987). The scope here is broader, covering all kinds of third parties and all kinds of armed conflict. There are some obvious difficulties in any analysis of third-party activity. In many instances, information is not available, because few participants are willing to publish material on failures and because others might be quicker to claim involvement in case of success than the real actors. Also, governments may have reasons not to reveal their involvement, either to protect their own interests or those of the third parties. Thus, there is a constant element of underreporting with respect to mediation attempts. Furthermore, parties might be involved on a personal or associational basis that is not recorded by the parties or by public media. From this point of view, it might be argued that there is more mediation or other type of third-party conflict resolution activity going on than will ever be known.

This section relies on recent information on wars and armed conflicts between 1945 and 1984 developed by Hans Jürgen Gantzel and Jörg Meyer-Stamer (1986). It also includes data from the project on armed conflict and negotiated settlement at the Department of Peace and Conflict Research, Uppsala University, Uppsala, Sweden, which contains information from the 1980s on mediation and conflict resolution attempts. For 1984, it is consequently possible to answer some questions on the frequency of third-party activity. Also, 1984 is interesting because it was one of the low points in relations between the nuclear superpowers.

Gantzel and Meyer-Stamer (1986) list 159 wars during the 40 years since 1945. Of these, 32 wars were still going on in 1984, whereas 126 wars had been terminated during this period. The data suggest that the number of ongoing wars increased in every decade since 1945, making the 1980s among the most war-prone. Thus, Gantzel and Meyer-Stamer provide ample evidence that the issue of conflict resolution is particularly pertinent to our times. In addition, their study gives information on the termination of the armed conflicts, but without an analysis of different outcomes. A cursory reading suggests that victory or defeat is a most frequent ending.

Information on mediation and third-party involvement (cases mentioned in recent literature, media information) has been available on armed conflicts during the 1980s through the Uppsala project. For our present purpose we selected the 32 wars that were still going on in 1984 to analyze the extent of third-party involvement in different types of conflicts. Only a few armed conflicts of the 1980s had ended through negotiations by 1984, notably the war between South and North Yemen in 1979 and the war between Peru and Ecuador in 1981. These few negotiated conflict resolutions cannot be meaningfully compared. Thus, the analysis concentrates on ongoing conflicts. The conflicts are listed in the Appendix to this chapter.

From available information, we can say with confidence that a third-party was involved with the conflicting primary parties in order to find a solution to the basic incompatibility at one time or another in 16 of the 32 cases. That is, from fairly easily accessible sources we can observe that third parties tried (on their own initiative or on the inspiration of the primary parties) to settle the conflict in half of the total ongoing conflicts. If our assumption about under-reporting is correct, this would suggest that third parties are perhaps involved in more than half of the ongoing conflicts in order to promote a settlement. This means that third parties are perhaps more frequently involved in conflict settlement activity than might be assumed from present studies on the topic.

However, this should not be overstated: it does not necessarily mean that there is constantly a third-party working for settlement, only that initiatives have been taken some of the time. Thus, the dissatisfaction with frequency of mediation attempts might still be warranted. But the data also suggest that the parties to the conflict do not normally decline offers of third parties to establish contact or make proposals. As some of the literature points out, there are important benefits for the primary parties to establishing contacts with one another, even without ceasing armed struggle.

Third Parties and Types of Conflicts

Gantzel and Meyer-Stamer (1986) provide a categorization of conflicts in types, which basically refers to legal categories—that is, whether the conflict is internal or international and to what extent there is military involvement by an outside, "foreign" party (their term, "third parties", becomes confusing in the context of this chapter). The first distinction is more readily understood. The second one, outside military involvement, requires some comment. Here situations are included where a state is actively involved with its own military troops in actual warfare, in addition to the fighting by the "local" primary parties. Such involvement includes regular units as well as "volunteers," but not mercenaries or military advisors who are not actively fighting (Gantzel and Meyer-Stamer, 1986:12–13). Outside involvement often means military intervention, such as an outsider supporting a party in an internal conflict. The outsider's intention may be to "solve" the conflict by contributing to a military victory. This, of course, is different from the third-party involvement we are interested in here, which is a peaceful involvement, where the third party does not side with the primary parties but rather is there to promote a solution for those at war.

In the Gantzel and Meyer-Stamer (1986) data, the wars are closely categorized along the two dimensions mentioned (see Table 4.1). According to Table 4.1, most of the ongoing wars in 1984 were internal wars (26 of 31). In most of the wars, there was no outside military involvement (20 of 31). The most frequent type of war was the internal one with no outside military involvement (19 of 31). Using information on mediation and other third-party conflict resolution activity, it is now possible to calculate the extent of such activity in all conflicts of a particular type, bearing in mind an unknown degree of underreporting of such activity. Table 4.2 presents the number of conflicts with some such conflict resolution activity out of all wars of that category.

Table 4.2 shows that in all ongoing international wars in 1984 (whether an outside party was militarily involved or not) mediation was going on or had been attempted. Examples are the Iran–Iraq war (by the U.N., the Gulf states, and the Organization of Islamic Countries), the war between Ethiopia and Somalia (by Cuba, the United States, and the Soviet Union), the conflict over Kampuchea (by Thailand and the Association of Southeast Asian Nations [ASEAN] countries), and South African's conflicts with Angola and Mozambique (by the U.N., Zambia, and Portugal).

Furthermore, conflict resolution attempts were made in 71 percent of all internal wars with an outside party militarily involved. Examples are the proposals made for Lebanon (by Syria and other Arab states, often resulting in short-lived cease-fire arrangements between different parties); Chad (by African countries and the Organization of African Unity [OAU], resulting in a cease-fire in 1987); Central America (first, the Contadora process headed by South American countries, and then in 1987 the Equipulas II process, initiated by the Central American governments themselves); and the war in Afghanistan (which Gantzel and Meyer-Stamer [1986] classify as an internal war into which the Soviet Union intervened; indirect negotiations via the U.N., later resulting in an agreement of Soviet withdrawal in 1988, effectuated by February 15, 1989). In all of these cases, covering three of four cells

TABLE 4.1   Types of Wars Ongoing in 1984
(Absolute Numbers)

	Outside Military Involvement		
Type of War	Yes	No	Total
Internal	7	19	26
International	4	1	5
Total	11	20	31

Note: One conflict not classified.

Source: Gantzel and J. Meyer-Stamer (1986).

TABLE 4.2   Percentage of Ongoing Wars in 1984
in Which Third-Party Conflict Resolution Activity
Has Been Recorded

	Outside Military Involvement					
	Yes	(N)	No	(N)	Total	(N)
Internal	71	(7)	26	(19)	38	(26)
International	100	(4)	100	(1)	100	(5)
Total	82	(11)	30	(20)	48	(31)

Note: One conflict not classified.
Percentages are calculated for each cell.
Source: Gantzel and J. Meyer-Stamer (1986).

in Table 4.2, the conflicts are, in fact, highly internationalized. In some cases, the neighbors are directly affected by the armed conflict; in others, involvement by major powers prompt mediation. Furthermore, as the examples make clear, it is often international action that can be documented: other governments initiate mediation, either through existing international organizations (the U.N. and the ASEAN) or by forming special groups (the Contadora and Equipulas groups) that might have influence in the region. Nongovernmental organizations are also involved in these conflicts (and perhaps in some others).

In these three categories of armed conflict, there is no apparent lack of attempt at establishing indirect contact among the fighting parties. On the contrary, there is a rather impressive array of links being established. This also corresponds to what other studies have shown: there is considerable mediation activity in internationalized conflicts involving two or more states. Using Butterworth's (1976) data, Bercovitch shows this to be the case in 82 percent of 310 international disputes from 1945 to 1974; in his own data set, Bercovitch (1986:159) finds this to be true in 61 percent of 72 international disputes from 1945 to 1984; and Holsti (1966) finds this to be the case in 64 percent of 77 international disputes from 1919 to 1965 (obviously the authors apply different definitions of an international dispute). Combining the three categories of internationalized conflicts in Table 4.2, the comparative figure for 1984 data is 83 percent.

However, the picture is different with respect to the fourth category of conflicts in Table 4.2, internal wars that have no military involvement by outside parties. In some sense, these conflicts are more effectively sealed off from the international system than the others. As noted in Table 4.1, this category contains a considerable number of all ongoing wars, 19 of the 31. Table 4.2 shows that mediation attempts have only been recorded in about one-quarter of the cases, or five conflicts. This category of conflicts is not frequently covered by other studies. Thus, there is a need to discuss what separates this category of armed conflicts from the others. Also, we need to distinguish between those wars that involve third-party conflict resolution activity and those that do not, within this very category of wars. Light can be shed on both these questions by analyzing the 19 cases more closely.

First, there are five cases where mediating activity has been reported. In the Ethiopian conflict, the Sudan at times has established contact between the Ethiopian central government and Eritrean guerilla movements. The Sudan as a neighbor is directly affected by the war and the flow of refugees, as well as by Ethiopian and Eritrean incursions over the border. Also, in this case, the Soviet Union through the German Democratic Republic (GDR) is known to have attempted to find a solution. A second case is southern Sudan, where a solution was reached between the central government and the south Sudan movement, partly through the good offices of Ethiopia, in 1972. In 1983 the conflict resumed, and again the Ethiopian neighbor plays a role for contacts.

In the conflict over Irian-Jaya (West Irian), Australia has reportedly been active, at least in reducing the tensions resulting from the tense border situation between Indonesia and Papua New Guinea. In the case of Sri Lanka, India has been active in finding a solution. This conflict affects India through, for example, the ethnic affiliations among Tamils in India and in Sri Lanka. In 1987, significant changes took place when India promoted an agreement and stationed troops on the island. This in turn led to conflict between India and Tamil organizations and to a questioning of India's presence by Singhalese organizations.

These four cases concern ethnic minorities where neighbors are affected through refugees or through ethnic affiliations across the border.

The fifth case is a different one—namely, the conflict over the apartheid system in South Africa. The neighbors are committed to majority rule in South Africa. Nevertheless, they have sometimes served as channels of contact between white groups and the leading opposition movement, the African National Congress (ANC). A series of decisions by the U.N. Security Council formed the basis for international action in this case. The involvement of the European Community (EC) and the U.S. Congress in 1986 suggested a more mediating role, but not in a pure fashion, as they were at the same time putting pressure on the South African regime. In this way, neighbors and the international community are trying to create, through the use of nonviolent means, the conditions that would make serious negotiations between minority and majority possible.

Thus, all these internal conflicts have obvious international ramifications. This is what makes international conflict resolution activity possible, either by neighbors or through the U.N. These five wars are therefore not necessarily different from the internationalized wars described above.

Let us now proceed to investigate the remaining 14 cases. Several of these conflicts are also ethnic in nature and would thus be similar to some of the conflicts just discussed. For example, there are cases in which ethnicities cross borders, but instead of neighbors supporting or trying to mediate these groups, the opposite is true. The neighbors have a similar negative view of this particular group's aspirations. The prime example is the Kurds, who are parties to three wars—against Iran, Iraq, and Turkey. None of these neighboring countries has seen any reason to mediate in the Kurdish affairs of the neighbor. Rather, Kurds have been supported or suppressed when it has suited the goals of the central administration, but the issues have never been resolved.

In some other cases, the neighboring country has been more helpful to the kith and kin on the other side, but its actions can hardly be labeled mediation: The Republic of Ireland has supported the aspirations of the nationalists in Northern Ireland, but without trying to mediate in the conflict. The reason might well be that the decision makers believe there is already a solution to the problem, namely, the inclusion of Northern Ireland in the Irish Republic. Also, Ireland might not want to further complicate relations with Great Britain. An agreement was signed in 1985 between the two governments pertaining to the status of Northern Ireland, but again this reflects certain common interests between conflict parties more than third-party conflict resolution activity.

What we have seen so far is that crosscutting ethnic loyalties do not necessarily involve the neighboring country involved in conflict resolution attempts. The overall relationship between the neighboring countries seems to be decisive. If, for some reason, there is a desire to avoid war or conflict in the relations between the two neighboring states, there might be a consequent desire to find a solution to the "internal" conflict. In such circumstances, moreover, mediation might be more readily acceptable to the country on whose territory the conflict is being fought. However, if overall relations between the two countries are strained, the ethnic issue might be viewed differently—it can be used as an instrument against the other. Alternatively, an offer to contribute to the conflict resolution could be regarded as interference motivated by designs other than peaceful ones.

Another set of nonmediated ethnic conflicts concern ethnic groups that have very few or no ties to the outside world. The Basque, Oromo, and Tigray conflicts have some similarities in this respect. Although there is a Basque population in the south of France, it seems to offer little support to the armed Basque struggle in Spain. The Oromo and Tigrayan peoples are located well inside Ethiopia and have no "ethnic relatives" outside the country. Political alliances are still possible, for example, with Somalia or with Eritrean organizations, but there is no state or government obviously close enough to become a self-motivated mediator. In these cases, where the struggle does not relate directly to any other party, the lack of conflict resolution activity might play a role in prolonging the conflict. This does not preclude the possibility of the parties themselves initiating talks and inviting a third party. In fact, this happened in October 1989, when the Ethiopian and Tigrayan parties met for the first time. In case no side can coerce the other, the fighting parties have to endure a protracted stalemate with occasional outbursts of war. Burma (now Myanmar) is an example where de facto independent zones have been created in the interior, self-sufficient and with only a few ties to the outside world.

Two other wars add more information to this analysis: the conflicts over East Timor and over the Sikhs in India. In the case of East Timor, a U.N. General Assembly resolution defines the conflict as a decolonization issue. The former Portuguese territory of East Timor was, in accordance with U.N. decolonization policy, to become an independent state. However, Indonesia intervened and, during the end of the 1970s, secured military control over the area. The U.N. General Assembly has, in this case, almost become a party to the conflict, and this might reduce the possibilities for the U.N. to act in conflict resolution. More important is that Indonesia has de facto military control and has been unwilling to accept any negotiations on the issue. Although an international platform for mediation actually exists, it has so far not been used to settle the underlying conflict.

The Sikh issue has also been closed to international governmental action. India constantly warned neighboring Pakistan from exploiting the situation. Due to the overall state of affairs, Pakistan would not be an acceptable mediator. Furthermore, there is no Sikh state elsewhere to pursue the issue, and there is no strong Sikh regional concentration outside of India that can induce other governments to act as mediators. Thus, no outside government or state has so far seen itself in a position to mediate in this conflict. The Sikh conflict is a remarkable contrast to the Tamil one in Sri Lanka, where India, as an outsider, initially was an active mediator and later took on a more complex role.

Other internal wars may face international isolation, notably those in Colombia, Peru, the Philippines, and Uganda. In one of these, the war ended with the fall of the incumbent government (Uganda, in 1985, followed by conscious attempts of the new government to reintegrate a considerable number of the factions of the country into the political process); in others, temporary case-fires were negotiated without leading, however, to a solution of the basic issues (Peru, 1985; the Philippines, 1986–1987). These three conflicts could be described along a left–right continuum. The United States supported the governments facing the armed struggle. This does not necessarily mean that the Soviet Union or China would be potential supporters of the guerrillas. But it might suggest that mediators could be sought, either among neighbors, among parties taking a middle position on the left–right dimension, or among parties operating on a religious basis. At times, there have been mediation attempts by human rights groups, peace coalitions, and political parties in the cases of Colombia, Peru, and the Philippines. In the case of Colombia, direct talks between the government and leading guerilla movements were initiated, producing results in 1989.

Conclusion and Discussion

This analysis suggests that third-party conflict resolution activity by other states often is requested or is possible in the following situations:

- Interstate conflicts without an outside party militarily involved in the conflict—a classic case for the U.N., regional organizations, or neighbors to act.
- Interstate conflicts with an outside party militarily involved—third-party activity for conflict resolution might be requested but might also be strongly complicated by major-power involvement.
- Internal wars with military involvement by outside parties—the U.N. (indirectly), regional groupings, or neighbors are possible actors (major-power involvement might make mediation difficult).
- Internal wars without outside military involvement—neighbors might be called in as third parties if the conflict is over ethnic issues, there are existing ethnic cross-border affiliations, and a general state of peaceful relations prevails.

From this investigation, it appears that third-party conflict resolution activity is more frequent the more internationalized the war. At the same time, wars are probably more dangerous to a larger group of people when more parties are involved. Conflict resolution activity, in other words, is related to the dangers a war poses to a larger community. In that sense, the offer of mediation is a self-interested reaction to prevent geographical or vertical (superpower) escalation of war.

The forms of internationalization vary. In a war between two states, the interest of the larger community is quite obvious, because there are agreements and treaties to refer to (not the least of which is the U.N. Charter). To the extent that third parties are militarily involved in such a war, the interest in finding resolution by others might increase. However, a considerable number of internal wars has such international components—for example, through military assistance to one of the sides by outside parties, through ethnic and other affiliations, or through the history of the conflict. Because internal war is the largest category, it might be important for the international community to constantly develop new criteria by which internal conflict can be opened to international mediation. Here, human rights should provide a possible channel, for example, with respect to conflicts in Ethiopia, India, and South America. There is considerable scope for nongovernmental organizations to act, using human rights and other concerns for involvement (Bailey, 1985).

The superpowers are actors in a number of the internationalized wars. That, however, does not seem to prevent conflict resolution activity by other parties. In the war in Afghanistan, the U.N. was given a mandate to act in spite of the dominant Soviet role in that war. In the Central American conflicts, with a determining U.S. involvement, a mediation process was allowed. In these cases the third parties have been militarily and politically weak, thus not posing any direct threat to the superpowers. None of them has been in a position to bring pressure on the major powers. Rather, the resolution attempts have had to accommodate the wishes of the major powers concerned. It is still notable that the efforts have been continuing and that it probably would be difficult for the superpowers to prevent them from going on. Their success will, however, depend on the superpowers more than on the activity of the mediator.

It is possible that a closer review would find some interesting information concerning the timing of conflict resolution attempts. The literature contains some discussion of this. From this overview of cases, it appears that there are more intensive attempts at settlement immediately before an armed conflict breaks out and immediately after the first armed actions have been taken. As the conflict escalates, the frequency and intensity of mediation attempts seem to be reduced, only to emerge again at particular junctures of the armed conflict. A hypothesis is that mediation (and other third-party conflict resolution activity) will be related to development of the armed struggle. Before fighting has broken out and immediately after the onset of fighting, the military situation is uncertain, a situation that might be conducive to finding a solution. As fighting intensifies, however, the primary parties might be less prone to initiate and respond to diplomatic contact, directly or indirectly. Instead the armed struggle takes priority, and conflict resolution only becomes interesting again when both parties draw the conclusion that neither can win and that a solution would be preferable to continued fighting (Pillar, 1983). Mediation, in other words, is partly victim to the "fortunes" of the battlefield. But it also suggests that early action is very important—that is, to intervene for settlement in the period before a crisis, before all positions have been cemented, and before too much suffering makes a settlement appear as surrender.

Timing could also be viewed in another way. Conflict resolution activity is often undertaken by neighboring countries. Their actions do not necessarily come from only a concern with the potential and actual suffering of the fighting parties and their populations. There is probably also a fear of becoming involved in the military struggle itself. Conflict resolution work, then, stems from a wish to contain a war. The mediators will most likely be most active before the war has started. Like everybody else, they are uncertain about what a war would entail. Also, they would be more active when the war approaches a stalemate, whereas when one side appears to be winning, the neighbors might prefer to orient themselves in the direction of the apparent winner. In other words, the efforts by neighboring third parties might also vary with the "fortunes" of the war. The significance of early reaction was clearly understood in the serious dispute that flared up in December 1987 between Uganda and Kenya. Reportedly, President Kaunda of Zambia immediately approached both parties and a threatening war was avoided. Related to this is the possibility of third parties contributing to the establishment of contacts between some of the parties to the conflict using opportune moments. A particular case is the contribution by Sweden in laying the groundwork for contact between the Palestinian Liberation Organization (PLO) and the United States in December 1988, drawing on the new conditions created by the *intifada* (Palestinian uprising) and the PLO statement accepting the right of Israel to exist (*New York Times*, 16 December 1988).

Six of the 32 ongoing conflicts in 1984 came to an agreement pertaining to parts of the conflict by the end of 1988. All of these agreements emerged from conflicts where third parties had been active for some time, and third parties did have a role in these achievements. These were the conflicts fought on the territories of Afghanistan, Angola, Chad, Mozambique, and Namibia, and the war between Iran and Iraq. Most of the agreements related to withdrawal of forces, cease-fires, or nonintervention, leaving out the solution to some central issues (for example, the regime in the country). Thus, some conflict activity was scaled down, but considerable fighting remained between other parties (Afghanistan: between Communist government and Muslim opposition; Angola: between the Popular Movement for the Liberation of Angola [MPLA] government and the National Union for the Total Independence of Angola [UNITA]; Mozambique, between the Frelimo government and South-African-backed rebels). For Namibia, a full-scale solution was found through a jointly agreed procedure for independence of the country. Cease-fire was agreed and initiated in the Iran–Iraq war in August 1988, but the basic grievances still remained.

It is interesting to note that all these conflicts were highly internationalized either by being interstate conflicts or by having outside military presence. The aspect that was most readily resolved was also the international one: a stop to cross-border fighting and the removal of outside troops. This, on the one hand, illustrates a certain strength of the international community, but, on the other hand, it also points to its weakness. Many of these conflicts might now be defined as internal ones without international involvement, and thus enter into a category that is more difficult for international peace activity. They threaten to be "hidden" from the international community, and, not less significantly, from international press coverage.

Four of the agreements were concluded through the U.N. and with the support of the superpowers (Afghanistan, Angola, Namibia, Iran–Iraq). The agreements were more frequently regarded as indications of the achievements of a renewed détente between the two superpowers rather than real victories for the U.N. system. Perhaps they do illustrate both aspects: agreements on highly internationalized conflicts are more dependent on the state of international relations in general, and changes in that regard open or close possibilities for third-party activity. In contrast, solutions to internal conflicts might depend more on the state of internal affairs, and would, thus, show more autonomous dynamics. Neither external third parties nor superpowers might easily involve themselves in such issues.

In addition, promising activities were, by the end of 1988, underway in several conflicts (Kampuchea, Nicaragua, Sri Lanka, and the western Sahara). In one case, one party withdrew (Israel, largely but not completely, from Lebanon in 1985). Again, these were highly internationalized conflicts, and in all of them some third-party activity was recorded. Still, by the end of 1989, 5 years later, most of the wars were going on as before, in spite of attempts at conciliation. Recalling Kerr's question, "Does mediation matter?," there is reason for concern. However, because few wars had ended after still another 5 years of fighting, we could also ask, equally legitimately: Does war solve conflicts? As more human effort, undoubtedly, has gone into ending a war militarily, the lack of a positive result in that respect is more appalling than the apparent lack of success in the conflict resolution attempts.

The review throws some light on the literature on third-party conflict resolution efforts and on five general propositions on why there is so little success in resolving armed conflicts:

1. There is a lack of mediation attempts. The overview presented suggests, but does not conclusively prove, that this is not true, at least not with internationalized disputes. There are, normally, ample opportunities for exchange of resolution ideas among the parties. This is, however, not to suggest that efforts to organize institutionalized conflict resolution are futile. On the contrary, such measures can be important for internationalized conflicts, and even more for noninternationalized wars. Perhaps, however, the following conclu-

sion can be formed: there is a lack of mediation in the early phases of a conflict, in periods of precrisis. Thus, forms of early involvement need to be developed.

2. There is a lack of ability in the mediation attempts. A considerable proportion of the literature on mediation is devoted to making mediators more perceptive, more effective and, thus, ultimately more successful. This is most worthwhile, but it is questionable whether this is the entire explanation of success or failure. There is little evidence that the low success rate is due to a lack of competence among the mediators actually involved. Many of the skills required relate to cross-cultural understanding, language skills, ability to make independent judgment, and diplomatic feeling. Such skills do exist, perhaps in some countries more than in others. Although we cannot directly relate lack of such skills to lack of success in mediation, it might affect the availability of this option in dealing with conflicts. If there are no mediators available, using mediation is a nonalternative to decision makers. Furthermore, our analysis suggests that, for the future, internal conflicts might require the involvement of third parties. Then, obviously, the question of skills and training becomes very important. Many of these skills relate to university training in general. Thus, internationalized educational programs become important.

3. There is a lack of material power to convince the primary parties. As noted, self-interest is a significant motive for mediators. It could be argued that this motive makes third parties try harder. Thus, lack of success might not be due to lack of motivation or ability, but rather, to the distribution of power among the primary parties and the third party. It might be that powerful mediators are more successful than those coming from international organizations or associations of small countries. This perspective is further explored in the section "Power Relations and Third-Party Activity."

4. There is a lack of willingness among the primary parties to allow successful mediation attempts. This was alluded to in the discussion of timing. There are important phases of a war when the primary parties are uninterested in conflict resolution. The armed struggle demands more, and the solution is secondary. Put differently: if the conflict hurts too much, there is no willingness to solve it. Also, a lasting stalemate may reduce interest in a solution. A stalemate might be preferable both to renewed fighting and to negotiations. A stalemate might signify some success and could be regarded as a step to final victory. An agreement would mean giving up such long-term expectations. The "hurting stalemate" is suggested as an important precondition for a negotiated settlement, and something on which the mediator can build to create an agreement (Zartman, 1986). In this case, however, it is not the skills of the third party that lead to success, but the simultaneous perception among the

parties that an agreement is preferable to continued war or other alternatives. Again, this gives the third party the role of convincing the primary parties that there is, in fact, a stalemate.

5. There is a lack of interest in a successful mediation among important segments of the global society at large. If there is no international consensus on conflict resolution, it will be more difficult to achieve. If, on the other hand, there is détente among the major powers, conflict resolution would be easier. We find some evidence for this in the review of the 1980s, using the ongoing wars of 1984 as measure. It has often been mentioned in connection with the Iran–Iraq war that the superpowers did not want either of the primary parties to win. Rather, they preferred a return to the status quo ante. An opportunity for that emerged in 1987 and was brought about in 1988, with an armistice. The interest in continued conflict should not, of course, be underestimated. There are primary parties who will see their interests better enhanced with continued battle. However, the function of the U.N. in general, and the U.N. Security Council in particular, is to maintain global peace and security. Thus, the problem is to bring this common interest to the forefront. There are also other situations where important actors prevent the attainment of agreement. It has been suggested that some hijackings and hostage-takings have been aimed at preventing resolution of conflicts, for example, in the Middle East. A spectacular violent action can halt promising moves toward settlement. Again, the problem is one of common interest, or at least sufficient common interest, to not allow such provocations to succeed, at times when there is progress toward equitable settlement. That is another challenge to the global community.

How does this analysis relate to the question of prevention of nuclear war? First, resolution of local conflicts, as well as the lack of resolution, is a strong indicator of the relations between the major nuclear powers, the United States and the Soviet Union. Much of their competition takes place through their presence in various conflicts. Thus, escalation of such conflicts relates to confrontation between the two, and resolution of such conflicts suggests détente between them. The 1980s testify to this observation with a general absence of resolution of conflicts until a renewed détente began in the later years of the decade. This pattern suggests that a set of outstanding, unsolved local conflicts could also jeopardize relations between the nuclear powers. In this sense, war in one part of the world threatens the stability in other parts of the world.

Second, solutions, when sought and found, often relate to international aspects of conflicts, more particularly those aspects of direct concern of the promoters of resolution. Other issues remain untackled. Therefore, third parties might play a role that is different from the one of the major nuclear powers: taking in less internationalized issues and, thus, contributing to a more comprehensive solution.

Third, there might be some knowledge gained from the Sarajevo scenario and the Munich syndrome for the major nuclear powers. The dangers of local conflicts escalating may be a reason why a joint approach to some conflicts was developed (Afghanistan, Iran–Iraq, Angola–Namibia). Another danger is that some of these involvements become increasingly expensive in human lives, as well as in material resources, to the major powers themselves. The experience from these incomplete solutions may lead to an interest in developing alternative forms and fora for conflict resolution.

Fourth, the question of precrisis involvement is potentially very significant, both to prevent local escalation among the primary parties and to preempt major-power alignment to different parties. Again, third parties can have a special role in this context.

Power Relations and Third-Party Activity

Overview

The review of the literature and the analysis of ongoing wars show that power cannot be neglected in mediation or third-party activity for conflict resolution. There are at least two different ways in which it becomes relevant. First, there is the question of the power of the primary parties. Figure 4.1 distinguishes conflicts on this dimension. To what degree are third parties allowed to interfere in relations among major powers? Can major powers become third-party mediators in particular situations? In the nuclear age, we are particularly interested in relations between major nuclear weapon powers. Will nuclear weapon states act as major powers have done in the prenuclear age? The overall frequency of wars is not lower in the post-1945 period than in the pre-1945 period. The frequencies of major-power confrontations are actually higher (Wallensteen, 1981; Small and Singer, 1982; Gochman and Maoz, 1984). This would suggest that traditional behavioral patterns have changed very little, although there is no way to know the actual answer to this suggestion. Let us assume that knowledge of behavior prior to nuclear weapons is of sufficient relevance today.

Second, there is the question of the power of the mediator vis-à-vis the primary parties. In this situation, a mediator with power in some material or physical sense can offer more to the parties than a mediator relying solely on skills and creativity. However, there is also a danger. Mediation may become more difficult if the conflict is complicated by the interest of a powerful third party. Mediation of the "original" conflict becomes peripheral and secondary.

As we have seen, some writings point to the importance of the self-interest of mediators. Whether this makes mediation more successful remains debatable and unproven. The evidence suggests, however, that there is a role in conflict resolution that could be taken by actors with power. Conflict resolution, in other words, provides a challenge to the major powers. Normally, these powers play a considerable role in making conflict: initiating, encouraging, and sustaining conflict, or preventing its unfavorable solution for the major power. As these actions threaten the relations between the major powers themselves, they might have come to reconsider their roles.

Let us briefly consider the involvement of major nuclear weapon powers in negotiating agreements between countries in conflict. Since the early 1970s, high-level U.S. officials have been involved in mediation at many times. Also, Soviet efforts in the same vein are known. Some examples are:

• Cyrus Vance as U.S. President Johnson's special envoy in the conflict over Cyprus between Greece and Turkey in 1967.
• Henry Kissinger as U.S. Secretary of State performing "shuttle diplomacy," resulting in agreements between Israel and Egypt, and Israel and Syria in 1973–1974 (Rubin, 1981).
• Alexander Haig as U.S. Secretary of State commuting long-distance between Argentina and the United Kingdom during the South Atlantic war in 1982.
• Lord Carrington as Foreign Secretary and the Lancaster House negotiations in London concerning Rhodesia (Zimbabwe) in 1979.
• Nikolai Podgorny, president of the Soviet Union, and Fidel Castro, president of Cuba, trying to prevent a conflict between Ethiopia and Somalia in early 1977 (George, 1983; Napper, 1983:230; Zartman, 1983:348).
• Soviet efforts to mediate between warring Communist factions in South Yemen in 1986.
• U.S. efforts to contain the Shaba crisis to avoid a war between Zaire and Angola in 1977 and 1978 (Zartman, 1983:345).

If we go further back in history, the number of cases increases. A most interesting and well-described case is the Trieste conflict in 1954, in which Great Britain and the United States served as mediators between Italy and Yugoslavia (Campbell, 1976).

The record of "success" is mixed. Some of these efforts resulted in durable agreements, but most did not. Thus, there is no complete correlation between the power of the mediator and the degree of success. Although the major powers do have, in comparison with other mediators, considerable resources to draw on, this does not mean that they can dictate solutions. Also, "success" means different things. In some cases, "success" might have been simply to avoid allies fighting each other, leaving the conflict unsolved (for example, Greece and Turkey).

A cursory reading of this incomplete list suggests that mediation for the major powers is closely linked to global or regional concerns. Mediation activity often is "conflict management" more than "conflict resolution." The effort, at a minimum, is directed to not harm overall interests of one major power, and, at a maximum, it is a means to establish or solidify influence, often at the expense of the other major power. Many of the conflicts involve allies of a major power (for example, U.S. efforts with respect to Greece and Turkey, and Great Britain and Argentina; Soviet efforts with respect to Ethiopia and Somalia, and South Yemen), thus suggesting that the major power is more concerned about avoiding disruption in alliances (which could be used by the adversary) than mediating in the issues at hand. Also, some other situations indicate that the mediation attempt was made to extend influence, not only to achieve conflict resolution (for example, the "shuttle diplomacy" of Kissinger).

These efforts are largely pact-building or pact-maintaining work. There is obviously much more successful activity than can be recorded here. Building and maintaining pacts might even involve routine, behind the scene behavior of a major power. In fact, the absence of conflict between some states with known disagreements might be credited to such major power activity. This is true of some Latin American conflicts (for example, the Peru–Ecuador border dispute, which included a short border war in 1981) and Eastern European conflicts (for example, Hungary–Rumania), as well as among former French colonies in Africa (for example, the border dispute between Burkina Faso and Mali in 1984). The arrangements of various pact or military treaties concluded between small states and major ones sometimes give major powers a mediating role, whether intended or not.

Third Parties in Major-Power Relations

The literature on mediation and conflict resolution suggests a number of functions of mediators in relations where there is some symmetry between the parties. However, there is little consideration of the special circumstances prevailing on the very top of a hierarchy, or in conflicts between two competing hierarchies. In these cases, there are few norms and rules to refer to, little common interest and common understanding, and most certainly, no paramount power to appeal to for support or decision. At the top, decisions have to be made with less precedence and with potential consequences of creating precedents. In fact, this is the way international rules are created. This, at least, is likely to be the perception of the decision makers. What guidance can the literature offer?

First, in historical or modern political records of conflicts between two major powers, third parties are rarely mentioned in a mediating function. There are examples of other majors acting as intermediaries, bringing messages. An example is the visit by British Prime Minister Harold Macmillan to Moscow in 1959 in connection with the Berlin crisis. In this case, however, Great Britain was itself a party to the conflict. Other examples include foreign minister conferences that were set up—for example, to end the war in Indochina in 1954, where some major powers mediated among some of the others. It is important to note the practice of the 1950s of such conferences involving all the leading states seems to have been completely abandoned. The pattern of the 1970s and 1980s is instead one of bilateral dealings between the United States and the Soviet Union, both in due course informing their allies, but not involving them in direct negotiations. This, seemingly, is a testimony to the increasing difference between the superpowers and other major powers. In a superpower perspective, this might be seen as functional and efficient, even natural: after all, much of their discussions concern "their" weapons and "their" interventions. The effect, however, is one of exclusion. In time, a pattern of a paradoxical "partnership in conflict" emerges, where no other actors can become involved in times of crisis.

Second, there are some arguments for why it is unlikely that major powers would accept mediation in conflicts between themselves. One hypothesis is that major powers tend to deal with one another and do not let others in except in peripheral functions (for example, as messengers), on a very high level, and on special occasions. Also, it is possible that the more powerful the actors in conflict, the more powerful the mediator required. A corollary to this is that the more powerful the actors in conflict, the fewer mediators available. Thus, we would expect very few open attempts at mediation between major powers.

An additional hypothesis is that major-power conflicts are more difficult to solve than other conflicts. A considerable amount of literature on international politics would argue that major-power conflicts are built into the system of states. Major powers are, almost by definition, in conflict with one another. Thus, conflicts cannot yield durable solutions; they can only be handled temporarily. Sooner or later, these theories would suggest, the rivalries will reappear.

This might be an unnecessarily gloomy prediction, because a considerable number of such rivalries have turned into cooperative relations, for varying reasons. Two obvious examples are the American–British relations, starting from the Boston Tea Party in 1772 and leading to alliance in all major wars in the twentieth century; and Great Britain and France, which were major rivals in Africa in the nineteenth century, but allies during the twentieth century. The rivalries, in other words, do not necessarily have to be of permanent character and do not need to take armed forms.

The known cases of mediation among major powers are few, but there is at least one from which something could be learned—the mediation between Russia and Japan by the United States in 1905 (Esthus, 1967, 1970; Harbaugh, 1975, Trani, 1969). President Theodore Roosevelt was mediator in this major war, in what has become known as the Portsmouth (N.H.) Peace Conference; he was awarded the Nobel Peace Prize for his efforts. The mediation illustrates mechanisms of both hypotheses, but suggests that they can operate to enhance mediation. First, there is the status aspect (major powers require major mediators). A corollary to this is that in a major-power conflict, it might, at certain moments, be impossible for the parties to refuse an offer by a major power to mediate. Thus, when the U.S. president offered his assistance, it was hard not to take it seriously. The United States certainly was a power of considerable status, and it was not allied directly to either of the primary parties. In addition, it was not a traditional European power (something that appealed to Japan). Thus, its high status made the United States a well-placed mediator, once it decided to take on that role. This could mean, as a more general observation, that mediation offers by major powers are difficult to dismiss.

Second, there is the rivalry aspect ("major powers have their own conflicts; thus, none is impartial enough"). The United States was a rising power in 1905, with interest in the area of contention. It was a country with an industrial potential that would make it useful as a future partner to both combatants. Thus, it was an important player in future rivalries. In sum, the United States had enough status at the time, and enough importance for the future, not to have its offer dismissed out of hand. There may have been other aspects to this as well—for example, a U.S. "silent partnership" with the Anglo–Japanese alliance, something which might not have been generally known at the time. This could have made it important for Japan to accept the United States as mediator. (Harbaugh, 1975:263). This case suggests that status can be a resource and that rivalries can make mediation more likely, not the reverse.

The timing of the mediation effort may have been equally important for the acceptance of the offer, as well as for its success. The U.S. efforts were initiated after some dramatic changes in the conflict, creating an opportunity for settlement. The Japanese victory at Tsushima in May 1905 showed that Japan was very strong militarily and that it might be difficult for Russia to reassert itself. However, the Japanese apparently took the initiative by accepting Roosevelt's offer of mediation, and Russia followed only after pressure from Germany (Harbaugh, 1975:268). It is argued that Japan was economically exhausted by the war, and thus seized upon an opportunity to end it as soon as possible (Marks, 1979:65-66). An opportunity presented itself, although it is questionable if it can be termed a "mutually hurting stalemate" (cf Zartman, 1986:219).

The dynamics of this mediation attempt seem different from "normal" practices. For example, according to some accounts, it was the direct intervention of President Roosevelt with the Japanese leadership that finally made strategic Japanese concessions possible, breaking the deadlock in the negotiations (Harbaugh, 1975:270). Again, the strength and position of the United States may have been decisive, compared to any other mediator.

The Portsmouth experience also points away from a traditional conception of mediation as one party going between two combatants. Despite the conference format, the conference was not where the decisions were made. Roosevelt had an undisputed authority vis-à-vis the other participants, who continuously consulted their home governments. Using his authority, President Roosevelt could direct himself straight to the leaderships. Perhaps a conference with all leaders rather than representatives would have made more direct communication and quicker decisions possible. However, in the midst of a war, that is an unlikely event.

Roosevelt appeared active in promoting a particular solution. This role is outside the traditional role of a mediator. It illustrates some of the dangers in major-power mediation. In Japan, it was alleged that the United States forced Japan to accept an agreement that was not optimal and not consonant with its military success. Anti-American sentiments rose on this point. The United States became identified with Japan's failure to realize the fruits of its victories (Harbaugh, 1975:273). This might be a special problem not afflicting less powerful mediators. The power and position, which is partly the basis for success, can turn into the cause of defeat of an agreement. This is true particularly if the mediated agreement leaves crucial aspects of the incompatibility unsolved. Thus, in the Portsmouth Peace Conference, the status of Korea seemed not to have been an issue. Possibly, the de facto U.S. acceptance of the Japanese occupation of Korea was a precondition for its role as a mediator. This also affected the outcome, in that a particular issue was left untouched.

One case is a limited basis for more general conclusions. Still, it might be interesting to discuss the implications for current U.S.–Soviet Union relations and the theorizing it illustrates. Many of the functions performed by President Roosevelt at the Portsmouth negotiations are those traditionally given to mediators: urging that concessions be made; devising new, integrative options; helping to undo commitments; and so forth. Also, Roosevelt could act with authority, but without really exerting power and pressure on either of the parties. The Portsmouth case, in other words, has many of the traits of mediation, as discussed in the literature: impartiality, but relevance; providing services, not incentives or pressure. All of this was possible because the United States had status and was of interest as a potential partner in ongoing rivalries. Is there, in the present world, a leading country or a grouping that could perform such a role between the superpowers if needed? Of the three permanent members of the Security Council other than the United States and the Soviet Union, two are allies of the U.S. and, thus, are not in a position for a mediating role in a conflict between U.S. and the Soviet Union. There are other intermediary functions that could be performed, however. The third member, China, would then be the only possibility. It might be an interesting and seldom considered notion. Certainly, China itself has not moved in this direction. Also, some of the issues discussed between the U.S. and the Soviet Union, such as strategic and intermediate range nuclear missiles, concern China, as a nuclear power itself, in a very direct way. Probably China could not or would not like to become involved in these issues. However, Chinese mediation might remain a possibility in cases of a crisis concerning other, more regional issues. The choice of an acceptable mediator among major powers is probably a delicate one: for the mediating power there has to be some interest and relevance to the issue in conflict, but not too great an involvement.

Beyond the permanent members of the U.N. Security Council, the usefulness of other countries for third-party activity is severely reduced. The power status requirement is one limitation. Many countries and leaders are in a position to convey messages, but communication might not be the central problem in a confrontation between the two superpowers. The nonaligned movement of the 1950s and 1960s offered to play a mediating role; however, it never did.

The U.S. mediation at Portsmouth had a conference character. Are the current, largely bilateral contacts between the U.S. and the Soviet Union preferable to the conference format as it was practiced in the "Four-Power" meetings of the 1950s (Weihmiller, 1986)? The results of bilateral meetings (for example, arms control agreements in 1972, 1979 and 1987) might speak favorably of this format, but the lack of result and the lack of contact for long periods (for example, no summits from 1974 to 1979 and from 1980 to 1985) must also be considered. In addition, conference settings involving the United States and the Soviet Union have been effective (for example, the Indochina agreement of 1954 and the Helsinki Final Act of 1975), although some failures are documented as well. Bilateral settings are vulnerable because they usually lack "smoothing elements," in case negotiations do not work out. The summit meeting in Reykjavik in 1986 is a telling example, where the leaders simply left in frustration. A third party, available in a multilateral negotiation setting, might have found ways to continue the negotiations. Thus, a return to a conference format might have advantages for all parties, although one cannot convincingly claim that this will make matters more efficient. Conferences can fail, and their failure may have a long-term impact. A frequently cited example is the 1960 Four Powers meeting in Paris. However, this particular failure was not due to conference dynamics, but to the shooting down of the U.S. U-2 plane over Soviet territory 2 weeks before the scheduled meeting. In fact, no discussion ever took place (Weihmiller, 1986:39–40). The Paris meetings followed a pattern established during World War II (Weihmiller, 1986) and would, consequently, best be suited for issues relating to that particular conflict. However, a structured revival of this pattern, in a different setting, might help to eliminate the swings between euphoria and fear that have largely colored direct superpower relations since 1945. The use of a preplanned and agreed schedule of meetings might be the most conducive device in this respect.

Still, it should be recalled that relations among major powers are vulnerable to many events in the world. In spite of their claim to superpower status, events in less powerful nations, such as a revolution in Iran or a rebellion in Afghanistan, seem to affect the relations between the United States and the Soviet Union. This suggests that the determinates of major-power relations are to be found not so much in the availability of third parties and links of communication, but in the general stability and instability in the world, and their interpretation of world conditions. Thus, it might be argued that the "real" swings are those between particularistic and universalistic views in the major powers themselves. In phases of particularism, it is the direct, egotistic interests of one or several major powers that color the relations among them all. In phases of universalism, however, the powers are also giving priority to the interests of others. In the former set of circumstances, most major wars break out; in the latter, there are no wars between major powers, historically speaking (Wallensteen, 1984). What then accounts for such swings? Internal changes? International experiences? Can the swings be predicted? Whatever their answers, these questions are arguments for always having forms and mechanisms of mediation available to be used if (and when) such swings occur. A degree of institutionalization might be helpful—a set of scheduled summit meetings, for example. Imagine two separate sets: annual bilateral meetings (United States–Soviet Union, Soviet Union–China, China–United States, etc.) and an annual summit meeting of the entire U.N. Security Council, including the U.N. Secretary General. This would provide a mixture of effective bilateralism and means of third-party reconciliation, a repetitive pattern where there would be no loss of prestige when contacts are renewed after tension. The pattern is not unknown. It is found in the relations within the EC, with bilateral meetings between the Federal Republic of Germany and France, and with ministerial meetings of the EC. For the major powers, the U.N. is the closest equivalent.

Asymmetric Situations

Several of the examples of major-power mediation listed above concern actions by foreign ministers and heads of states in conflicts between smaller, often allied countries. In these conflicts, major powers have, as already observed, particularly strong interests of their own to intervene. The mediation attempts might be, in these circumstances, only the tip of an iceberg of activities. The most typical example is U.S. involvement in settlements of conflicts in the Middle East. The lessons to be drawn from this need to be closely watched. However, before venturing into this problem, there is another, more extreme situation: a conflict between a major power and a subordinate country. This section explores whether outside third parties are likely to be allowed into such situations.

CONFLICTS BETWEEN MAJOR POWERS AND DOMINATED COUNTRIES

This type of conflict can be referred to in different ways—for example, as intrabloc, intraregional, and intrahemispheric conflicts. The terms imply that there are regions in the world controlled by certain major powers. Inside those regions, conflicts will occur that threaten the cohesion of the region and the leadership of the major power. Can and should such conflicts be mediated? Are they, in fact, mediated? Among the conflicts of this type, open third-party involvement for conflict resolution seems to be rare. When a major power has decided to make an intervention and is well underway carrying it out, the international community has little possibility to involve itself, as witnessed in many cases—for example, Soviet Union–Hungary, Soviet Union–Czechoslovakia, United States–Dominican Republic, United States–Grenada, and France-Central African Empire. The mediation literature has little to offer with respect to such highly asymmetric conflicts. Few of the services normally performed by third parties are relevant. The concessions that can be advocated will all have to deal with a central and principal problem of the legality of the action and the interference of the foreign troops. Concessions on these dimensions will be difficult to wrestle from either party, and asking concessions from one might be interpreted as partisan. Third parties might still contribute to schemes (such as for agreed withdrawal) but generally, it seems that third parties achieve a role only as a result of outside, international reactions (such as widespread condemnation, objections to interpretation of international law, or imposition of sanctions—the case of Rhodesia/Zimbabwe is most interesting from this perspective). The danger, then, is that the acceptance of third-party activity (such as in the United States–Dominican Republic example, when a U.N. observer team was sent to the island) is more pro forma and has little measurable impact on the conflict itself.

The recent conflicts in Central America bear considerable testimony to the fact that major powers rarely appreciate independent third-party activity. Thus, the Contadora group (which included states such as Mexico and Venezuela), trying to work out a solution for the conflicts in the region, was not well received by the U.S. administration. Similarly, the peace plan developed by five Central American presidents in Esquipulas, Guatemala, in August 1987 met with considerable resentment from the Reagan administration— including the resentment of awarding the Nobel Peace Prize to President Oscar Arias of Costa Rica for his work on this plan. This is not to suggest that third-party actions should not be undertaken in such circumstances. Rather, it is to point out some of the problems that they are likely to meet. In general, the literature on mediation seems to not have sufficiently highlighted the particular problems of these strongly asymmetric, but quite frequent conflicts.

CONFLICTS WITH MAJOR POWERS AS "INTERESTED" THIRD PARTIES

Of the many conflict cases referred to in the literature on mediation, the ones where a major power is mediating between states with links to the major one are probably the most frequent. Some of these are conflicts between alliance members; U.S. efforts in the conflict between Greece and Turkey are a prime example. Others are cases where one contending party is an ally and the other is related in other ways (U.S. efforts in British–Argentine conflict, Soviet efforts in the Horn of Africa, and Yemen conflicts). Finally, there is a set of cases where the major power is allied to one of the parties in the conflict but has a neutral or uncertain relation to the other side (the United States in conflicts between Zaire and Angola, and Israel and Syria; and Soviet efforts in the conflict between India and Pakistan). The conflicts of the Middle East exemplify a number of these relations.

From the point of view of some of the mediation literature, these conflicts are "ideal:" the major powers are involved (and have their own strong reasons for being so), they have resources to bring into the situation (sticks and carrots), mediation by the major powers might be attractive for all sides (not the least for the expectation of their being able to influence the other side), and, thus, communication can be established with all sides. These conflicts are also significant for the prevention of nuclear war: they involve many uncertainties as to the actions and reactions of the opposing sides, and therefore pose dangers of escalation. Such conflicts seem so "ideal" for mediation that the importance of power is overlooked. The study of mediation in such cases is informative for the practice of mediation. But this sort of mediation is different from the simple provision of services and findings of creative solutions that are the conventional conception of mediation. This is "interested mediation," not "disinterested" mediation.

Consider two cases in which major-power third-party mediation achieved the termination of wars and where the mediators were different in background and tradition. In these cases, the mediators were also heads of government: Prime Minister Alexei Kosygin mediating between India and Pakistan, Tashkent, Soviet Union, 1966; and President Jimmy Carter mediating between Egypt and Israel, Camp David, Maryland, United States, 1978–1979.

These two cases of mediation were both spectacular and drew considerable attention. They resulted in agreements with some durability. These mediation attempts had a summit meeting character and the principal parties were present in a mixture of face-to-face and indirect communication over many days. This means that the complex web of interstate and interpersonal relations came to play, in a context involving the power of the host, the mediator. The latter is underscored by the fact that these negotiations took place on the territory of the major power mediating. In only one case has the mediator himself told his story of what went on (Carter, 1982). Other participants have given detached analysis of the negotiations (Quandt, 1986). About the meeting in Tashkent little is known, but an analytical account is available (Thornton, 1985). Both conflicts had recently resulted in war—in the Camp David negotiations, less than 5 years earlier; and in the Tashkent talks, only some months before the meeting. There were serious dangers of a resumption of fighting in both cases.

It was argued before that the more powerful the actors in conflict, the more powerful the mediator required. A corollary to this is that the more powerful the actors in conflict, the fewer the mediators available. These two conflicts illustrate this pattern, with a considerable number of previous mediation attempts in the Arab–Israeli conflict, where the parties are less powerful, globally speaking, and very few in the Indo–Pakistani conflict, which involved two major regional powers. In the latter case, it was probably more difficult to find a mediator both sides would agree to listen to.

The choice of mediator came about in a similar way: a major-power leader offering his services on his own initiative. An invitation to mediation by a major power is an offer few actors can refuse. At the same time, the two cases illustrate another general proposition offered in the literature on mediation: there is no requirement that the mediator be completely impartial or equidistant to the parties. In both these cases, the mediating state was closer to one of the parties. The Soviet Union was closer to India, particularly after 1962, than to Pakistan, which had been allied to the United States since the 1950s. The U.S. was potentially closer to Israel than to Egypt, being Israel's chief supplier of military goods and financial and political support. It has been argued that this nonneutral position makes the mediator more attractive. The closeness in relations provides leverage that makes the mediator interesting to the other primary party. It might be possible to wrench concessions that nobody else could deliver. Thus, a mathematically exact in-between position might not be necessary.

However, two other requirements are very important: honesty and impartiality in the mediation task. This is constantly underlined by President Carter in his account of the Camp David negotiations. This is impartiality in another way: the correct reporting of what the other party says, the honest assessment of what the other can realistically offer and implement, and so forth. Particularly in a complex confrontation like the Arab–Israeli one, there are high demands on fairness. The primary parties pay attention to the personal qualities of the mediator, not only to his or her national origin and position. This, then, is an example of how intersocietal and personal variables interact. In President Carter's account of the Camp David negotiations, the personal relations between the mediator and the two opposing sides played a considerable role. The personal relations between the Pakistani leader, President Ayub, and the Soviet leadership has been used to explain the outcome of the Tashkent negotiations (Thornton, 1985:144, 150).

The mediation attempts were initiated after dramatic changes in the conflict, creating opportunities for settlement. The Tashkent conference is hard to relate to the emergence of a "hurting" stalemate. The war of August–September 1965 had ended with a cease-fire that was uncomfortable rather than hurting. It seems instead that an opportunity was created by the entrance of a new, unexpected factor—the Soviet offer to mediate. Also, the parties came to Tashkent without high expectations (Thornton, 1985:146). The Camp David negotiations followed another logic, but again they seem to spring from a political opportunity rather than from a military or political stalemate as such. President Sadat's visit to Jerusalem created a new momentum in the old conflict. The ensuing dialogue between Israel and Egypt was rapidly deteriorating, and the opportunity seemed to be lost. In order to renew the peace efforts, President Carter invited the two leaders to the U.S. (Carter, 1982:316). The rule seems to be that successful mediation follows important changes in the conflict, either in the relationship between the primary parties or in a new unexpected factor, too important to ignore. The fact that the opportunity was related to a major power may be important but so probably are the timing and the lack of alternatives. However, in none of the cases does it seem that the mediation efforts were initiated because of uncertainties in the military situation. On the contrary, weapons were silent in both cases (truces were in effect along the Indo–Pakistani and Egyptian–Israeli cease-fire lines). A considerable part of the literature deals with the mediation process, suggesting different functions mediators can perform. Many of these concern the provision of services, such as establishing contact, clarifying issues, and defusing tension. However, the cases of major-power mediation involved a much more active role for the third party. When the Indo–Pakistani negotiations appeared to reach a dead end, Prime Minister Kosygin took the initiative, providing "active and creative help" according to *Pravda* (Thornton, 1985:153). This seems to have changed the Tashkent meeting from an imminent failure to a success. In the Camp David negotiations, a considerable amount of the drafting was done by the U.S. team. In fact, President Sadat and Prime Minister Begin did not meet personally for several days. President Carter and the other Americans instead worked in parallel on the Israeli and Egyptian teams. Again, this heavy involvement seems to have changed a looming failure into a success. These examples testify to a difference between "normal" mediators and major-power mediation. The activity that was undertaken by Kosygin and Carter would probably be difficult to accept were it to come from mediators equal or inferior in status and power to the primary parties. It is a type of behavior not normally expected in diplomacy. Also, the available literature suggests that third-party mediators are aware of their limited resources and thus prefer to take a servicing rather than a promoting role. Perhaps the difference is the cost of antagonizing the primary parties. For a "normal" mediator, such consideration might carry a lot of weight. Too active promotion that fails might have negative long-term effects for the organization or group that the mediator represents. Major powers have greater leeway, although there are limits for them also. Because of their power, major powers face a different problem from the less powerful mediators, a problem seen in connection with Roosevelt's mediation: promotion of a settlement can become an imposition that is unacceptable in the long run. As we observed, this problem is particularly important if the mediated agreement leaves crucial aspects of the incompatibility unresolved.

A difference between a major power proposing a negotiation and a "normal" mediation might be the commitment on the mediator's part. A failure is not only a failure to the primary parties but also to the major power. It is not a failure of one person who can be easily exchanged for another, but a failure of foreign policy for a major power. Thus, the mediation proposal will not come unless the major power is prepared to work hard for an agreement. A failure is not likely to result easily in a renewed effort. In both Tashkent and Camp David, moreover, the efforts received considerable international support, suggesting that there might not have been many more chances in the near future.

In short, finding an agreement becomes part of the foreign policy of the major power. This makes an agreement more important and ensures a very powerful commitment that could not easily be made by other mediating third parties. These conclusions are reflected in the negotiation strategy employed by both Kosygin and Carter. Both seem to have been clear from the outset which were the most difficult questions to resolve. Both apparently concluded that the meeting would fail if these issues were tackled first. Instead, both concentrated on other issues, thus making agreement possible. They returned to the sticking points later. This strategy means attempting to reduce the significance of the difficult issues. And indeed, they would of course become "smaller," if agreements have been reached on other accounts. In both these cases, the strategy seems to have worked. It becomes more difficult to overturn an agreement if there are only a few issues remaining to be solved. Thus, formulas were found, for example, for the new Israeli settlements on the West Bank, during the final days (Carter, 1982:371, 397; Thornton, 1985:152).

Agreements were signed and implemented. They implied some territorial and military changes, particularly in the case of Egypt and Israel, where the Sinai peninsula was returned to Egypt. However, some issues were left unsolved, particularly those relating to weaker parties in the conflict that were not represented at the meeting: the Kashmir and Palestinian disputes were untouched. In the Tashkent negotiations, the status of Kashmir was evidently raised, but with no result. This later contributed to the downfall of President Ayub (Thornton, 1985:162). In the Camp David negotiations, the Palestinian issue was strongly discussed, and a continued peace process was outlined. In this case, the acceptability of the agreement in the Arab world depended on its reaching a procedure on this issue. As of 1989, however, the peace process on this issue had not continued beyond the stage agreed on in 1979.

The fact that the agreements did not resolve all the issues has several implications. First, it might be a good negotiation strategy to solve what is immediately solvable first. The limited time and energy available to the negotiators make this a reasonable approach. However, leaving problems out may make it more difficult to achieve comprehensive support for the agreement. There were serious frictions within the Pakistanian team, particularly between President Ayub and his foreign minister, Zulfiqar Ali Bhutto, who later was to become president (Thornton, 1985:154, 161–162). Within the Egyptian team there was also discontent. The assassination of President Sadat in 1981 may be related to such dissatisfaction within Egypt. President Carter could build on the close relations between the United States and Israel, participating, for example, in a cabinet meeting of the Israeli government and trying to reassure Israeli critics of the agreement (Carter, 1982:383, 422). For the durability of an agreement, comprehensiveness might be highly desirable. At the same time, achieving this is highly cumbersome, thus making attractive the possible solution suggested at Camp David: to view a mediated agreement as the first step in a process. To make the planned continuation credible, its general direction has to be outlined, relevant parties have to be included, and the first steps have to be carefully implemented as agreed. International support is important for this. Such support is highly dependent on the credibility of the envisioned process. Because a major power is involved, its commitment and power to supervise the continued process becomes crucial.

Again, differences appear between major-power mediation and "normal" mediation. Normally, a mediator is not expected to be a permanent party to the agreement, and the mediator is not given a role in implementation. The organization that the mediator comes from might have some such long-term responsibilities, but those are hardly related to the mediator and his or her political influence. The mediator, normally, is providing services of a more temporary nature. The mediator may gain in credibility by virtue of having no vested interest in the continued relationship, apart from the agreement itself. However, if an agreement is part of a longer process, such a vested interest is required. In this case, normal mediation effort cannot succeed. Here lies some of the potential advantages of a permanent mediation structure. Such a structure could provide the responsibility for supervision and resolution of minor disputes within the negotiated framework, as well as for the continuation of the negotiation process.

In summary, these two cases of major-power, third-party activity in conflict resolution suggest that there is a special role available to major powers. Major powers can actually promote conflict resolution in a way not open to other possible mediators. Among the advantages are commitment of resources, continuity of involvement, and support for a protracted peace process. However, there are also serious problems facing this type of third-party mediation that do not afflict other mediators. Major powers have vested interests that might be incompatible with the peace efforts, and their role might appear to be an imposition rather than a mediation, or an intervention rather than a resolution. This means that to take on a role in mediation, the leadership of the major power needs to be highly skillful and perceptive. Honesty and reliability are part of building confidence for such a role. It also means that alternative, permanent mediation structures, without major-power bias, might be needed.

CONFLICTS AMONG STATES WITHOUT LINKS TO MAJOR POWERS

Our focus is conflicts that threaten to escalate and lead to a nuclear war. Thus, conflicts with linkages to major powers are important. There is, nevertheless, a set of conflicts where the major powers have less interest, and where, as a consequence, direct conflicts between the two might not be expected. This is an interesting group of conflicts, because it contains issues where major powers could jointly play a more impartial and constructive role, without entangling their own economic or military ambitions. These are also cases where other actors, notably international governmental and nongovernmental organizations, neighboring states, and others, might be most effective. Such cases include the Beagle Channel dispute between Chile and Argentina, concluded with a mediated agreement in 1984 through the services of the Vatican; and the internal war in the Sudan, concluded with the help of the World Council of Churches in 1972. These examples illustrate that there are a number of conflicts in the world that have not been drawn into the rivalries between major powers. Such conflicts present relatively little danger of escalating local fighting. Third parties might intervene to avoid having major powers drawn into the dynamics of particular conflicts. For this objective, international organizations might be eminently well suited.

Summary

Power is an important, but elusive, factor in mediation and conflict resolution. This is clear from the foregoing discussion of relations between parties of different status and of the participation of major powers as mediators. Two situations are most relevant for the problem of nuclear war: the relations between major powers themselves, and the relations between major powers and regional conflicts with a potential of escalation. These situations differ in ways that affect the possibilities and usefulness of third-party activities. Some conclusions on mediation can be drawn for each specific category and for more general ones.

Third-party activity in conflicts between major powers seems to be rare, at least in the form of open mediation. A promising field of inquiry is to examine the diplomatic and semiofficial connections that do exist. The status of a major power makes it, as already argued and illustrated, difficult to find mediators of similar stature. Thus, there is little open mediation of major-power conflicts. There is, however, a possibility to make mediation more likely by institutionalizing meetings, directly among the major powers as well as among groups of major powers and other countries. The preplanned and fixed schedules would eliminate some of the drama surrounding summit meetings. Using both bilateral and multilateral fora means allowing for needed direct contacts and contexts where others can play useful functions as go-betweens. This means, in addition, that contacts can take place both before, during, and after a crisis, allowing for the prevention, handling, and healing of a crisis. Also, we have pointed out that China might have a special role in some issues between the U.S. and the Soviet Union, where China is relevant but not too obviously guided by its own interests. The precedent is the U.S. third-party role between Russia and Japan in 1905. Although it did not take place in the nuclear age, this case is still relevant as an example of how some usual obstacles to third-party activity in major-power relations can be circumvented.

In more asymmetric and complex relationships with escalation potential, there have been a number of mediation attempts by major powers. These are the cases on which much of the literature is concentrated. Here, the most powerful actor is the mediator and some successes have been recorded—that is, durable solutions have been found, at least to some central elements of important conflicts. There can be little doubt about the attraction of using power in this way. For the primary parties, major powers bring resources and leverage and can help with implementation of agreements. A crucial problem is that the asymmetry can backfire, as is the case when the resulting agreements do not become durable because they are seen as imposed or, in fact, are imposed. Thus, the delicacy of such negotiations is that the parties must not only find integrative options, but also make sure that the options are founded in the political and cultural environment in which the agreement is going to be implemented. This delicacy is a general problem in mediation, but it is more pronounced when major powers function as mediators.

A major-power offer of mediation is difficult to refuse. Thus, it might help provide a way out for the primary parties, which might otherwise dismiss mediation offers. There is, for example, the danger that a refusal will color relations between countries for a considerable period of time. Those unwilling to negotiate would therefore feel pressure to try. It is possible that the initial offer is not an empty one, that there have been contacts with the other primary party, and that it might contain substantial proposals. It is also plausible to assume that major powers are sensitive to having their offers turned down. All these considerations make it likely that a major-power offer will be accepted.

Successful mediation requires some changes in the conflict that present an opportunity for settlement. This is not simply a question of a "hurting stalemate," but rather one of a political opportunity. Such opportunities probably present themselves at many junctures during the course of a conflict. The question is whether such opportunities are seen and utilized. As in the Indo–Pakistani conflict, even the offer of mediation may in itself be such an opportunity. Opportunities are created by (the perception of) changes in the conflict, whether these are military, political, or other. They look different in different conflicts. The task of the skillful observer or participant is to perceive them and use them for conflict resolution.

The cases of major-power mediation give some insight into negotiation tactics, where some surprising similarities in behavior can be seen across time and culture. President Carter recalls that, after days of discussion, Secretary of State Cyrus Vance came running to explain that the Egyptians were packing their bags and had ordered an helicopter for their departure (Carter, 1982:391). Similarly, the Pakistanis suddenly announced that they would be leaving the conference in 2 days unless a result was achieved (Thornton, 1985:153). In the account of the Portsmouth negotiations, Marks writes that "Roosevelt felt that his last-minute intercession as the Russians were packing their bags and threatening to bolt had been decisive. Packing your bags might be a most important strategy. . . . the servants of the Czar were not the first diplomats in history to pack their bags under pressure . . . " (Marks, 1979:66). They were not the last either.

With major powers as mediators, it is very difficult to leave the meeting. It has been argued that President Ayub stayed on in Tashkent because Prime Minister Kosygin convinced him that failure to agree would be an affront to Soviet hospitality (Thornton, 1985:156).

From these cases, one can conclude that third-party activity for conflict resolution is possible between major powers, but that special forms and circumstances may be required to make it acceptable. Also, major powers can play a role in mediating certain types of conflicts, when they appear willing and able to offer something to the parties. These are the advantages of major powers, beyond what other mediators can add to conflict resolution. This implies that if the major powers are not prepared to offer something, their activities are unlikely to yield positive results.

Third Parties and the Prevention of Nuclear War

A nuclear war between the major powers could result from the Sarajevo scenario, the Munich syndrome, or a combination of the two. A nuclear war is not likely to emerge as a sudden attack. It is related to contention and crisis. Historical investigation shows that major-power war often grows from conflicts involving smaller states. Escalation of such conflicts, via alliances and commitments, to a major-power confrontation is a distinct possibility. From the Sarajevo scenario, the lesson is that inflexibility in commitments makes escalation more possible; the Munich syndrome teaches that commitments have to be made credible to deter an aggressor. If both lessons are equally valid, it means that commitment has to be combined with negotiation and that contacts are appropriate, given that each side understands the seriousness of the other. This understanding can be communicated only through dialogue. Thus, contact between the major powers is crucial.

The review of literature and results from studies of conflict resolution, however under-researched the field may be, suggest some important roles for third parties in major-power relations. Some dilemmas for third parties were outlined earlier in this chapter in Figure 4.1, with respect to the constellation of power as well as the dynamics of conflicts. The solution to these question is relevant to the roles of third parties in preventing nuclear war, as summarized in the following eight propositions.

1. Relating to direct contacts between major powers, to avoid crisis: There is some evidence in favor of institutionalized, routinized contact on a high level and in a multilateral forum. Routinization reduces drama and gives a chance for finding out real positions. Since the 1960s, there has been a preference in the U.S. and the Soviet Union for bilateral contacts. This seems to correspond to a historical pattern among major powers. There is a tendency among major powers to deal with one another directly, not allowing others to interfere. Although there are important issues that, strictly speaking, only concern these two powers, most of their discussions also affect others. Furthermore, the evidence suggests, from the course of summit meetings, for example, that the two do not necessarily and easily agree. These arguments suggest having *several sets of institutionalized high-level meetings at regular intervals*. There could be one set of bilateral contacts and one set of meetings, for example, of the 15-member U.N. Security Council. The format of two sets of regular meetings provides a combination of closed "business" talks and meetings where third parties can help solve issues of contention and inject new ideas and where some degree of global representation is achieved.

Furthermore, following the precedent of U.S. mediation in the war between Russia and Japan in 1905, it is suggested that major states should not hesitate to undertake a similar role today, in the event of crisis between the U.S. and the Soviet Union. Offers by major powers to mediate are difficult to refuse and can significantly affect the direction of events, as seen from some of the examples analyzed in this chapter.

In fact, given the plurality of actors in today's world, there is nothing to prevent other states and nonstate actors from involving themselves in third-party activity also for direct major-power relations. The historical patterns speak against the effectiveness of such initiatives, but studies do not cover the whole spectrum of activity in crisis situations. Effective mediation, however, requires the consent of parties and that might still be difficult to obtain with respect to direct issues between superpowers.

2. With respect to armed conflicts involving major and nonmajor states: The number of unresolved armed conflicts in the world remains at a very high level, probably higher than any other time since 1945. These conflicts are dangerous not only to the societies directly affected, but to the world at large.

In some of these, major powers are strongly involved. Thus, escalation of conflicts remains a possibility. As a consequence, *equitable conflict resolution has to have a central role in international relations*. There is considerable third-party activity in many of these conflicts. From open and easily accessible sources, such activity can be documented in about half of all ongoing conflicts. The regulation of some of these (for example, during 1988, Iran–Iraq, Afghanistan, Angola, Namibia) has involved the major powers as third parties, however self-motivated they may have been. This is a role frequently not taken up by major powers, so their involvement should be seen as an encouraging sign.

Many of these major-power conflict regulations have concerned international aspects of the conflict rather than full and comprehensive settlement of all issues. This reflects an inadequacy of solutions building on major-power initiatives and makes it important to search for other third parties as well: international organizations, neighboring states, and nongovernmental organizations.

3. The problem of conflicts that are not internationalized: from the point of view of escalation to nuclear war, such conflicts may not be of greatest urgency. They are largely contained within one country, with possible links to neighbors. However, the repercussions may be severe if they are left without attention: arms purchases may involve other states, economic difficulties may induce interventions, and so forth. Thus, there is a need to consider how the international community (rather than the superpowers) can become involved and contribute to equitable conflict resolution. *Measures to strengthen human rights and other humanitarian conventions* can prove very significant. They provide a legal basis for the international community at large to be concerned. They can be a point of departure for negotiations between third parties and the primary actors. In these cases, nongovernmental organizations may prove to be among the most useful.

4. Military interventions of major powers into other states: Third parties have seldom found a role in such conflicts, as can be seen from literature and historical evidence. Nevertheless, there are interesting developments. The international court procedures have become useful in some asymmetric conflicts (Iran, Nicaragua). In fact, *international law* might provide forms of regulation for such conflicts. This means that the role of third parties might be to enhance the legal alternative, rather than to supply complete solutions to particular conflicts: finding commonly agreed procedures for handling conflicts is a significant contribution to preventing escalation. Legal procedures have not been of interest to many actors, major powers preferring to use their power and Third World countries being skeptical of a legal system developed by former colonial states.

A special and significant recent development is the formation of *regional groupings*, which have strong interventionary features, for negotiating conflicts. Examples are the ASEAN grouping in Southeast Asia and the Esquipulas II process in Central America. Such independent initiatives may have important effects on particular conflicts, and the formation of such groupings can contribute to the prevention of escalation of conflicts. This is a type of collective third-party activity for which there is little historical precedent.

5. Timing for third-party involvement in a protracted conflict: There is no way of objectively determining when the right time has arrived, so continuous activity is required. The literature on third-party mediation contains different arguments on what moments are the most appropriate for action. There is a search for stalemates and pauses in the military struggle, as well as ways of estimating war destruction. All that can be said is that *an opportunity for settlement may arise, even will arise, in most conflicts*. But it is subjectively determined: it is when the parties perceive that victory is no longer possible, defeat is not imminent, and continued destruction is therefore of no use. The delicacy is that the opposing sides have to come to the same conclusion at the same moment.

Because these perceptions cannot be predicted, continuous third-party activity is important, however unsuccessful it might appear. Consequently, third-party involvement has to be a long-term commitment. Potential mediators need to develop familiarity with the situation and develop the confidence of the parties. Patience is a central quality in successful third-party involvement.

6. Third-party involvement in the early phases of an armed conflict: because this may be the most effective time for intervention, *systems of early warning* are called for. There is little systematic inquiry into this aspect of third-party activity, but practitioners' insights as well as conflict accounts give some validity to this point. Also, much activity undertaken by major powers vis-à-vis allies in conflict illustrates the significance of early intervention. The question, then, is whether systems of early warning can be established and made available to countries other than the major powers themselves. Global news media would be a significant element in this, as would systems under the aegis of international organizations or, perhaps, neutral countries, with free access provided for all interested. Information undoubtedly is important for the exercise of power. Information in the hands of third parties can be significant also for the promotion of conflict resolution. The U.N. Secretariat has now begun to construct such a system. The urgency cannot be denied.

The real problem is the step from "early information" to "early action:" how can third parties really interject themselves in issues that governments would find sensitive, embarrassing, or even offensive to discuss with outsiders? In a world of inequitable distribution of power, safeguarding your secrets may be a way of maintaining independence. This consideration speaks in favor of nonmajor powers as third parties.

7. *Training and education of third parties:* Although there is no lack of mediation attempts in many conflicts, the potential uses of third parties are probably greater than the present uses, involving, for example, conflicts defined as "internal" by many states. The skills required include cross-cultural empathy, language training, understanding of history, and social and diplomatic training. Some training in these skills is provided today by ministries of foreign affairs. However, this training is often carried out within a one-nation framework: the participants learn how to deal with other nationals from a particular perspective. The workshop approach reviewed in this chapter suggests that there is a need for developing new tools of training: thinking of conflict analysis as international dialogue and contact. These thoughts suggest having an international training program for diplomats, international experts, staff of international organizations, and so forth, to help bring about more understanding or at least reduced misunderstanding. The principles should be the same as in proposition 1: a multilateral forum is preferable to a unilateral or bilateral one. There have been initiatives in this direction, but the proposition here is that the training should be more directly geared to the needs for developing third-party skills for conflicts that are difficult for mediators to address today.

8. Research: A review of a field that raises more questions than can be answered needs to conclude that *more research is required.* The topics are important, and some real contributions have been made. However, many concerted efforts are needed, and the outstanding issues remain central. In fact, propositions 7 and 8 are interlinked. More training will require more research, and more research is needed to provide more training. There are new centers being created for conflict resolution, peace research, and negotiation studies, all witness to the significance of the issues. If this trend continues, a completely different review of the state of the art might be made in the next decade.

Appendix

Ongoing Wars in 1984

War is defined as a struggle directly between two or more armed forces where:

1. at least on one side are regular forces of the government,
2. on both sides there is a central leading organization, and
3. the armed operations have a certain continuity (Gantzel and Meyer-Stamer, 1986:8)

Conflict (Location)[a]	Gantzel Reference Number[a]	Year Begun[a]	Open Third-Party Mediation Activity[b]
Burma	(021)	1948	—
Eritrea	(063)	1961	Recorded
Chad	(092)	1966	Recorded
Namibia/Southwest Africa	(093)	1966	Recorded
Northern Ireland	(105)	1969	—
Basques (Spain)	(106)	1969	—
The Philippines	(109)	1970	—
Lebanon	(120)	1975	Recorded
East Timor (Indonesia)	(121)	1975	—
Tigre (Ethiopia)	(121)	1975	—
Western Sahara (Morocco)	(123)	1975	—
South Africa vs. Angola	(124)	1976	Recorded
South Africa	(125)	1976	Recorded
Kurdish issue (Iraq)	(126)	1976	—
Ogaden War (Ethiopia–Somalia)	(127)	1976	Recorded
West Irian (Indonesia)	(130)	1977	Recorded
Oromo (Ethiopia)	(131)	1977	—
Colombia	(137)	1978	—
South Africa vs. Mozambique	(138)	1976	Recorded
Kampuchea (Vietnam)	(139)	1978	Recorded
El Salvador	(140)	1978	Recorded
Afghanistan	(141)	1976	Recorded
Kurdish issue (Iran)	(144)	1979	—
Guatemala	(146)	1980	—
Peru	(147)	1980	—
Iraq vs. Iran	(148)	1980	Recorded
Nicaragua	(151)	1981	Recorded
Uganda	(152)	1981	—
Sikh issue (India)	(155)	1982	—
Sri Lanka	(157)	1983	Recorded
Sudan	(158)	1983	Recorded
Kurdish issue (Turkey)	(159)	1984	—

[a]Data from Gantzel and Meyer-Stamer (1986).
[b]Data from the project on armed conflict and negotiated settlement, Department of Peace and Conflict Research, Uppsala University, Uppsala, Sweden.

References

Azar, E., and J.W. Burton, eds. 1986. *International Conflict Resolution: Theory and Practice.* Boulder, Colo.: Lynne Rienner.

Bailey, S. 1982. *How Wars End: The UN and the Termination of Armed Conflicts, 1946–1974.* 2 Vols. Oxford: Clarendon.

———. 1985. Non-official mediation in disputes: Reflections on Quaker experience. *International Affairs* 61:207–222.

Bendahmane, D.B., J.W. McDonald, Jr., eds. 1986. *Perspectives on Negotiation. Four Case Studies and Interpretations.* Center for the Study of Foreign Affairs, Washington, D.C.: Foreign Service Institute, U.S. Department of State.

Bercovitch, J. 1986. International mediation: A study of the incidence, strategies and conditions of successful outcomes. *Cooperation and Conflict* 21:155–168.

Brecher, M., and P. James. 1988. Patterns of crisis management. *Journal of Conflict Resolution* 32:426–456.

Burton, J.W. 1969. *Conflict and Communication: The Use of Controlled Communication in International Relations.* London: Macmillan.

Butterworth, R.L. 1976. *Managing Interstate Conflicts, 1945–1974: Data with Synopses.* Pittsburgh: University of Pittsburgh, Center for International Studies.

Campbell, J.C., ed. 1976. *Successful Negotiation: Trieste 1954. An Appraisal by the Five Participants.* Princeton, N.J.: Princeton University Press.

Cancio, H.R. 1959. Some reflections on the role of mediation. *Labor Law Journal* 10:720–723.

Carter, J. 1982. *Keeping Faith: Memoirs of a President.* London: Collins.

Claude, I. 1971. *Swords into Plowshares,* 4th rev. ed. New York: Random House.

Curle, A. 1971. *Making Peace.* London: Tavistock.

Doob, L.W. 1974. A Cyprus workshop: An exercise in intervention methodology. *Journal of Social Psychology* 94:161–178.

Doob, L.W., ed. 1970. *Resolving Conflict in Africa: The Fermeda Workshop.* New Haven and London: Yale University Press.

Doob, L.W., and W.J. Foltz. 1973. The Belfast workshop: An application of group techniques to a destructive conflict. *Journal of Conflict Resolution* 17:489–512.

———. 1974. The impact of a workshop upon grassroots leaders in Belfast. *Journal of Conflict Resolution* 18:237–256.

Druckman, D. 1977. *Negotiations: Social-Psychological Perspectives.* Beverly Hills, Calif.: Sage.

Esthus, R.A. 1967. *Theodore Roosevelt and Japan.* Seattle: University of Washington Press.

———. 1970. *Theodore Roosevelt and the International Rivalries.* Waltham, Mass.: Ginn Blaisdell.

Fisher, R.J. 1980. A third-party consultation workshop on the India/Pakistan conflict. *Journal of Social Psychology* 112:191–206.

———. 1983. Third-party consultation as a method of intergroup conflict resolution: A review of studies. *Journal of Conflict Resolution* 27:301–334.

Fisher, R.J., and W. Ury. 1981. *Getting to Yes. Negotiating Agreement without Giving In*. Boston: Houghton Mifflin.

Galtung, J. 1965. Institutionalized conflict resolution. *Journal of Peace Research* 2:348–397.

Gantzel, H.J., and J. Meyer-Stamer. 1986. *Die Kriege nach dem Zweiten Weltkriegbis, 1984. Daten und erste Analysen*. Munich: Weltforum Verlag.

George, A.L., ed. 1983. *Managing U.S.–Soviet Rivalry: Problems of Crisis Prevention*, Boulder, Colo.: Westview Press.

Gochman, C., and Z. Maoz. 1984. Militarized interstate disputes, 1816–1976. *Journal of Conflict Resolution* 28:585–616.

Haas, E.B. 1983. Regime decay: Conflict management and international organizations, 1945–1981. *International Organization* 37:189–256.

Harbaugh, W.H. 1975. *The Life and Times of Theodore Roosevelt*, rev. ed. New York: Oxford University Press.

Holsti, K. 1966. Resolving international conflict: A taxonomy of behavior and some figures on procedures. *Journal of Conflict Resolution* 10:272–297.

Kelman, H.C. 1972. The problem-solving workshop in conflict resolution. In R.L. Merritt, ed., *Communication in International Politics*. Urbana: University of Illinois Press.

———. 1982. Creating the conditions for Israeli–Palestinian negotiations. *Journal of Conflict Resolution* 26:39–75.

Kelman, H.C., and S.P. Cohen. 1976. The problem-solving workshop: A social-psychological contribution to the resolution of international conflict. *Journal of Peace Research* 13:79–90.

Kerr, C. 1954. Industrial conflict and its mediation. *American Journal of Sociology* 40:230–245.

Marks, F.W., III. 1979. *Velvet on Iron: The Diplomacy of Theodore Roosevelt*. Lincoln: University of Nebraska Press.

Merrills, J.G. 1984. *International Dispute Settlement*. London: Sweet & Maxwell.

Mitchell, C.R. 1981. *Peacemaking and the Consultant's Role*. Farnborough, England: Gower.

Napper, L.C. 1983. The Ogaden war: Some implications for crisis prevention. In A.L. George, ed., *Managing U.S.–Soviet Rivalry: Problems of Crisis Prevention*, pp. 225–253. Boulder, Colo.: Westview Press.

Ott, M.C. 1972. Mediation as a method of conflict resolution. *International Organization* 26:595–618.

Pillar, P.R. 1983. *Negotiating Peace: War Termination as a Bargaining Process*. Princeton, N.J.: Princeton University Press.

Pruitt, D.G. 1971. Indirect communication and the search for agreement in negotiation. *Journal of Applied Social Psychology* 1:205–239.

———. 1986. Trends in the scientific study of negotiation and mediation. *Negotiation Journal* 2:237–244.

Quandt, W.B. 1986. *Camp David: Peacemaking and Politics*. Washington, D.C.: The Brookings Institution.

Raymond, G.A. 1980. *Conflict Resolution and the Structure of the State System.* Montclair, N.J.: Allanheld and Osmun; Alphen aan den Rijn, the Netherlands: Sijthoff and Noordhoff.

Raymond, G.A., and C.W. Kegley, Jr. 1985. Third-party mediation and international norms: A test of two models. *Conflict Management and Peace Science* 9:33–52.

Rubin, J.Z., ed. 1981. *Dynamics of third-Party Intervention: Kissinger in the Middle East.* New York: Praeger.

Sherman, F. 1987. *Part-Way to Peace: The United Nations and the Road to Nowhere.* Ph.D. dissertation, Department of Political Science Pennsylvania State University.

Small, M., and J.D. Singer. 1982. *Resort to Arms: International and Civil Wars, 1816–1980.* Beverly Hills, Calif.: Sage.

Thornton, T.P. 1985. The Indo–Pakistani conflict: Soviet mediation at Tashkent, 1966. Reprinted in S. Touval and I.W. Zartman, eds., *International Mediation in Theory and Practice,* pp. 141–171. Boulder, Colo.: Westview.

Touval, S. 1982. *The Peace Brokers: Mediators in the Arab–Israeli Conflict, 1948–1979.* Princeton, N.J.: Princeton University Press.

Touval, S., and I.W. Zartman, eds. 1985. *International Mediation in Theory and Practice.* Boulder, Colo.: Westview.

Trani, E. 1969. *The Treaty of Portsmouth: An Adventure in American Diplomacy.* Lexington: University of Kentucky Press.

Wall, J.A. 1981. Mediation: An analysis, review and proposed research. *Journal of Conflict Resolution* 25:157–180.

Wallensteen, P. 1981. Incompatibility, confrontation and war: Four models and three historical systems, 1816–1976. *Journal of Peace Research* 18:57–90.

———. 1984. Universalism vs. particularism: On the limits of major power order. *Journal of Peace Research* 21:243–257.

Walton, R.E. 1970. A problem-solving workshop on border conflicts in Eastern Africa. *Journal of Applied Behavioral Science* 6:453–489.

Weihmiller, G.R. 1986. *U.S.–Soviet Summits: An Account of East–West Diplomacy at the Top 1955–1985.* New York: University Press of America.

Young, O. 1967. *The Intermediaries: Third Parties in International Crises.* Princeton, N.J.: Princeton University Press.

———. 1971. Intermediaries: Additional thoughts on third parties. *Journal of Conflict Resolution* 16:51–65.

Zartman, I.W. 1983. The strategy of preventive diplomacy in Third World conflicts. In A.L. George, ed., *Managing U.S.–Soviet Rivalry: Problems of Crisis Prevention.* Boulder, Colo.: Westview Press.

———. 1986. Ripening conflict, ripe moment, formula, and mediation. In D.B. Bendahmane and J.W. McDonald, Jr., eds., *Perspectives on Negotiation: Four Case Studies and Interpretations.* Washington, D.C.: Foreign Service Institute, U.S. Department of State.

Zartman, I.W., and M. Berman. 1982. *The Practical Negotiator.* New Haven, Conn.: Yale University Press.

5

Sources of Moderation in Soviet Security Policy

MATTHEW EVANGELISTA

In December 1987, Mikhail Gorbachev and Ronald Reagan signed the first bilateral U.S.–Soviet arms control agreement since the ill-fated SALT II treaty was completed in 1979. After a period of serious deterioration in U.S.–Soviet relations during the late 1970s and much of the 1980s, the treaty eliminating intermediate- and shorter-range missiles appeared to herald a new atmosphere of international cooperation. How can we account for such a dramatic change from what some observers characterized as a "new cold war" to what appeared to be a new détente?

Historians and political analysts will continue to debate the sources of Ronald Reagan's apparent turnaround on policy towards the Soviet Union (Lapidus and Dallin, 1989; Gaddis, 1989). According to William Safire, the main candidate explanations are "fatigue, lameduckiness and place-in-history Nancyism" (*New York Times,* 10 March 1988). In attempting to understand the change in U.S. policy, analysts will have the benefit of interviews with Reagan advisers and, eventually, whatever becomes available of the documentary record.

How can we account, however, for comparable changes in Soviet policy? Soviet officials are not as accessible for interviews; even if they were, there is no Freedom of Information Act to provide documents as a check against self-serving accounts of recent history. Yet one should not overstate the paucity of evidence for Soviet decisions. Much can be learned from an eclectic mixture of sources, including memoir accounts, U.S. intelligence analyses, the negotiating record, and the Soviet press. Furthermore, the policy of *glasnost* promises further access both to Soviet officials and to archival materials. Analysts of Soviet policy would do well to prepare for the increasing availability of new data by identifying the gaps in their knowledge and setting priorities for the acquisition of new information. Finally, by employing deductive theory to generate the questions that most need to be addressed, analysts can make the best use of existing evidence and know what to look for in the future (Snyder, 1984/1985, 1988*b*).

The behavioral and social sciences offer a number of potentially promising theoretical frameworks that could be applied to the question of change toward moderation in Soviet security policy. These include regime theory, notions of learning, and game-theoretic and psychological approaches to cooperation and conflict. In the policy realm as well, several candidate explanations enjoy wide currency. Among the most common are the view that the Soviets change their policy in response to pressure from adversaries who pursue "negotiation from strength;" or that the Soviets react to conciliatory policies and compromise by moderating their own policies; or that Soviet moves toward moderation are driven by internal constraints, such as economic stringency.

The purpose of this chapter is to review the academic theories and to integrate them with more popular explanations into a larger framework that seeks to illuminate the sources of change in Soviet policy. It then attempts to evaluate the components of the framework in light of available evidence and, where evidence is lacking, to suggest the kind of information that would be required to test competing explanations. The chapter concludes with a discussion of the most promising methodological approaches to understanding the sources of Soviet change and a presentation of hypotheses, linking aspects of the various explanations, that could be tested in future research. From a policy standpoint, it is particularly important to propose hypotheses and to adopt methods that help identify factors that encourage moderate behavior on the part of the Soviet Union, especially those factors that may be susceptible to influence by the United States and other countries.

The evidence presented in this chapter, however, indicates that the factors most commonly assumed to induce Soviet moderation—economic constraints or U.S. negotiation from strength, for example—do not typically work in a direct or deterministic fashion. Rather, they become subject to domestic debates between opponents and proponents of moderation. Understanding the sources of moderation in Soviet security policy ultimately depends on understanding how Soviet policy entrepreneurs and domestic coalitions prevail in foreign policy debates.

Assessing Change in Soviet Security Policy

The problems of applying generalizations derived from the behavioral and social sciences to specific policy questions are myriad (Tetlock, 1989). Moreover, the study of Soviet security policy is less developed than many of the social sciences, and, given the impossibility of conducting controlled experiments, its conclusions are always subject to dispute. Trying to account for, or even recognize, change toward moderation in Soviet policy is further complicated by problems of definition and the fact that analyses are often heavily influenced by unspoken biases and assumptions that are essentially nonfalsifiable.

Definitions

The first problem that we encounter is simply trying to define "change toward moderation" in Soviet policy. Although one of the goals of this chapter is to examine what constitutes meaningful change in Soviet security policy, we still need a working definition to start. Many obvious definitions would entail tautological reasoning if used to explain the sources of moderation. For example, if we define moderation as a reduction in resources allocated to the military, we automatically call attention to explanations that focus on economic stringency. We must also distinguish moderation from cooperation. Keohane (1984:51) defines "intergovernmental cooperation" as that which "takes place when the policies actually followed by one government are regarded by its partners as facilitating realization of their own objectives, as the result of a process of policy coordination" (for a similar definition, see Weber, forthcoming). Thus, if we equate Soviet moderation with actions that lead to formal or tacit bilateral or multilateral cooperation, we make our judgments dependent on the perceptions of the Soviet Union's adversaries as to whether Soviet actions facilitated achievement of their own objectives. If these objectives include *avoidance* of cooperation, then the unwillingness of Soviet adversaries to come to agreement to coordinate policies might make us overlook instances of Soviet moderation. Consider, for example, how U.S. policymakers in 1956 publicly dismissed Soviet troop reductions as insignificant because the Eisenhower administration was not interested in coordinating arms reductions with the Soviet Union (Evangelista, 1990a), or, more recently, how the Reagan administration ignored the 19-month Soviet unilateral nuclear test moratorium, because it opposed in principle negotiation of a test-ban agreement (Evangelista, 1986). By emphasizing cooperation, we would have to exclude such initiatives as evidence of Soviet moderation—regardless of actual Soviet intentions.

For our purposes, we should define a change toward moderation broadly enough to encompass most such initiatives that could have policy implications for the United States. Therefore, we include in the definition any actions that meet one of the following three criteria: (1) they limit actual or potential future Soviet military capability; (2) they could plausibly be intended to reduce the adversary's perception of threat; or (3) they could plausibly be intended to signal willingness to restrain the arms race through tacit cooperation or to negotiate formal agreements limiting the competition. By employing this definition, we obviously risk including actions that could be interpreted as moderate but were not intended so (such as temporarily reorienting resources from military to civilian uses to gain a "breathing space") or policies that were simply declaratory in nature with no substantive content. For policy purposes it seems worth erring on that side for now, to make sure to evaluate all the possible signals of Soviet moderation. Later in the chapter, when we consider the specific evidence from Soviet cases, we can be more discriminating in identifying what constitutes significant change.

For the purposes of this study, *security policy* is defined as military policy regarding nuclear weapons, conventional ground and air forces, and related arms control policies. These appear most immediately relevant to the objective of this series of books—contributing to "the prevention of nuclear war." This chapter limits consideration of such issues as Soviet policy toward the

Third World, military intervention abroad, and naval policy, although these are surely relevant to the question of nuclear war. The chapter also excludes discussion of topics appropriate to a broader definition of security—economic welfare, human rights, environmental policy, and so forth—except where they are explicitly raised by Soviet officials in their attempts to pursue moderation in the more narrowly defined security realm.

Assumptions, Bias, and the Problem of Nonfalsifiability

Among social-scientific endeavors, the study of Soviet security policy is certainly one of the most difficult to pursue "objectively," in isolation from current policy concerns and the individual analyst's policy preferences and prejudices. Disagreements among analysts often stem from divergent assumptions about such basic issues as the nature of the Soviet Union, the structure of the international system, and the appropriate role of force in interstate relations. Assumptions are rarely made explicit, yet they influence fundamentally the policy implications an analyst draws. A more serious barrier to analysis of Soviet security policy stems from Herrmann's (1985) observation that the three dominant "models" for understanding Soviet motives (communist expansionism, realpolitik expansionism, and realpolitik self-defense) are nonfalsifiable. Most evidence can fit any of the models, especially given the imprecise definitions of such key concepts as defense, provocation, risk, and opportunity. To take the most prominent example, a status-quo-oriented Soviet Union is difficult to distinguish from an expansionist-yet-cautious Soviet Union. In the absence of overt aggression, one could plausibly argue either that the Soviet Union was expansionist, but deterred from aggression, or that the Soviet Union was simply not interested in aggression.

One of the most fundamental disagreements among analysts of Soviet security policy concerns the nature of Soviet nuclear doctrine and strategy. As Jack Snyder (1988b) characterizes the debate, one side argues that the Soviets accept the implications of a deterrent relationship based on the threat of mutual assured destruction (MAD), whereas the other side maintains that the Soviets reject Western conceptions of deterrence and pursue a war-winning capability. Both explanations seem impervious to falsifying evidence. Evidence that appears to undercut the former view of Soviet acceptance of MAD—such as deployment of the SS-18 missile and other "counterforce" systems—are explained away as vestigial hedges against the failure of deterrence. Evidence that seems to contradict the latter view of a war-winning posture—such as Soviet acceptance of the treaty limiting antiballistic missile systems (ABMs)—are described as temporary expedients imposed by technological constraints.

Underlying this debate about Soviet strategy is an even more fundamental one about the nature of nuclear weapons. Different interpretations of Soviet nuclear strategy apparently reflect analysts' divergent beliefs about such issues as whether nuclear weapons can be considered to fulfill actual combat functions during a war, whether there are meaningful advantages to striking first, given the existence of virtually invulnerable retaliatory forces, and whether one can conceive of "victory" in nuclear war (Green, 1987:9) Probably an analyst who believes that it makes no sense under any circumstances to initiate first use of nuclear weapons, given the near certainty of devastating retaliation, would be more inclined to find Soviet acceptance of MAD plausible. By contrast, an analyst who believes that meaningful military advantages accrue to the side that strikes first and pursues a war-winning, counterforce strategy would find it incredible for the Soviets to foreswear such an option. Divergent views about the political utility of a nuclear war-fighting posture or "nuclear superiority" are similarly based on axiomatic beliefs and therefore not easily subject to falsification.

In principle one could devise ways to test competing explanations that appear nonfalsifiable by linking them to propositions derived from deductive theory. Snyder (1988b), for example, evaluates competing interpretations of Soviet nuclear strategy by introducing game-theoretic deductions about the links between nuclear weapons and crisis behavior. In a similar fashion, Herrmann (1985) develops propositions deductively from theories of cognitive psychology to evaluate contrasting interpretations of Soviet intentions. Unfortunately, however, such efforts are extremely rare.

Given the state of knowledge in Soviet security studies, a review essay of this sort cannot systematically evaluate all of the competing assumptions inherent in the many possible explanations for Soviet policy change. Ideally, one would need to identify the underlying assumptions of each explanation, link them to propositions derived from deductive theory, and test them against appropriate empirical evidence (Snyder, 1988b)—a task well beyond the scope of this chapter. The goals of this essay are more modest: to present a range of explanations for change toward moderation, calling attention to areas of overlap as well as dispute; to indicate when underlying assumptions contribute to disagreements about causal factors; and to be sensitive to the effect of competing assumptions when reviewing the empirical evidence.

Explaining Change Toward Moderation

Over the years, a number of scholars have written about change in Soviet security policy with an eye toward policy implications for the United States.

By and large, however, they have not taken advantage of the theoretical literature on cooperation and change, perhaps because much of its is based in another subfield of political science—the study of international political economy. Nor have Sovietologists made a systematic effort to evaluate even such popular notions as "negotiation from strength" or economic stringency, although these explanations are implicit in much of their work. Making valid generalizations about the sources of moderation in Soviet security policy is not an easy matter then, because much of the work still needs to be done.

This survey of the research on Soviet security policy confronts problems familiar to those who have undertaken such efforts in the past (Horelick, Johnson, and Steinbruner, 1973; Meyer, 1984; Green, 1987). The conclusions of a 1973 Rand Corporation survey are still valid today (Horelick, Johnson, and Steinbruner, 1973:27): "only a small portion of the Soviet foreign policy literature contains a self-conscious and reasonably systematic effort to employ an explicit theoretical framework. . . . There is little cumulation of comparable propositions and hypotheses." Another shortcoming identified by the Rand study—sparsity of case studies on Soviet foreign policy—no longer obtains to the same extent (Meyer, 1984). At the same time, however, the existing case-study literature is largely descriptive, does not seek to evaluate competing theoretical perspectives or test hypotheses, and has yielded little cumulative knowledge about the sources of Soviet policy (Snyder, 1984/1985, 1988b). Thus, a review of this sort in Soviet studies cannot, as in some other disciplines, even fully spell out the main hypotheses in operational terms, let alone present "findings" from the existing body of research.

Academic Theories

This section reviews the academic literature on foreign policy change relevant to understanding the sources of Soviet moderation. It draws particularly from the literature on sources of cooperation in international economic policy. The section proceeds "backwards," as it were, in that it presents theories of cooperative outcomes—as represented in this case by international regimes—and then inquires into the means by which such outcomes are obtained. The inquiry relies on theories at different levels of analysis, many of which are complementary rather than competing. In general, the discussion covers those theories at a higher—systemic—level first, and then moves increasingly towards lower-level theories that focus on political coalitions, bureaucracies, and individuals. Theories that link across levels—for example, notions of "transnational alliances"—are also considered.

REGIME THEORY

Students of international political economy often view regimes as the main goal of efforts at interstate cooperation. In the widely accepted definition, regimes are a set of "implicit or explicit principles, norms, rules, and decision-making procedures around which actors' expectations converge" (Krasner, 1983:2). If we seek to understand the process leading to moderation in Soviet security policy and U.S.–Soviet cooperation, we might benefit from considering how a U.S.–Soviet international security regime could emerge. A number of analysts have already attempted to apply regime theory to security policy. Some have been skeptical of its relevance (Jervis, 1983), while others have found some of the insights of regime theory valuable (Caldwell, 1981; George, Farley and Dallin, 1988, Nye, 1987).

If regimes matter, they should serve to constrain states' behavior in ways that the existing distribution of power in the international system does not already do (Krasner, 1983). According to Jervis (1983:190), for example, if the fear of retaliation deters nuclear attack, one need not invoke strategic arms control as a "regime" in order to explain the prevention of nuclear war. To demonstrate the existence of a regime in the sphere of arms control, one must show that the rules, principles, and norms associated with arms treaties have "the potential to alter unilateral decision-making" within states in ways that would not have been done otherwise (Rice, 1988:298), or—by related criteria—that the states exercise restraint in the pursuit of narrow, short-run self-interest in favor of longer-term goals of cooperation (Jervis, 1983:186–187; Nye, 1987:396).

Assuming that regimes could exist in the security sphere and that they would influence behavior in the direction of moderation, one is still left with the question of how regimes are established. As Alexander George and his colleagues put it (George, Farley, and Dallin, 1988:716–717), "How, under what circumstances, and why do incentives for security cooperation emerge?" They found that a prerequisite for U.S.–Soviet security cooperation was a perception on the part of the leaders of both countries of mutual interests that could be served better by cooperation than by unrestrained competition. The question then becomes what leads policymakers to change their estimates of the relative merits of unilateral versus cooperative policies. Or, as Axelrod and Keohane (1985:229) argue, "to understand the degree of mutuality of interests (or to enhance this mutuality) we must understand the process by which interests are perceived and preferences determined." Yet the conditions under which a perception of mutual interests emerges are not well specified, and the regime literature's lack of attention to domestic politics exacerbates the problems (Haggard and Simmons, 1987).

COOPERATION THEORY

Students of international political economy have only begun to consider how preferences and interests are determined (see for example, Stein, 1983). They have paid more attention to the structural limitations and possibilities for cooperation. Even if two adversaries perceive a mutual interest in cooperation, these analysts maintain, the structure of their interaction may make cooperation difficult to achieve. The anarchic international system, unlike most domestic polities, has no central government to enforce cooperative agreements. States operate on the basis of self-help and feel obliged to provide for their own security through arming rather than trust their opponents to abide by a disarmament agreement. Game theorists have described this situation as a "prisoners' dilemma" game, where each side would prefer to cooperate, but continues to arm for fear that the other side would defect rather than adhere to mutual disarmament.

A number of analysts have proposed solutions to the prisoners' dilemma. Robert Axelrod, for example, has suggested that a strategy of "tit-for-tat" reciprocity holds great potential for inducing cooperation in such cases (Axelrod, 1984; see also Brams, 1985). He argues that if one side takes the initiative and adopts a "nice" strategy (by not being the first to defect), and both sides follow a rule of reciprocity, cooperation can evolve through a tit-for-tat mechanism. The main condition is that the two sides anticipate interacting many more times, so that the "shadow of the future" is cast over present actions. Axelrod has explicitly suggested that his cooperation theory should apply to U.S.–Soviet arms negotiations: "Certainly, the fact that the United States and the Soviet Union know that they will both be dealing with each other for a very long time should help establish the necessary conditions [for arms control]" (Axelrod, 1984: 181).

One assumption of the prisoners' dilemma is that mutual interest in cooperation exists, but that it is difficult to establish. Some analysts have argued, however, that many arms races are not actually prisoners' dilemmas, where each side would prefer to cooperate, but the game of deadlock, where at least one side prefers conflict (defection) to cooperation (Downs, Rocke, and Siverson, 1985). As Kenneth Oye puts it, "When you observe conflict, think Deadlock—the absence of mutual interest—before puzzling over why a mutual interest was not realized" (Oye, 1985:7). Others have argued that the pursuit of relative advantage severely limits the scope of mutual interests and makes efforts at cooperation even more difficult than advocates of strategies of reciprocity admit (Waltz, 1979; Grieco, 1988).

Even if mutual interests do exist, one or both sides may fail to recognize that the opponent favors cooperation. Deborah Larson has argued, for example, that if the target of a conciliatory action "has an inherent 'bad faith' image of the initiator, a single cooperative action may be ignored, reinterpreted to conform to preexisting beliefs, or discounted as a ploy to trick the target into letting down its guard" (Larson, 1987:30–31). In her view, the potential for such misperceptions poses barriers to implementing a strategy of tit-for-tat reciprocity (Larson, 1987:30–31; Lebow and Stein, 1987:41–47; Van Evera, 1985).

Another problem with the prisoners' dilemma, and therefore the tit-for-tat solution, is that a state's actions cannot always be understood as the product of a unitary rational actor but must often be seen as the consequence of struggle between competing domestic institutions and individuals (Gowa, 1986:138). If some of those substate actors argue against the existence of mutual interests and manage to prevail, the situation becomes a deadlock, even if objectively cooperation could have benefited both sides. Writing of Soviet–U.S. security relations, Alexander George argued that internal U.S. "disagreements over the correct image of the Soviet Union can call into question the scope as well as the desirability of cooperative arrangements with the Soviets and reinforce a preference for relying on unilateral policies for assuring U.S. security interests" (George, Farley, and Dallin, 1988:660). Factors at the substate level may also hinder implementation of strategies of reciprocity: "Internal factional, organizational, and bureaucratic dysfunctions may limit the ability of nations to implement Tit-for-Tat strategies. It may be easier to sell one unvarying line of policy than to sell a strategy of shifting between lines of policy in response to the actions of others" (Oye, 1985:16).

A number of analysts have argued in favor of alternative strategies that take account of psychological barriers, the possibility of misperception induced by mistrust, and the existence of hardliners in domestic coalitions. A strategy of graduated reciprocation in tension-reduction, or GRIT, some maintain, can promote cooperation through a series of unilateral initiatives and concessions aimed at dispelling the opponent's "enemy image" (Osgood, 1962; Plous, 1985, 1987; Larson, 1987). Lebow and Stein (1987) favor a mixture of strategies, including reciprocity and limited security regimes, all under the rubric of "reassurance."

The perception of mutuality of interests appears to be central to the success of both tit-for-tat and GRIT. As George points out, tit-for-tat seems to apply mainly "when mutuality of interests clearly exists in a particular issue-area and is recognized by the two sides" (George, Farley, and Dallin, 1988:705). GRIT, by the same token, acknowledges that psychological barriers and mistrust may obscure the mutuality of interests between adversaries, but it assumes that one side recognizes the problem and sets out on a course of unilateral initiatives in order to persuade the other side that cooperation is in their mutual interest. In order for these approaches to be adopted as a means of securing cooperation, at least one side (for GRIT) or both sides (for tit-for-tat) must come to believe that a mutuality of interests exists. In game-theoretic terms, they must change their perception of the competition from one of deadlock to one of prisoners' dilemma.

The recognition of mutual interest, then, is a prerequisite for establishing cooperation through tit-for-tat or GRIT mechanisms as well as for institutionalizing cooperation through regimes. But is it possible for states to change their perceptions in order to recognize a mutuality of interests where none was visible before? This would appear to entail a redefinition of their interests. One problem with game-theoretic approaches that posit a unitary rational actor and a structure of fixed preferences is that they fail to account for the possibility that substate actors may change the definition of national interest (Haas, 1980; Lebow and Stein, 1987:46; Nye, 1987:378). Because the payoff matrix defines the game, game theorists can represent a change in preferences (the "national interest") only by changing the game itself (Axelrod and Keohane, 1985:229–230). But as Jervis (1988:324) points out, "by taking preferences as given we beg what may be the most important question on [sic] how they are formed." International relations theorists increasingly recognize that accounting for changes in preferences "requires an examination of the internal politics of states" (Morrow, 1988:96). Thus, both regime theory and cooperation theory point us in the direction of actors at the substate level of analysis (Haggard and Simmons, 1987).

COALITION THEORY

By focusing on the domestic level of analysis, one can identify a number of ways that definitions of the national interest can change. The most straightforward is a change in political leadership, resulting from an election, a coup, or longer-term generational change (Nye, 1987:378; Jervis, 1988:326–327). Students of international political economy have also identified links between international pressures and the formation of domestic coalitions as a means of explaining policy changes (Gourevitch, 1986; Kurth, 1979; Gershenkron, 1962).

Soviet studies provides a relevant literature that explains policy change by focusing on the process of coalition-building among important institutions, such as the military, the heavy industrial sector, the party apparatus, and so forth (see, for example, Breslauer, 1982). Applied to foreign policy, this analysis suggests that changes in Soviet external behavior result from new alliances between domestic institutions (Snyder, 1987/1988). The members of the new coalition criticize the policies of the old coalition as atavistic and dysfunctional. The new coalition pursues new policies and new goals, in effect manifesting a changed definition of the national interest that in some cases could favor more cooperative relationships with adversaries.

Some coalition theorists see changes in the coalitions that determine Soviet foreign policy as a consequence of domestic stimuli, generated by such factors as the "objective requirements of the stage of intensive development" of the economy, the "natural processes of modernization," or opportunistic political maneuvering (Snyder, 1987/1988:110). In this view, foreign policy ideas play a role mainly "in rationalizing and reconciling group interests" of the domestic coalitions (Snyder, 1987/1988:99). An alternative explanation, however, holds that new foreign policies are adopted because the old policies have failed and become discredited, because they cannot meet changing international conditions, or because they become too costly (Bialer, 1988:475–490). In such cases, scholars often write of a country's ability to adapt its foreign policy in terms of learning, rather than in terms of the product of domestic political realignment.

The coalition and learning explanations are not necessarily incompatible; it might be possible to use them together and in combination with other approaches. One could argue, for example, that groups which have learned important foreign policy lessons may come to achieve political power because the governing coalition's inability to learn has resulted in foreign policy failures. Several advocates of regime theory also try to incorporate notions of learning into their explanations for international cooperation. In order for policymakers to support the establishment of international regimes, it is argued, they often need to learn that such cooperative efforts serve their interests better than unilateral policies do. At the same time, argue some analysts, international regimes themselves can enhance learning in a number of respects, particularly through providing contacts with, and information about, the other participants (Keohane and Nye, 1977; Keohane and Nye, 1987:751; Nye, 1987:400–401). Thus, for many analysts, understanding the potential for strategies of reciprocity and for the establishment of international regimes depends on knowing how foreign policy learning takes place (Lebow and Stein, 1987:46, 62–63; Keohane, 1984:132; Keohane and Nye, 1987:752–753; Nye, 1987).

Unfortunately, however, the literature on learning is not sufficiently developed to fit in so neatly with theories of coalitions and regimes, and in some cases the approaches make competing claims. The disagreements have been highlighted in studies of international political economy. Odell, for example, favors cognitive learning explanations for change in U.S. monetary policy and approvingly quotes Keynes' famous dictum that "the power of vested interests is vastly exaggerated compared with the gradual encroachment of ideas" (Odell, 1982:12–13). Gourevitch, by contrast, maintains that "ideas for solving economic problems are plentiful, but if an idea is to prevail as the actual policy of a particular government, it must obtain support from those who have political power. . . . The victorious interpretation will be the one whose adherents have the power to translate their opinion into force of law" (Gourevitch, 1986:17). Naturally, there are points of overlap in the two explanations for change. Odell's attention to the notion of policy "triggers" that facilitate change, for example, bears some resemblance to Gourevitch's focus on international economic crises as stimulants to policy change.

Before trying to disentangle the competing interpretations offered by the learning and coalition approaches, we must inquire into the various conceptions of learning available in the literature and their potential application to moderation in Soviet security policy.

LEARNING

Several analysts have recently attempted to explain changes in Soviet security policy under Gorbachev by applying the concept of learning. One should consider then whether the concept could prove useful in accounting for change toward moderation in Soviet security policy in general. The task is hindered, however, by a number of factors, not the least of which is the interdisciplinary nature of the original body of literature on learning and the plethora of competing and overlapping definitions. The two problems are related in the sense that definitions of learning depend in part on whether they are used, for example, by psychologists, students of organizational behavior, or specialists in artificial intelligence. Political scientists who use learning to account for foreign policy change are often inclined to propose their own definitions, subdefinitions, and categories. Furthermore, as Steinbruner (1974) points out, different models of decision making have associated with them different processes of learning, so that "learning" to those who favor a rational, analytic model is something very different from what those who favor a cognitive model would understand.

A useful starting point for examining the various definitions is the National Academy of Sciences' project on learning in U.S. and Soviet foreign policy, organized by George Breslauer and Philip Tetlock. Tetlock proposes five definitions of learning: minimalist, cognitive content, cognitive structural, efficiency, and institutional. A *minimalist* definition "posits that learning can be said to have occurred whenever, as a result of experience, there has been a discernible change in the probability of a verbal or policy response" (Tetlock, 1988:3). This definition draws on the behaviorist tradition in psychology and does not take into account cognitive variables. The *cognitive content* definition, by contrast, focuses on individual belief systems and sees learning essentially as a change in beliefs resulting from experience or knowledge.

Belief systems are understood to be hierarchically organized "with general policy objectives or values at the apex of the system, strategic beliefs and preferences at the intermediate level, and tactical beliefs and preferences at the base of the system." Tetlock (1988:4–5) proposes a three-part hypothesis to the effect that decision makers faced with the failure of existing policy will seek first to change tactics; then, after tactical solutions repeatedly fail, they consider shifting strategies; and, finally, only after both tactical and strategic solutions meet with repeated failure do they reconsider basic goals.

Cognitive structural learning "involves the acquisition by policy-makers of progressively more differentiated understandings of the workings of the political environment with which they must cope and of the complex trade-offs that policy-making requires" (Tetlock, 1988:7). Whereas beliefs (cognitive content) can shift without entailing structural change, a change in structure necessarily leads to changes in beliefs. *Efficiency* learning relates not to the content or structure of beliefs but to the process and outcome of policies: "According to this definition, learning has occurred whenever policy-makers have learned to match means and ends in more efficient and effective ways" (Tetlock, 1988:8). To learn in this sense means either to "discover more effective strategies or means for pursuing one's original goals" or "to redefine one's goals in more realistic ways" (Tetlock, 1988:8). Finally, Tetlock (1988:16–17) proposes an *institutional* definition of learning. It concerns the ability of policymakers to translate their new cognitive beliefs or structures into actual policy by overcoming institutional and domestic political barriers.

Notions of learning have appealed to students of Soviet policy, probably because many of the definitional distinctions resonate with common debates about Soviet intentions and behavior. Consider, for example, Nye's definitions of "simple" and "complex" learning (which are similar to the two types of efficiency learning proposed by Tetlock). *Simple* learning "uses new information merely to adapt the means, without altering any deeper goals in the end-means chain" (Nye, 1987:380). It leads to changes in tactics. *Complex* learning, "by contrast, involves recognition of conflicts among means and goals in causally complicated situations, and leads to new priorities and trade-offs" (Nye, 1987:380). Much of the debate over the significance of changes in Soviet security policy centers around whether they entail only a change in tactics or whether they constitute a meaningful long-term reassessment of goals (Griffiths, 1972:449–478; Lynch, 1989). Soviet gestures of moderation give rise to such questions as: Have Soviet leaders abandoned the goal of world revolution, or are they merely seeking a breathing space? Is the Soviet Union's renunciation of nuclear superiority genuine, or is it merely a ploy to lull its adversaries into a false sense of security? Questions such as these lie at the heart of the debate over the so-called new thinking in foreign and security policy under Mikhail Gorbachev and probably account in part for the growing academic interest in notions of learning.

Whereas the definitions considered so far concern the individual and organizational levels of analysis, Robert Legvold (1988*b*) has proposed three additional definitional distinctions that bear on relations between countries: *independent* learning "is the kind that occurs apart from or even contrary to the learning taking place in other societies;" *joint* learning "occurs when two or more societies learn simultaneously;" and *interactive* learning "occurs when one society learns from another." He finds that all of these types of learning have occurred at various times in U.S.–Soviet relations, although independent learning has probably been most prevalent.

Despite the high level of interest, there is reason to question how much the literature on learning is able to contribute to understanding moderation in Soviet security policy. This is due partly to the fact that many of those who write about learning are pursuing questions that are sufficiently different from the focus of this essay so as to make it difficult to apply their hypotheses. The National Academy of Sciences study, for example, uses notions of learning in part to try to understand "the processes by which governments adapt or fail to adapt to changing circumstances" (Tetlock, 1988:22). It focuses on the question of whether or not learning has occurred, rather than on the question of how to account for change (for example, toward moderation) while considering learning as only one possible explanation. So far there has been little systematic testing of a "learning hypothesis" against competing explanations for a given phenomenon.

Learning hypotheses that are grounded in the literature of cognitive psychology, while better substantiated than some of their competitors from other fields, present problems when applied to foreign policy. The most apparent problem is the familiar one of levels of analysis (Tetlock, 1989). How can one take theories developed to analyze the belief systems of individuals and apply them to the behavior of nation-states? One must consider also the higher level of organizations and bureaucracies that make up governments. Most analysts would agree with Nye (1987:381) in this regard that "individual learning is a necessary, but insufficient, basis for organizational learning." So far, however, the literature on foreign policy learning does not stand on a foundation of theoretical knowledge about organizational learning comparable to what is available for individual, cognitive learning.

To the extent that foreign policy analysts have drawn on existing theories of organizational learning, they have probably exacerbated rather than resolved the problems inherent in attempting to apply learning to foreign policy. Many proponents of learning explanations emphasize, for example, the importance of avoiding normative definitions of learning. As Nye (1987:380) puts it, "the question is whether the new information or skills [that could contribute to learning] have enabled the actors to achieve their purposes better, regardless of whether the observer likes those purposes or not" (see also Tetlock, 1988). Yet much of the literature on organizational learning comes from a field— business management—that explicitly advocates a normative goal, namely improving the operation of a business firm. The text by management professors Chris Argyris and Donald Schön (1978), most frequently cited by foreign policy analysts seeking insights into organizational learning, is explicit on this point: "We believe that a preoccupation with a normative theory of intervention provides the best starting point for a theory of organizational learning" (Argyris and Schön, 1978:iv). Indeed the normative focus is embedded in the authors' very definition of their subject: "Organizational learning involves the detection and correction of *error*" (Argyris and Schön, 1978:2, emphasis added).

The notion of error presupposes that one can judge unambiguously what is right and what is wrong. For a business, whose main goal is increasing market share or profitability, such a judgment may be relatively straightforward. For countries pursuing "security," it is far more difficult to identify good and bad policies. Not only are errors difficult to detect, but policymakers frequently disagree over the impact of policies because they disagree over fundamental questions about the nature of international relations. Political scientists who define foreign policy learning in such terms as a "growth of *realism*," or an increase in understanding "processes actually operating in the world" (Etheredge, 1985:66, original emphasis) neglect the extent to which differences in perception and interpretation of reality among policymakers render notions of learning problematic. There is a considerable risk that analysts' own normative views influence their assessment of whether learning has taken place.

Some of the best-known studies of the "lessons" of foreign policy—the works of Richard Neustadt and Ernest May—are normative in the tradition of Argyris and Schön (1978) in that they seek to improve the performance of policymakers. The case studies used in their collaborative project (Neustadt and May, 1986) were originally developed for teaching a public-policy course mainly to midcareer professionals. May's earlier (1973) study was also intended to help policymakers use history more effectively. Their work assumes that historical "reality" can be ascertained and that one can reliably detect error in the uses of history by policymakers (at least in retrospect). In focusing on performance, the authors evince an implicit normative agreement with the goals of policy. Thus, they tend to neglect the self-serving or opportunistic uses to which policymakers can put historical "lessons" in their struggles over policy objectives.

In contrast to the professional-school approach to foreign policy learning,

John Lovell (1984) has deliberately formulated an operational definition of organizational learning that avoids normative assumptions. Perhaps most importantly, he recognizes the central role of politics by conceptualizing "lessons" as "the product of an organizational *and political* dynamic, rather than as products of the application of logic and pure reason to analysis of the past" (Lovell, 1984:134, emphasis added). He defines learning not only as the changes that organizations make in response to experience but also the "political accommodations that they make in order to cope with the effects of experience" (Lovell, 1984:134). Operationally, his definition of learning includes the following "discernible effects of policy experience" on the organization:

> modifications of the doctrine and "conventional wisdom" that provide institutionalized guideposts for action; changes of policy procedures and processes in ways that acknowledge the "lessons" of experience; an alteration of policy structures to reflect such lessons; a revision of policy-related personnel systems to bring incentive structures into accord with the felt needs of experience; and a revision of policy commitments and budgetary commitments on the basis of experience (Lovell, 1984:134–135).

Perhaps most notable about Lovell's definition, besides its rare operational specificity, is that it is most suitable to studying a particular bureaucracy or organization, rather than a government as a whole. Indeed, in his preliminary use of the framework, he compared the lessons learned by the U.S. State Department versus those learned by the U.S. Army regarding U.S. military involvement abroad (Lovell, 1984). Lovell's approach could be useful for studying change in the organizations that make up the Soviet security-policy apparatus. Unfortunately, however, most analysts have attempted the more ambitious and dubious task of generalizing about learning at the level of the Soviet government as a whole. Moreover, they have rarely done so with the requisite degree of precision in setting forth their operational definitions of the phenomenon.

These problems with applying learning to foreign policy are certainly not unfamiliar to serious students of the subject. In discussing efficiency learning, for example, Tetlock acknowledges the difficulty of determining whether it has occurred. In the absence of "well-designed evidential standards for determining success and failure," if it is impossible "to conduct controlled experiments to test and eliminate alternative causal hypotheses," and if policymakers are unable "to get quick and unambiguous feedback concerning the correctness of their predictions," then we cannot definitively establish that efficiency learning has taken place (Tetlock, 1988:9–10). Analysts must rely on counterfactual reconstructions of history that are always subject to dispute.

The epistemological problems associated with the study of learning in foreign policy are evident from attempts to apply the concept to the Soviet Union. In the Sovietological literature learning has generally been associated with shifts away from ideological thinking in Soviet foreign policy toward more pragmatic or "realistic" views of the world (Zimmerman, 1969; Breslauer, 1987). Because traditional Soviet ideological tenets entail such ambitious goals—such as the ultimate victory of communism worldwide— any recognition of impediments to achieving those goals seems to represent a more realistic picture of the external environment, a process that is often characterized as learning (in the efficiency sense, as Tetlock defines it). If such learning becomes the basis for changes in Soviet foreign policies, those policies are likely to be more moderate in that they are less ambitious in the face of newly acknowledged barriers. The relevance to understanding moderation in Soviet security policy appears obvious.

Yet problems arise in trying to identify which picture of the world is accurate or realistic as compared to the one seen through an ideological prism. Robert Darst has made the provocative claim that U.S. academic analysts tend to credit the Soviet government with learning when it begins to view the international system in terms compatible with those favored by the analysts themselves (Darst, 1989:155–157). William Zimmerman, for example, writing in the late 1960s, argued that Soviet foreign policymakers had "learned" because they had come to accept the notion of states as the primary actors in an international system, and had called into question the ideological stereotype of the "two camps" of socialism and imperialism (whose conflict would inevitably result in war) (Zimmerman, 1969, 1970). Robert Legvold (1988b), by contrast, describes as learning the process by which Soviet policymakers began to stress the importance of thinking of international relations as more than the interaction of nation-states; rather than focus exclusively on national interests, for example, Soviet leaders have called attention to such concepts as "common security" and "interdependence," and have emphasized the importance of international organizations such as the United Nations in furthering common goals. For Darst, Zimmerman's view of reality reflects the dominant paradigm in U.S. academic study of international relations—often called "structural realism"—whereas Legvold's reality represents the competing paradigm that emerged during the 1970s as "complex interdependence." Darst concludes that "the gap between 'reality' as Zimmerman perceives it and 'reality' as Legvold perceives it suggests that determining the standard against which Soviet learning is to be measured is no simple task" (Darst, 1989:156). It may be that both Zimmerman and Legvold accurately describe shifts in the dominant views of Soviet foreign policymakers. The difficulty lies in attributing such shifts to "learning."

Despite such difficulties, academic interest in learning persists, and many analysts find the notion particularly persuasive in accounting for changes in Soviet policy under Gorbachev (Legvold, 1988*b;* Weber, 1989). There is no doubt that policies pursued by Gorbachev and his reform-minded colleagues differ from those of previous leaders, and that the "new thinking" in foreign policy is fundamentally new in many ways (for example, its rejection of zero–sum thinking in favor of notions of common security and interdependence, and its devaluation of the military instrument in foreign policy in favor of diplomacy and domestic economic health). Yet Gorbachev is not the Soviet Union; and even the Politburo, not to mention the armed forces, contains people whose views differ substantially from those of the general secretary (Parrott, 1988; Lynch, 1989). Here the anthropomorphism of the concept of learning becomes highly problematic. How can one speak of shifts in belief systems of a *government* or *state,* when serious differences in beliefs among foreign policy influentials persist, and it is not clear that any particular individual's views have actually changed? As Goldmann (1988:35) points out, cognitive factors "operate only at the individual level. Hence, the structure of officially adopted beliefs—a foreign policy doctrine, a party program—is relevant only insofar as the official beliefs are also widely shared by the members of the policymaking system."

Ernst Haas, a political scientist who began discussing foreign policy learning before the current wave of interest, emphasized this point as well. Learning, for Haas, is a change in the definition of the national interest. In order for learning to occur, there must be acquisition of *consensual knowledge.* "A claim to knowledge becomes consensual whenever it succeeds in dominating the policy making process—and that implies acceptance by all major actors involved in that process" (Haas, 1980:370). Although he writes mainly in regard to policymaking between rather than within states (he is interested in how states agree to form international regimes), the same arguments would apply to the domestic decision-making process. One cannot argue that a state has learned if important members of the policymaking community disagree about the lessons.

Proponents of learning explanations vary in the extent to which they take into account disagreements between policymakers. They often anthropomorphically represent the state as a unitary, cognitive actor even while employing language that suggests otherwise. Nye, for example, argues that learning may occur when "leaders notice changes in the structure of the situation which affects their effectiveness, and they adapt their behavior as a result of anticipation or experience . . .or learning may occur simply through *perceptions* of change in the structure of the situation" (Nye, 1987:388–389, emphasis added). He gives as an example that the United States and Soviet Union may have perceived a decline in the bipolar nature of the international system in the mid-1960s, which reinforced their interest in nuclear nonproliferation. But states do not "perceive" anything—only individuals do. And individuals disagree in their perceptions of such vague concepts as the polarity of the international system. Current disagreements about the relative decline of the U.S. economy (and the attendant academic debates on "hegemonic stability") attest to the importance of avoiding assumptions of consensus when there is none. Even the appearance of consensus may deceive. As Breslauer (1987:447) points out, even if all relevant policymakers learn the same lesson, they may do so for different reasons: thus, "their perspectives are likely to evolve in diverse directions, for objective circumstances to which they point may change at differential rates."

Proponents of learning explanations do at some point take account of substate-level disagreements about how to interpret the international environment. An appreciation of the role of domestic politics underlies Nye's observation that "shifts in social structure and political power determine whose learning matters" (Nye, 1987:381). He admits that "some changes in 'national interest' depend not upon new affective or cognitive views in the society at large, but merely on changes of political elites. Such political change may occur because of domestic issues largely unrelated to foreign policy" (Nye, 1987:378). Breslauer argues that generational change and political leadership succession in the Soviet Union "facilitate regime learning by providing the impetus, political incentive, and political opportunity for a significant reevaluation of assumptions" (Breslauer, 1987:443). Tetlock (1988:22–23) observes that fundamental forms of learning "appear to require major personnel shifts" (see also Steinbruner, 1974:136–137). This observation leads him to wonder whether "a political version of a natural-selection model may provide a more appropriate description of how governments adapt to a changing international environment than does a learning framework." He discusses other possible explanations that put more emphasis on politics, personal opportunism, and chance—including the "garbage can model" developed by Cohen, March, and Olsen (1972).

Tetlock and others believe that many of the competing explanations for how governments adapt are not necessarily incompatible with a learning framework. For the purposes of this chapter, however, it is important to call attention to points of disagreement between competing approaches. Considering the significance for policy, we should especially try to identify the explanations that provide the best understanding of whether Soviet moderation is likely to be of a temporary or enduring character. Although learning explanations do not focus specifically on moderation, they do give attention to reversions to past policies following a learning-induced change of some duration.

Analysts tend to speak in such cases of "unlearning" or "forgetting." As Tetlock (1988:17) describes: "Lessons drawn from experience at one time can be 'forgotten' or 'unlearned'—either because the individuals who originally drew the lessons no longer see them as useful guides to policy or because these individuals have been replaced by a new cohort who subscribe to a different set of goals or strategic and tactical beliefs." Only the first possibility seems best understood by cognitively based notions of learning at the individual level of analysis. In the second case, when foreign policymakers are actually replaced, it makes more sense to concentrate on political explanations at higher levels of analysis. Notions of learning, unlearning, and forgetting in such cases seem superfluous, as when Nye writes of "occasional forgetting as coalitions shift in domestic politics" (Nye, 1987:382). If one is interested in explaining change, the explanation in this case is a domestic political realignment. "Forgetting" is merely a descriptive term of limited explanatory value.

Despite problems with the metaphor itself, those who have used notions of learning to account for change in Soviet foreign policy have captured an important aspects of Soviet behavior. Soviet academic writing on such subjects as the international system and the determinants of U.S. policy has evinced a growing sophistication since the foundation of international relations as a field of research in the Soviet Union (Zimmerman, 1969). Much of the sophistication became evident in the rhetoric and actions of top policymakers as well, many of whom were apparently influenced by academic analysts in their capacity as policy advisers. Learning is a suitable description for what academic researchers do. It is not so clear, however, that the learning metaphor is appropriate for describing policymakers who adapt to events in the international environment, even with the help of new knowledge and advice—especially given the existence of competing policy options and contrary advice.

Yet Sovietologists have been drawn to learning metaphors largely, it seems, in reaction to the tenacity and longevity of explanations focusing on *ideology*. In only slightly caricatured form, these explanations hold that "the ideological imprint of Marxism-Leninism on the Soviet political mentality is so strong that the Soviet vision of international relations has stood fast before the challenges posed by the contemporary world" (Lynch, 1987:1). In countering such generalizations analysts such as Griffiths (1972, 1984), Zimmerman (1969, 1970, 1980), Breslauer (1987), and Lynch (1987) have made an important contribution. But one does not need to invoke learning to argue that Soviet leaders managed to adapt their views and policies to such ideologically uncomfortable developments as the emergence of a Communist Chinese threat or the continued viability of capitalist economies—unless one assumes that ideology constrains Soviet foreign policy like a straightjacket. From

Brest-Litovsk on, however, Soviet foreign policy has manifested considerably more flexibility than that, as advocates of a learning approach themselves have pointed out. The problem is not with the reality that these analysts describe, but with the metaphors that they employ.

Cognitive psychological theories of learning have the potential to make a strong contribution to understanding foreign policy change. An important obstacle is the difficulty of reconciling individual-level psychological approaches and political theories of coalition-building without reifying the concept of learning. Notions of learning would appear most valuable in cases where one can demonstrate that a coalition had fallen from power and had been replaced precisely owing to general agreement that foreign-policy failures had resulted from the erroneous beliefs or defective cognitive structures held by members of the coalition. The important assumptions here are that the coalition was replaced for reasons of foreign, rather than domestic, policy; that there was close to consensus within the policymaking community that faulty cognitive beliefs were responsible for foreign policy failures; and that the new coalition came to power owing to its alternative conceptions of foreign policy. Notions of learning may still be useful even if such stringent requirements are not fulfilled. If the requirements were met, however, learning would demonstrate a clear superiority over rival explanations that seek to account for change in foreign policies.

POLICY ENTREPRENEURSHIP

If foreign policy changes come about as the result of new internal political alignments, as coalition theories suggest, and if these shifts in coalition are the product of learning, as some advocates of that approach assert, there is still a piece missing from the puzzle. We must explore the mechanism by which these new alignments themselves come about, or—if the learning metaphor is appropriate—how individuals who have changed their minds manage to produce a change at the organizational and governmental levels. An important body of literature in U.S. politics suggests that policy entrepreneurs play a key role in promoting new ideas in order to build political coalitions around them (Kingdon, 1984; Lewis, 1980; Ferguson, 1984). In the field of Soviet politics, a comparable argument has appeared that focuses on the role of policy specialists in influencing the top leadership, who then in turn put together coalitions around the policies they find attractive (Löwenhardt, 1981; Solomon, 1978; Gustafson, 1981; Bunce, 1981).

A key insight of the literature on policy entrepreneurs concerns the concept of the "policy window" (Kingdon, 1984). It refers to an opportunity that typically appears in the form of a new problem. Individuals or groups seize the opportunity to promote the policies they have long favored in order to deal with the new problem. This phenomenon, of "an answer actively looking for a question," has been termed the "garbage can model" of organizational choice (Cohen, March, and Olsen, 1972:3).

Policy entrepreneurs may play a role in foreign policy learning if their arguments are persuasive enough to form the basis for "consensual knowledge" (Haas, 1980). If, however, decision makers are "uncommitted thinkers," in Steinbruner's (1974) terms, and there are other entrepreneurs promoting competing policies, the learning metaphor seems less useful. For by definition such a "high-level policy maker, beset with uncertainty and sitting at the intersection of a number of information channels, will tend at different times to adopt *different* belief patterns for the same decision problem" (Steinbruner, 1974:129, original emphasis). To the extent that the policies that flow from the different belief patterns contradict one another, learning theorists would probably have to speak of a process of learning (and unlearning) contradictory lessons in potentially rapid succession—a pattern that calls into question what it means to learn.

On a number of occasions Sovietologists have used notions of learning that are compatible with policy entrepreneurship but are very different from the ones discussed in the previous section. Rather than anthropomorphize the Soviet Union as a unitary actor, William Zimmerman (1980:560), for example, emphasizes the "widespread differences in Soviet foreign policy priorities" among elites. In his view, competing elite "perspectives are formed out of divergent values, career backgrounds, and political roles" (Zimmerman, 1980:558). Thus, when he and Axelrod (1981) write of "learning" in the Soviet context, they describe a highly politicized process by which different institutions promote self-serving "lessons" from international events such as the U.S. withdrawal from Vietnam: "Our survey of Soviet lessons of Vietnam shows that the notion of monolithic Soviet preferences is flatly wrong. When one speaks of Soviet goals, it is necessary to specify the particular individuals, institutions, or media sources, as well as the context" (Zimmerman and Axelrod, 1981:17). The language here is quite far from notions of learning as development of "consensual knowledge" or changes in individual cognitive structures. By implicitly describing "lessons" of Vietnam as policy windows through which entrepreneurs push their preexisting preferences for Soviet policy Zimmerman seems much closer to the coalition-building and policy-entrepreneurship perspectives on Soviet foreign-policy change than to the cognitive learning approaches. Griffiths (1972, 1984), while rejecting (as Zimmerman does as well) overly schematic divisions of Soviet policymakers into moderates and hardliners, still stresses competition between contrasting "tendencies" in Soviet foreign policy and uses "learning" to describe a political process of promoting competing images of the adversary. In this case, reconciling the competing approaches of coalition-building/entrepreneurship and learning demands fundamentally reinterpreting the latter.

LEADERS

Learning approaches could be useful for explaining at the individual level of analysis how top Soviet leaders change their views about foreign policy. Various types of content-analysis techniques have been developed to evaluate the views of leaders (see, for example, Axelrod, 1976; Hermann, 1980). Although emphasizing the individual level of analysis always risks ignoring more important explanatory factors, the approach may be more appropriate for a highly centralized system such as the Soviet Union than for other polities. Margaret Hermann's (1989) personality profile of Gorbachev is a useful start. One would especially be interested, however, in analyzing leaders of long tenure, in order to assess the degree of change over time in their foreign policy views. Notions of learning could be particularly valuable in explaining changes in the "operational codes" of decision makers (George, 1969).

Unfortunately, Sovietologists have not devoted a great deal of attention to a systematic evaluation of changes in the individual foreign-policy views or operational codes of Soviet policymakers. Richard Herrmann's work (1985, 1988) indicates, however, that the data and methods are available for undertaking such efforts. Even if one found evidence of changes in views, in order to support a learning explanation one would still need to demonstrate that leaders were not simply "uncommitted thinkers," temporarily influenced by the most persuasive policy entrepreneurs they encountered. Studies of this sort would also have to control for factors at other levels of analysis.

Within Soviet studies, more attention has been focused on the influence of new leaders than on changes in views of old ones. The Gorbachev phenomenon has led many observers to focus on the role of new leaders in instigating foreign policy change, and, in this case, change toward moderation. In studies of Soviet domestic politics, debates about the impact of new leaders have generated considerable interest if not definite conclusions (Breslauer, 1982; Bunce, 1980, 1981; Roeder, 1985; Bunce and Roeder, 1986). One major obstacle to generalization is the paucity of cases: even if we include leaders with extremely short terms of office, such as Malenkov, Andropov, and Chernenko, we generate barely more than a half-dozen cases since Lenin. The same problem applies to security policy. Even if we broaden consideration beyond the person of the general secretary to include other members of the security policy elite (for example, Politburo and Defense Council), the number of new leaders who have dealt extensively with issues of security policy and international cooperation in the nuclear age is not many.

There is a body of literature in Soviet security studies that puts particular emphasis on the role of individual leaders. The most explicit presentation of this view is Karl Spielmann's (1978) articulation of a "national leadership model," which he counterposed to rational-actor and bureaucratic-politics models. Spielmann was interested mainly in the determinants of Soviet force posture and weapons, but one could also apply his model to arms control negotiations and other aspects of security cooperation and moderation, as many analysts have been inclined to do since Gorbachev came into office. In his review of literature on Soviet national security policy, Stephen Meyer agrees with Spielmann that "leadership preferences have been a dominating influence in Soviet defense decision making," but he maintains that "the national leadership model offers little in the way of predictive capability" (Meyer, 1984:265–266).

Meyer's (1988) own recent work on the sources of new Soviet thinking on security suggests consistency with his earlier views. He argues that "if one looks carefully at the history of military doctrinal change in the Soviet Union, one inescapable conclusion is clear: individual general secretaries do matter. . . . It is not so much a matter of 'personalities' as it is personal policy agendas, priorities, and images of what has gone before and what needs to be done now" (Meyer, 1988:127–128). Meyer's article also reinforces his skepticism about the ability of leadership models to generate accurate predictions. Discussing, for example, the possibility of unilateral reductions in Soviet military forces, Meyer (1988:147) wrote, "I fail to find any evidence that such notions reflect policy at the present time." He argued that a bold advocacy by three Soviet academics (Zhurkin, Karaganov, and Kortunov, 1987) of unilateral reductions "is not a widely shared perspective among new thinkers" (Meyer, 1988:147). With regard to conventional forces, he maintained that "Gorbachev seems to be more in line with the old thinkers than he is with the new thinkers" in countenancing Soviet reductions "only with strictly matched compensating reductions on the NATO side" (Meyer, 1988:149). Meyer concluded his article with the observation that "it may be that the period of Gorbachev's greatest freedom of action in arms control is passing" (Meyer, 1988:163).

Within weeks of the publication of Meyer's article, Gorbachev announced a unilateral Soviet reduction of 500,000 troops, 10,000 tanks, 8,500 artillery pieces, and 800 combat aircraft—an initiative that even the most skeptical observers of Soviet military policy welcomed as significantly reducing the capabilities for a Soviet conventional attack (U.S. House of Representatives, 1989). Since then the Soviets have announced a 14.2 percent decrease in their military budget and a 40 percent cut in tank production; they have welcomed U.S. observers to inspect laser test ranges and laboratories and ballistic missile silos and launch facilities; and they have unilaterally withdrawn some of their tactical nuclear weapons from Europe.

Of course, Meyer is not the only analyst to have been surprised by Gorbachev's initiatives; it has become more the rule than the exception among Sovietologists. His article reinforces his own point that leadership models may serve well for ex post facto explanation of policy, but fare poorly for prediction. As Meyer himself is well aware, to understand the sources of change in Soviet security policy, one needs to incorporate other levels of analysis besides the individual preferences of the general secretary.

TACIT TRANSNATIONAL ALLIANCES

The theoretical perspectives discussed so far have emphasized the international, domestic, and individual levels of analysis. Another possibility, suggested by the literature on interdependence, focuses on transnational or transgovernmental relations, with actors participating simultaneously in interstate relations and domestic politics (Keohane and Nye, 1977). The notion of a "tacit alliance" between actors in different countries promoting their domestic goals through the pursuit of an international agreement seems compatible with the literature on policy entrepreneurs and policy windows. In international relations, presumably, arguments or information received from counterparts in the adversary country who are fellow members of a tacit alliance could serve as a window to help policy entrepreneurs pursue their goals. Here a link to coalition theory is evident. "Where a nation may lack a winning coalition domestically," Haggard and Simmons (1987:517) wonder, "can pressure or support from external actors tip policy in the direction favored by the cooperative minority?" The hypothesis seems plausible for such issue-areas as economic relations (Putnam and Bayne, 1987; Putnam, 1988) and environmental policy (Haas, 1989; Young, 1989), and the approach has been proposed specifically as a means to security cooperation as well (Singer, 1984:245–255, 267–269). Analysts have suggested that international contacts, say between U.S. and Soviet scientists discussing arms control issues at international meetings, or even between arms negotiators themselves, can lead to tacit alliances to promote moderation in their respective countries' policies (Dallin, 1981:382–386; Legvold, 1988*b*; York, 1987).

In the security realm, such tacit alliances are more likely to be successful if they serve to change the image of the adversary from hostile to benign. Changes in enemy images can be an important contributor to foreign policy change and would probably constitute examples of "cognitive content" learning, in Tetlock's definition (Holsti, 1967; White, 1984; Larson, 1985; Tetlock, 1988). Sovietologists have paid considerable attention to how Soviet views of the United States change, and have related Soviet perceptions of a more benign U.S. adversary to a greater propensity for cooperative behavior on the part of the Soviet Union. There is some disagreement, however, over whether views of the adversary are used merely to rationalize domestic political goals or whether they represent genuine beliefs or "tendencies" (Griffiths, 1972, 1984; Dallin, 1981; Snyder, 1987/1988; Jackson, 1981). If tacit alliances genuinely change beliefs, we could speak of them as enhancing "interactive" learning, in Legvold's (1988b) sense.

Popular Notions

In the popular U.S. discourse on Soviet foreign policy, a number of explanations claim to account for change toward moderation in Soviet security policy. Integrating them into the academic literature poses certain problems for the analyst. Some of the explanations—those that give prominence to individual Soviet leaders, for example—appear both in academic and popular discussions, so the only problem is the possible arbitrariness of placing them in one category or another. Other popular explanations—such as "negotiation from strength" or economic stringency—have clear counterparts in the academic literature, but where to situate them in an overall framework for understanding sources of Soviet policy depends in large measure on the analyst's own theoretical proclivities. Analysts inclined to "black box" Soviet internal decision-making and treat the state as a unitary actor would consider such factors as declining growth rates and military pressure from Soviet adversaries as exogenous or independent variables. In this view, they relate directly to the degree of Soviet moderation—the dependent variable—that we seek to explain.

As the preceding review indicates, however, there is criticism as well as support for such realist assumptions about international politics within the theoretical literature on international cooperation. Robert Putnam (1988:432), for example, maintains, that "on nearly all important issues, 'central decision-makers' disagree about what the national interest and international context demand" (see also Young, 1989). Competing policies for dealing with external or internal pressures become the stuff of coalition politics (Gourevitch, 1986). Seemingly objective or exogenous factors become "endogenized" in domestic political debates and the outcome cannot easily be predicted. In this interpretation, factors such as military pressure or economic constraints become intermediate rather than independent variables; they affect the prospects for Soviet moderation in indeterminate ways.

Although in reviewing the empirical material on Soviet security policy I will be sensitive to the possibility of straightforward relationships between "exogenous" factors and Soviet policy outcomes, in the theoretical framework developed here I treat them as mediating rather than determining influences. There are a number of reasons for this approach. First, statistical tests of correlations between, say, U.S. hostile behavior and Soviet conciliatory behavior or change in Soviet economic growth and change in security policy do not indicate a simple causes-and-effect relationship (Bennett, 1989). Second, in U.S.–Soviet security affairs, perhaps more than most areas, it is difficult to determine the appropriate policy for dealing with even the starkest evidence of economic decline or increase in the adversary's hostility. It is nearly as difficult, in internal debates about security, to persuade opponents that a given policy has failed—that it is too costly, too conciliatory, or too conflictual: the most clear-cut indication of a failed security policy would be the outbreak of superpower war or the collapse of a national economy, neither of which has happened. In the absence of those events, advocates of competing policies are unlikely to yield to their opponents. Even obvious failures short of superpower war—for example, U.S. withdrawal from Vietnam—are subject to contradictory interpretations at home and abroad, as Zimmerman and Axelrod (1981) point out.

One way to incorporate seemingly "objective" factors such as external military pressure and economic constraints is to consider them as windows that entrepreneurs can use to try to build coalitions in support of their preferred policies. Thus, the notion of the policy window can provide a bridge between academic theories of policy change and explanations current in the public debate. Specifically, it can point to the kinds of internal and external pressures that are often credited with inducing changes in Soviet security policy, and it can also incorporate events, such as the advent of new leaders, that otherwise have little predictive power.

MILITARY EXIGENCIES

One common explanation for changes in Soviet security policy maintains that they are dictated by military requirements. Given a limited military budget, the argument goes, the Soviets cannot give the same priority to all of their military programs at once. One should expect to see restraint in certain programs (for example, strategic nuclear weapons) at times when other programs (say, conventional forces) are receiving higher priority. When applied to instances of moderation in Soviet security policy, this view maintains that what appears as moderation is not in fact moderation but merely a shift in priorities. At its extreme, this explanation can account even for absolute decreases in Soviet military budgets and substantial reductions in forces (for example, through disarmament agreements). These actions are described as "breathing spaces," necessary to prepare the Soviet Union for future military competition.

This explanation begs the question, however, of how military requirements are formulated, what gives rise to new ones, and how priorities are set and changed. One argument that we have already encountered holds that military requirements reflect the desires of domestic political coalitions (Snyder, 1987/1988:123–126). Other arguments, however, focus on the role of external factors in shaping Soviet military requirements and priorities, in particular military developments by Soviet adversaries (MccGwire, 1987). To the extent that changes in priorities are viewed as rational responses that enhance Soviet security, this explanation accords with—and shares the drawbacks of— notions of "efficiency" learning. For our purposes, the controversial questions remain: Are external threats likely to produce change toward moderation in Soviet security policy or merely a reorientation of Soviet military efforts? How can one distinguish genuine, enduring moderation from a temporary breathing space? Explanations that focus narrowly on military exigencies do not provide satisfactory answers.

NEGOTIATION FROM STRENGTH

A popular notion in the U.S. policy debate holds that external pressure and threats do induce moderation—specifically, that moderation in Soviet security policy results from a U.S. practice of negotiation from strength. In some versions, the notion is narrowly defined to mean that Western military programs, in the form of "bargaining chips," are necessary to secure reductions or limitations in Soviet forces (Einhorn, 1985; Rose, 1988). More expansive versions focus on strength more than on negotiation, in that their proponents often oppose negotiations on principle. Consistent in some respects with the coalition-theory approaches, they maintain the Soviet moderation is only possible as a result of internal social, economic, and political change. Such change can be induced only by external Western pressure, in the form of both military programs and economic warfare, until the Soviet leadership sees no alternative but to reform (Pipes, 1984). An unwavering policy of U.S. "strength" will contribute to that end, even without formal negotiations.

The negotiation-from-strength approach resembles some of the more mechanistic (for example, "minimalist") notions of learning, in that repeated failures of Soviet policy in the face of U.S. firmness are understood to lead to changes in Soviet behavior. It is also consistent with George Kennan's predictions about the consequences of a U.S. policy of "containment" of the Soviet Union: he maintained that the Kremlin could not "face frustration indefinitely without eventually adjusting itself in one way or another to the logic of that state of affairs" (Kennan, 1947:581). Such adjustment would entail either the "break-up or the gradual mellowing of Soviet power" (Kennan, 1947:581;

also Hough, 1987). The latter possibility implies a change consonant with transformation of cognitive content or structure, as learning approaches hold. Contrary to coalition theorists, but consistent with some learning approaches, proponents of negotiation from strength typically do not differentiate Soviet policymakers into hardliners and moderates or argue that U.S. policy should try to support the latter. A conception of a monolithic Soviet decision-making system is implicit in arguments that U.S. military pressure would put such a strain on the Soviet economy "that the Soviet leadership would have little choice but to make substantial concessions on arms control" (Gaddis, 1989:13). Unrecognized—because their arguments did not prevail—is the possibility that some Soviet policymakers would be willing to strain the economy even further to meet the challenge, whereas others would seek to minimize the threat posed by U.S. pressure by appealing to arguments about the adequacy (and "overkill" potential) of the existing Soviet nuclear arsenal.

ECONOMIC STRINGENCY

An important assumption of the expansive negotiation-from-strength perspective is that economic pressure will force the Soviets to limit their military spending and therefore show restraint in their security policy. A corollary of this assumption is that the U.S. must continue to maintain external pressure until Soviet internal reform is complete; otherwise the Soviet leaders will try to use foreign policy successes as a means of diverting the populace from demanding reform (Pipes, 1984). This argument, however, entails a logical fallacy. If Soviet leaders need to distract their citizens, they should be able to do so at least as effectively by invoking foreign threats as by mounting successful foreign adventures. Foreign threats could create a "rally 'round the flag" response that would attract attention away from the popular desire for reform. There is some precedent, dating back to the 1920s, for Soviet leaders to use "war scares" for internal political purposes (Meyer, 1978; Shlapentokh, 1984). Even if hardline U.S. policies managed to discredit Soviet hardliners (rather than reinforce their image of a hostile adversary), there is a danger that U.S. proponents of pressure, as those most skeptical of Soviet intentions, would not recognize a Soviet change toward moderation. At that point, continued pursuit of a hostile U.S. policy could undercut the Soviet reformers' efforts (Snyder, 1989).

An alternative view holds that the Soviets are already concerned about the economic consequences of military spending and would welcome the opportunity to limit it through arms control agreements. In this view, inducements in the form of favorable trade agreements will tend to encourage Soviet cooperation in disarmament, whereas efforts at economic pressure will probably be counterproductive (Clemens, 1973:65–66; Cohen, 1979, 1988). In the words of one "Doonesbury" cartoon character (a freshman in Dr. Kissinger's seminar), "the Soviets don't mind being bribed, but they hate being black-mailed." According to the notion of "linkage," conciliatory Soviet behavior in arms negotiations is more likely if the U.S. makes economic cooperation contingent upon Soviet moderation (Skinner, 1987; Druckman and Hopmann, 1989). This view does often distinguish between hardline and moderate elements in the Soviet leadership, but it does not spell out the mechanism by which moderates use U.S. actions to promote their preferred policies or to consider how such efforts might backfire.

Another view simply relates Soviet military programs to the state of the Soviet economy. When the growth rate declines, when competition for resources between the civilian and military sectors becomes particularly severe, when major bottlenecks occur, the Soviets will be inclined to slacken their military efforts, even without a formal agreement, if in their view the international situation permits. Under such conditions, one could argue, policy entrepreneurs who favor reductions in military spending could promote a more benign image of the adversary in order to bolster their case. Certainly the actual policies of the adversary make a difference as well. Contrary to the negotiation-from-strength perspective, this view would maintain that extreme external pressure at a time of tight resource stringency would make it more difficult for proponents of reduced military spending to argue their case persuasively.

UNILATERAL INITIATIVES

In contrast to the negotiation-from-strength view, many analysts argue that the Soviet Union will not show restraint in its military programs in response to U.S. pressure, but will reciprocate U.S. unilateral initiatives of restraint. This view is the equivalent in the public debate of academic notions of tit-for-tat and GRIT. Its supporters often cite historical examples from the U.S.–Soviet nuclear arms race, particularly nuclear testing moratoria of the late 1950s and early 1960s. The view also seems to inform a number of congressional initiatives aimed, for example, at maintaining the integrity of the Strategic Arms Limitation Talks (SALT) agreements, preventing an arms race in antisatellite weapons, and securing a comprehensive nuclear test ban. A comparative study of five cases in which the U.S. attempted unilateral initiatives of restraint (of various degrees of seriousness) reported mixed results for the technique (Rose, 1988).

SOVIET STRENGTH

Although not very common in the U.S. debate today, the argument is at least logically tenable that the Soviets are willing to moderate their behavior and come to mutually beneficial agreements only when they have caught up or are ahead in the arms race. Indeed, in the Soviet debate, the notion was rather widespread, at least during the 1970s, that the "correlation of forces" had shifted in the Soviet Union's favor and, for that reason, the United States was finally willing to negotiate strategic arms control (Payne, 1980; Schwartz, 1978; Zagladin, 1986). Similar reasoning did often appear to underlie the Nixon administration's pursuit of arms control, especially its efforts to curtail the emerging Soviet advantage in "heavy" intercontinental ballistic missiles (ICBMs). It is worth considering, then, whether moderation in Soviet security policy correlates with periods of relative Soviet strength.

A related Soviet argument links this proposition about military strength to the overall state of the economy. It suggests that the U.S. will be better disposed toward superpower cooperation in the security realm at times when the Soviet economy is performing well, whereas the U.S. will take advantage of periods of Soviet economic weakness to pursue a confrontational policy. Thus, in this view, the prospects for security cooperation are positively related to the performance of the Soviet economy or at least to the seriousness of Soviet attempts to accelerate economic growth (Zagladin, 1986).

PUBLIC OPINION

A state may moderate its foreign policy under pressure from domestic or international public opinion. It may do so to gain a propaganda advantage over an adversary or to sow discord among the adversary's allies. It may try merely to give the appearance of moderation for any of these reasons. These points are frequently raised in the course of debates about Soviet intentions in the security realm—especially when the Soviets conduct "public diplomacy" by announcing initiatives related to ongoing arms control negotiations in an effort to induce U.S. concessions. Explanations that focus on public opinion as a source of cooperation or moderation also figure prominently in certain academic approaches, including regime theory (for example, its focus on norms) and GRIT.

Distinguishing between sincere, voluntary gestures of moderation and feigned moderation or moderation resulting from pressure would at first appear a crucial task. In fact, however, for many purposes the distinction is not essential. A state that is only feigning moderation in some particular initiative risks having its bluff called, so to speak. In response, it would either have to come through with a genuinely cooperative gesture or sacrifice whatever propaganda advantage it had anticipated. For the GRIT approach, the initiatives by definition have to be of some significance in order to break the opponent's "enemy image" (Osgood, 1962; Larson, 1987). If they are intended as propaganda gestures, they will not trigger a response. Only when they become widely recognized at home and abroad as significant will the target state feel obliged to respond—even if its central decision makers (as the ultimate repository of the enemy image) are still not convinced of the initiator's sincerity. For the long-term objective of tension-reduction and cooperation, it does not matter if the decision makers are still skeptical. As Larson (1987:33) points out, "regardless of whether the response is motivated by internal conviction or by domestic political pressures, the result is the same; the target state reciprocates with another cooperative act." If the process is to continue, the initiator must reciprocate with further meaningful, cooperative gestures, leading to changes in attitudes about the adversary on both sides and ultimately a reduction in tensions.

Reluctant reciprocation or initiation of moderate policies under pressure of public opinion need not be considered less significant than comparable policies pursued with conviction. Support for this argument comes from, among other places, theories of social and cognitive psychology. Cognitive dissonance theory, for example, would argue that policymakers forced to pursue certain policies come to adopt belief systems that justify them. The policies then are viewed as appropriate and correct. Self-perception theory, using competing assumptions and for different reasons, comes to a similar conclusion (Larson, 1985:29–34, 42–50). These theories, if valid, would suggest that policymakers caught in a spiral of conciliatory initiatives—reciprocated originally for reasons of "public relations"—would come to believe that moderation is in any case a sound policy. Presumably they would also respond to "positive reinforcement" (to mix psychological metaphors) from the public opinion that initially pressured them to pursue moderation. Counterintuitive as these arguments may appear, they do find some support in the empirical material considered below.

Evidence from the Soviet Case

There are a number of possible ways to organize the evidence on change in Soviet security policy. One is to focus on particular chronological periods— for example, the tenure in office of the major Soviet leaders. Another is to look at specific areas of security policy—for example, strategic weapons procurement, nuclear testing, military doctrine, or arms control. Some theoretical concepts would seem to lend themselves to one approach over the other, although there are ambiguities. One might not expect a security regime, for example, to exist in only a narrow sphere of the East–West military competition. Nye (1987), however, has argued that the concept does apply to the issue-area of nuclear nonproliferation but not to the U.S.–Soviet security relationship as a whole. By the same token, coalition theorists would not expect a different constellation of domestic forces to form in each security-related issue-area, but the relative influence of hardline and conciliatory groups might vary from issue to issue. For both of these approaches, analysis by chronological leadership period would seem necessary, but not sufficient.

For evaluating other approaches, analysis by leadership period would not seem particularly appropriate. It would be difficult, for example, to consider the merits of a tit-for-tat strategy if every action relevant to the arms race during a given leader's tenure had to be taken into account; it would make more sense to focus on a particular issue-area, such as nuclear testing or the SALT I negotiations. Choosing the best approach for evaluating other theoretical approaches is even less clear-cut. Learning, for example, could take place in fairly narrow issue-areas, or in relation to the overall pattern of foreign policy behavior. In a similar sense, one could equally expect to find policy entrepreneurs favoring specific new approaches to strictly defined problems or promoting a reconceptualization of policy as a whole. Strategies such as GRIT would appear to lend themselves to testing in specific issue-areas (Etzioni, 1967), but according to some versions GRIT specifies that the "initiatives should be diversified in sphere of action and geographical location" (Larson, 1987:32).

A comprehensive study of change in Soviet security policy should probably combine both the chronological and issue-area approaches. For the purposes of this chapter, we settle on a compromise. The following sections are organized by chronological leadership period (including Andropov and Chernenko as part of "The Brezhnev Era") and selectively by issue-area within each period. It is not possible in a single chapter to "test," or even to give systematic attention to each of the dozen or so theoretical approaches and variations enumerated above. The requisite research has simply not been done; in many cases, the historical data have not even been compiled. Instead, the chapter highlights those explanations that for a given issue-area or chronological period seem to have strong explanatory value, appear to receive little support from the evidence available, or might be promising but require more empirical research before we can know for sure.

Table 5.1 provides a list of simple hypotheses, derived from the preceding literature review, to help guide the reader through the discussion of historical cases. It must be emphasized, however, that the discussion that follows does not constitute a test of the hypotheses, for several reasons. First, the cases do not represent a random sample: their selection was based on availability of secondary accounts, and, to some extent, primary materials. Thus, it is not possible to indicate conclusively which hypotheses were validated and which were disproved. Second, the hypotheses are formulated in a general way,

TABLE 5.1   Hypothescs on Soviet Moderation

1a.	Moderation results from a security regime.
1b.	Moderation leads to a security regime.
2.	Moderation results from learning.
3.	Moderation results from domestic political realignments.
4.	The *appearance* of moderation results from changes in military requirements.
5a.	Transnational alliances facilitate moderation.
5b.	Transnational alliances hinder moderation.
6a.	Soviet policymakers who desire moderation will use GRIT to induce international cooperation from Soviet adversaries.
6b.	GRIT works to facilitate moderation.
7a.	Soviet policymakers who desire moderation will use tit-for-tat to induce international cooperation from Soviet adversaries.
7b.	Tit-for-tat works to facilitate moderation.
8a.	Unilateral U.S. concessions or initiatives of restraint produce Soviet moderation.
8b.	U.S. negotiation from strength produces Soviet moderation.
8c.	Moderation is more likely to occur under conditions of relative Soviet strength rather than weakness.
9.	Moderation results from efforts of policy entrepreneurs to take advantage of policy windows.
10a.	Moderation is most likely under conditions of relative Soviet economic weakness.
10b.	Moderation is most likely under conditions of relative Soviet economic strength.
11.	Leadership preferences determine the degree to which the Soviets will pursue policies of moderation.
12a.	Concern for public opinion leads policymakers to pursue moderation.
12b.	Public opinion reinforces reciprocity in gestures of moderation.

rather than in more precise, operational terms. This choice was dictated by the nature of the existing secondary literature. Most of the relevant work in the field is of a descriptive and historical nature, and virtually none presents and tests propositions. Relying on this secondary literature does not permit the degree of specification that one would use to develop hypotheses in an original research design. Finally, even a chapter of this length cannot give systematic attention to 20 hypotheses over 3 major leadership periods for several issue-areas.

Although it cannot present conclusive findings from the field of Soviet security studies, let alone provide specific policy prescriptions, the following review should, nevertheless, prove useful to indicate the nature of the evidence available to support policy-relevant hypotheses about Soviet behavior.

It also suggests areas where future research could fill in gaps, and, along with the preceding literature review, forms a basis for the more specific hypotheses with which the chapter concludes.

The Khrushchev Era

East–West security cooperation was absent throughout the Stalin period and most of the Khrushchev era as well. One certainly cannot speak of anything resembling a *security regime*. Under Nikita Khrushchev there were a number of major changes in security policy, but many of them—the nuclearization of the Soviet armed forces, for example—were not in the direction of moderation. On the other hand, the advent of nuclear weapons and the "mutual hostage" relationship between the two superpowers led Khrushchev to make a major ideological pronouncement that portended a change in Soviet attitudes toward nuclear arms control.

MILITARY DOCTRINE

At the Twentieth Party Congress in 1956, Khrushchev declared that war between the two rival social systems—capitalism and socialism—was no longer "fatalistically inevitable" (Holloway, 1983:84–86). This declaration apparently called into question Lenin's analysis of war as an inevitable consequence of imperialism, the "highest stage of capitalism." It set in motion a process that resulted in a more differentiated view of U.S. politics, one that identified "realists" who were willing to resist the pressures of the "military-industrial complex" and come to some agreements with the Soviet Union to slow the arms race.

Some analysts would argue that the Khrushchev pronouncements constitute evidence of *learning* (Zimmerman, 1969; Griffiths, 1972). Certainly there were changes in the means pursued to achieve Soviet security objectives, especially with the addition of limited cooperation with the United States in the form of arms control. Probably there were changes in ends as well—the demise of the capitalist world was no longer considered the sine qua non of the Soviet Union's survival. Perhaps there were changes in the cognitive structures of Khrushchev and other leaders—their views of the sources of U.S. policy were probably more differentiated than those they held before coming to power. Yet not all members of the Soviet foreign-policy community accepted these views. Even after the Twentieth Party Congress, Khrushchev faced opposition from hardliners such as Viacheslav Molotov, who had served as Stalin's foreign minister and was later a member of the "anti-Party group" that tried to depose Khrushchev in 1957. Throughout Khrushchev's tenure, far more simplistic and hostile images of the United States (especially, but not exclusively, in the military) competed with his own views and dogged his efforts to pursue arms control (Jönsson, 1979; Griffiths, 1972; Kolkowicz, 1967).

As Tetlock (1988) points out, it is always difficult to evaluate whether "efficiency" learning has taken place. Certainly those of Khrushchev's colleagues who successfully conspired to remove him from power in 1964 doubted that his policies had achieved Soviet objectives more effectively than the alternatives. For descriptive purposes, one might nevertheless argue that certain types of learning did occur but that "institutional" learning was not fully achieved or that some lessons were "unlearned" or quickly forgotten. Such arguments, however, are mainly ways to save the learning metaphor. Accounts that incorporate the domestic political struggles over competing images and policies would seem to provide more satisfactory explanations for changes during the Khrushchev period.

THE TROOP REDUCTIONS

Among the more concrete signs of change in Soviet policy was a greater flexibility and willingness to compromise in the pursuit of arms control agreements with the West. Disarmament negotiations had been held under the auspices of the U.N. since 1946, but by most accounts—including recent Soviet ones—the Soviet Union did not take them seriously until the mid-1950s, after Stalin had died (Bloomfield, Clemens, and Griffiths, 1966; Shevchenko, 1985:78; Zubok, 1988). Starting in 1954, talks were conducted by a subcommittee of the U.N. Disarmament Commission, with representatives from the United States, the Soviet Union, France, Great Britain, and Canada (Bechhoefer, 1961). The most significant indication of Soviet interest in an agreement came on May 10, 1955, when the Soviet delegation put forward a proposal that incorporated the main features of an earlier Western memorandum including, among other things, the total prohibition of the use and manufacture of nuclear weapons, major reductions in all armed forces and conventional armaments, and the establishment of adequate organs of control and inspection (Noel-Baker, 1958:12–30; Griffiths, 1972:399–407; Evangelista, 1990a). The Soviet Union's adherence to the plan would have entailed cutting back the Soviet armed forces from 5.7 million to between 1 and 1.5 million men. These figures, proposed originally by the Western powers, would have constituted a significantly disproportionate reduction in Soviet forces, compared to those of France, Great Britain, or the United States. In return the Soviets would benefit from the eventual destruction of stocks of U.S. nuclear weapons, but their own would have to be destroyed as well.

The fact that the Western powers, on U.S. initiative, retracted their earlier proposal instead of pursuing an agreement makes it difficult to evaluate Soviet intentions (Bloomfield, Clemens, and Griffiths, 1966; Noel-Baker, 1958). In order to identify the May 1955 proposal as constituting a meaningful change in Soviet policy, one would have to cite evidence that the proposal was not merely a bluff, but that the Soviets were willing to carry out the disarmament measures they had proposed. Evidence for such counterfactual reconstructions is by definition difficult to obtain. In this case, however, we have a number of promising leads. For example, a Soviet defector, who had specialized in disarmament at the Foreign Ministry, reports that a major change in the Soviet Union's approach took place following the death of Stalin. He quotes his superior as revealing that "we're starting a new policy that will mean serious negotiating on disarmament" (Shevchenko, 1985:78). A Yugoslav diplomat, whom Khrushchev treated somewhat as a confidant, presents further evidence, from their conversations, of the new leader's interest in the issues (Mičunović, 1980:157, 166). Western scholars as well recognize Khrushchev's willingness to make concessions in the disarmament sphere and on related issues, such as the status of Austria (Bloomfield, Clemens, and Griffiths, 1966; Larson, 1987). Perhaps the strongest corroboration of Soviet interest in disarmament was provided by Soviet actions following the U.S. rejection of the May 1955 plan. In the wake of failure to obtain Western agreement on mutual, large-scale reductions in the conventional forces, the Soviets reduced their army unilaterally. From 1955 through 1957, the Soviet Union cut back its armed forces by an estimated 1.84 million men (*Pravda*, 15 January 1960; Wolfe, 1970:162–166). If the Soviets were willing to undertake such measures unilaterally, one would assume that they would much prefer to have had the Western powers limit their forces as well.

A number of explanations have been put forward to account for Khrushchev's reductions. Indeed, the case provides a typical example of overdetermination of causes that is so common in the study of the arms race (Kurth, 1971). The best that can be done here, as in the rest of this section, is to call attention to explanations that do not appear to fit the evidence, indicate the several candidate explanations that do, and, later, in the section on methodology and future research, propose how to go about choosing between equally plausible competing explanations.

One explanation holds that Khrushchev's reductions were not a sign of moderation in security policy at all, but merely a product of *military exigencies*. In this view, mass armies of the traditional type were no longer necessary in an age of battlefield nuclear warfare: the extensive demobilization of ground and tactical air forces was a sensible means to "modernize" the Soviet armed forces. From this perspective, the troop reductions were entirely in the Soviet interest and should not be considered as concessions intended to demonstrate a new cooperative attitude towards disarmament. In some interpretations, the initiative might constitute a form of "efficiency" *learning*, because the Soviet Union successfully adapted itself to the nuclear age.

The interpretation that the reductions did not hurt but rather benefited Soviet military capabilities apparently stems from the belief that nuclear weapons—especially tactical nuclear weapons—compensated for cuts in conventional forces. The "more bang for the buck" argument was widely promoted in the United States by the Eisenhower administration to support nuclearization of NATO forces on grounds of cost-effectiveness. Khrushchev put forward his own version—often dubbed "more rubble for the ruble"—to justify his disarmament proposals and his unilateral troop cuts (Evangelista, 1988). As it turned out, many prominent U.S. Army officers disagreed with Eisenhower, starting with the Army chief of staff himself. In 1954, General Matthew Ridgway claimed that the deployment of tactical nuclear weapons "does not warrant the assumption that the need for soldiers will become less. On the contrary," he argued, "there are indications that the trend will be in the opposite direction" (quoted in Evangelista, 1990a). He cited several reasons for needing more forces: the increased depth of the battlefield, the need for greater dispersion of forces, and the multiplication of maintenance and support facilities to supply large numbers of small, mobile combat units (Evangelista, 1990a). Prominent Soviet military officers cited such arguments by U.S. Generals Bradley, Collins, Ridgway, Taylor, and others to support a case for maintaining mass armies, arguing that the prospect of a nuclear battlefield "calls not for the reduction of the numbers of combatants, but for their logical further increase, since the threat of wiping out divisions grows, and large reserves will be needed for their replacement" (Krasil'nikov, 1956, discussed in Garthoff, 1958:124–125; Zubok, 1988). Such borrowing of arguments suggests that a *tacit transnational alliance* was at work, in this case between opponents rather than proponents of arms control.

In retrospect, it seems possible that Khrushchev did not view the reductions merely as a means to modernize the Soviet armed forces. Such a limited objective would hardly seem worth the risk of alienating important segments of the military, as he evidently did. Although military criticism of Khrushchev's reductions became particularly vocal following the announcement of a new round of cuts in 1960 (Gallagher, 1964; Wolfe, 1965:238–242; Tiedtke, 1985:54–62; Ritvo, 1962), recent evidence attests to the demoralization and discontent that even the initial reforms of the mid-1950s engendered. A commander of a Soviet air defense division writes in his memoirs, for example, that the late 1950s were "a difficult time for us military people. We still hadn't managed to survive the first unilateral reduction of the Soviet armed forces when a second began. Some of us didn't take the so-called reforms very cheerfully. Sometimes it seemed that everything we had done up until then was now unnecessary" (Lavrinenkov, 1982:225). In addition to their effect on military capability, the cuts also entailed problems of morale and dislocation, as hundreds of thousands of soldiers and officers were forced to reintegrate themselves into the civilian work force (*Krasnaia zvezda*, 20 January 1960; Tiedtke, 1985:157–179). Thus, the argument that the reductions were solely the product of military exigencies or efficiency learning is problematic at best. There were disagreements at the time concerning the wisdom of the cuts, and they have recently been revived in the context of the current debate about the similar initiatives of Gorbachev (Zhurkin, Karaganov, and Kortunov, 1987; Tret'iak, 1988).

Economic stringency evidently played a role in Khrushchev's reductions as well as in his other disarmament proposals. In the transcript of his tape-recorded reminiscences, Khrushchev mentions the reductions directly after expressing his belief that the United States was using the arms race to destroy the Soviet economy "and by that means to obtain its goals even without war" (Khrushchev, 1971:403). Khrushchev would probably have liked to curb the arms competition by negotiated agreement, but failing that, he thought that he could achieve some economic benefits through the transfer of labor from the army to the civilian work force; therefore, he was willing to carry out the reductions unilaterally (Tiedtke, 1985; Zubok, 1988). In this case, Khrushchev's moderation was not a response to *unilateral initiatives* from the U.S. side, but was a means by which he hoped, in vain, to gain U.S. reciprocation.

If we assume that Khrushchev genuinely wanted to lessen the military burden on the Soviet economy, then bargaining strategies associated with *cooperation theory* (such as tit-for-tat or GRIT) are consistent with his actions. Khrushchev does seem to have hoped that the United States would view the reductions as a concession that would improve the prospects for a disarmament agreement. In his reminiscences, he justified the cuts by associating them with his broader disarmament proposals: "to fight for disarmament or arms reductions at the time the Soviet Union had such an enormous army—no one would believe it" (Khrushchev, 1971:403–404). Because Khrushchev carried out the reductions without demanding or receiving tit-for-tat reciprocity from the West, it seems plausible that he was pursuing a GRIT strategy intended to moderate his adversary's enemy image of the Soviet Union. Remarks he made in retirement suggested that he had grasped the basic insight of the security dilemma—that "frightening the opponent" can be counterproductive (Khrushchev, 1971:406). One might characterize such insights as instances of foreign policy *learning* (of the cognitive structural sort) on the part of Khrushchev (Griffiths, 1972:310–312), but they did not become "consensual knowledge" in any sense and were not institutionalized.

The standard account of Khrushchev's effort to break through the cognitive barriers of U.S. leaders—specifically Secretary of State John Foster Dulles—describes it as a failure (Holsti, 1967). In fact, while publicly the U.S. dismissed as propaganda such initiatives as the unilateral reductions in Soviet armed forces, in closed meetings of the National Security Council, Dulles argued that "the Soviets had effected a complete alteration of their policy. Their policy had been hard and was becoming soft." According to Dulles, the Soviets were seeking "some limitation on the arms race, some easing of the armaments burden. This they were seeking not merely as a trick, but because they could ill afford to sustain this burden" (quoted in Evangelista, 1990a). Dulles's perception of Khrushchev's genuine interest in an accord was not sufficient to get the U.S. government to put forward a negotiable proposal as a basis for compromise. The failure to come to an agreement owed mainly to opposition from the Joint Chiefs of Staff (JCS) and the Atomic Energy Commission (AEC).

In game theoretic terms, the disarmament negotiations in the mid-1950s were not a prisoners' dilemma, in which both sides prefer mutual cooperation (bilateral disarmament) to mutual defection (an arms race), but a deadlock, in which at least one side prefers to continue the arms race regardless of whether the other side would be willing to disarm. This was explicitly the position of the JCS and the AEC at the time (Evangelista, 1990a). Thus, while Khrushchev's GRIT strategy worked in other issue-areas during the same period—most notably in the Austrian settlement (Larson, 1987)—it failed in the disarmament sphere. *Public opinion* did not, as suggested above, pressure the U.S. to respond favorably to the Soviet disarmament plan. It did, however, figure prominently in the Eisenhower administration's "Open Skies" counterproposal, an initiative that U.S. policymakers were confident the Soviets would reject (Evangelista, 1990a). Thus, public opinion did not in this case reinforce moderate tendencies.

The fact that Soviet disarmament initiatives during the 1950s stemmed in part from economic concerns, and that prominent U.S. policymakers such as Dulles recognized that fact, raises the possibility that the United States was pursuing a policy of *negotiation from strength,* and that we can attribute Soviet moderation to that policy. There is little doubt that some of Khrushchev's initiatives were intended to induce the United States to restrain its military programs. Indeed, that is one of the main purposes of pursuing arms agreements. Specifically, some authors have suggested that Khrushchev wanted to tie his troop reductions to restraints on U.S. deployments of tactical nuclear weapons in Europe and the rearming of West Germany (Bloomfield, Clemens, and Griffiths, 1966:85–86; Evangelista, 1988:265–267). The U.S. weapons might have served as bargaining chips to achieve further Soviet concessions, as the narrow version of negotiation-from-strength would prescribe. In the event, however, the chips were never cashed in, because the U.S. government—divided internally, but dominated by opponents of arms control—was not interested in a negotiated outcome. The policy of strength-without-serious-negotiation proved counterproductive. The Soviets built up their own force of tactical nuclear weapons in Europe and with the ouster of Khrushchev began a conventional-force buildup as well (Evangelista, 1988).

To what extent did *Soviet strength* constitute a prerequisite for Soviet concessions and moderation? A number of analysts, including a prominent Soviet defector, have argued that the change in the international atmosphere, characterized by the "spirit of Geneva" in 1955, resulted from the Soviet Union's growing confidence in its military power (Shevchenko, 1985:82–83). Even reform-oriented Soviet commentators, who in recent years have criticized excessive Soviet military spending, give Khrushchev credit for achieving nuclear parity with the United States, viewing it as a necessary starting point for negotiating arms control (Burlatskii, 1988a, 1988b; Zubok, 1988). In the case of the 1955 proposal, the record is mixed. The Soviets were clearly ahead in overall numbers of troops, but behind in most indices of nuclear capability. Their proposal sought to trade off their strengths for U.S. ones. If they had been ahead in all respects, it is unlikely that the Soviets would have proposed such a compromise. On the other hand, the fact that the Soviets were by the mid-1950s achieving success with their thermonuclear weapons program probably gave them the confidence to pursue negotiations with the United States, because some very basic form of nuclear parity appeared in sight (Holloway, 1983:25–27; Shevchenko, 1985:83).

Some of the insights of *coalition theory* are useful for understanding how Khrushchev implemented his troop reductions, despite opposition from certain sectors of the military. In order to prevail, Khrushchev evidently relied on Marshal Georgii Zhukov's authority and prestige within the military (Zubok, 1988). Zhukov was brought back from the virtual exile imposed on him by Stalin and was made defense minister in 1955. He became part of the first secretary's political coalition and proved his value during the attempt by the "antiparty group" to oust Khrushchev in June 1957 (Burlatskii, 1988a). Presumably Zhukov was also helpful in countering the arguments of army officers who wanted to maintain mass armies even as nuclear weapons became available.

Later Khrushchev adopted a similar coalition-building strategy when he decided to emphasize missiles as the main delivery vehicle for Soviet strategic and tactical nuclear weapons. In 1959, he coopted Chief Marshal of the Artillery Mitrofan Nedelin to head the Strategic Rocket Forces, whose ranks were made up of troops from the artillery and air defense forces (Tolubko, 1979:188). Khrushchev announced a new round of troop reductions in January

1960 when he argued that nuclear "firepower" now mattered more than "how many soldiers we have under arms, how many people are wearing soldiers' greatcoats" (*Pravda*, 15 January 1960). Because the new emphasis on nuclear weapons entailed substantial reductions in artillery and air forces, it was useful for Khrushchev to have cultivated allies within those services (Evangelista, 1988:228–229).

One should not, however, overstate the importance of coalition-building in this case. Khrushchev evidently did not see Zhukov as an indispensable ally, considering that he fired him in October 1957, but continued to pursue reductions in the armed forces (Burlatskii, 1988*a*). The coalitions were useful but they were not the impetus behind the changes in Soviet policy. Here economic stringency seems to have been a more important motivation (Tiedtke, 1985; Zubok, 1988); the desire to use unilateral initiatives to persuade the United States to agree to further arms restraint also played an important role (Evangelista, 1988, 1990a); and the limits of Khrushchev's ability to pursue a greater degree of moderation in his policy were probably more influenced by external factors—namely, U.S. unwillingness to reciprocate—than by internal power politics.

THE TEST BAN

The case of nuclear testing is worth reviewing for several reasons. The Limited Test Ban Treaty of 1963 was the only major arms control accord successfully negotiated during Khrushchev's tenure in office, and, furthermore, it was the first significant agreement of the nuclear age. From a theoretical standpoint, the series of U.S. and Soviet initiatives leading up to the treaty appear to constitute a good test for *cooperation theory*. Other theoretical approaches may be useful for understanding Khrushchev's motives for pursuing a test ban.

The first international proposal for a nuclear test ban came from Indian Prime Minister Jawaharlal Nehru in 1954, largely in reaction to the danger of radioactive fallout posed by U.S. and Soviet thermonuclear tests in the atmosphere. The Soviet Union put the test ban on the agenda of the U.N. Disarmament Commission as part of its May 1955 proposal, but the test ban became tied to disputes over other aspects of a comprehensive disarmament plan and made no progress. On March 31, 1958, following an extensive series of nuclear tests, the Soviet Union announced a unilateral moratorium on further testing and invited the Western powers to reciprocate. If we assume that the nuclear arms race could at this time be represented as a prisoners' dilemma, a tit-for-tat strategy would have prescribed Western reciprocation of this seemingly cooperative Soviet move. Instead, the United States reacted as psychological theories would predict, by calling into question the Soviet Union's good faith (Jacobson and Stein, 1966:45–49).

On August 22, 1958, the United States suggested a multilateral moratorium to accompany test ban negotiations, which it proposed to convene in Geneva starting on October 31. The Soviets had meanwhile begun preparing to resume testing and probably saw President Eisenhower's announcement as a propaganda ploy, because this time it was the United States that had just completed a major test series. Although one could view Eisenhower's August proposal as a positive response to the Soviet moratorium, in the sense of tit-for-tat, each country still had reason to suspect the other's motives (Divine, 1978:229).

The Soviets would not commit themselves to a moratorium in the autumn of 1958; they did, however, agree to the negotiations in Geneva. The United States proposal for a moratorium led to "a last-minute rash of testing by all three nuclear powers"—the United States, Soviet Union, and Great Britain (Divine, 1978:231). The United States completed its tests the day before the conference opened; the Soviet Union broke its unilateral moratorium on September 30 and continued testing until November 3. Thereafter a multilateral moratorium remained in effect until the fall of 1961, but indications of its fragility were evident many months before. In December 1960, Eisenhower announced that the United States was formally ending its moratorium but would not test without prior warning. He urged President-elect Kennedy to resume testing (Seaborg, 1981:25). In February 1961, France became a nuclear power by testing its first atomic weapon; at the United Nations, the United States delegate supported the French right to nuclear testing, even though the Soviets had warned that they considered a test by France, a NATO member, as equivalent to one by the United States or Great Britain. On September 1, the Soviets resumed testing, and 2 weeks later the United States followed suit.

The series of events resemble in some respects a pattern of tit-for-tat reciprocity of both cooperative acts and defections. In fact, however, many of the ostensibly cooperative moves were viewed by the other side as propaganda maneuvers and did little to induce genuine cooperation. Furthermore, it seems apparent that the situation approximated a prisoners' dilemma only intermittently, if at all. Internal policymaking in the United States was fragmented, as critics of tit-for-tat would predict (Gowa, 1986); the situation frequently gave test ban opponents a veto over U.S. cooperative gestures (Divine, 1978; Neidle, 1988). In the Soviet Union, as well, internal pressure to continue testing meant that the government did not always favor mutual cooperation (Jönsson, 1979; Khrushchev, 1971:940–942; Garthoff, 1972). The nearly 3-year moratorium, from autumn 1958 to autumn 1961, is not easily explained, it seems, as the result of a straightforward tit-for-tat mechanism. It is unlikely that a GRIT strategy can be credited with the mutual moratorium. If Khrushchev wanted to use test suspensions as part of GRIT, he was often stymied by internal opposition from hardliners such as fellow Presidium (Politburo) members Frol Kozlov and Mikhail Suslov (Jönsson, 1979; Slusser, 1973). Soviet policy did not demonstrate the degree of unilateral concession and risk that GRIT entails; at best the Soviet Union pursued a strategy of contingent restraint. As for the U.S. side, it is doubtful that Eisenhower changed his view of Soviet intentions in response to Soviet test-ban initiatives, as GRIT would suggest. He seemed to be more influenced by the scientific (and pseudoscientific) arguments concerning verifiability, and his support for a test ban waxed and waned with his understanding of the technical prospects for detection of cheating.

Considerations of *military exigencies* appear to account in some measure for the inconsistencies of Soviet test-ban policy. The Soviets were generally behind in nuclear-warhead technology. At times they evidently anticipated falling further behind and preferred that both sides maintain the status quo by observing a moratorium and negotiating a comprehensive test ban. At other times—especially following the U.S. test series in the summer of 1958 and the French tests in 1961—the Soviets apparently found their lag intolerable and initiated tests to catch up. In the latter case, as analysis of the tests suggested, the Soviets were particularly interested in understanding the effects of high-altitude atmospheric explosions useful for antiballistic missile defense. They also used the 1961 series to narrow the gap with the United States in large-yield warhead technology (Seaborg, 1981:119–123; Garthoff, 1972: 187–190; Jönsson, 1979:37). These goals were sufficiently pressing for a dominant faction in the leadership to decide to break the 3-year test moratorium with the United States and Great Britain. Khrushchev, moreover, saw an opportunity to use the test resumption as part of his war of nerves during the 1961 Berlin deadline crisis (Seaborg, 1981:70; Slusser, 1973; Sakharov, 1974:32). Although U.S. advantages in warhead technology at times motivated the Soviets to seek a test ban, explicit U.S. attempts at negotiation from strength had mixed results. The Soviets occasionally took the position that because the United States had tested nuclear weapons first (in 1945), the Soviet Union had the right to test them last. In 1958, for example, they were unwilling to enter a moratorium until they had matched the U.S. test series with one of their own. In 1963, Soviet Ambassador Anatolii Dobrynin complained—perhaps disingenuously—that U.S. resumption of underground testing, although intended by the Kennedy administration to pressure the Soviets into making concessions in the test ban negotiations, actually helped the Soviet proponents of testing; they argued for the need to keep up to the

United States and they questioned the administration's good faith (Seaborg, 1981:202).

Economic stringency does not appear to have been an explicit motive behind the test ban policy. In a general sense, any resources transferred from the military to the civilian sector would be welcome (Garthoff, 1972:68–69), but during the mid-1950s the most substantial benefits were anticipated to come from troop reductions. During the months preceding negotiation of the Limited Test Ban Treaty in 1963, Khrushchev did, however, accelerate his efforts to shift investments from military to civilian purposes. Especially following the signing of the treaty, he emphasized the opportunities that the emerging U.S. détente provided for decreasing military expenditures (Kolkowicz, 1967:292–293).

Evidently it is not difficult to explain the lack of cooperation or moderation in nuclear testing—that is, the inability of the nuclear powers to agree to a comprehensive test ban. Indeed, the outcome is overdetermined, beginning with the explanation that states facing a security dilemma are likely to pursue unilateral policies rather than risk cooperation (Jervis, 1978). More difficult to account for, however, is the nuclear test moratorium that the United States, Soviet Union, and Great Britain maintained for 3 years. *Military exigencies* certainly shed some light on the question—the United States wanted to freeze its lead, the Soviet Union wanted to keep from falling further behind (Neidle, 1988). Yet given the vast disagreements within each country concerning the merits of a test ban and the relative advantages that would accrue to each side, this explanation is hardly determining. Concern for *public opinion*—for attaining a propaganda coup or limiting the propaganda benefits of the adversary's initiative—appears to have played a crucial role at key junctures. Public concern about radioactive fallout was an early and persistent stimulus to the various test-ban initiatives (Divine, 1978; Sakharov, 1974). The fact that negotiations were conducted under the auspices of the United Nations reinforced the saliency of international public opinion (Jacobson and Stein, 1966). Although focusing on public opinion would not allow one to predict continuation of the moratorium at any given point, the factor clearly figured in decisions on each side about whether to pursue it (Seaborg, 1981; Jönsson, 1979).

How well do the various hypotheses explain the successful achievement of the Limited Test Ban Treaty in 1963? Amitai Etzioni argues that the pattern of events starting with John F. Kennedy's American University speech on June 10, 1963 and continuing through the signing of the treaty on August 5 and up until Kennedy's death provide a test of the theory that "psychological gestures initiated by one nation will be reciprocated by others with the effect of reducing international tensions" (1967:361). Although sometimes misunderstood as a test of the GRIT strategy, Etzioni's approach is closer in some respects to tit-for-tat. GRIT consists of a series of moderately risky concessions that continue for some time even without reciprocation. Tit-for-tat entails a cooperative move of unspecified risk, and demands immediate reciprocity by the other side in order for cooperation to continue. Etzioni's strategy involves merely a symbolic initiative that entails no risk, and he would not prescribe more than a few such gestures in the absence of reciprocity. He specifically distinguishes his strategy from Charles Osgood's GRIT according to these criteria (Etzioni, 1967:364–365). Etzioni considers Kennedy's speech to have been precisely the kind of symbolic, low-risk initiative that his theory prescribes, although it is possible that Khrushchev and his advisers viewed it as more of a gamble, given their notions of the power of a U.S. military-industrial complex (Adzhubei, 1988:118–119). (Bunn and Payne, 1988:14 also consider it to have been an "extraordinary" political risk.)

In practice, Etzioni describes the steps that the United States and Soviet Union took during the summer of 1963 as an exercise in tit-for-tat reciprocity (1967:366–369). The process worked as Axelrod (1984) would predict. Indeed, when the U.S. government decided to cease reciprocating Soviet initiatives in late October, in apparent concern for the "psychological disarmament" of the U.S. public, the process ground to a halt (Etzioni, 1967:371–372). In game-theoretic terms, defection was met with defection. Here is further evidence that concern for *public opinion* cuts both ways.

There were other factors at work besides the resolution of a prisoners' dilemma game through a tit-for-tat mechanism. Unlike the classic prisoners' dilemma, which assumes unitary rational actors and no communication between the "prisoners," the test ban debate involved internal lobbying by *policy entrepreneurs* on both sides and *tacit transnational alliances* of test ban proponents. Scientists, for example, played an important role in several respects. At the Conference of Experts in Geneva they provided the first agreed technical basis for verifying a test ban, even through subsequent research disputed some of their conclusions (Jacobson and Stein, 1966). Soviet scientists and officials met with U.S. counterparts at international meetings of Pugwash and the Dartmouth Conference, and they often employed the arguments that they heard at those meetings in later internal Soviet debates about the test ban (Seaborg, 1981:177; Richmond, 1987:118–119). For example, E.K. Fedorov, a former participant in the Conference of Experts, published an article in the Soviet Union in support of a test ban at a time when Khrushchev was apparently the only top leader who strongly endorsed the measure (Jönsson, 1979:149–151). Fedorov, whose article had originally been presented at a Pugwash meeting, appeared to be trying to bolster Khrushchev's position (Fedorov, 1959). International concern about radioactive fallout gave such

Soviet scientists as Andrei Sakharov a *policy window* through which to promote their proposals for test moratoria (Divine, 1978: 161, 233–234; Sakharov, 1962, 1974). Sakharov specifically claims that the arguments of Soviet scientists, including himself, helped to persuade Khrushchev to agree to the Limited Test Ban Treaty (Sakharov, 1974:33–34; Sakharov, 1982:216). Khrushchev could placate international *public opinion* by removing the source of fallout (atmospheric tests), but still avoid alienating the Soviet military (or so he hoped) by allowing them to continue tests underground. Much the same logic convinced Kennedy to pursue only a limited test ban (Seaborg, 1981).

One should not assume that *transnational alliances* between proponents of moderation on each side always enhance the prospects for cooperation. The early history of the test ban debate provides a strong counterexample. During the 1956 presidential campaign in the United States, Adlai Stevenson, the Democratic contender, seized on the issue of a test ban to rally popular support for his candidacy. The Soviet leadership, which had been pressing the United States to agree to a test ban, wrote to President Eisenhower in September, renewing the offer and remarking favorably that "certain prominent public figures in the United States" supported the move as well (Divine, 1978:98–99). The administration released the letter to the press, which interpreted it as a Soviet endorsement of Stevenson—the kiss of death for his campaign, and a major setback for the test ban. Ironically, Eisenhower appeared to be close to agreeing to explore the possibility of a test ban with the Soviets in September 1956. According to Divine (1978:111), "Stevenson brought the issue into the presidential campaign and made a diplomatic initiative impossible."

The test ban case suggests that *coalition theory* has something to contribute to understanding the possibilities for and constraints on moderation in Soviet security policy. Clearly Khrushchev's test ban proposals had many opponents; the zig zags of his initiatives appear to correlate to some extent with the domestic constellation of forces favoring or opposing a détente policy at a given time (Jönsson, 1979). While the formation of a coalition in favor of moderation is dependent on a number of domestic political and economic factors (Snyder, 1987/1988), international events play an important role as well. In the case of the test ban, for example, Kremlin hardliners evidently took advantage of a *policy window*—the flight of Gary Powers's U-2 spy plane over the Soviet Union on May 1, 1960—to derail a process that seemed to be leading to a test-ban accord. By most accounts, including recent Soviet ones, Khrushchev felt pressured by test ban opponents to use the U-2 as a pretext to scuttle the upcoming Paris summit, at which he apparently had hoped to finalize a treaty (Jönsson, 1979:166–168). After the Soviet Union shot down the plane and captured the pilot, Khrushchev demanded an apology from Eisenhower and a promise of no further aerial espionage missions.

Eisenhower refused and Khrushchev broke up the summit (Adzhubei, 1988:113–114).

An even more dramatic international event—the Cuban missile crisis—is often credited with providing the impetus to the improvement in East-West relations that ultimately resulted in the Limited Test Ban Treaty (Seaborg, 1981:176, 199). One could argue that the incident contributed to Khrushchev's *learning* about his adversary. In this view, the U.S. willingness to give the Soviets an opportunity for a face-saving retreat (the commitment not to invade Cuba) and to compromise (the promise to remove U.S. missiles from Turkey) gave Khrushchev a new understanding of U.S. interest in achieving a mutually beneficial outcome to the test ban negotiations. Judging by Khrushchev's interpretations of U.S. policymaking before and after the crisis, however, his view did not change substantially. He had already differentiated, for example, between "sober" elements and "lunatics" among U.S. decision makers, and he used the outcome of the crisis to reinforce his view that the lunatics could be overruled (Garthoff, 1972:80). The fact that Khrushchev's views continued to meet resistance at high levels—and in particular that his image of the United States was rejected (Jönsson, 1979:200–207)—calls into question the utility of the learning metaphor. An alternative explanation would view the crisis as another example of a *policy window* that test ban proponents, including Khrushchev, used to bolster their arguments both about the danger of the arms race and about the prospects for getting it under control.

The Brezhnev Era

The Brezhnev period saw the emergence of negotiated arms control as a major component of U.S.–Soviet relations. If regime theory were to account for developments in the security sphere, it should apply to this time when the Soviets voluntarily entered into agreements to restrict their nuclear capability. One also would want to investigate whether these cooperative agreements stemmed from military or economic pressure, came about as a result of the entrepreneurial efforts of longtime proponents of cooperation, or should be attributed to policymakers who had experienced some form of learning that made them more amenable to cooperative approaches to security policy. Did bargaining strategies such as tit-for-tat or GRIT prove useful in achieving cooperative outcomes? Ideally one would also want to account for failures to achieve moderation. Even under the terms of the SALT agreements, for example, the Soviets increased their nuclear capability substantially and engaged in a program of conventional-force modernization as well.

ORIGINS OF SALT

Most analysts argue that SALT became possible only after the Soviet Union had achieved an approximate parity with the United States in strategic nuclear forces. In this sense, considering that the Soviets endured most of the 1960s in a position of relative strategic inferiority vis-à-vis the United States, it was the growth of *Soviet strength* that helped bring about SALT. There is, however, an argument that the most important agreement resulting from SALT—the 1972 Antiballistic Missile Treaty—came about as a consequence of *U.S. negotiation from strength*. Specifically, the argument goes, it was the 1969 decision by the U.S. Senate (passed by a single vote) to fund Phase I of the Nixon administration's Safeguard ABM system that motivated the Soviets to agree to negotiate a treaty limiting ABMs (Einhorn, 1985:2–3; Hampson, 1987:84–85; Rose, 1988:87–102). Although the U.S. program probably did increase Soviet incentives to limit ABMs, there was far more behind Soviet reevaluation of strategic defense and the merits of a treaty than the prospect of a few U.S. ABM complexes (Garthoff, 1984; Garthoff, 1985:182–183; Holloway, 1985). In fact, since the Soviet ABM system around Moscow had appeared several years before Safeguard was even proposed, one could equally argue that it was the Soviet system and the prospect of a race in both offensive and defensive weapons that induced the United States to pursue arms control seriously (Farley, 1988).

The precise link between economic motives were relevant to Soviet decisions about entering into arms control negotiations. An arms race in both defensive and offensive weapons would surely have put a major burden on the Soviet economy. Much of the internal Soviet debate about technology and the economy in the early 1970s appears to have been linked to disagreements about the economic implications of arms control (Parrott, 1983:242–256). Brezhnev expressed the optimistic view that the United States had originally wanted to ruin the Soviet economy by means of an arms race, but had come to believe that such a policy was futile: "Now everyone can see that socialism is sufficiently powerful to secure both reliable defense and the development of the economy, although, of course, without large defense expenditure we would be able to drive our economy forward even faster" (Brezhnev, 1971:390). On the other hand, Brezhnev did impose restraints on the growth rate of Soviet military spending starting in the mid-1970s (Kaufman, 1985, 1988).

The precise link between domestic economic concerns and Soviet arms control policy in the SALT era could still use further exploration. Did *economic stringency* give the United States any bargaining leverage in inducing Soviet concessions? There appears to be general agreement that when the United States makes economic cooperation explicitly contingent on Soviet behavior in other spheres, the tactic backfires. A number of Soviet émigrés who were involved in the policy process during the détente period have argued that economic pressure—for example, in the form of the Jackson-Vanik amendment linking U.S. trade concessions to emigration of Soviet Jews—

works against the Soviet proponents of cooperation (Dallin, 1981:383–386; Garthoff, 1985:465–467). On the other hand, U.S. willingness to agree to arms control measures that would save the Soviets money would probably bolster the case of the Soviet moderates. It could serve as a *policy window* for them to promote their own agenda for reallocating resources to the civilian sector.

Clearly, the origins of the ABM treaty and Soviet acceptance of constraints on offensive and defensive systems are too complex to be encompassed by simple notions of negotiation from strength, whether Soviet or American, or economic pressure. For the purposes of this chapter, the key question is what changed Soviet views about the desirability of limiting defenses.

Among the explanations that could account for the Soviet change are those that focus on *learning,* and, especially, the role of *transnational alliances.* There is evidence, for example, that some prominent Soviet scientists, military officers, and political officials heard the views of their U.S. counterparts, and perhaps changed their minds, through meetings in groups such as Pugwash; the Soviet–American joint study group, organized by Paul Doty of Harvard; and the Dartmouth Conference (Garthoff, 1984; Newsom, 1987). One could argue that these individuals experienced cognitive structural learning as they became aware of the complexities and paradoxes of offense, defense, and crisis stability in the nuclear age. Some of the Soviet participants in international meetings, and others who followed the discussions from inside the Soviet Union, became *policy entrepreneurs* advocating arms control measures such as ABM restrictions (Sakharov, 1972:197–205).

The result of transnational alliances and policy entrepreneurship was to fashion a new domestic coalition that redefined Soviet national interests to include the pursuit of arms control and, in particular, limitations on Soviet ballistic missile defenses. The fact that not everyone in the Soviet security policy community accepted arguments about the destabilizing consequences of ABM (it is well to remember that not everyone accepts them in the United States today) has made a number of analysts unwilling, however, to maintain that the 1972 ABM Treaty constitutes Soviet *learning* (Blacker, 1989; Weber, 1989). *Military exigencies* appear to have played an important role, in that Soviet ABM technology was substantially inferior to that of the United States and, regardless of their views about stability, the Soviets would not have wanted to be on the losing side of an ABM race. Moreover, because the Soviets continued to pursue military programs that portended similarly destabilizing consequences (namely, multiple-warhead missiles with counterforce capabilities), many analysts deny that they grasped the essence of the arms controllers' critique of ABM (Blacker, 1989; Weber, 1989).

Coalition theory may account for the apparent inconsistency of the simultaneous Soviet pursuit of arms control and counterforce advantage—the argument being that Soviet policy resulted from a process of log-rolling (Snyder, 1987/1988). The apparent support that some officers of the Strategic Rocket Forces showed for the ABM Treaty—in particular by countering the claims of the Air Defense Forces, the service responsible for Soviet ballistic missile defenses (Parrott, 1987)—indicates the presence of particularly strange bedfellows of the sort that log-rolling interpretations would expect.

As George and his colleagues (1988:705) point out, once two sides have identified a mutuality of interests, bargaining strategies associated with *cooperation theory* become relevant to understanding subsequent outcomes. One possible outcome is the establishment of a regime. In the case of the SALT negotiations, the process of bargaining from the end of 1969 until SALT II was signed in 1979 was clearly one of reciprocal concessions (Jensen, 1984). Although the pattern was not regular enough to represent tit-for-tat, it suggested that concessions were mostly met with concessions. In general, there were few retractions; those that occurred sometimes precipitated a period of nonreciprocating behavior, but in other cases the Soviet Union would respond to a hardening of the U.S. negotiating position by increasing its rate of concessions (Jensen, 1984:539–541). It appears evident that the SALT treaties did not result from a GRIT strategy, in which one side makes a series of moderately risky concessions in order to break the cognitive barriers of the other side's leaders and convince them of its willingness to cooperate. Both sides seemed to recognize a mutuality of interests by 1969, despite actions such as the U.S. escalation of the war in Vietnam and the Soviet invasion of Czechoslovakia that should have reinforced stereotypical enemy images.

MILITARY DOCTRINE

Despite apparently successful bargaining strategies that resulted in the SALT treaties, Robert Jervis has argued that SALT did not evolve into a *regime*. His notion of a regime is based on the Concert of Europe, which lasted from 1815 until the outbreak of the Crimean War in 1854. Jervis calls the Concert "the best example of a security regime," because "the regime influenced the behavior of the states in ways that made its continuation possible even after the initial conditions had become attenuated [as early as 1823]" (1983:178, 181–182). In the case of U.S. and Soviet security policy, Jervis argues that one cannot speak of a regime that constrained state behavior. Even within the limitations posed by the SALT treaties, both sides continued unilaterally to pursue military doctrines aimed at achieving "war-fighting," counterforce advantages. The core problem is that each "state may believe that its security requires making others insecure" by threatening their retaliatory capabilities (Jervis, 1983:191). Thus there is no basis for a security regime.

Jervis calls particular attention to the problems posed by Soviet military doctrine: "If the Soviets believe that in order to deter American expansionism or cope with an American attack they need the capability to come as close as possible to military victory, then, even if they do not think that their security requires infringing on U.S. vital interests, forming a security regime will be extremely difficult" (Jervis, 1983:191). Jervis, in keeping with many analysts of Soviet military policy, singles out the apparent contradiction—that Soviet officials of the Brezhnev era refused to recognize—between the goals of preventing a nuclear war and preparing to wage one (Holloway, 1983:55–58). It is worth considering, then, the extent to which Soviet military doctrine of the Brezhnev period did inhibit the formation of a security regime that would serve to moderate Soviet (and U.S.) policy.

Although the tension between the deterrent and war-fighting aspects of Soviet military doctrine was never resolved during the Brezhnev era (Kokoshin, Sergeev, and Tsymburskii, 1988), there were significant doctrinal changes. In particular, the Soviets rejected pursuit of their long-declared goal of military superiority in favor of parity; they unilaterally foreswore the first use of nuclear weapons; and they denied the possibility of victory in a nuclear war. How can one confidently judge such declaratory policies as signifying meaningful change? The problem is especially acute when the characteristics of the Soviet nuclear force posture permit analysts to argue that it supports a strategy of preemptive attack aimed at victory and that in several important numerical indices it is superior to the U.S. force. In this view, the declaratory statements are false and intentionally misleading.

The means traditionally used to resolve this dilemma are rather eclectic. First, one seeks to determine whether the public statements disavowing superiority, first use, and victory are consistent with internal, nonpublic, especially military, sources. Then, one looks to evidence from the record of arms negotiations and the Soviet nuclear force posture itself for further corroboration.

In June 1982, Leonid Brezhnev made a formal, unilateral pledge that the Soviet Union would not be the first to use nuclear weapons. It seems clear, in retrospect, that the decision was taken many years earlier. In the early 1970s the Soviet military evidently was instructed to base its planning on the assumption that the Soviet Union would use nuclear weapons only if an opponent used them first. According to a 1975 article in *Military Thought,* the confidential journal of the Soviet General Staff, the military "was guided by the instructions of the Central Committee of the CPSU [Communist Party of the Soviet Union] that the Soviet Union shall not be the first to employ nuclear weapons" (quoted in Garthoff, 1987:42). In subsequent years, indications of the no-first-use decision appeared in other authoritative Soviet military publications, although Western analysts did not appreciate their significance at the time. In the key article on "Military Strategy" in the *Soviet Military Encyclopedia*, for example, Marshal Nikolai Ogarkov described the principle of no-first-use as the foundation of Soviet military strategy (Garthoff, 1987:44).

Further evidence for the seriousness of the Soviet no-first-use pledge comes from a combination of the strategic logic of the Soviet Union's military situation and the character of its force development since the 1960s. Unlike the United States, which relies on the threat of first use of nuclear weapons to help deter a Soviet conventional attack against its European allies, the Soviet Union does not require such "extended deterrence." Soviet territory is contiguous with that of its Warsaw Pact allies. Therefore the Soviet Union can rely directly on defense of those territories against a conventional invasion. While the U.S. first-use policy risks Soviet nuclear retaliation in the event of a European war, the Soviet Union can at least put the onus to escalate on U.S. decision makers by foreswearing first use. No-first-use appears to make strategic sense for the Soviet Union.

The trend in development of Soviet military forces presents evidence both consistent and inconsistent with a no-first-use policy. Since the late 1960s, the Soviet Union has invested enormous sums to improve its conventional forces, intending them to meet any contingencies short of nuclear war. At the same time, according to the Central Intelligence Agency (CIA), the growth rate of spending on Soviet strategic nuclear forces has evidently stagnated (Kaufman, 1985, 1988; MccGwire, 1987). For some analysts, the serious attention paid to conventional capabilities demonstrates an intent to avoid nuclear escalation; in their view, a no-first-use policy contributes to that goal as well. That the Soviets were willing to cap the growth of their missile force through arms control appears to support this reasoning. One must, however, consider important counterarguments. Even though spending on the strategic arsenal and the growth rate of the missile force itself flattened out, the counterforce capabilities of Soviet strategic forces nevertheless increased substantially during the 1970s and 1980s through the process of putting multiple warheads (MIRVs—or multiple, independently targetable reentry vehicles) on a fixed number of missiles.

For many analysts, the presence of considerable Soviet counterforce potential belies a no-first-use policy. This argument is not entirely sound, however. Certainly a Soviet minimum deterrent force of clearly retaliatory weapons would appear more compatible with no first use. Yet counterforce does not presume first use. Reasoning by analogy to the U.S. case might give that impression, in that U.S. pursuit of counterforce has often been justified as a means of enhancing the credibility of extended deterrence (the threat of nuclear first use). The Soviets, however, have probably pursued counterforce for different reasons, most prominently perhaps for "damage limitation." In this reading, they would not equate *preemption* with first use, because they would intend to launch their weapons only after unambiguous evidence of a U.S. decision to initiate nuclear use. Of course, no U.S. decision maker would feel reassured to know that Soviet nuclear restraint depended on the accuracy of Soviet leaders' perceptions of U.S. intentions in the heat of a major conventional war. Moreover, the fact that one has to delve so deeply into the arcana of Soviet nuclear strategy to make no first use appear consistent with the pursuit of counterforce capabilities makes it easily understandable why the Soviet pledge was not taken as evidence of moderation.

Even if the Soviet no-first-use pledge were accompanied by the "de-MIRVing" of missiles and reduction down to a few hundred systems, the simultaneous strengthening of offensively oriented conventional forces would continue to raise doubts about what constitutes moderation. Apparently the Soviet conventional buildup was intended to enable Soviet forces to destroy NATO nuclear weapons with nonnuclear attacks at the outset of a war to prevent nuclear escalation. Such a strategy could, however, have the opposite effect. NATO military leaders might fear an early loss of their nuclear weapons and press their political superiors to give them more flexibility in deciding when to use them. In a crisis situation, the offensive Soviet conventional posture could bring about the outcome—nuclear escalation—that the no-first-use policy was supposed to prevent (Lebow, 1985; Snyder, 1987/1988:123–124).

Should the no-first-use pledge be considered a sign of moderation at all? In particular, did the Soviet leadership intend the pledge to signify moderation? Here the arguments again cut both ways. The timing of the pledge was clearly designed to affect *public opinion* and, in particular, to help derail the NATO decision to deploy new U.S. missiles in Europe. Hypothetically, the United States could have called the Soviet Union's bluff by insisting on operational changes in strategic and conventional forces that would appear more compatible with a no-first-use posture. If any of these were forthcoming, the pledge could have evolved into a series of reciprocal initiatives of restraint, as the previous discussion of public opinion suggested. Yet NATO and the United States had no interest in bolstering the credibility of a Soviet no-first-use pledge for fear of undermining the U.S. commitment to use nuclear weapons first in defense of its European allies ("flexible response").

The significance of the pledge as a gesture of restraint *from the Soviet perspective* should not be dismissed simply because no first use makes strategic sense for the Soviet Union and creates problems for NATO doctrine. Many analysts believe that it makes sense for the United States and NATO as well (Bundy, et al., 1982; Steinbruner and Sigal, 1983). The Soviets clearly see the U.S. threat of first use as a hostile posture; presumably they would view a U.S. no-first-use pledge as a sign of moderation and considered their own pledge in the same light, despite the anticipated propaganda benefits. Brezhnev evidently did not find it easy to make the Soviet policy public, judging by the near decade that separated the secret Central Committee decision from the public announcement. The 1982 unilateral pledge prompted some criticism in Soviet military circles along with demands for further strengthening conventional forces and nuclear readiness (Tetekin, 1982; Ustinov, 1983). If the pledge were intended for propaganda purposes alone, one would not anticipate such a reaction.

THE SALT AGREEMENTS

One can find evidence in the internal Soviet literature, including *Military Thought* (Garthoff, 1987), for a change in Soviet doctrine toward rejection of both victory in nuclear war and superiority as a goal of Soviet policy. Evidence from Soviet negotiating behavior and force posture is somewhat more ambiguous, however, but points in the same direction. The issue here is whether the Soviets accepted the principle of numerical parity and whether they were willing to constrain their counterforce capabilities to the extent necessary to dispel concerns that they believed in the possibility of military victory in nuclear war.

Michael MccGwire (1987) maintains that by the late 1960s the Soviets came to accept an ICBM force equal in size to the U.S. one and that this entailed cutting the annual production rate of their missiles by 60 percent. He argues further that "in the course of the SALT negotiations, the Soviets accepted a cap on 'heavy' ICBMs that was probably 40 percent less than they had originally planned" (MccGwire, 1987:269). This argument is plausible, although it depends on assumptions about planned Soviet missile production runs that we cannot know for certain. Raymond Garthoff argues in a similar fashion that the Soviets signaled their willingness to constrain their forces during the SALT I negotiations by curtailing construction of ICBM forces already underway. He points out that the Soviet Union started launch sites for at most 80 new missiles during the 2½ years of the negotiations, compared to some 250 to 350 new launchers in each of the preceding 3 years (Garthoff, 1985:183). These arguments focus perhaps too extensively on launchers to the neglect of warheads. As with the United States a few years earlier, the stabilization of numbers of Soviet launchers coincided with the process of "MIRVing" the missiles, thereby increasing the number of warheads and the overall counterforce threat.

Looking specifically at the SALT treaties, one does nevertheless find evidence to support the arguments of MccGwire and Garthoff that the Soviets did constrain their counterforce capabilities more than they would have done in the absence of an agreement. By limiting their SS-18 force to 308 missiles with 10 warheads each in the SALT II treaty, and at the same time allowing the United States to deploy MX missiles in a mobile mode, as was then envisioned, the Soviets gave up the possibility of destroying the U.S. land-based missile force in a counterforce attack: they simply would not have enough warheads to barrage the mobile force. Even if the Soviets intended to limit the SS-18 force to a few hundred missiles, they need not have deployed only 10 MIRVs on each: the missiles are apparently capable of carrying two or three times that many—although perhaps not with the same degree of accuracy. By accepting the overall limits of SALT II and the restrictions on antiballistic missile systems from SALT I, in combination with the characteristics of the U.S. force posture (thousands of warheads on invulnerable submarines, plus the possibility of deploying mobile land-based missiles), the Soviet political leadership acknowledged the impossibility of achieving a meaningful damage-limitation capability. The Soviets could not expect to launch a first strike against U.S. forces without suffering tens of million of casualties in retaliation (Levi, von Hippel, and Daugherty, 1987/1988). The Soviet military nevertheless appear to have pursued damage limitation within the constraints posed by the SALT agreements and budgetary considerations, thus encouraging U.S. observers to dismiss the political renunciation of victory and superiority as propaganda.

It may be, as Jervis suggests (1983:191–192), that the U.S. perception of Soviet military doctrine as committed to victory in nuclear war posed a major barrier to making SALT into a security regime. Ironically, however, the Soviet political leaders seem to have desired to establish a regime to sanction their own doctrinal changes, such as the principle of no first use. As Garthoff (1987) describes, the Soviets made persistent efforts to get the United States to agree to a bilateral no-first-use pledge. The issue was raised once unsuccessfully during the SALT negotiations at the end of 1970; subsequently efforts were pursued through unpublicized diplomatic contacts between Henry Kissinger and Soviet Ambassador Anatolii Dobrynin, and later through a series of Soviet, Warsaw Pact, and United Nations proposals (Garthoff, 1985:182, 335; Garthoff, 1987). The latter proposals were presumably intended to influence *public opinion* and fulfilled in part a propaganda function, whereas the backchannel overtures to Kissinger probably represented a more serious attempt to solicit U.S. interest in a bilateral no-first-use pledge. In any case, the importance that the Soviets attached to this initiative—as well as to those "paper agreements" that were achieved, such as the 1973 statement on Prevention of Nuclear War—suggests that the political leadership believes in the constraining power of principles, norms, and rules associated with *se-*

curity regimes. That they were willing to be constrained themselves is suggested by their later adoption of a no-first-use pledge unilaterally and its apparent use as a tool for reorienting Soviet military doctrine and forces to prevent nuclear escalation. No first use would no doubt have been easier for Brezhnev to impose domestically if it had been sanctioned by an international regime.

Condoleezza Rice has made the argument, contrary to Jervis's views, that the SALT agreements can be considered part of a limited security regime. She identifies three principles on which the regime was based: (1) "acceptance of parity as a virtually irreversible condition;" (2) "the recognition of mutual vulnerability as an objective technological fact of the nuclear age;" and (3) the offense-defense link: "the recognition that the acquisition of defensive weapons would drive the other side to acquire more offensive firepower in order to overwhelm the defense" (Rice, 1988:297). In support of her view that the SALT regime actually constrained unilateral decisions, or short-range self-interest, as Jervis (1983:186–187) or Nye (1987:396) would put it, Rice points to several pieces of evidence. First, in implementing the accord, the Soviet Union removed over 1,200 land-based and submarine-based strategic missiles and 20 strategic missile-carrying submarines (SSBNs); the United States dismantled 8 Polaris SSBNs. Second, the SALT subceilings constrained the Soviet military from developing an optimal counterforce posture. Third, both sides have complied with the main provisions of SALT II, even though the treaty was never ratified. Moreover, until 1986, the Reagan administration, despite its evaluation of the SALT treaties as "fatally flawed," agreed not to undercut the treaty so long as the Soviets abided by its limits. As Rice points out, "the existence of this unratified treaty made the President's job of breaking out of the SALT limitations very difficult" (1988:298–299). Even when the administration moved to exceed the SALT limits, and especially with its plans eventually to violate the ABM treaty by testing and deploying a strategic defense system, the SALT regime had a constraining role. As Rice argues, the administration was at pains to justify "its decision to break out of the treaty limits through a skillfully orchestrated campaign of charges that the Soviets have already violated the treaty" (Rice, 1988:299). It was considered necessary, at least for the sake of *public opinion,* to demonstrate that it was the Soviet Union that defected from the regime first (Rice, 1988:299).

Three additional factors relevant to consideration of SALT as a security regime pertain to *learning,* particularly in its institutional definition. First, SALT created or reinforced domestic institutions and processes favorable to a continuation of the regime. The U.S. Congress, NATO allies, and until 1986, the Joint Chiefs of Staff argued for continued compliance with the SALT limitations (Rice, 1988:298). Second, as Keohane and Nye (1987:751) might argue, SALT contributed to "incremental" learning by changing the standard operating procedures of national bureaucracies. In the Soviet Union, for example, new institutions, such as the General Staff's Legal and Treaty Department, were set up to monitor Soviet military programs to ensure compliance (Rice, 1988:299). Third, the SALT process established *transnational alliances* with the potential to enhance compliance in the face of recalcitrant governments. In the view of Keohane and Nye, such "new coalition opportunities" are the product of regimes, which also contribute to incremental learning by providing "information about compliance with rules, which facilitates learning about others' behavior" (1987:751). Whether the use of the term "learning" to describe these various processes risks reifying the concept is an open question. Much of the behavior that proponents of learning approaches find relevant does, however, appear to be present in the case of SALT.

There are a number of good examples of *transnational alliances* working to maintain the arms control achievements of the 1970s and to continue the process. After the Soviets broke off official negotiations with the United States in late 1983, following deployment of new U.S. missiles in Europe, semi-private delegations of prominent arms control supporters on each side continued to meet to discuss possible ways out of the impasse (Stewart, 1987; Mattison, 1987). More recently, Soviet proponents of arms control have attempted tacit cooperation with the U.S. Congress to make sure that the research program of the Reagan administration's Strategic Defense Initiative (SDI) did not exceed the limits of the ABM treaty. Soviet science advisers, notably Evgenii Velikhov, persuaded the Soviet leadership to allow a U.S. congressional delegation to visit the Krasnoiarsk radar—suspected of being a violation of the ABM treaty—in order to improve the domestic climate for arms restraint in the United States. Given the close attention that Congress had paid to SDI and the question of treaty compliance up to that time (Crawford and Hildreth, 1987), it was reasonable for such *policy entrepreneurs* as Velikhov and his U.S. "allies" to hope that such a dramatic initiative would have some impact on the U.S. domestic debate (Huber, 1989:122–124). It could, for example, have been expected to create a *policy window* that would improve prospects for restraining SDI. In the event, however, the outcome of the Krasnoiarsk visit was indeterminate. Experts in the U.S. delegation found Soviet claims of a space-tracking role for the radar implausible, but dismissed as well the Pentagon's claim that the system would be useful for "battle management" as part of a nationwide ballistic missile defense system. They found it best suited for early warning of a missile attack, although they were not particularly impressed with its capabilities even in this area (*New York Times,* 7 September 1987). Finally, the transnational alliance succeeded: the Soviets admitted that the radar violated the treaty and agreed to tear it down. Subsequent coordinated efforts by Soviet and U.S. entrepreneurs have been equally successful: visits by U.S. delegations to top-secret Soviet laser test ranges and laboratories have revealed far less relevance and capability for ABM purposes than the Pentagon had claimed (von Hippel and Cochran, 1989).

Despite the apparent compatibility of the SALT legacy with aspects of theories of regimes and learning, Rice argues that SALT was only a *limited* regime. In her view, it never succeeded in providing a set of *norms* around which the two sides' expectations converged (see also Weber, 1989; Blacker, 1989)—an important component of the generally accepted definition of regime (Krasner, 1983). On the other hand, she does describe the maintenance of parity as an example of agreed expectations: "since arms control is premised on the implicit understanding that neither side will accept inferiority, periodic demonstrations of resolve in defending parity should be expected" (Rice, 1988:297). In Rice's assessment, the recognition that each side was obliged to maintain parity—because the achievement of parity itself was a condition for successful negotiation of the treaties—introduced "a self-reinforcing dynamic into the agreement" (Rice, 1988:296–297). The problem is that by basing the regime on such an ambiguous notion as parity, the parties to the SALT treaties opened the way for persistent accusations that each was striving to overturn parity and achieve superiority (Holloway, 1983:48–55). In the atmosphere of deteriorating relations in the late 1970s and early 1980s, the delicate balance of cooperation and competition inherent in the maintenance of a regime based on parity could not be sustained.

Ironically, the desire to maintain parity was, in Rice's view, both the motivation for and the demise of the SALT regime. Unlike Jervis, who argued that the superpowers were sufficiently confident in the stability of mutual deterrence to rule out the need for a regime, Rice maintains that from the Soviet vantage point, "the fact of mutual deterrence was not deemed to be enough. . . . [T]he real demand for the regime stemmed from the realization that mutual deterrence needed to be codified" (Rice, 1988:296). The codification of parity was important politically for domestic purposes—to give Brezhnev a justification to contain military spending—and for reasons of international prestige. Jervis, by contrast to Rice, doubts "whether there will ever be strong political pressures in favor of a regime unless there is dramatic evidence that individualistic security policies are leading to disaster" (Jervis, 1983:194).

The Gorbachev Era

The period since Mikhail Gorbachev came into office in March 1985 provides an important body of evidence against which to evaluate competing theories of change in Soviet security policy. Changes in both word and deed indicated a shift toward greater moderation in Soviet policy and greater interest in cooperation. Starting in the mid-1980s, Soviet officials began to acknowledge publicly the existence of a security dilemma—the fact that actions intended as defensive by one side are often interpreted as offensive by the other (Litherland, 1986). Gorbachev (1986*b*:25) himself renounced the "egoistical attempts to strengthen one's security at another's expense" that Jervis (1983) had identified as a barrier to establishment of a U.S.—Soviet security regime. The language reflects what the Soviets call the "new thinking" about the nature of national security.

Soviet analysts credit the new thinking with several major precedents in Soviet arms control policy under Gorbachev, including: the agreement eliminating all U.S. and Soviet intermediate- and shorter-range nuclear missiles, known as the INF treaty; extensive on-site verification procedures associated with that treaty; the unilateral moratorium on nuclear testing that the Soviet Union maintained for 19 months without U.S. reciprocation; the invitation for Western scientists to set up seismic monitoring equipment adjacent to Soviet nuclear test sites to verify the moratorium (Schrag, 1989); the unilateral reduction of 500,000 Soviet troops and 10,000 tanks; the willingness to consider further asymmetrical reductions and restructuring of conventional forces in Europe; the Soviet withdrawal from Afghanistan; and greater Soviet interest in international organizations such as the United Nations, the World Bank, and the International Monetary Fund. In order to understand the relationship between the changes in word and the changes in deed, and how the various explanations account for both types, we should examine issue-areas that encompass both rhetoric and action.

MILITARY DOCTRINE

In the Soviet Union changes in military doctrine are often articulated at the highest level before they are fully developed and implemented. The changes under Gorbachev fit this pattern. At the Twenty-Seventh Party Congress in 1986, Gorbachev (1986*a*) announced that "reasonable sufficiency" should serve as the criterion for the Soviet military posture, but he did not explicitly define the term. Many civilian analysts and politicians were quick to interpret sufficiency as a less demanding alternative to the strict maintenance of parity that had characterized Soviet objectives during the SALT period (Zhurkin, Karaganov, and Kortunov, 1987; Garthoff, 1988). Military officials, by contrast, were more reluctant to renounce parity and were more inclined to make Soviet moderation contingent on comparable U.S. behavior (Garthoff, 1988; Phillips and Sands, 1988; Parrott, 1988).

A second important change in Soviet doctrine is the emphasis on preventing war as its primary goal. Although this change has in some respects been an evolutionary one, the magnitude of the transformation is suggested by a comparison of authoritative statements on military doctrine from the early 1970s with those of the Gorbachev period. In 1971, for example, Marshal Andrei Grechko, Soviet defense minister at the time, described Soviet doctrine as "a system of scientifically founded and officially endorsed views on questions of the preparation and the victorious waging of war in defense of the interests of the Soviet Union and the countries of the socialist commonwealth" (quoted in Garthoff, 1988:137). Gorbachev's defense minister, Army General Dmitrii Iazov, by contrast, stressed that Soviet military doctrine is "a system of fundamental views on the *prevention of war*" as well as the waging of it (Garthoff, 1988:136–137, emphasis added). In May 1987, the Warsaw Pact issued a declaration that its military doctrine, as well as that of the Soviet Union itself, "is *subordinated* to the task of preventing war, nuclear and conventional," a point also emphasized by Iazov (quoted in Garthoff, 1988:137, emphasis added).

A third change relevant to Soviet military doctrine is consistent with the emphasis on preventing war, but has deeper roots and broader implications for Soviet foreign policy as a whole. In a sharp, ideological departure from official rhetoric, Soviet analysts and political leaders have spoken of the need for "all-human values," most notably the preservation of peace, to take precedence over the narrower interests of class struggle (Shenfield, 1987; Shevardnadze, 1988; Lynch, 1989). This new formulation has evident implications for U.S.–Soviet competition in the Third World, but it also implies a willingness to cooperate on a wide range of issues in order to strengthen the foundations of "mutual security." Soviet officials have emphasized the necessity of resolving the security dilemma through such cooperative policies. They stress the importance of norms, principles, and trust in international relations (Dobrynin, 1986; Falin, 1988; Gorbachev, 1987; Iakovlev, 1987, 1988; Shevardnadze, 1988).

Soviet officials have clearly begun to use the language of *regime theory* to express their preferences for the evolution of the U.S.–Soviet security relationship. Their rhetoric does not, of course, mean that one can speak of the existence of a security regime under Gorbachev. Regime theory is nevertheless useful for understanding the likely goals of Gorbachev and his civilian advisers. They appear to want to embed Soviet security policy in an international regime in order to justify restraints on their own military policy—much as Brezhnev would have liked an international sanction for his no-first-use pledge. This goal is one possible interpretation of the Warsaw Pact's offer to NATO of mutual consultation on the military doctrines of the two alliances

(*Pravda,* 30 May 1987). Subsequently, representatives of 85 countries met in Vienna in early 1990 for a doctrinal "seminar." Such initiatives make even the operational aspects of Soviet military doctrine a subject of international political scrutiny, and therefore the responsibility of Soviet diplomats rather than the narrow purview of the Soviet military. An international regime that created expectations that military doctrine would be open to examination by the Soviet Union's adversaries—as a means of alleviating the security dilemma—would also widen the scope for participation by other Soviet analysts from outside the uniformed military, including natural and social scientists (Kokoshin, 1988c). It would be consistent with calls by prominent Soviet political figures for civilian academic analysts to become more involved in studying Soviet military doctrine (Dobrynin, 1986; Iakovlev, 1987; Shevardnadze, 1988). Civilian reformers have also called explicitly for international—and transnational—cooperation in a program of conversion of military industry to civilian purposes. Although such measures could be carried out unilaterally, Soviet reformers seek international participation—including publication of national plans and development of joint proposals—deliberately in order to gain leverage over the Soviet military whom they do not trust to oversee the demilitarization of the Soviet economy (Izyumov, 1988; Melman, 1989; Vasilchuk, 1989).

Western analysts are generally not satisfied with declaratory changes in Soviet military doctrine or mere proposals from reformist intellectuals. They seek evidence in actual Soviet behavior, preferably in force posture or—if it is too early to identify operational indicators of doctrinal changes—in positions taken in arms negotiations (which eventually affect force posture). In looking for signs of substantive change in Soviet security policy under Gorbachev, analysts would expect to find more than the tacit acceptance of mutual societal vulnerability that characterized the SALT regime. In Soviet arms control proposals, for example, one would expect to see evidence of greater willingness to limit those forces that appear threatening to the U.S. side, a less rigid adherence to "parity" as the main objective of the accords, and a decrease in the propensity to interpret parity in ways that favor the Soviet side at the expense of the United States. All of these characteristics are apparent in the rhetoric of Gorbachev and his advisers, and the emerging evidence from the arms proposals themselves seems generally consistent.

THE START TALKS

One sign of willingness to take U.S. concerns into account is the Soviet acceptance of deep cuts in the SS-18 force (for details of the negotiations, see Hardenbergh, 1985–1990). In his memoirs, Andrei Gromyko, Soviet foreign minister at the time, described the Carter administration's March 1977 proposal for a 50 percent reduction of Soviet heavy SS-18 missiles as "not only unacceptable, but absurd" (Gromyko, 1988, vol. 2:218). Gromyko's opinion probably never changed, but with the advent of Gorbachev, Soviet negotiators began to accept such reductions as part of an agreement in the Strategic Arms Reduction Talks (START). At the 1986 summit meeting in Reykjavik, Marshal Sergei Akhromeev, then chief of the Soviet General Staff, apparently offered explicitly to cut the SS-18 force in half, a position confirmed in subsequent Soviet statements (Garthoff, 1988:136). Despite this offer, however, some Western analysts, including General Brent Scowcroft, expressed concern that a START agreement would give the Soviets counterforce advantages over the United States by decreasing the ratio of vulnerable U.S. targets to accurate Soviet warheads (Hardenbergh, 1987:611.B.429; 1988: 611.C.53–54).

There is a fundamental problem inherent in scrutinizing Soviet arms proposals for evidence of a decision to deemphasize the pursuit of counterforce advantages. In some respects the only indisputable evidence would be a shift to a minimum deterrent force, manifested by Soviet willingness to take deep asymmetrical cuts in their most potent counterforce weapons (something that could actually be done without an arms control quid pro quo from the U.S. side). Gorbachev would, presumably, have great difficulty carrying out such a unilateral restructuring, even if he wanted to do so. For one thing, most of the existing Soviet missile force possesses the technical capability for counterforce attacks, and the Soviets could hardly be expected to build a new retaliatory force of inaccurate, single-warhead missiles. Here *economic stringency* as a factor influencing Soviet moderation plays an ambiguous role. On the one hand, Gorbachev wants arms agreements as a way to signal the Soviet military to reduce their demands for future weapons. On the other hand, to satisfy its negotiating partner by building a new missile force that would lower the U.S. perception of threat would be prohibitively expensive.

The START negotiations are unlikely to yield an unambiguous Soviet minimum deterrent force. Studies of bargaining strategies associated with *cooperation theory* suggest that a treaty would result from a series of moderate mutual concessions (Jensen, 1984) or from a pattern of tit-for-tat reciprocity (Axelrod, 1984). Given that the U.S. negotiating position assumes retention of extensive counterforce capabilities in the U.S. arsenal, it is doubtful that the positions of the two sides would converge around an agreement that would eliminate comparable Soviet capabilities. Looking at the domestic level of analysis reinforces this conclusion: any Soviet leader who tried to move to a minimum deterrent in the face of U.S. efforts to extend its own counterforce capabilities against Soviet forces would encounter considerable internal opposition. Evidence of such U.S. efforts is readily available. Even while negotiating for reductions in Soviet counterforce potential, the United States has continued developing earth-penetrating warheads to destroy the hardened facilities of the Soviet command and control system (*Wall Street Journal*, 13 September 1988). The U.S. Strategic Air Command has been revising its war plans to enhance its counterforce capabilities; it is particularly interested in destroying the Soviet leadership and in trying to find ways to target Soviet mobile missiles (*New York Times*, 2 November 1988, 23 November 1988). Finally, SDI is interpreted on the Soviet side, and by most U.S. analysts, as part of an offensive, counterforce strategy and, as such, it serves as an additional barrier to potential Soviet efforts to abandon counterforce—or even to carry out substantial reductions, given the possible future need for sufficient redundancy in retaliatory capability to overwhelm a defense.

The strategic arms negotiations will probably not produce evidence to convince diehard skeptics of a change toward moderation in Soviet military doctrine. This is in part, however, a question of self-fulfilling prophecies. As the literature on *tacit transnational alliances* would suggest, the proponents of counterforce strategies on the U.S. side reinforce the arguments of their counterparts on the Soviet side (Griffiths, 1984; Singer, 1984:245–271), especially when there is good evidence of official U.S. pursuit of counterforce. Or, as the Soviet poet Evgenii Evtushenko put it, "your hardliners help our hardliners, and our hardliners help your hardliners" (*Moscow News*, 23–30 October 1988). Hypothetically there is a possibility that the Soviet Union would make dramatic reductions in its counterforce capabilities as part of a GRIT strategy. Such a move would constitute an effort by conciliatory forces in the Soviet Union to form a tacit alliance with their counterparts in the United States, a possibility that a number of Soviet analysts have advocated and that has numerous historical precedents (Kokoshin, 1988d; Shevardnadze, 1988).

Initially it appeared that the "doves" on each side were too busy trying to maintain existing restraints on the arms race, such as the ABM treaty and the moratoria on testing antisatellite weapons, to consider promoting radical unilateral actions (Kokoshin, 1988c). Thus, the December 1988 announcement of unilateral conventional-force reductions took most analysts by surprise; it appears to have stemmed from proposals by academic policy advisers whose role had been generally underestimated in the West (U.S. House of Representatives, 1988, 1989; Meyer, 1988). Several prominent Soviet academics have now put forward proposals for a unilateral Soviet shift to a minimum nuclear deterrent posture, some even going so far as to argue that the threat of retaliation by only a few nuclear weapons would be enough to deter the United States (Bogdanov and Kortunov, 1989). These *policy entrepreneurs* are aware of the barriers to implementation of such a unilateral posture—indeed in some respect their work is inspired by the desire to make those barriers irrelevant. The difficulty of achieving deep reductions and reorientation toward a minimum deterrent via the arms-control route has, for example, spurred some analysts to advocate unilateral Soviet initiatives "without waiting for Washington to endorse our vision of the future" (Kortunov, 1989). The economic expense entailed in developing an unambiguous second-strike retaliatory force has led analysts to present imaginative proposals for working within the existing Soviet force structure to produce a comparable end. The plans focus on both the offensive and defensive components of counterforce by including reductions in the most destabilizing and redundant offensive systems (for example, MIRVed missiles), along with paring back air defenses and halting modernization of the Moscow ABM complex (Arbatov, 1988, 1989). Although proposals for a unilateral Soviet minimum deterrent have already generated strong opposition in the press (see, for example, Dvorkin and Torbin, 1989), they are now nevertheless on the agenda for further public debate. Despite the caveats raised above, we should not be surprised by future Soviet initiatives pointed in this direction. If the fact that such proposals are openly discussed in the Soviet Union today is not enough to persuade U.S. skeptics of meaningful change in Soviet security policy, the implementation of unilateral reductions of an order of magnitude might make a difference.

THE INF TREATY

For many analysts, the clearest evidence of change in Soviet security policy under Gorbachev was the INF treaty. A number of explanations have been put forward to account for Soviet acceptance of the "zero option" to eliminate U.S. and Soviet intermediate- and short-range missiles. They include military exigencies, economic stringency, and reaction to U.S. negotiation from strength. One could also imagine the Soviet signing of the INF treaty as part of a GRIT strategy to induce U.S. cooperation in other spheres, notably trade, or as part of a series of tit-for-tat gestures. In many respects, one's choice of explanation for this particular incident bears on one's interpretation of the overall degree of change in Soviet security policy.

Analysts who see Soviet acceptance of the zero option as a function of *military exigencies* attach little importance to the INF agreement as a herald of more fundamental change. They maintain that the INF treaty was in the Soviet Union's military interest and was firmly supported by the military because it removed the threat of the U.S. Pershing II missile (Larrabee, 1988:1022–1023). This analysis begs the question why the Soviets waited until Gorbachev came into office to accept the zero option, rather than doing so when West German Chancellor Helmut Schmidt suggested it in 1978, when NATO decided to deploy the new missiles in 1979, when the Reagan administration put forward the zero option in 1981, or when the first Pershing II missiles became operational in Europe in December 1983 (Risse-Kappen, 1988). The fact that the Pershing II missiles were removed made the INF treaty more palatable for the Soviet military, but it was not necessarily the most important reason for the agreement. The shift in Soviet negotiating behavior following Gorbachev's ascendancy lends particular weight to explanations that incorporate the role of new *leaders* (see, for example, Meyer, 1988).

What needs to be explained is why the Soviets were willing to accept unequal reductions in forces in 1987, whereas in the mid-1970s—long before the deployment of U.S. Pershing II and cruise missiles—they perceived a need to augment their forces by deploying the SS-20. A number of analysts have offered plausible explanations for the original deployment. They have called attention to Soviet preoccupation with U.S. forward-based systems (FBS) around Europe and the growing French and British nuclear forces (Berman and Baker, 1982; MccGwire, 1987; Gromyko, 1988, vol. 2:210). The Soviets have tried since the beginning of strategic arms negotiations to gain some compensation for these systems. Their deployment of the SS-20 as a counter to FBS can be understood in part as a consequence of their inability to eliminate the threat through arms control (Garthoff, 1983). While not every analyst agreed with this rationale for the SS-20 deployment, virtually no one predicted that the Soviets would be willing to do away with the missiles altogether.

Even though they did not predict Soviet acceptance of the zero option, some analysts maintain that the INF treaty and Gorbachev's overall arms control strategy are consistent with Soviet military requirements, but that the requirements themselves have changed. Thus, they downplay the importance of Gorbachev's leadership and doubt that he is pursuing a security agenda incompatible with military preferences. They argue that "Gorbachev's call for radical arms control can be justified within current Soviet military doctrine," owing to a new Soviet emphasis on conventional operations (FitzGerald, 1987:16). They maintain that "Gorbachev and the Soviet military are now in agreement on an arms control and nuclear weapons development program" (Weickhardt, 1987:24). A number of writers have called particular attention to the statements by Marshal Nikolai Ogarkov, former chief of the General Staff, denigrating the role of nuclear weapons and stressing the importance of advanced-technology conventional systems (Ogarkov, 1985:88–89). Yet Gorbachev's unilateral conventional-force reductions, military budget cuts, and disparaging remarks about Ogarkov's favored high-technology weapons (Gorbachev, 1987) would appear to call this interpretation into question.

Moreover, the argument that the Soviet elimination of the SS-20 and shorter-range missiles makes obvious strategic sense fails to account for the apparent uneasiness within the Soviet military and the public about the treaty. At the treaty ratification hearings, for example, General V.M. Arkipov, commander of the Moscow Military District, reported that some in the military "think we are weakening the country's defense capacity by the unequal reduction of those missiles," although he maintained that the majority supported the treaty (*Izvestiia*, 16 March 1988). Defense Minister Iazov also spoke at the hearings in support of the treaty, but he mentioned that "letters from the Soviet people are reaching the Ministry of Defense which express concern either directly or indirectly: will not harm be done to the security of the Soviet Union and the countries of the socialist community through the Soviet Union's destruction of more missiles under the treaty than are to be destroyed by the United States?" (*Krasnaia zvezda*, 10 February 1988; see also Utkin, 1988:6). It would not be surprising if much of this "opposition" to the treaty were intended primarily for foreign audiences, in order to exaggerate the extent of Soviet concessions. On the other hand, public opinion surveys conducted by foreign and Soviet polling organizations have also found considerable unhappiness with the treaty among the Soviet public (Carrère d'Encausse, 1987:48; Ivanov, 1987). Soviet citizens apparently expressed concern about the extensive verification of the agreement (Hardenbergh, 1988:403.B.622–623). One would expect members of the military to feel even more strongly about these issues. Furthermore, there was evidence of opposition to the treaty at the highest political levels, including from the head of the KGB and conservative Politburo members (Parrott, 1988:22–23).

The INF treaty provides a good case for illustrating how popular and academic explanations for moderation in Soviet security policy overlap. Implicit in some of the military arguments focusing on the Pershing II deployment is the argument that Soviet acceptance of the zero option was a product of U.S. *negotiation from strength*. A comparable argument in the academic literature on *cooperation theory* uses the notion of tit-for-tat to account for Soviet behavior. In this interpretation, the United States responded to a Soviet defection (deployment of SS-20) with a reciprocal defection (deployment of U.S. missiles). The low payoff from mutual defection induced the Soviets to try a cooperative move next time, by accepting the zero option. The United States reciprocated and the INF treaty resulted (Zimmerman and Jacobson, 1987). One problem with these arguments is that they fail to account for the timing of the Soviet decision. The first Pershing II missiles were deployed in December 1983 and the Soviets' initial reaction to this U.S. "defection" was another defection: they broke off the arms talks in Geneva. It was only during the summer of 1985, after Gorbachev came into office, that the Soviets began to make concessions leading to the final agreement (Evangelista, 1986). Another problem is the suggestion that the U.S. pursuit of a tit-for-tat strategy worked. Tit-for-tat cannot account for the Soviet concessions that brought about the treaty. On the basis of strict reciprocity, it would have predicted an endless spiral of mutual defections. We need an explanation that helps us understand why the Soviets abandoned tit-for-tat in order to secure the INF treaty.

One such explanation would view Gorbachev's initiatives as an example of GRIT. In this interpretation, Gorbachev sought to induce U.S. cooperation through a number of unilateral concessions, such as the 19-month test moratorium and the willingness to exclude French, British, and U.S. forward-based nuclear systems from an INF accord (Evangelista, 1988:275; Zimmerman and Jacobson, 1987). Zimmerman and Jacobson (1987) have argued that the INF treaty resulted from a U.S. strategy of tit-for-tat combined with a Soviet strategy of GRIT. They also draw the normative conclusion that the appropriate strategy for the United States as a status quo power is strict reciprocity, whereas the Soviet Union as an expansionist power must bear the burden of convincing its adversary of its good intentions through a series of multiple concessions.

Of course, status quo is in the eye of the beholder. That is the main insight of the literature on the security dilemma. In the case of INF, for example, the Soviet Union maintained that it was the Americans who upset the status quo; they violated the spirit of SALT II by deploying new "strategic" missiles in Europe that undercut the treaty's limitations. The SS-20s, according to this argument, were fully in keeping with the spirit of the treaty, even though they were not in any case formally limited by it: they were simply modernized versions of existing systems, the SS-4 and SS-5 (Garthoff, 1983; Garner, 1983). One also hears from the Soviet side the argument that the INF accord resulted from *Soviet strength,* that the SS-20s were bargaining chips intended to be cashed in to get an agreement on European systems (Haslam, 1989). A Soviet engineer who works at the Votkinsk plant that produced the SS-20 argued, for example, that "if we did not have these missiles, the West would not be talking with us on equal terms." Although he harbored some doubts about the INF treaty, he reassured himself "that we have sufficient strength left to make anyone see reason" (*Pravda,* 27 January 1988). The problem with the argument about Soviet strength and the use of SS-20 as a bargaining chip is that, even cashing in all their chips, the Soviets never achieved what they wanted: there are still no restrictions on FBS or British and French systems.

The popular arguments about negotiation from strength, U.S. or Soviet, as well as the academic arguments about tit-for-tat versus GRIT all fail to account for Gorbachev's INF initiatives. Why did he make the cooperative moves at all? Why did he not continue to respond with further defections, as his predecessors did by deploying "countermeasures" to the new U.S. systems (in the form of more missiles in Eastern Europe and submarines off the U.S. coast)? One argument, not inconsistent with negotiation from strength, is that Soviet concessions were a response to the threat of the U.S. Strategic Defense Initiative and an attempt to avoid a costly new arms race in space (McConnell, 1988; Zimmerman and Jacobson, 1987). This explanation would appear to account for the Soviets' decision to return to the negotiating table in 1984, even before Gorbachev came in, and for the fact that their willingness to return hinged on U.S. agreement to negotiate space weapons along with INF and strategic forces.

SDI undoubtedly figured prominently in Soviet calculations. Moreover, the Soviet Union's willingness to make concessions in its areas of strength (for example, land-based intermediate and strategic missiles) in return for curbing a new round of the technological arms race (in this case, SDI) has ample precedent (Evangelista, 1988; Bloomfield, Clemens, and Griffiths, 1966). Yet there is also precedent for the Soviets to respond to U.S. initiatives by developing their own analogous systems. Why have the Soviets under Gorbachev put so much rhetorical emphasis on asymmetrical responses to U.S. initiatives? Why have they stressed the need to meet military challenges by improving the economy rather than wasting resources on matching every U.S. weapon (Zhurkin, Karaganov, and Kortunov, 1987; Shevardnadze, 1988; Evangelista, 1989, 1990b)? It is difficult to avoid the conclusion that the "new political thinking" on security played some role in a number of Soviet decisions, including the acceptance of unequal cuts in intermediate-range nuclear forces and the rejection of a Soviet "Star Wars" system.

NEW THINKING

The closest academic counterpart to the popular notion of "new thinking" as an explanation for the changes in Soviet policy is the literature on *learning*. Indeed, much of the Soviet commentary about the new thinking refers explicitly to the failures of the Brezhnev policy and suggests that the new policies are a product of having learned from those difficult lessons (Primakov, 1987; Shevardnadze, 1988). The very language of the reformers appears to reinforce the inclination of some analysts to describe learning as a reaction and accommodation to "reality," in defiance of outmoded ideological preconceptions: an important Party document from 1988 reported that previous Soviet foreign policy "did not escape dogmatic and subjective attitudes. It trailed behind fundamental changes that occurred in the world" (Lynch, 1989:1). Gorbachev has argued that "life has corrected our notions of the laws and rates of transition to socialism, our understanding of the role of socialism on the world scale" (Lynch, 1989:36).

In some respects the academic debate about learning as an explanation for Gorbachev's security policy has fallen into the pattern of distinguishing changes in tactics from changes in long-term goals. Analysts who focus on *military exigencies*—for example, the signing of the INF treaty to eliminate the threat of Pershing II missiles—find only tactical adjustments in Soviet policy. Others stress the external function of new thinking in influencing *public opinion*. Given the extent to which the Soviets oriented their propaganda activities to prevent deployment of U.S. INF systems in the early 1980s (Haslam, 1989), it is not surprising that analysts interpreted acceptance of the zero option in the same light. With this background in mind, Joseph Nye made the case that only simple learning had taken place in Soviet policy. He understood Gorbachev's initiatives, including signing the INF treaty, as attempts to overcome the legacy of insensitivity to the impact of Soviet actions on the perceptions of adversaries. As Nye (1988:389–390) put it, "one need only compare the heavy-handed Soviet handling of the INF issue that united NATO in 1983 with the subtle dilemmas Gorbachev's agreement to remove nuclear weapons posed for NATO in 1987 to see the significant change that has occurred in tactical sophistication." This argument appears to assume that the Soviet Union's main goal, both in 1983 and in 1987, was to disrupt NATO. By Nye's definitions only simple learning (about tactics) had occurred. Complex learning had not taken place because the long-term objective of damaging NATO remained the same.

Some analysts do perceive more fundamental forms of learning in Gorbachev's security policy. Robert Legvold, for example, uses Nye's definitions, but comes to different conclusions, arguing that Gorbachev, in pursuit of arms control, has demonstrated "the beginning of complex learning. When he subordinates military values in choosing an arms control posture, as he apparently has in negotiating the INF agreement and in discussing strategic arms cuts at Reykjavik, he is altering basic Soviet *priorities*" (Legvold, 1988b:123, original emphasis). Using Tetlock's (1988) definitional distinctions, Blacker (1989) maintains that the Gorbachev changes represent both cognitive-content learning and efficiency learning; Weber (1989:49) finds evidence of cognitive structural learning in Gorbachev's acceptance of asymmetric and unilateral reductions and of intrusive verification of arms control treaties, and especially in his decision to "de-emphasize military force as a source of power in world politics"—all elements that contradict the "strategic model" that Weber believes guided previous Soviet security policy.

The debates about a learning *explanation* would be relatively easy to resolve if proving that learning had occurred required only that one demonstrate that changes in goals rather than merely tactics had taken place. As many analysts point out, the discussions in the Soviet press about Brezhnev's foreign policy and, in particular, the SS-20 decision do suggest a redefinition of Soviet goals and of the meaning of security itself (Blacker, 1989; Weber, 1989; Holloway, 1989; Evangelista, 1990b). As Foreign Minister Eduard Shevardnadze put it in criticizing the Soviet deployment of SS-20 and the reaction it triggered, "a second strategic front against us was created in Europe, not without our help. Its appearance could have been avoided if our genuine national interests at the time had been correctly evaluated" (Shevardnadze, 1988:37). The Brezhnev leadership had a conception of Soviet interests—and, by extension, goals—different from that of the reformers. Gorbachev understands what Brezhnev could not be made to understand: that by striving to achieve military gains, the Soviet Union can incur high political costs that ultimately undermine the putative security benefits of the original action. Gorbachev recognizes the corollary as well: there may be political benefits to be gained by sacrificing some military capability.

Many of the aspects of learning definitions that focus on individual cognition seem to apply to people such as Gorbachev and Shevardnadze, given how radically their world views and conceptions of Soviet national interests differ from those of their predecessors. Yet it is really appropriate to say that they learned? Neither man was responsible for Soviet foreign policy before 1985, and we have little evidence of their views about the subject before that time. They began implementing aspects of the new political thinking almost as soon as they assumed office. The thinking—in particular, the critique of the Brezhnev-era policy—may not have been new to them at all. If they were skeptical of the policy, but merely kept silent, then one cannot say that they learned. Nor did the policymakers who formulated Soviet foreign policy under Brezhnev learn. Rather, they were removed from office, they died, or—as in the case of former Foreign Minister Andrei Gromyko—both. In fact, Gromyko is a particularly important test of a learning explanation for the changes since 1985. In his memoirs published in 1988, he continued to defend the policies of the Brezhnev era (and the Stalin era, for that matter)—including, for example, the invasion of Afghanistan and Soviet arms control positions on the SS-18 and SS-20 missiles—policies that Gorbachev and Shevardnadze have criticized and reversed. Even after his retirement from the Foreign Ministry in 1985, Gromyko continued to express reservations about the new course from his position on the Politburo (Parrott, 1988).

The massive replacement of personnel in the foreign and security policy-making apparatus, combined with a long-awaited generational turnover (Parrott, 1988; Hough, 1988), make it difficult to sustain arguments that learning as an individual cognitive process accounts for change toward moderation in Soviet security policy since 1985. Recognizing the importance of these developments, proponents of the learning metaphor have tended to speak of learning at the level of the Soviet *government*, rather than in terms of individuals. If there were general agreement within the Soviet foreign policy community about the failures of Brezhnev's security policy, and if Gorbachev and his advisers were recruited for their alternative views, one might justifiably speak of governmental learning. Yet on both counts the evidence appears to point in the opposite direction. As Blacker (1989:48) argues, the pre-Gorbachev foreign policymakers did not acknowledge their mistakes:

> Given their own roles in the development of Soviet policy over the course of the preceding 10 or in some cases 20 years, as well as their identification with and commitment to the goals these policies had been designed to serve, it would have taken an extraordinary set of circumstances to induce these Brezhnev-era policymakers to abandon their handiwork. In their own view, no such set of circumstances had arisen, despite the admittedly troubled state of the Soviet economic, political, and social system.

It is not only retired policymakers who reject the criticism of the Brezhnev era and doubt the wisdom of the new thinking. The public debate on security policy in the Soviet Union since the advent of Gorbachev has continued to expand, providing ample evidence of the persistence of the "old thinking." Divergence in views between civilian reformers and military traditionalists is particularly striking (Phillips and Sands, 1988; Evangelista, 1989; Wallander, 1989). Even Politburo members openly express their disagreements about fundamental issues such as the relevance of class versus "all-human" values in international relations; whether there is any tension between the preservation of peace and the pursuit of socialism, and, if so, which should take precedence; and the relative merits of unilateral arms reductions versus negotiated ones versus none at all (Parrott, 1988; Holloway, 1989; Shenfield, 1987; Lynch, 1989). One careful analysis goes so far as to conclude that "the dedicated exponents of the new *thinking*, as opposed to just new language, appear to be limited to a very few politicians and advisors, judging by the analytical rather than the rhetorical content of what the Soviet leadership has been saying" (Lynch, 1989:53 original emphasis). One finds little evidence of a new, widely held "consensual knowledge" (Haas, 1980) about security affairs that would support notions of governmental learning as a source of the new thinking.

Nor can one speak of recruitment of new thinkers to replace the unsuccessful policymakers of the previous era, as a natural-selection version of learning might suggest. Foreign policy issues are rarely salient in any country for the selection of new leaders. Moreover, in the Soviet Union new leaders are not chosen on the basis of public opinion as expressed at the ballot box. The Communist Party Politburo and Central Committee members recruit their successors from within; they would not knowingly choose people who disagreed with their approach. Even if Gorbachev were chosen in anticipation that he would undertake major changes, his background—and the most pressing Soviet problems—was in domestic economic administration and agriculture. His ability to cope with those issues probably figured most prominently in his selection. To the extent that Gorbachev's colleagues took into consideration his views on Soviet security policy, they probably assumed that he would pursue what Bruce Parrott (1988) calls the "dual-track" approach of the Brezhnev era: expansion of Soviet military power as the ultimate guarantor of security, combined with efforts at arms-control negotiations to moderate the superpower competition. According to Parrott, the approach came under attack from Soviet hardliners in response to the worsening of relations with the United States that began during the Carter administration and intensified under Reagan. Gorbachev was expected to reestablish the consensus on a dual-track policy that had prevailed during the 1970s.

Another problem with a learning explanation for changes in Soviet security policy concerns the fact that a number of policy analysts appear to have held for a long time the views now associated with the new thinking. The works of Shenfield (1987) and Lynch (1987, 1989) persuasively demonstrate that many of the ideas associated with the new thinking appeared in academic studies dating back to the 1970s and earlier: the devaluation of the class factor in international relations, and the irrelevance of superiority and the meaninglessness of victory in nuclear war, for example. Zimmerman's (1969) work finds antecedents to these ideas even during the Khrushchev period—indeed many of the personalities associated with the ideas at that time cut a high profile in the Gorbachev administration today. Ideas about the long-term viability of capitalism and the nature of change in the Third-World—important components of the new thinking on security—also have a demonstrably long pedigree (Hough, 1986). Some Soviet analysts even claim to have warned the Brezhnev leadership about the deleterious effect of Soviet activity in the Third World on détente and arms control both long before and immediately after the invasion of Afghanistan (Bogomolov, 1988a, 1988b). This sensitivity to linkage between issue-areas in East–West relations is often identified as one of the characteristics of the new thinking. Recognition of the security dilemma and the need to abandon zero-sum thinking in favor of international cooperation, devaluation of the military instrument in foreign policy, and stress on economic interdependence—all of these ideas were expressed in somewhat muted form before Gorbachev came into office (see, for example, Burlatskii, 1982; Gromyko and Lomeiko, 1984; Arbatov, 1984).

The point is not to argue that academic policy analysts have not changed their views or "learned" anything since the 1970s. On the contrary, their job, by definition, is to develop an increasingly sophisticated and "realistic" interpretation of international politics. The fact is, however, that their "lessons"— about intervention in the Third World, and about insensitivity to the adversary's security concerns—were rejected by policymakers and continue to be rejected by prominent elements of the security-policy community today. Even so seemingly obvious a lesson as the unwinnability of nuclear war is subject to sharp, polemical disputes about its implications. The policy prescriptions that emerge from such competing interpretations are diametrically opposed (Grachev, 1988; Proektor, 1988; Grachev et al., 1989). Many Soviet political and military figures reject the basic lesson of the new thinkers that Soviet military policy under Brezhnev failed because it provoked a U.S. response. Arguing that "imperialism" is inherently militaristic, these analysts reject Soviet responsibility for the deterioration of détente, the acceptance of which is fundamental to Gorbachev's new approach (Grachev et al., 1989). Even the "lessons" of Afghanistan have not been learned by all: in 1989, a group of veterans of the war called for the Soviet government to send "volunteers" to help defeat the rebel forces still receiving U.S. military aid (Kondrashov, 1989).

Learning metaphors obscure what is fundamentally a political process of change toward moderation—one that is in no way irreversible. "Lessons" of the Brezhnev era have become instruments of Gorbachev's *coalition-building* strategy (Snyder, 1987/1988). The new thinkers are those *policy entrepreneurs* who have been promoting their ideas, albeit somewhat cautiously, since before Gorbachev's tenure began. Gorbachev has latched onto these ideas, which are probably compatible with his own instincts in any case, in order to redistribute the relative power of the institutions involved in formulating and carrying out Soviet security policy. In Meyer's (1988:129) words, "Gorbachev's agitation for new political thinking on security is more a product of instrumental necessity than of military-strategic enlightenment." As he himself has made clear on many occasions, Gorbachev views changes in Soviet security policy as a prerequisite for the successful implementation of his domestic reforms.

Thus, as Lynch (1989:3) argues, the new thinking "is first of all a political rather than an intellectual or conceptual act. It reflects preestablished political priorities of the Gorbachev leadership, which in turn has assiduously coopted strains of thinking—some of it actually new, much of it developed quietly by specialists during the Brezhnev period—which suits its purposes and long-term goals." These purposes and goals differ markedly from those of the Brezhnev leadership, except in the most abstract sense that all Soviet leaders seek to ensure the "security" and "well-being" of the Soviet Union, as they understand those notions. To argue that the Gorbachev changes constitute learning in the "efficiency" sense, one would have to make normative assumptions in favor of Gorbachev's goals over Brezhnev's—in particular, that it is "better" to emphasize economic, diplomatic, and political instruments in foreign policy, rather than military ones; that economic integration into the world capitalist system can achieve security and well-being more effectively than pursuit of military parity or superiority; and even that a détente relationship with the West is preferable to ideological, political, and military competition. Given that there is sharp disagreement on these issues among Soviet foreign policy influentials, it would be rash for an outside observer to stake the case for the validity of concepts such as learning on normative assumptions.

In this context, the various factors to which the Soviet changes have been attributed take on new meaning. The Reagan military buildup, the U.S. Strategic Defense Initiative, the costly Afghanistan war, the economic crisis in Poland, and the domestic situation in the Soviet Union, all could be seen as *policy windows* that allowed proponents of restraint in Soviet security policy to come to the fore. Their arrival was in no sense preordained, however, as use of the learning metaphor as well as the popular negotiation-from-strength arguments often imply. Here the focus on *leaders* is appropriate: "there is no reason to believe that Andropov or Chernenko (had they lived), or Romanov (had he been selected instead of Gorbachev) would have chosen to travel Gorbachev's path of doctrinal reform" (Meyer, 1988:128). In this sense, new leaders are a form of policy window as well.

Unlike explanations keyed to specific external factors—such as the Reagan administration policies or declining Soviet fortunes in the Third World—a focus on policy windows emphasizes the indeterminacy of outcomes. The case of the Strategic Defense Initiative provides a good example of how *policy entrepreneurs* try to take advantage of such factors. According to most technical assessments, SDI poses at most a long-term threat to the Soviet Union, mainly in the form of possible technological spin-offs to other weapons systems. Yet Soviet proponents of moderation could see how sectors of the Soviet military might demand an immediate response. Already in the mid-1970s, some military officers and scientists tried to reopen the debate on strategic defenses that was ostensibly settled by the 1972 ABM treaty (Parrott, 1987:32–35; Velikhov, 1988). In the wake of the Reagan administration's strong anti-Soviet rhetoric, military demands for more resources became increasingly strident—even before Reagan's announcement of SDI in March 1983 (Parrott, 1987:45–52). Soviet reformers portrayed SDI as a U.S. plan to bankrupt the Soviet Union by forcing it into a futile and wasteful technological arms race. For them this was a familiar pattern of past U.S.–Soviet competition. But this time they were able to put forward their alternatives, thanks to a new, sympathetic general secretary.

Proponents of Soviet moderation used SDI as a window in two respects—

first, they made the case for asymmetrical responses as a cheaper alternative to emulation of the U.S. program, and second, they argued that economic modernization was necessary now in order to compete with U.S. advanced military technology in the future (Evangelista, 1986). Emboldened by their apparent success in convincing Gorbachev to embrace their alternatives, the reformers opened the window wider. Now they advocated asymmetrical responses to a broad range of military threats, in effect enshrining a new general principle of Soviet security policy; they criticized strict adherence to parity in favor of "reasonable sufficiency;" and they promoted unilateral gestures of restraint explicitly modeled on the Khrushchev troop reductions (Zhurkin, Karaganov, and Kortunov, 1987). Instead of hinting that economic reform would favor a future high-technology Soviet military machine, they began to downplay the value of the military instrument altogether and to stress that economic strength in itself makes the biggest contribution to security (Evangelista, 1989). They began to imply that if the U.S. goal were to bankrupt the Soviet Union with an arms race, then the less the Soviets spent on the military the better. As Shevardnadze put it (1988:36), "we have agreed that war cannot be a rational means of politics. But couldn't the arms race be such a means? However paradoxical it seems—it can. Yes, the arms race can exhaust and bleed the opponent dry, with the goal of undermining its very economic and social base."

Economic stringency clearly plays a role in the efforts of Gorbachev and his supporters. If the Soviet economy were growing at a robust rate, proponents of moderation would have a more difficult time denying the military the chance to compete with the United States in strategic defensive systems. The state of the economy gave the proponents of moderation an effective argument for not even trying to imitate SDI and for embracing more radical conceptions of security. Evidently, in addition to the political and diplomatic benefits, Gorbachev and his allies do hope to reap economic dividends from the new Soviet security policy. Major conventional reductions benefit the economy, at least in the sense of reducing the opportunity cost of keeping young men out of the civilian labor force. In the nuclear and strategic area, Gorbachev's proposals would also entail some economic benefit by foregoing emulation of SDI and putting limits on the development of future strategic systems.

But economic problems did not dictate the change in the Soviet approach to security. As Parrott points out, the initial Soviet response to the increased U.S. hostility of the early 1980s was to adopt a more confrontational policy to replace the dual-track approach of the 1970s, despite the economic sacrifice that such policies would entail: "Largely hidden from view, the breakdown of the Brezhnevian security consensus under hard-line criticism created intellectual uncertainty within the elite and provided an opening for the liberal alternatives that had been quietly developing in academic think-tanks" (Parrott, 1988:35). Gorbachev and his allies were able to make the case that future economic welfare depended on radical reform in both foreign and domestic policy. To make the arguments appeal to a new generation of Soviet citizens, they were aided by long-term secular trends in Soviet society, such as urbanization, increasing education, and the rise of the *intelligentsiia* as the fastest-growing segment of society (Lewin, 1988). Yet there were (and are) alternative arguments based on more sanguine assessments of the prospects of the Soviet political-economic system or more pessimistic analyses of the consequences of reform. If these views had prevailed, the Soviet reaction to external and internal pressures could have been very different from the Gorbachev approach.

Although we do not understand the precise means by which Gorbachev, rather than his more conservative rivals, came to power, we do have good insight into how the new Soviet leader set about institutionalizing his changes. Basically, he has sought to give civilian reformers a greater role in the determination of military policy. A number of U.S. political scientists have called attention to the importance of civilian control of security policy as a means of countering the military's usual preference for ambitious, offensively oriented strategies (Van Evera, 1983; Snyder, 1984; Posen, 1984). Gorbachev appears to be following the logic of these arguments precisely. He has attempted to institutionalize his new thinking by putting people with military expertise into the Central Committee staff; by relying on civilian scientists as an alternative source of advice on military-technical matters; and by borrowing many ideas from the scholarly community (Litherland, 1986; Parrott, 1988; Lynch, 1989; Evangelista, 1989).

Gorbachev's ambitious disarmament diplomacy has not only seized the initiative from the United States, but also from the Soviet military. As Raymond Garthoff (1985:186) has pointed out, during the SALT period "the initiative in proposing direct limitations on weaponry was reserved in Moscow to the Ministry of Defense and the General Staff, reporting to the Defense Council." Civilians in the Ministry of Foreign Affairs and the Central Committee apparatus were more successful at exerting their influence when responding to U.S. proposals (Garthoff, 1985:186). Now it seems evident that a number of major initiatives are being proposed by Gorbachev's civilian advisers, who are becoming increasingly bold in treading on territory formerly reserved for military specialists—particularly on the topic of conventional-force reductions and restructuring (Kokoshin, 1988*b; Kokoshin and Larionov, 1988; Legvold, 1988*a; Snyder, 1988*a).

The civilians have sought to challenge military expertise by taking advantage of *transnational alliances*. Soviet academic specialists have adopted a number of ideas concerning "nonprovocative defense" or "defensive defense," mainly, it seems, from West European scholars and peace researchers (Tiedtke, 1986; Zhurkin, Karaganov, and Kortunov, 1987; Kokoshin, 1988a, 1988b; Kokoshin and Larionov, 1988; Dragsdahl, 1988). The alliances have become quite explicit, leading in one case to a joint proposal for a conventional arms control regime—the product of an unlikely collaboration between a Polish and a West German scholar (von Müller and Karkoszka, 1988a, 1988b). Legvold (1988b:121) would probably term such activity "interactive" learning. The important point is not only that Soviet academics learned from their Western counterparts, but that they were able to forge transnational alliances to affect the outcome of domestic political debates (Putnam, 1988).

The links between international relations and domestic politics evident in the Gorbachev period reinforce the emphasis on the interaction between levels of analysis highlighted in the theoretical discussion in the first half of this chapter. In the Soviet Union, we observe a process by which policy entrepreneurs can take advantage of policy windows in the form of economic and military pressure to influence new leaders and contribute to formation of domestic political coalitions in favor of moderation. They appeal to "lessons" of past policy failures and sometimes join transnational alliances to gain further influence in domestic political debates. Proponents of moderation often seek to establish international security regimes in order to constrain the actions of domestic political opponents of moderation. The following section proposes some hypotheses for indicating under what conditions such a course of events is likely to take place.

Hypotheses and Methodology for Future Research

Unlike some areas of social science, the study of Soviet security policy has yielded little in the way of cumulative knowledge. Few scholars have attempted systematically to identify the sources of moderation in Soviet policy. The preceding discussion has not, therefore, been able to present the "findings" of the Soviet studies field on this important topic. Rather, it has suggested on the basis of the historical record how particular theoretical approaches might be applied. This section assembles some of the more promising approaches into a series of hypotheses and suggests how they might be tested.

Simple Tests of Straightforward Hypotheses

The hypotheses that seem most easily tested by quantitative, statistical methods are those that posit a simple relationship between two variables. In studying negotiations, for example, one can evaluate the extent to which concessions from one side induced concessions from the other side, one can determine the effectiveness of bargaining chips, tit-for-tat strategies, negotiation from strength, and so forth (Jensen, 1962, 1968, 1984, 1988). Assuming that one can develop convincing coding rules for distinguishing and rating concessions and retractions—no mean feat, in any case—this method seems preferable to those that review the negotiating record in a descriptive, unsystematic fashion (Einhorn, 1985; Skinner, 1987).

Some of the assumptions of coalition theory might benefit from rigorous testing by statistical methods. Is it true, for example, as Snyder (1987/1988) has suggested, that a domestic coalition between the military, the heavy industrialists, and the party ideologues is likely to produce an aggressive, expansionist foreign policy, whereas an alliance of the *intelligentsia* and the consumer-industry sector will produce a more moderate, conciliatory policy? If it were possible to determine the nature of the domestic coalition, one could use "event data" to establish correlations between internal and foreign policy, along the lines of Roeder's (1984) study of a related question. The main problem would be in specifying the independent variable—the nature of the domestic coalition. One might, for example, count the number of representatives from a given group (the military, the heavy industrialists, and so on) who are members of the Central Committee of the Soviet Communist Party at a particular time, or the number of articles in the most influential Soviet newspapers and journals that represent the views of a certain institutional interest. Methods that rely on content analysis of the Soviet press or speeches might provide information about attitudes of coalition partners and their likely prominence (Holsti, 1969; Zimmerman and Axelrod, 1981; Phillips and Sands, 1988). Unfortunately, one could never come up with a completely uncontroversial specification of the independent variable, especially given the disagreement in the Soviet studies field about the very applicability of the notion of "interest group" to Soviet politics (Skilling and Griffiths, 1971; Skilling, 1983; Odom, 1976; Hough, 1977). The dependent variable would be more straightforward, in that event data sets have been compiled that specifically identify cooperative and conflictual behavior (see, for example, Azar, 1980), although these have not been above criticism (Howell, 1983; McClelland, 1983).

Some of the popular explanations about the effects of military and economic pressure on Soviet policy could be tested statistically. One could, for instance, relate some indicator of Soviet economic performance (for example, change in growth rate) to an indicator of Soviet behavior in arms negotiations (for example, patterns of concessions and retractions, as in Jensen [1962, 1963, 1968, 1984]); one could compare U.S. force levels to Soviet negotiating behavior, and so forth. A review of the history of changes in Soviet security policy suggests, however, that such tests might not be particularly revealing (see also Bennett, 1989). The Soviets rarely exhibit consistently conciliatory or conflictual behavior in all aspects of their security policy at the same time, so it seems evident that a gross indicator such as economic growth does not influence each aspect in the same fashion. The same holds true in regard to the relationship between U.S. military programs and Soviet security policy. During the same historical period, the Soviets might respond to some programs by imitation, others by countermeasures, and yet others by ignoring them. The Khrushchev period, with its development of tactical nuclear weapons, its pursuit of missiles and ballistic missile defenses, and its unilateral troop reductions and test moratoria constitutes an especially good example (Evangelista, 1988). Another would be the Brezhnev period, with its limitations on strategic nuclear forces and buildup of conventional forces. For studying the influence of economic stringency as well, one would need a more fine-grained analysis that examined, for example, the effect of troop reductions on the labor force (Tiedtke, 1985), or the trade-offs between production of machine tools and military equipment.

Some aspects of theories that focus on policy entrepreneurs and transnational alliances could be evaluated using quantitative methods. For identifying the issues promoted by policy entrepreneurs, for example, one could code answers to interviews, as Kingdon (1984) did for U.S. health and transportation policy, or, more likely for the Soviet case, one could code published articles. Interviews with Western participants in transnational alliances— members of Pugwash, arms negotiators, or international peace activists, for example—would identify the issues that they pursued with their Soviet counterparts. One could then try systematically to assess the influence of these transnational contacts on the Soviet debate.

If the policy of *glasnost* continues to provide information about the Soviet past and present, a number of explanations for Soviet moderation could be subject to fairly rigorous evaluation. Access to former policymakers would be useful, particularly if archival material becomes available to confirm their recollections. Interviews with former and current policymakers are also more likely than in the past. Understanding Soviet motivations will be further facilitated if foreign policy debates are conducted publicly, for example, in committees of the Supreme Soviet. Opinion surveys of elite-level policy influentials (see, for example, Melville and Nikitin, 1988) as well as the general populace (Carrère d'Encausse, 1987; Ivanov, 1987) could be employed to test explanations that incorporate coalition-building and leaders' perceptions of public opinion, military exigencies, economic stringency, the adversary's behavior, and so forth. Greater availability of information would benefit pursuit of nonquantitative methods as well. Opening up of historical archives, already beginning for Soviet scholars, would be especially welcome.

Testing Policy-Relevant Hypotheses

It appears unlikely that most of the theoretical approaches that hold implications for U.S. policy could satisfactorily be evaluated by quantitative, statistical methods alone. The actions of policy entrepreneurs, the nature of learning, and the perceptions of conciliatory and conflictual behavior do not seem easily quantifiable. Focused, comparative case studies would be useful here, especially if they identify variables of policy relevance that are subject to influence by actors outside the Soviet Union (Snyder, 1984/1985, 1988b).

In order to undertake such studies, one would need hypotheses that link the most promising approaches and focus on policy-relevant variables. The following hypotheses are intended only to be suggestive of the kind that might be useful for such an exercise. They try to link military and economic factors, policy entrepreneurship, domestic Soviet coalitions, learning, bargaining, and regimes.

DETERMINANTS OF SUCCESSFUL POLICY ENTREPRENEURSHIP
The first hypothesis begins with three assumptions: that the definition of the national interest is a political matter; that foreign policy "learning" can be used as a political tool in internal debates over the appropriate policy; and that, in principle, transnational alliances can operate in such a way that the actors on each side influence "domestic interests [to] pressure their respective governments to adopt mutually supportive policies" (Putnam, 1988:444).

1. Policy entrepreneurs who favor moderation in security policy will enhance their chances of implementing their conception of the national interest if, other things being equal, they are able: (a) to form successful transnational alliances with likeminded groups in the adversary's country; (b) to associate hardline policies with past foreign policy failures and make the case that learning from those failures means adopting a more moderate approach; (c) to take advantage of a policy window in the form of a foreign threat that will impose unacceptably high costs if addressed in the usual manner; (d) to identify important trade-offs between military spending and the health of the economy; and (e) to gain the support of a new leader who is open to the possibility of new thinking and new coalition partners.

It would be useful to evaluate this hypothesis through a series of comparative, historical case studies in order to ascertain, for example, whether any or all of these factors must be present in order for moderation in Soviet security policy to occur. Such a study would help answer some of the key questions about recent changes in Soviet security policy. Was the U.S. Strategic Defense Initiative necessary to induce Soviet moderation? Was Gorbachev or someone like him necessary? How poor must Soviet economic performance be before policy entrepreneurs can use it as a justification for restraining military demands? It would also help identify conditions under which transnational alliances succeed (as with scientists who advocated an atmospheric test ban to prevent fallout) or fail (as with the Soviet Union's attempt to pressure Eisenhower to adopt a test ban by siding with Stevenson in 1956). Finally, it would shed light on how Soviet policy entrepreneurs successfully invoke the "lessons" of foreign policy failures to promote change.

DETERMINANTS OF COOPERATIVE AGREEMENTS

The second hypothesis assumes that once a reformist coalition gains enough power to put forward policy initiatives, it will probably seek to solicit cooperative behavior from its adversary because, according to 1.a earlier, reciprocation enhances its chances to pursue a moderate policy.

2. The coalition's choice of bargaining strategy for securing the adversary's cooperation depends on the degree of change it desires and its perception of the constellation of domestic forces in the adversary's country: (a) the coalition is more likely to pursue a tit-for-tat strategy if it favors only modest change toward cooperative arrangements and believes that it can get agreement from the adversary's government without dispelling the adversary's "enemy image" or inducing any change in its balance of domestic interests; (b) it is more likely to pursue a GRIT strategy if it desires radical change and believes that, in order for its initiative to be accepted, it has to dispel the enemy image by appealing to the public or the government's opposition or by shifting the weight of bureaucratic influences within the adversary's government; and (c) if the coalition is unstable and divided over its perception of the adversary, it will not be able to pursue any consistent strategy of reciprocity.

I refer here to tit-for-tat and GRIT as "bargaining strategies" not in terms of formal negotiation, but in the sense that policymakers can use one of the two approaches to induce a certain response by the other side that they can in turn use to influence the character of their domestic coalition. The basic argument is that tit-for-tat reciprocity often leads to agreements based on the "least common denominator," because governments that are uncertain about their preferences between competitive and cooperative strategies, or favor an uneasy mixture, will hesitate to commit themselves to agreements that entail significant cooperation at the expense of short-term interest, especially if obtaining the agreement entails unreciprocated concessions (see Bunn and Payne [1988;223–224] for a related argument). The safer approach is to adopt tit-for-tat reciprocity. In effect, however, such strict reciprocity can produce tacit collusion between the status quo-oriented factions within the super-powers to avoid meaningful change. In this regard, Axelrod (1984:180–181) has warned that the tit-for-tat strategy, while enhancing beneficial cooperation in some cases, can also be used to promoted collusive practices, such as oligopolies. (Keohane [1984:73] has made a similar point in regard to certain types of regimes that result from reciprocity.)

GRIT strategies, by contrast, are deliberately designed to produce out-comes that transform the status quo by reorienting internal coalitions on each side or by transforming the cognitive frameworks of decision makers. Finally, unstable coalitions are likely to be characterized by yet another constellation of images of the adversary and a different bargaining strategy. Here I assume that Alexander George's observations about the United States apply as well to the Soviet Union: that internal Soviet "disagreements over the correct image of the [United States] can call into question the scope as well as the de-sirability of cooperative arrangements with the [Americans] and reinforce a preference for relying on unilateral policies for assuring [Soviet] security interests" (George, Farley, and Dallin, 1988:660). In other words, an unstable coalition will prefer defection to tit-for-tat reciprocity or GRIT.

Notions of a "least common denominator" appear to underlie criticism that the United States and Soviet Union use the "game of disarmament" as a cover for continuing the arms race (Myrdal, 1978). They seem, as well, to have some empirical support—for example, the Limited Test Ban Treaty that was followed by an accelerated program of underground testing on both sides; the SALT I interim agreements that allowed a proliferation of multiple-warhead (MIRVed) missiles; and the unratified SALT II accord that appeared to en-dorse the next generation of weapons that each side planned to deploy.

Perhaps understandably, we have fewer examples of successful GRIT strat-egies to enable us to evaluate their domestic causes and consequences. The conclusion of the Austrian State Treaty in 1955 would, however, appear to support the hypothesis (Larson, 1987). Khrushchev evidently believed that the Soviet Union needed to make significant concessions in order to get the U.S. government to agree to a cooperative settlement. In the event, Soviet conces-sions contributed to a reordering of bureaucratic influence in the U.S. govern-ment, diminishing the objections of the U.S. military that had often con-stituted a veto over proposals for cooperation, for example, on disarmament (Evangelista, 1990a). Khrushchev's ability to make concessions in turn de-pended on a reshuffling of his own domestic coalition and the defeat of his rivals (Larson, 1987:40–46). The outcome of the treaty was certainly a pro-found change: it entailed, among other things, the end of four-power military occupation of Austria and a guarantee of its neutrality. The value of testing this hypothesis would lie in further specifying the conditions under which GRIT could lead to meaningful U.S.–Soviet security cooperation, perhaps, if necessary, by counterfactual analyses of failed attempts.

PROSPECTS FOR A SECURITY REGIME

The third hypothesis assumes that cooperation that is institutionalized in the form of an international regime is likely to be more enduring than ad hoc agreements.

> 3. The type of bargaining strategy that a state employs in attempting to estab-
> lish a regime helps determine the character and longevity of the regime: (a) a
> regime that results from a tit-for-tat strategy is more likely to codify the status
> quo than to produce significant change; it will tend to be limited and relatively
> fragile because, according to 2a above, the coalition that sponsored it has not
> abandoned competitive policies in its pursuit of modest cooperative measures,
> and has not had to generate consensus beyond the government itself; and (b) a
> regime that results from a GRIT strategy will produce more significant change
> and will prove more durable because, according to 2b above, it was formed by
> altering the enemy image of the adversary and changing the structure of the
> domestic coalitions on both sides.

These hypotheses appear to find support in the legacy of the SALT treaties. As Rice (1988) points out, the main objective of establishing a "limited security regime" was the desire of both sides to codify mutual deterrence and nuclear parity. Yet owing to the ambiguous nature of parity, they also tacitly agreed to continue pursuit of new weapons that could raise the specter of an attempt to achieve a military advantage. In game theoretic terms, the situation seemed to reflect the generalization that "the key conditions for the successful operation of reciprocity are that mutual cooperation can yield better results than mutual defection, but that temptations for defection also exist" (Axelrod and Keohane, 1985:244). The demise of the regime, and of U.S.–Soviet détente in general, came about "because each side concluded that the other was not practicing reciprocity, but was, on the contrary, taking unilateral advantage of its own restraint" (Axelrod and Keohane, 1985:245). This conclusion is not surprising for a regime that imposed so few concrete or meaningful restraints in any case. As for the domestic aspect, the consensus on the U.S. side was so fragile that even arms negotiators such as Edward Rowney (and earlier Paul Nitze) broke ranks before SALT II was signed (Talbott, 1979). In the end the treaty was never ratified.

The Austrian State Treaty again provides the clearest example of an agreement that established an enduring regime. Neither side has sought to challenge Austria's neutrality, and a country that seemed so contentious in the Cold War atmosphere of the mid-1950s was hardly noticed during the subsequent ups and downs of the U.S.–Soviet relationship. Another possible candidate to support the second part of the hypothesis is the INF treaty. It entailed significant concessions on the Soviet side that resembled a GRIT strategy, and it probably required the advent of a leader who, in assembling a new political coalition, could reduce the influence of the Soviet military as an institution (Evangelista, 1989; Snyder, 1987/1988). The structure of the U.S. domestic coalition changed as well with the departure of inveterate hardliners such as Richard Perle; and President Reagan, at least, abandoned his enemy image of the Soviet Union as the evil empire. Finally, the treaty's terms are unambiguous, in that they entail the complete destruction of two classes of weapons worldwide.

It is premature to speak of the INF treaty as establishing a new security regime. Some of its provisions—particularly on-site verification—do, however imply a convergence of expectations and norms concerning the positive relationship between openness and security, as a number of Soviet analysts have suggested (Zhurkin, Karaganov, and Kortunov, 1987; Zubok, 1988; Shevardnadze, 1988). One could also argue that the INF treaty has begun to constrain unilateral decision making in ways that a regime would do: NATO finds it difficult to agree on "modernization" of nuclear weapons that are not limited by the treaty, because such action would appear to undercut the spirit if not the letter of the document. The Soviet Union, in turn, finds it increasingly necessary to address concerns about its offensively oriented conventional forces, because the INF treaty has raised the specter of "denuclearization" of Europe and called attention to disparities at the conventional level.

None of the three sets of hypotheses proposed here needs to be restricted to the U.S.–Soviet security relationship. It is reasonable to assume that factors such as the influence of new leaders, the ability of actors to forge transnational alliances, and the way entrepreneurs invoke "lessons" in support of preferred policies will differ from country to country, based on divergent political cultures and domestic structures (presumably they differ between the United States and the Soviet Union). All the same, however, the plausibility of these hypotheses would be strengthened if they found support for other sets of countries, and—with some modifications—even in other issue-areas.

Conclusions

The paucity of systematic research on the sources of change in Soviet security policy rules out neat prescriptions for U.S. policymakers. There are, however, a number of observations that follow from this review of the existing evidence that may be of value. The first is that many of the most straightforward policy prescriptions, such as "negotiate from strength," do not find empirical support across a range of cases over time. If both sides pursue negotiation from strength, they are unlikely to find much to negotiate about. Indeed, many U.S. proponents of the policy appear skeptical of negotiations with the Soviet Union and believe that U.S. strength in itself will yield the desired outcome. Yet there is no body of evidence to support the notion that an unrelentingly hostile U.S. posture will induce Soviet moderation. A more narrowly defined conception of negotiation from strength that focuses on the role of bargaining chips in achieving arms treaties may be useful, but more systematic research is necessary to assess its real value. More often than not, one would expect bargaining chips to take on a life of their own and develop constituencies in both countries that resist cashing them in (Lynn-Jones, 1988). Negotiation from strength is not an automatic mechanism that functions independently from the internal politics on each side.

Beliefs that deterioration of the Soviet economy will inevitably produce moderation in Soviet security policy reflect an equally mechanistic view of the Soviet Union and a neglect of the political dimension of Soviet economic decisions. In a similar sense, explanations for Soviet security policy that focus on changing Soviet military requirements narrowly defined also miss the fundamentally political nature of debates over resource allocation and "how much is enough." Trade-offs between guns and butter—or, more accurately, among investment, consumption, and military spending—are a permanent fixture of the Soviet economy. The ability of the economy to sustain high military spending is not an objective judgment, but rather a matter of internal political debate. The willingness of society to put up with a large military burden is influenced, no doubt, by levels of education, urbanization, and material expectations. Yet even democracies with large, educated, and relatively affluent middle classes (for example, Chile) have succumbed to authoritarian rule, sometimes with dangerous consequences for foreign policy (for example, Argentina in the Falklands/Malvinas War). Regardless of the state of the Soviet economy, one should never rule out the possibility of an authoritarian leadership pursuing a militaristic course at home and abroad.

Perhaps the most definite conclusion one can draw from this review is that U.S. policymakers should be sensitive to the potential diversity of opinion on security matters in the Soviet Union (Payne, 1980; Schwartz, 1978; Melville and Nikitin, 1988; Utkin, 1988). U.S. actions are not unambiguously interpreted by the other side. They become "evidence" for debates between opponents and proponents of cooperation. Soviet actions are subject to debate at home as well. They are interpreted as successes or failures, depending in part on how they are received abroad; they become the "lessons" that are learned and promoted by actual or prospective members of domestic political coalitions.

At any given point in time, it is not easy for an outside observer to assess the balance of political forces in the Soviet Union. Perhaps in retrospect it is possible to recognize lost opportunities for supporting moderates, such as Malenkov or, at times, Khrushchev. Given the ambiguities and uncertainties about links between U.S. behavior and the fortunes of those promoting Soviet restraint, however, it is unclear how much U.S. policy can influence the Soviet Union in the direction of moderation. It is probably more certain that the West could inhibit Soviet changes if, in Snyder's (1987/1988:131) words, it "creates an environment that is inhospitable to their survival." As David Holloway (1979:31) put it, "if the West seeks restraint, co-operation and effective arms control from the Soviet Union, then it must adopt these policies itself and at least provide for the possibility that the Soviet Union may pursue them too."

As our information about the internal politics of Soviet security policy increases—through historical research as well as the growing openness of the Soviet system—we may be able to recognize more clearly the possibilities for establishing transnational alliances in support of cooperation and moderation. If these alliances are based on shared norms and expectations, they may help to establish enduring regimes and institutions to promote mutual security. Whether or not these opportunities are pursued, however, depends as much on how Americans define their own national interests as on changes in the Soviet Union.

Notes

I would like to acknowledge support from the Presidential Initiatives Fund of the University of Michigan, the research assistance of Marc Bennett and Yury Polsky, and the sources of their support: the MacArthur Foundation and the University of Michigan's Program on International Peace and Security Research. For comments on an earlier version of this chapter, I am grateful to Robert Axelrod, Alexander George, Charles Glaser, Philip Tetlock, the participants of the Stanford Soviet Nuclear History Workshop, and several anonymous reviewers.

References

Abzhubei, A. 1988. Te desiat' let. *Znamia*. No. 7:80–133.
Arbatov, A. 1984. *Voenno-strategicheskii paritet i politika SShA*. Moscow: Politizdat.
———. 1988. Parity and reasonable sufficiency. *International Affairs*. 10 (October).
———. 1989. How much defence is sufficient? *International Affairs*. 4 (April).
Argyris, C., and D.A. Schön, D.A. 1978. *Organizational Learning: A Theory of Action Perspective*. Reading, Mass.: Addison-Wesley.

Axelrod, R., ed. 1976. *Structure of Decision: The Cognitive Maps of Political Elites.* Princeton: N.J.: Princeton University Press.

———. 1984. *The Evolution of Cooperation.* New York: Basic Books.

Axelrod, R., and R.O. Keohane, 1985. Achieving cooperation under anarchy: strategies and institutions. *World Politics* 38(1):226–254.

Azar, E.E. 1980. The Conflict and Peace Data Bank (COPDAB) project. *Journal of Conflict Resolution* 24:143–152.

Bechhoefer, B.G. 1961. *Postwar Negotiations for Arms Control.* Washington, D.C.: Brookings Institution.

Bennett, M. 1989. A look at the pros and cons of event data. University of Michigan Department of Political Science: Ann Arbor, Mich.

Berman, R.P., and J.C. Baker. 1982. *Soviet Strategic Forces: Requirements and Responses.* Washington, D.C.: The Brookings Institution.

Bialer, S. 1988. The Soviet Union and the West: Security and foreign policy. In S. Bialer and M. Mandelbaum, eds., *Gorbachev's Russia and American Foreign Policy.* Boulder, Colo.: Westview.

Blacker C.D. 1989. Learning in the nuclear age: Soviet strategic arms control policy, 1969–1989. Paper prepared for National Academy of Sciences conference on Learning in U.S. and Soviet Foreign Policy, November 1988 (revised version).

Bloomfield, L.P., W.C. Clemens, Jr., and F. Griffiths. 1966. *Khrushchev and the Arms Race: Soviet Interests in Arms Control and Disarmament, 1954–1964.* Cambridge, Mass.: MIT Press.

Bogdanov, R., and A. Kortunov. 1989. Minimum deterrent: Utopia or real prospect? *Moscow News,* 23.

Bogomolov, O. 1988a. Afghanistan as seen in 1980. *Moscow News,* 30, 30 July–6 August. Selections from "Some considerations on the foreign policy results of the 1970s (main points)," report submitted to the CPSU Central Committee and the KGB, 20 January 1980.

———. 1988b. Kto zhe oshibalsia? *Literaturnaia gazeta.* 17 March.

Brams, S.J. 1985. *Superpower Games: Applying Game Theory to Superpower Conflict.* New Haven, Conn.: Yale University Press.

Breslauer, G.W. 1982. *Khrushchev and Brezhnev as Leaders: Building Authority in Soviet Politics.* London: Allen and Unwin.

Breslauer, G.W. 1987. Ideology and learning in Soviet Third World policy. *World Politics* 39(3):429–448.

Brezhnev, L.I. 1971. Interesy naroda, zabota o ego blaga—vysshii smysl deiatel'nosti partii. *Leninskim kursom-rechi i stati.* Vol. 3. Moscow Politizdat.

Bunce, V. 1980. The succession connection: Policy cycles and political change in the Soviet Union and Eastern Europe. *American Political Science Review* 74(4):966–977.

———. 1981. *Do New Leaders Make a Difference? Executive Succession and Public Policy under Capitalism and Socialism.* Princeton, N.J.: Princeton University Press.

Bunce, V., and P.G. Roeder. 1986. The effects of leadership succession in the Soviet Union. *American Political Science Review* 80(1).

Bundy, McG., G. Kennan, R. McNamara, G. Smith. 1982. Nuclear weapons and the Atlantic alliance. *Foreign Affairs* 60:753–768.

Bunn, G., and R.A. Payne. 1988. Tit-for-tat and the negotiation of nuclear arms control. *Arms Control* 9:207–233.

Burlatskii, F. 1982. Filosofiia mira. *Voprosy filosofii,* 12:57–66.

———. 1988*a*. Brezhnev i krushenie ottepeli. *Literaturnaia gazeta,* 14 September.

———. 1988*b*. Khrushchev: shtrikhi k politicheskomu portretu. *Literaturnaia gazeta,* 24 February.

Caldwell, D. 1981. *American–Soviet Relations: From 1947 to thhe Nixon-Kissinger Grand Design.* Westport, Conn.: Greenwood.

Carrère d'Encausse, H. 1987. Les contradictions d'une société conformiste. *Le Point,* 789, 2 November.

Clemens, W.C., Jr. 1973. *The Superpowers and Arms Control: From Cold War to Interdependence.* Lexington, Mass.: Lexington Books.

Cohen, M.D., J.D. March, and J.P. Olsen. 1972. A garbage can model of organizational choice. *Administrative Sciences Quarterly* 17:1–25.

Cohen, S.F. 1979. Soviet domestic politics and foreign policy. In F.W. Neal, ed., *Detente or Debacle: Common Sense in U.S.—Soviet Relations.* New York: Norton.

———. 1988. Will we end the Cold War? The next president's historic opportunity. *The Nation* 247(9):293–314.

Crawford, R.J., and S.A. Hildreth. 1987. *Congress and the Strategic Defense Initiative: A Detailed Overview of Legislative Action, 1984–1987.* Report No. 87–749 F. Washington, D.C.: Congressional Research Service.

Dallin, A. 1981. The domestic sources of Soviet foreign policy. In S. Bailer, ed., *The Domestic Context of Soviet Foreign Policy,* pp. 335–408. Boulder, Colo.: Westview.

Darst, R. 1989. Unitary and conflictual images in the study of Soviet foreign policy. In *Analyzing the Gorbachev Era: Working Papers of the Students of the Berkeley–Stanford Program in Soviet Studies.* Berkeley, Calif.: Berkeley-Stanford Program in Soviet Studies, University of California.

Divine, R.A. 1978. *Blowing on the Wind: The Nuclear Test Ban Debate, 1954–1960.* New York: Oxford University Press.

Dobrynin, A. 1986. Za bez"iadernyi mir, navstrechu XXI veku. *Kommunist,* 9.

Downs, G.W., D.A. Rocke, and R.M. Siverson. 1985. Arms races and cooperation. *World Politics* 38(1):118–146.

Dragsdahl, J. 1988. Are the Soviets really serious? *Nuclear Times* (May/June):22–25.

Druckman, D., and P.T. Hopmann. 1989. Behavioral aspects of negotiations on mutual security. In P.E. Tetlock, J.L. Husbands, R. Jervis, P.C. Stern, and C. Tilly, eds. *Behavior, Society, and Nuclear War.* Vol. I. New York: Oxford University Press.

Dvorkin, V., and V. Torbin. 1989. On real sufficiency of defence. *Moscow News*, 26, 2–9 July.

Einhorn, R.J. 1985. *Negotiating from Strength: Leverage in U.S.–Soviet Arms Control Negotiations*. New York: Praeger.

Etheredge, L.S. 1985. *Can Governments Learn?* New York: Pergamon.

Etzioni, A. 1967. The Kennedy experiment. *Western Political Quarterly* 20:361–380.

Evangelista, M. 1986. The new Soviet approach to security. *World Policy Journal* 3(1):561–599.

———. 1988. *Innovation and the Arms Race: How the United States and the Soviet Union Develop New Military Technologies*. Ithaca, N.Y.: Cornell University Press.

———. 1989. Economic reform and military technology in Soviet security policy. *The Harriman Institute Forum* 2(1):1–8.

———. 1990a. Cooperation theory and disarmament negotiations in the 1950s. *World Politics* 42(4).

———. 1990b. Soviet strategic arms control policy. In B. Parrott, ed., *The Dynamics of Soviet Defense Policy*. Washington, D.C.: Woodrow Wilson Center, Smithsonian Institution.

Falin, V. 1988. People need to learn listening skills. *Moscow News*, 41, 16–23 October.

Farley, P.J. 1988. Strategic arms control, 1967–87. In A.L. George, P.J. Farley, and A. Dallin, eds., *U.S.–Soviet Security Cooperation: Achievements, Failures, Lessons*. Oxford: Oxford University Press.

Fedorov, E.K. 1959. Soglashenie o prekrashchenii ispytanii iadernogo oruzhiia dolzhno byt' zakliucheno bezotlagatel'no. *Vestnik Akademii Nauk SSSR*, 10:11–16.

Ferguson, T. 1984. From normalcy to New Deal: Industrial structure, party competition, and American public policy in the Great Depression. *International Organization* 38(1):41–94.

FitzGerald, M.C. 1987. The strategic revolution behind Soviet arms control. *Arms Control Today* 17(5):16–19.

Gaddis, J.L. 1989. Hanging tough paid off. *Bulletin of the Atomic Scientists* 45(1):11–14.

Gallagher, M. 1964. Military manpower: A case study. *Problems of Communism* 13(3):53–62.

Garner, W.V. 1983. *Soviet Threat Perceptions of NATO's Eurostrategic Missiles*. Paris: Atlantic Institute for International Affairs.

Garthoff, D.F. 1972. The domestic dimension of Soviet foreign policy: The Kremlin debate on the test ban treaty. October 1962 to October 1963. Ph.D. dissertation, Johns Hopkins University, Baltimore.

Garthoff, R.L. 1958. *Soviet Strategy in the Nuclear Age*. New York: Praeger.

———. 1983. The Soviet SS-20 decision. *Survival* 25:110–119.

———. 1984. BMD and East–West relations. In A.B. Carter and D.N. Schwartz, eds., *Ballistic Missile Defense*. Washington, D.C.: The Brookings Institution.

————. 1985. *Detente and Confrontation: American–Soviet Relations from Nixon to Reagan*. Washington, D.C.: The Brookings Institution.

————. 1987. Continuity and change in Soviet military doctrine since the 1960s. Paper prepared for a conference on the Dynamics of Soviet Defense Policy, Kennan Institute, Wilson Center, Washington, D.C.

————. 1988. New thinking in Soviet military doctrine. *Washington Quarterly* 11(3):131–158.

George, A.L. 1969. The "operational code": A neglected approach to the study of political leaders and decision making. *International Studies Quarterly* 13:190-222.

George, A.L., P.J. Farley, and A. Dallin. 1988. *U.S.–Soviet Security Cooperation: Achievements, Failures, Lessons*. Oxford: Oxford University Press.

Gerschenkron, A. 1962. *Economic Backwardness in Historical Perspective*. Cambridge, Mass.: The Belknap Press of Harvard University Press.

Goldmann, K. 1988. *Change and Stability in Foreign Policy: The Problems and Possibilities of Detente*. Princeton, N.J.: Princeton University Press.

Gorbachev, M.S. 1986a. *Politicheskii doklad tsentral'nogo komiteta KPSS XXVII s"ezdu kommunisticheskoi partii Sovetskogo Soiuza*. Moscow: Politizdat.

————. 1986b. Rech' na torzhestvennom sobranii, posviashchennom vrucheniiu Vladivostoku ordena Lenina. 28 July. Reprinted in *Izbrannye rechi i stat'i*. Vol. 4. Moscow: Politizdat, 1987.

————. 1987. Za bez"iadernyi mir, za gumanizm mezhdunarodnykh otnoshenii. *Literaturnaia gazeta*, 18 February.

Gourevitch, P. 1986. *Politics in Hard Times: Comparative Responses to International Economic Crises*. Ithaca, N.Y.: Cornell University Press.

Gowa, J. 1986. Anarchy, egoism, and third images: *The Evolution of Cooperation* and international relations. *International Organization* 40(1):167–186.

Grachev, N. 1988. Nuclear war and its consequences. *International Affairs*, 2 (February).

Grachev, N., et al. 1989. Letters to the editor. *International Affairs*, 1 (January).

Green, W.C. 1987. *Soviet Nuclear Weapons Policy: A Research and Bibliographic Guide*. Boulder, Colo.: Westview.

Grieco, J.M. 1988. Anarchy and the limits of cooperation: A realist critique of the newest liberal institutionalism. *International Organization* 42(3):485–507.

Griffiths, F. 1972. Images, politics, and learning in Soviet behavior toward the United States. Ph.D. dissertation, Department of Political Science, Columbia University.

————. 1984. The sources of American conduct: Soviet perspectives and their policy implications. *International Security* 9(2):3–50.

Gromyko, A., and V. Lomeiko. 1984. *Novoe myshlenie v iadernyi vek*. Moscow: Mezhdunarodnye otnosheniia.

Gromyko, A.A. 1988. *Pamiatnoe*. 2 Vols. Moscow: Politizdat.

Gustafson, T. 1981. *Reform in Soviet Politics: Lessons of Recent Policies on Land and Water*. Cambridge, England: Cambridge University Press.

Haas, E.B. 1980. Why collaborate? Issue-linkage and international regimes. *World Politics* 32(3):357–405.

Haas, P.M. 1989. Do regimes matter? Epistemic communities and Mediterranean pollution control. *International Organization* 43(3):377–404.

Haggard, S., and B.A. Simmons. 1987. Theories of international regimes. *International Organization* 41(3):491–517.

Hampson, F.O. 1987. SALT I Interim Agreement and ABM Treaty. In A. Carnesale and R.N. Haass, eds., *Superpower Arms Control: Setting the Record Straight.* Cambridge, Mass.: Ballinger.

Hardenbergh, C., ed., (1982–1990). *The Arms Control Reporter* (monthly compendium). Brookline, Mass.: Institute for Defense and Disarmament Studies.

Haslam, J. 1989. *The Soviet Union and the Politics of Nuclear Weapons in Europe, 1969–1987.* Ithaca, N.Y.: Cornell University Press.

Hermann, M.G. 1980. Explaining foreign policy behavior using personal characteristics of leaders. *International Studies Quarterly* 24(1):7–46.

————. 1989. Personality profile data on Gorbachev. Developed for presentation at the annual meeting of the International Studies Association, London, England.

Herrmann, R.K. 1985. *Perceptions and Behavior in Soviet Foreign Policy.* Pittsburgh, Pa.: University of Pittsburgh Press.

————. 1988. The empirical challenge of the cognitive revolution: A strategy for drawing inferences about perceptions. *International Studies Quarterly* 32(2):175–203.

von Hippel, F., and T.B. Cochran. 1989. The myth of the Soviet "killer" laser. *New York Times,* 19 August.

Holloway, D. 1979. Decision-making in Soviet defence policies. In *Prospects of Soviet Power in the 1980s,* Part II, pp. 24–31. Adelphi Paper No. 152. International Institute for Strategic Studies, London.

————. 1983. *The Soviet Union and the Arms Race.* New Haven, Conn.: Yale University Press.

————. 1985. The strategic defense initiative and the Soviet Union. *Daedalus* 114(3):257–278.

————. 1989. Gorbachev's new thinking. *Foreign Affairs* 68(1):66–81.

Holsti, O. 1967. Cognitive dynamics and images of the enemy. In *Enemies in Politics.* D. Finlay, O. Holsti, and R. Fagan, eds. Chicago: Rand McNally.

————. 1969. *Content Analysis for the Social Sciences and Humanities.* Reading, Mass.: Addison-Wesley.

Horelick, A.A., R. Johnson, and J.D. Steinbruner, 1973. *The Study of Soviet Foreign Policy: A Review of Decision-Theory-Related Approaches.* Report R-1334. Santa Monica, Calif.: Rand Corporation.

Hough, J.F. 1977. *The Soviet Union and Social Science Theory.* Cambridge, Mass.: Harvard University Press.

————. 1986. *The Struggle for the Third World: Soviet Debates and American Options.* Washington, D.C.: Brookings Institution.

————. 1987. The "X" article and contemporary sources of Soviet conduct. In T.L. Deibel and J.L. Gaddis, eds., *Containing the Soviet Union.* London: Pergamon-Brassey's.

————. 1988. *Opening Up the Soviet Economy.* Washington, D.C.: Brookings Institution.

Howell, L.D. 1983. A comparative study of the WEIS and COPDAB data sets. *International Studies Quarterly* 27(2):149–159.

Huber, R.T. 1989. *Soviet Perceptions of the U.S. Congress: The Impact on Superpower Relations.* Boulder, Colo.: Westview.

Iakovlev, A.N. 1987. Dostizhenie kachestvenno novogo sostoianiia Sovetskogo obshchestva i obshchestvennye nauki. *Kommunist,* 8.

————. 1988. From an institute of counteraction towards an institute of interaction. *Moscow News,* 41, 16–23 October.

Ivanov, V.N. 1987. Bol'shinstvo odobriaet. *Pravda,* 17 December.

Izyumov, A. 1988. The other side of disarmament. *International Affairs,* 5 (May).

Jackson, W.D. 1981. Soviet images of the U.S. as nuclear adversary, 1969–1979. *World Politics* 33(4):614–638.

Jacobson, H.K., and E. Stein. 1966. *Diplomats, Scientists, and Politicians: The United States and the Nuclear Test Ban Negotiations.* Ann Arbor: University of Michigan Press.

Jensen, L. 1962. The postwar disarmament negotiations: A study in American–Soviet bargaining behavior. Ph.D. dissertation, University of Michigan, Ann Arbor.

————. 1963. Soviet–American bargaining behavior in the post-war disarmament negotiations. *Journal of Conflict Resolution* 9:522–541.

————. 1968. Approach-avoidance bargaining in the test ban negotiations. *International Studies Quarterly* 12:152–160.

————. 1984. Negotiating strategic arms control, 1969–1979. *Journal of Conflict Resolution* 28(3):535–559.

————. 1988. *Bargaining for National Security: The Postwar Disarmament Negotiations.* Columbia, S.C.: University of South Carolina Press.

Jervis, R. 1978.Cooperation under the security dilemma. *World Politics* 30(2):167–214.

————. 1983. Security regimes. In S.D. Krasner, ed., *International Regimes,* pp. 173–194. Ithaca, N.Y.: Cornell University Press.

————. 1988. Realism, game theory, and cooperation. *World Politics* 40(3):317–349.

Jönsson, C. 1979. *Soviet Bargaining Behavior: The Nuclear Test Ban Case.* New York: Columbia University Press.

Kaufman, R.F. 1985. Causes of the slowdown in Soviet defense spending. *Soviet Economy* 1(1):9–31.

————. 1988. Economic reform and the Soviet military. *Washington Quarterly* 11(3):201–211.

Kennan, G.F. (under pseudonym "X"). 1947. The sources of Soviet conduct. *Foreign Affairs* 25:566–582.

Keohane, R.O. 1984. *After Hegemony: Cooperation and Discord in the World Political Economy.* Princeton, N.J.: Princeton University Press.

Keohane, R.O., and J.S. Nye, Jr. 1977. *Power and Interdependence: World Politics in Transition.* Boston: Little, Brown.

———. 1987. *Power and Interdependence* revisited. *International Organization* 41(4):725–753.

Khrushchev, N.S. 1971. Transcript of reminiscences. Harriman Institute, Columbia University.

Kingdon, J.W. 1984. *Agendas, Alternatives, and Public Policies.* Boston: Little, Brown.

Kokoshin, A.A. 1988a. Razvitie voennogo dela i sokrashchenie vooruzhennykh sil i obychnykh vooruzhenii. *Mirovaia ekonomika i mezhdunarodnye otnosheniia,* 1, 20–32.

———. 1988b. Restructure forces, enhance security. *Bulletin of the Atomic Scientists* 44(7):35–38.

———. 1988c. Sokrashchenie iadernykh vooruzhenii i strategicheskaia stabil'nost'. *SShA,* 2.

———. 1988d. Tri "kita" stabil'nosti. *Krasnaia zvezda,* 16 September.

Kokoshin, A.A., and V.V. Larionov. 1988. Protivostoianie sil obshchego naznacheniia v kontekste obespecheniia strategicheskoi stabil'nosti. *Mirovaia ekonomika i mezhdunarodnye otnosheniia,* 6, 23–30.

Kokoshin, A.A., V.M., Sergeev, and V.L. Tsymburskii. 1988. Evolution of the concept of "victory" in Soviet military-political thought after World War II. Moscow: Institute of U.S.A. and Canada Studies.

Kolkowicz, R. 1967. *The Soviet Military and the Communist Party.* Princeton, N.J.: Princeton University Press.

Kondrashov, S. 1989. Haven't fought enough? *Moscow News,* 31, 6–13 August.

Kortunov, A. 1989. Why hurry? *Moscow News,* 17, 30 April–7 May.

Krasil'nikov, S. 1956. *Marksizm-Leninizm o voine i armii.* Moscow: Voenizdat.

Krasner, S.D., ed. 1983. *International Regimes.* Ithaca, N.Y.: Cornell University Press.

Kurth, J. 1971. A widening gyre: The logic of American weapons procurement. *Public Policy,* 19:373–404.

———. 1979. The political consequences of the product cycle: Industrial history and political outcomes. *International Organization* 33:1–33.

Lapidus, G.W., and A. Dallin. 1989. The pacification of Ronald Reagan. *Bulletin of the Atomic Scientists* 45(1):14–17.

Larrabee, F.S. 1988. Gorbachev and the Soviet military. *Foreign Affairs* 66(5):1002–1026.

Larson, D.W. 1985. *Origins of Containment: A Psychological Explanation.* Princeton, N.J.: Princeton University Press.

Larson, D.W. 1987. Crisis prevention and the Austrian State Treaty. *International Organization* 41(1):27–60.

Lavrinenkov, V. 1982. *Bez voiny.* Kiev: Politizdat Ukrainy.

Lebow, R.N. 1985. The Soviet offensive in Europe: The Schlieffen plan revisited? *International Security* 9(4):44–78.

Lebow, R.N., and J.G. Stein. 1987. Beyond deterrence. *Journal of Social Issues* 43(4):5–70.

Legvold, R. 1988*a*. Gorbachev's new approach to conventional arms control. *Harriman Institute Forum* 1(1):1–8.

――――. 1988*b*. War, weapons, and Soviet foreign policy. In S. Bialer and M. Mandelbaum, eds., *Gorbachev's Russia and American Foreign Policy.* Boulder, Colo.: Westview Press.

Levi, B.G., F. von Hippel, and W.F. Daugherty, 1987/1988. Civilian casualties from "limited" nuclear attacks on the Soviet Union. *International Security* 12(3):168–189.

Lewin, M. 1988. *The Gorbachev Phenomenon: A Historical Interpretation.* Berkeley, Calif.: University of California Press.

Lewis, E. 1980. *Public Entrepreneurship: Toward a Theory of Bureaucratic Political Power.* Bloomington: Indiana University Press.

Litherland, P. 1986. *Gorbachev and Arms Control: Civilian Experts and Soviet Policy.* Peace Research Report No. 12. School of Peace Studies, Bradford, England.

Lovell, J.P. 1984. "Lessons" of U.S. military involvement: Preliminary conceptualization. In D.A. Sylvan and S. Chan, eds., *Foreign Policy Decision Making.* New York: Praeger.

Löwenhardt, J. 1981. *Decision Making in Soviet Politics.* New York: St. Martin's Press.

Lynch. A. 1987. *The Soviet Study of International Relations.* Cambridge, England: Cambridge University Press.

――――. 1989. *Gorbachev's International Outlook: Intellectual Origins and Political Consequences.* Institute for East–West Security Studies Occasional Paper No. 9. Boulder, Colo.: Westview.

Lynn-Jones, S.M. 1988. Lulling and stimulating effects of arms control. In A. Carnesale and R.N. Haass, eds., *Superpower Arms Control: Setting the Record Straight.* Cambridge, Mass.: Ballinger.

MccGwire, M. 1987. *Military Objectives in Soviet Foreign Policy.* Washington, D.C.: Brookings Institution.

McClelland, C.A. 1983. Let the user beware. *International Studies Quarterly* 27(2):169–177.

McConnell, J.M. 1988. SDI, the Soviet investment debate and Soviet military policy. *Strategic Review* 16(1):47–62.

Mattison, J.V. 1987. Discussing nuclear issues and trade relations. In D.D. Newsom, ed., *Private Diplomacy with the Soviet Union.* Lanham, Md.: University Press of America.

May, E.R. 1973. *"Lessons" of the Past: The Use and Misuse of History in American Foreign Policy.* New York: Oxford.

Melman, S. 1989. We are ready to share information. *Moscow News*, 3, 22–29 January.

Melville, A., and A. Nikitin, 1988. Not everyone can think alike. *Moscow News*, 3, 14–21 August.

Meyer, A.G. 1978. The war scare of 1927. *Soviet Union/Union Sovietique* 5, Pt. 1:1–25.

Meyer, S.M. 1984. Soviet national security decisionmaking: What do we know and what do we understand? In J. Valenta and W. Potter, eds., *Soviet Decisionmaking for National Security*. London: Allen and Unwin.

———. 1988. The sources and prospects of Gorbachev's new political thinking on security. *International Security* 13(2):124–163.

Mičunovič, V. 1980. *Moscow Diary*. Trans. by David Floyd. New York: Doubleday.

Morrow, J.D. 1988. Social choice and system structure in world politics. *World Politics* 41(1):75–97.

von Müller, A., and A. Karkoszka. 1988a. An East–West negotiating proposal. *Bulletin of the Atomic Scientists* 44(7):39–41.

———. 1988b. A modified approach to conventional arms control. *Defense and Disarmament News* 1(3):1–8.

Myrdal, A. 1978. *The Game of Disarmament: How the United States and Russia Run the Arms Race*. New York: Pantheon.

Neidle, A. 1988. Nuclear test bans: history and future prospects. In A.L. George, P.J. Farley, and A. Dallin, eds., *U.S.–Soviet Security Cooperation: Achievements, Failures, Lessons*. Oxford: Oxford University Press.

Neustadt, R.E., and E.R. May. 1986. *Thinking in Time: The Uses of History for Decision-Makers*. New York: Free Press.

Newsom, D.D., ed. 1987. *Private Diplomacy with the Soviet Union*. Lanham, Md.: University Press of America.

Noel-Baker, P. 1958. *The Arms Race: A Programme for World Disarmament*. New York: Oceana.

Nye, J.S., Jr. 1987. Nuclear learning and U.S.–Soviet security regimes. *International Organization* 41(3):371–402.

———. 1988. Gorbachev's Russia and U.S. options. In S. Bailer and M. Mandelbaum, eds., *Gorbachev's Russia and American Foreign Policy*. Boulder, Colo.: Westview.

Odell, J.S. 1982. *U.S. International Monetary Policy: Markets, Power, and Ideas as Sources of Change*. Princeton, N.J.: Princeton University Press.

Odom, W. 1976. A dissenting view on the group approach to Soviet politics. *World Politics* 28:542–567.

Ogarkov, N.V. 1985. *Istoriia uchit bditel'nosti*. Moscow: Voenizdat.

Osgood, C.E. 1962. *An Alternative to War or Surrender*. Urbana: University of Illinois Press.

Oye, K.A. 1985. Explaining cooperation under anarchy: hypotheses and strategies. *World Politics* 38(1):1–24.

Parrott, B. 1983. *Politics and Technology in the Soviet Union*. Cambridge, Mass.: MIT Press.

———. 1987. *The Soviet Union and Ballistic Missile Defense*. Boulder, Colo.: Westview.

———. 1988. Soviet national security under Gorbachev. *Problems of Communism* 37(6):1–36.

Payne, S.B., Jr. 1980. *The Soviet Union and SALT.* Cambridge, Mass.: MIT Press.

Phillips, R.H., and J.I. Sands. 1988. Reasonable sufficiency and Soviet conventional defense: A research note. *International Security* 13(2):164–178.

Pipes, R. 1984. Can the Soviet Union reform? *Foreign Affairs* 63(1):47–61.

Plous, S. 1985. Perceptual illusions and military realities: The nuclear arms race. *Journal of Conflict Resolution* 29(3):363–389.

Plous, S. 1987. Perceptual illusions and military realities: Results from a computer-simulated arms race. *Journal of Conflict Resolution* 31(1):5–33.

Posen, B.R. 1984. *The Sources of Military Doctrine: France, Britain, and Germany between the World Wars.* Ithaca, N.Y.: Cornell University Press.

Primakov, E. 1987. Novaia filosofiia vneshnei politiki. *Pravda.* 11 July.

Proektor, D. 1988. Politics, Clausewitz and victory in a nuclear war. *International Affairs,* 5 (May).

Putnam, R.D. 1988. Diplomacy and domestic politics: The logic of two-level games. *International Organization* 42(3):427–460.

Putnam, R.D., and N. Bayne. 1987. *Hanging Together, Cooperation and Conflict in the Seven-Power Summits,* rev. ed. Cambridge, Mass.: Harvard University Press.

Rice, C. 1988. SALT and the search for a security regime. In A.L. George, P.J. Farley, and A. Dallin, eds., *U.S.–Soviet Security Cooperation: Achievements, Failures, Lessons.* Oxford: Oxford University Press.

Richmond, Y. 1987. Public diplomacy and other exchanges. In D.D. Newsom, ed. *Private Diplomacy with the Soviet Union.* Lanham, Md.: University Press of America.

Rissc-Kappen, T. 1988. *The Zero Option: INF, West Germany, and Arms Control.* Boulder, Colo.: Westview.

Ritvo, H. 1962. Internal divisions on disarmament in the Soviet Union. In S. Melman, ed., *Disarmament: Its Politics and Economics.* Boston: American Academy of Arts and Sciences.

Roeder, P.G. 1984. Soviet policies and Kremlin politics. *International Studies Quarterly* 28(2):171–193.

———. 1985. Do new leaders really make a difference? Rethinking the "succession connection." *American Political Science Review* 79(4):958–976.

Rose, W. 1988. *U.S. Unilateral Arms Control Initiatives: When Do They Work?* Westport, Conn.: Greenwood.

Sakharov, A.D. 1962. Radioactive carbon in nuclear explosions and nonthreshold biological effects. In A.V. Lebedinskii, ed., *What Russian Scientists Say About Fallout.* New York: Collier. Originally published in 1959 as *Sovetskie uchenye ob opasnosti ispytanii iadernogo oruzhiia.* Moscow: Atomizdat.

———. 1967/1972. Dialog mezhdu Ernstrom Genri i A.D. Sakharovym. In R. Medvedev, ed., *Politicheskii dnevnik, 1964–1970.* Amsterdam: Fond imeni Gertsena. Originally circulated in *samizdat* in 1967.

———. 1974. *Sakharov Speaks.* New York: Knopf.

———. 1982. Open letter to Anatoly Aleksandrov, President of the USSR Academy of Sciences. In Alexander Babyonyshev, ed., *On Sakharov*. New York: Vintage.

Schrag, P.G. 1989. *Listening for the Bomb: A Study in Nuclear Arms Verification Policy*. Boulder, Colo.: Westview.

Schwartz, M. 1978. *Soviet Perceptions of the United States*. Berkeley, Calif.: University of California Press.

Seaborg, G.T., with B. Loeb. 1981. *Khrushchev, Kennedy, and the Test Ban*. Berkeley: University of California Press.

Shenfield, S. 1987. *The Nuclear Predicament: Explorations in Soviet Ideology*. London: Routledge & Keegan Paul.

Shevardnadze, E. 1988. Doklad E.A. Shevardnadze. *Vestnik Ministerstva Inostrannykh Del SSSR*, 15, 15 August.

Shevchenko, A.N. 1985. *Breaking with Moscow*. New York: Knopf.

Shlapentokh, V.E. 1984. Moscow's war propaganda and Soviet public opinion. *Problems of Communism* 33(5):88–94.

Singer, J.D. 1984. *Deterrence, Arms Control, and Disarmament: Toward a New Synthesis in National Security Policy*. Lanham, Md.: University Press of America. Originally published in 1962.

Skilling, H.G. 1983. Interest groups and communist politics revisited. *World Politics* 36(1):1–27.

Skilling, H.G., and F. Griffiths, eds., 1971. *Interest Groups in Soviet Politics*. Princeton, N.J.: Princeton University Press.

Skinner, K.K. 1987. Linkage. In A. Carnesale and R.N. Haass, eds., *Superpower Arms Control: Setting the Record Straight*. Cambridge, Mass.: Ballinger.

Slusser, R.M. 1973. *The Berlin Crisis of 1961: Soviet–American Relations and the Struggle for Power in the Kremlin*. Baltimore, Md.: Johns Hopkins University Press.

Snyder, J. 1984. *The Ideology of the Offensive: Military Decision Making and the Disasters of 1914*. Ithaca, N.Y.: Cornell University Press.

———. 1984/1985. Richness, rigor, and relevance in the study of Soviet foreign policy. *International Security* 9(3):89–108.

———. 1987/1988. The Gorbachev revolution: a waning of Soviet expansionism? *International Security* 12(3):93–131.

———. 1988a. Limiting offensive conventional forces: Soviet proposals and Western options. *International Security* 12(4):48–77.

———. 1988b. Science and Sovietology: Bridging the methods gap in Soviet foreign policy studies. *World Politics* 40(2):169–193.

———. 1989. International leverage on Soviet domestic change. *World Politics* 42(1):1–30.

Solomon, P.H., Jr. 1978. *Soviet Criminologists and Criminal Policy: Specialists in Policy-Making*. New York: Columbia University Press.

Spielmann, K.F. 1978. *Analyzing Soviet Strategic Weapons Decisions*. Boulder, Colo.: Westview.

Stein, A.A. 1983. Coordination and collaboration: Regimes in an anarchic world. In

S.D. Krasner, ed., *International Regimes*. Ithaca, N.Y.: Cornell University Press.

Steinbruner, J.D. 1974. *The Cybernetic Theory of Decision: New Dimensions of Political Analysis*. Princeton, N.J.: Princeton University Press.

Steinbruner, J.D., and L.V. Sigal, eds., 1983. *Alliance Security: NATO and the No-First-Use Question*. Washington, D.C.: Brookings Institution.

Stewart, P.D. 1987. Informal diplomacy: The Dartmouth Conference experience. In D.D. Newsom, ed., *Private Diplomacy with the Soviet Union*. Lanham, Md.: University Press of America.

Talbott, S. 1979. *Endgame: The Inside Story of SALT II*. New York: Harper and Row.

Tetekin, N. 1982. Glavnyi pokazatel' kachestvennogo sostoianiia voisk. *Krasnaia zvezda*, 10 November.

Tetlock, P.E. 1988. Revised guidelines for contributors to the "Learning in U.S. and Soviet Foreign Policy" project, National Academy of Sciences, Washington, D.C.

Tetlock, P.E. 1989. Methodological themes and variations. In P.E. Tetlock, J.L. Husbands, R. Jervis, P.C. Stern, and C. Tilly, eds., *Behavior, Society, and Nuclear War*. Vol. 1. New York: Oxford University Press.

Tiedtke, J. 1985. *Abrüstung in der Sowjetunion: Wirtschaftliche Bedingungen und soziale Folgen der Truppenreduzierung von 1960*. Frankfurt/Main: Campus Verlag.

Tiedtke, S. 1986. *Abschreckung und ihre Alternativen: Die sowjetische Sicht einer westlichen Debatte*. Heidelberg: Forschungsstätte der Evangelischen Studiengemeinschaft.

Tolubko, V. 1979. *Nedelin: Pervyi glavkom strategicheskikh*. Moscow: Molodaia Gvardiia.

Tret'iak, I. 1988. Reliable defense, first and foremost. *Moscow News*, 8, 14–21 February.

U.S. House of Representatives, Committee on Armed Services. 1988. *General Secretary Mikhail Gorbachev and the Soviet Military: Assessing His Impact and the Potential for Future Changes*. Report of the Defense Policy Panel. 13 September.

U.S. House of Representatives. Committee on Armed Services. 1989. *Gorbachev's Force Reductions and the Restructuring of Soviet Forces*. Hearings before the Defense Policy Panel, 10 and 14 May.

Ustinov, D.F. 1983. *Borot'sia za mir, ukrepliat' oboronosponsobnost'*. Moscow: Voenizdat.

Utkin, A. 1988. Efforts must be mutual. *Moscow News*, 8 14–21 February.

Van Evera, S. 1983. The causes of war. Ph.D. dissertation, University of California, Berkeley.

———. 1985. Why cooperation failed in 1914. *World Politics* 38(1):80–117.

Vasilchuk, Y. 1989. Conversion issue should be in deputies' mandates. *Moscow News*, 2, 22–29 January.

Velikhov, E. 1988. Science for a nuclear-free world. *International Affairs*, 11 (November).

Wallander, C. 1989. Third world conflict in Soviet military thought: Does the "new thinking" grow prematurely grey? *World Politics* 42(1):31–63.

Waltz, K.N. 1979. *Theory of International Politics.* Reading, Mass.: Addison-Wesley.

Weber, S. 1989. Interactive learning in U.S.–Soviet arms control. Paper prepared for a National Academy of Sciences conference on Learning in U.S. and Soviet Foreign Policy, November 1988 (revised version).

Weber, S. 1990. *Explaining Cooperation in U.S.–Soviet Arms Control.* Princeton, N.J.: Princeton University Press.

Weickhardt, G.G. 1987. The military consensus behind Soviet arms control proposals. *Arms Control Today* 17(7):20–24.

White, R.K. 1984. *Fearful Warriors: A Psychological Profile of U.S.–Soviet Relations.* New York: Free Press.

Wolfe, T.W. 1965. *Soviet Strategy at the Crossroads.* Cambridge, Mass.: Harvard University Press.

———. 1970. *Soviet Power and Europe, 1945–1970.* Baltimore, Johns Hopkins University Press.

York, H.F. 1987. *Making Weapons, Talking Peace: A Physicist's Odyssey from Hiroshima to Geneva.* New York: Basic Books.

Young, O.R. 1989. The politics of international regime formation: Managing natural resources and the environment. *International Organization* 43(3):349–376.

Zagladin, V.V. 1986. Vystuplenie chlena TsK KPSS, pervogo zamestitelia zaveduiushchego Mezhdunarodnym otdelom TsK KPSS V.V. Zagladina na XXIII s"ezde Kompartii Turkmenistana. *Turkmenskaia Pravda,* 19 January.

Zhurkin, V., S. Karaganov, and A. Kortunov. 1987. Reasonable sufficiency—or how to break the vicious circle. *New Times,* 40, 12 October.

Zimmerman, W. 1969. *Soviet Perspectives on International Relations, 1956–1967.* Princeton, N.J.: Princeton University Press.

———. 1970. Elite perspectives and the explanation of Soviet foreign policy. *Journal of International Affairs* 24:84–98.

———. 1980. Rethinking Soviet foreign policy: Changing American perspectives. *International Journal* (Summer):548–562.

Zimmerman, W., and R. Axelrod. 1981. The "lessons" of Vietnam and Soviet foreign policy. *World Politics* 34(1):1–24.

Zimmerman, W., and H.K. Jacobson. 1987. Wither detente? Conflict and cooperation in U.S.–Soviet relations. Paper presented at International Studies Association meeting, Washington, D.C.

Zubok, V. 1988. SSSR-SShA: put' k peregovoram po razoruzheniiu v iadernyi vek (1953–1955 gg.). Paper presented at a conference at Ohio University, Athens, Ohio.

Contributors and Editors

GEORGE W. DOWNS is professor of politics and public affairs at Princeton University. He is also an editor of *World Politics*. His research has dealt with a variety of topics in nonmarket decision making at the domestic and international levels. Among his publications are *The Search for Government Efficiency* (Random House, 1986) and a series of articles on tacit bargaining and arms control. He received a Ph.D. in political science from the University of Michigan.

MATTHEW EVANGELISTA teaches Soviet and international politics in the Department of Political Science and is a faculty associate of the Institute for Social Research at the University of Michigan, Ann Arbor. He is the author of *Innovation and the Arms Race: How the United States and the Soviet Union Develop New Military Technologies* (Cornell University Press, 1988) and numerous scholarly and popular articles on international security and foreign policy. He received an A.B. from Harvard College and an M.A. and Ph.D. in international and comparative politics from Cornell University.

BARUCH FISCHHOFF is a professor of engineering and public policy and of social and decision sciences at Carnegie-Mellon University. He works in judgment and decision making with specializations in policy analysis, training, human factors, risk perception and management, and historiography. He serves on the editorial boards of *Policy Analysis, Journal of Risk and Uncertainty, Organizational Behavior and Human Performance, Accident Analysis and Prevention, International Journal of Forecasting,* and *Social Behavior.* He has served on a number of National Research Council panels and published various articles and a book, *Acceptable Risk* (Cambridge University Press).

Jo L. HUSBANDS is a senior research associate with the National Research Council. From 1982 to 1986, she was deputy director of the Committee for National Security in Washington, D.C. Her research interests include U.S. defense policy, international negotiations, and Third World security issues such as arms transfers and nuclear proliferation. Her recent publications include *Defense Choices: Greater Security with Fewer Dollars* (with William W. Kaufman; Committee for National Security, 1986) and "The conventional arms transfer talks" (with Anne H. Cahn) in *Arms Transfers Limitation and Third World Security* (Thomas Ohlson, ed.: Oxford University Press, 1988). She received a Ph.D. in political science from the University of Minnesota.

ROBERT JERVIS is Adlai E. Stevenson professor of political science and a member of the Institute of War and Peace Studies at Columbia University. He is currently working on problems of psychology, decision making, and cooperation. Among his publications are *Perception and Misperception in International Politics* (Princeton University Press, 1976), and *Psychology and Deterrence* (with Richard Ned Lebow and Janice Stein; Johns Hopkins University Press, 1985). He received his Ph.D. in Political Science from the University of California at Berkeley.

JANICE GROSS STEIN is professor of political science at the University of Toronto. Her research interests include crisis prevention and management, deterrence, international negotiation, and the international politics of the Middle East. She is coauthor of *Rational Decision Making: Israel's Security Choices, 1967* (with Raymond Tanter, Ohio State University Press, 1980) and *Psychology and Deterrence* (with Robert Jervis and Richard Ned Lebow; Johns Hopkins University Press, 1985). She recently edited *Getting to the Table: Processes of International Prenegotiation* (Johns Hopkins University Press, 1989). She received her B.A. from McGill University, her M.A. from Yale, and her Ph.D. in political science from McGill University.

PAUL C. STERN is study director of the Committee on Contributions of Behavioral and Social Science to the Prevention of Nuclear War and co-study director of the Committee on Human Dimensions of Global Change at the National Research Council. His current research is on the formation of social attitudes about environmental policy. His publications include *Evaluating Social Science Research* (Oxford, 1979) and *Energy Use: The Human Dimension* (with Elliot Aronson; Freeman, 1984). Stern received a B.A. from Amherst College, and M.A. and Ph.D. degrees in psychology from Clark University.

PHILIP E. TETLOCK is professor of psychology and director of the Institute of Personality Assessment and Research at the University of California at Berkeley. His major research interests include the study of international conflict, judgment and choice processes, and impression management. His recent publications include "Psychological advice on foreign policy: What do we have to contribute?" (*American Psychologist,* 1986) and "Monitoring the integrative complexity of American and Soviet foreign policy rhetoric: What can be learned?" (*Journal of Social Issues,* 1988). Tetlock received B.A. and M.A. degrees from the University of British Columbia and a Ph.D. in psychology from Yale University.

CHARLES TILLY is distinguished professor of sociology and history at the New School for Social Research, where he also directs the Center for Studies of Social Change. Most of his recent research and writing concerns political aspects and consequences of large-scale social change. His most recent books are *Big Structures, Large Processes, Huge Comparisons* (Sage, 1985), *The Contentious French* (Harvard University Press, 1986), and *States, Coercion, and Capital* (forthcoming). Tilly received his Ph.D. in sociology from Harvard University.

PETER WALLENSTEEN is Dag Hammarskjold professor of peace and conflict research at Uppsala University, Uppsala, Sweden. He is currently working on problems of conflict resolution and has a background in the study of causes of war as well as the impact of economic sanctions. His most recent books are *Peace Research: Achievements and Challenges* (Westview, 1988), *Global Militarization* (with Johan Galtung and Carlos Portales, Westview, 1985), and *Dilemmas of Economic Coercion: Sanctions in World Politics* (with Miroslav Nincic, Praeger, 1983). He received a Ph.D. in political science from Uppsala University and has been a visiting professor at the University of Michigan.

Index